T0356175

copaganda

also by alec karakatsanis

*Usual Cruelty: The Complicity of Lawyers
in the Criminal Injustice System*

copaganda

how police and the media
manipulate our news

alec karakatsanis

THE
NEW
PRESS

NEW YORK
LONDON

Requests for permission to reproduce selections from this book should be made
through our website: https://thenewpress.com/contact.

Published in the United States by The New Press, New York, 2025
Distributed by Two Rivers Distribution

ISBN 978-1-62097-853-5 (hc)
ISBN 978-1-62097-891-7 (ebook)
CIP data is available

The New Press publishes books that promote and enrich public discussion and
understanding of the issues vital to our democracy and to a more equitable world.
These books are made possible by the enthusiasm of our readers; the support
of a committed group of donors, large and small; the collaboration of our many
partners in the independent media and the not-for-profit sector; booksellers, who
often hand-sell New Press books; librarians; and above all by our authors.

www.thenewpress.com

Composition by Dix Digital Prepress and Design
This book was set in Janson Text LT Pro

Printed in the United States of America

2 4 6 8 10 9 7 5 3 1

Contents

copaganda

Introduction

What Is Copaganda?

If you're not careful, the newspapers will have you hating the people who are being oppressed, and loving the people who are doing the oppressing.

-Malcolm X[1]

On the morning of June 20, 2023, I stood outside the Genesee County Jail in Flint, Michigan. Like nearly every jail in the United States, the one in downtown Flint mostly detains people who are presumed innocent and awaiting their day in court. Most of them are jailed solely because their families do not have the cash to pay for their release. Many of them will never be convicted of anything. The U.S. and the Philippines are the only two countries that use for-profit cash bail companies to determine which human beings are confined to jail cells before trial and which human beings can go home to their families.

In 2014, the Genesee County Jail banned in-person family visits. It prohibited children from visiting their incarcerated parents, spouses from visiting their partners, and parents from visiting their children. While many human beings take for granted the ability to hug their mother or kiss their child on the forehead or look into the eyes of their lover, people in Flint could not.

That morning, I took a photograph. It shows the sidewalk outside the jail, where children had written messages of love and drawn hearts and flowers in chalk for their parents. From the jail windows, parents

could see the drawings and press their faces to the glass, hand-signaling hearts and other love symbols back down to their kids.

Why was this happening? Since the early 2010s, many U.S. jails eliminated free in-person family visits when they signed contracts with the multi-billion-dollar prison-and-jail telecommunications industry, which is largely owned by private equity companies. The theory was: if jails get rid of free in-person visits, desperate people will spend more money on phone and video calls to stay connected with their loved ones. The companies got monopolies on calls at each jail through contracts they negotiated with sheriffs. By locking in high exclusive rates, they made hundreds of millions of dollars each year from the denial of human contact. And the contracts promised sheriffs a percentage of the profits. In return, many of the contracts required sheriffs to end free in-person visits, and also required that the government keep the jail population above a specified minimum capacity to ensure a large enough market.[2]

The Genesee County sheriff, Chris Swanson, achieved national fame after the murder of George Floyd in 2020. On May 30, 2020, Sheriff Swanson put down his weapon and walked with protesters in Flint, declaring that police "love" them.[3] With cameras rolling, he pointed at a fellow police officer and told the protesters "that cop over there hugs people." A few years later, he would be a featured prime-time speaker at the Democratic National Convention that nominated Kamala Harris for president. National news stories did not mention that the hug-loving sheriff had banned family visits. Nor did they mention that he was collecting hundreds of thousands of dollars every year from the families of people he detained before trial, a disproportionate number of whom were Black and extremely poor.[4] Internal documents that my organization, Civil Rights Corps, obtained before we sued Swanson on behalf of children in Flint show that the contract he negotiated generates huge profits for the sheriff's office and the telecom monopoly, even though research shows that eliminating visits makes both the jail and society at large less safe. But as one county official put it in an internal email: "A lot of people will swipe that Mastercard." Children in Flint could no longer hug their parents because some people were making a lot of money, not because our society is better for it.[5]

Swanson was not alone. In the days after George Floyd was murdered, news stories across the country appeared, depicting police in city after city kneeling, marching beside, and even dancing the Macarena with protesters.[6] Local news quoted Louisiana sheriff Sid Gautreaux saying he was "sickened and heartbroken to see such callous disregard for another human being." The news reports of his compassion did not mention that more than forty human beings had died in Gautreaux's secretive jail between 2012 and 2020 or that sheriffs in Louisiana take a percentage cut of every cash bail posted.[7] The day after Swanson declared that police "love" and want to hug racial justice protesters in Flint, former Houston Police chief Art Acevedo removed his COVID-19 mask and appeared on the verge of crying as he offered reporters a chance to film his police escort to the funeral home for Floyd's body. The Houston Police Department updated its profile picture on social media to display Floyd's image. The coverage of Acevedo did not mention that Houston-area police had harassed, handcuffed, and caged Floyd repeatedly for years, ultimately prompting his relocation to Minnesota in search of a better life. While Chief Acevedo was grandstanding about his compassion for Floyd, he was quietly refusing to release video footage of six fatal Houston police shootings over a six-week period, the final one occurring on the same day Floyd was killed.[8]

There is a gulf between the image and the reality of the punishment bureaucracy. Copaganda creates that gulf. It is the system of government and news media propaganda that promotes mass incarceration, justifies the barbarities and profits that accompany it, and distorts our sense of what threatens us and what keeps us safe.

Watching police public relations officials across the country use the news media to portray themselves as social justice defenders after the murder of George Floyd marked a turning point in my career. It was an important time for copaganda, a rare moment when police, prosecutors, and prisons were vulnerable to exposure and mass rejection. More than a decade of widespread criticism against mass incarceration had made "criminal justice reform" a bipartisan issue. State and federal prison populations had been decreasing since 2009, and Michelle Alexander's thesis in her bestselling *The New Jim Crow*—that mass incarceration was a contemporary form of systemic racial oppression—had become conventional wisdom among liberals. During the first three months of the COVID-19 pandemic, the number of people in local jails dropped by 200,000 after advocates sucessfully pressured local officials to prioritize public health.[9] Mass movements led by the people most harmed by police and prisons led to Black Lives Matter protests in 2014 and 2015—and then, in 2020, the largest protests in U.S. history. Between 15 and 26 million people took to the streets in the first few weeks after the police murdered George Floyd.[10] In one major poll taken the week after the murder, 54 percent of Americans said that the burning of a Minneapolis police precinct was either "fully" or "partially" justified.[11] Calls to reduce the size and power of the punishment bureaucracy were ubiquitous, especially among young people and a new wave of political candidates running on that platform.

It was in that moment of mass movement, public consciousness, and potential change that I began to focus on how the news media supports the punishment bureaucracy. I had always been critical of how the news "manufactures consent" for inequality and oppression, to use Edward Herman and Noam Chomsky's phrase from their landmark examination of the political economy of the mass media.[12] But news media reactions to the 2020 uprisings alarmed me. Without subtlety or pretense to objectivity, the news seemed eager to undercut growing public consciousness about the failures of the punishment bureaucracy and to endorse a worldview that, by contrast, legitimized and valorized it. And so, starting in June 2020, I began to archive news stories on the punishment bureaucracy and to study the vested interests that use the news to shape the way we think about crime, safety, and the legal system.[13] Punishment bureaucrats understand something important: the news affects what and who we are afraid of, and in turn, which solutions we conjure to meet those fears.

Once I started looking more closely, I saw copaganda everywhere in coverage of crime and safety. In the aftermath of the 2020 uprisings, the news stoked a society-wide panic about one kind of crime or another despite police statistics demonstrating that we were, and still are, living in a period with among the lowest number of police-recorded crimes in modern U.S. history. These manufactured panics were not focused on all crimes, but on specific crimes that the news associated with poor people, strangers, immigrants, and people of color. And most striking of all, story after story built up a consensus—one utterly contrary to scientific evidence—that giving more money to the punishment bureaucracy was the only serious solution to achieve public safety.

I started asking myself questions that became themes of this book: Why is this story *news*? Why are other potential stories about things that harm us not in the news? How did *this* story get to *this* reporter? Who are the sources interviewed, and who counts as an expert? Whose perspective is included in this story, and whose perspective is left out?

Who benefits from how the story is framed, from what words are used, from what facts the reporter tells us, and from what the reporter ignores? *What kind of person* is created by consuming today's news about crime and punishment?

I started to document patterns of how news coverage makes us afraid of certain people, fails to inform us of the things actually most likely to harm us, and misleads us about what kinds of social policies best promote human flourishing. I worked with crime survivors, scholars, community organizers, students, people in jail and prison, and the families most targeted by the punishment bureaucracy to study the reality of public safety—that the key to reducing interpersonal harm is addressing the underlying causes of interpersonal harm and violence by investing in things like education, housing, health care, human connection, and reducing inequality. Yet I saw over and over again how news outlets distort and obscure this reality. I began collecting a public archive of copaganda on social media and producing hundreds of threads and dozens of essays in a newsletter to illustrate how copaganda operates with daily examples. I met with hundreds of reporters, editors, producers, and news executives, and I was invited to provide trainings for some of the most prominent news outlets in the country. This book documents some of what I found and learned.

Documenting copaganda was a very personal project, and I want to say something about my own biases. I began my career as a public defender in Alabama and Washington, DC, representing people who could not afford an attorney. Then, as now, the U.S. was confining people to cages at six times its own historical average, five to ten times as much as comparable countries, and caging Black people at six times the rate of South Africa during Apartheid.[14] I saw firsthand, in a way that I had not understood from books and law school, the sheer scope of the bureaucracy required to remove millions of people from their homes, schools, churches, jobs, and families and to transfer them into government-run courtrooms and cells. I also saw how the punishment bureaucracy transformed many of us working within it.

In 2013, I was fortunate to receive a grant from Harvard Law School that enabled me to quit my job and start a nonprofit organization that uses civil rights laws to challenge injustices in the punishment bureaucracy. I finally had the resources to take a deeper look at the punishment assembly line, and to try to do something about it. I made that career shift because I care about all people being safe.

Unnecessary violence—both violence perpetrated by the government and violence that exists because of our collective failure to promote the policies that will address it—has killed many of my clients and caused me and many people I care about to suffer enormously. If the U.S. had imprisonment rates comparable to other countries today or like those the U.S. itself had before 1980, U.S. life expectancy would be almost two years longer than it is now.[15] Hundreds of millions of human life years are lost because of our society's unparalleled focus on attacking social problems through punishment.

I have now been a civil rights lawyer for more than a decade, filing lawsuits and developing policies that challenge widespread violations of the Constitution. The organization I started, Civil Rights Corps, grew to over thirty-five employees. Our cases have ended modern debtors' prisons in many cities in which tens of thousands of people were jailed for nonpayment of debts; gotten hundreds of thousands of people out of jail who were or would have been illegally detained before trial solely because their families were poor; prevented hundreds of thousands of illegal convictions; prevented tens of thousands of families from being separated; shut down companies profiting from illegally extorting people for cash with threats of jail; returned tens of millions of dollars to tens of thousands of the poorest people in our society; vindicated the rights of sexual assault, domestic abuse, and gun violence survivors when prosecutors illegally threatened them; won civil rights cases against dozens of police officers for brutality and corruption; enabled the return of driver's licenses to hundreds of thousands of people who had been unable to drive anywhere because they owed debts; played a key role in blocking several billion dollars in new investments in policing and prisons; saved local governments hundreds of millions of dollars that they would have spent on jailing; and successfully sued more judges that anyone I am aware of in U.S. history.[16]

And yet, despite the success of our civil rights cases and the even greater successes of many other advocates, a core myth persists that the punishment bureaucracy is primarily concerned with, and effective at producing, public safety. That myth, which is consistently pushed in the news, has allowed the punishment bureaucracy to resist significant change and even to expand into new areas. Time and again, after our legal victories exposed corruption, ineffectiveness, and illegal government violence, the bureaucrats who created the problem would propose a "solution" that simply refashioned the profitable status quo: similar injustice, new label.

My years as an advocate for my indigent clients and their families led me to believe that things could be different if the news told different stories in different ways.

Who Benefits from Copaganda?

Copaganda is a specific type of propaganda in which the punishment bureaucracy and the powerful interests behind it influence how we think about crime and safety. I use the term "punishment bureaucracy" instead of "criminal justice system" in this book because it is a more accurate and less deceptive way to describe the constellation of public and private institutions that develop, enforce, and profit from criminal law.[17]

The government determines what things are considered a "crime" subject to punishment versus what things are permitted or tolerated even if they hurt people. Then, the government determines what kinds of punishments are appropriate for the conduct it prohibits. Across history and different societies, the definition of crime and how it should be punished has varied depending on who has power and what serves their interests, not an objective evaluation of what causes *harm*.

The following questions illustrate my point. Is it a crime to take food from a grocery store chain without paying for it if you're hungry? To terminate a pregnancy? To sleep on the subway or in a park? To beg on a sidewalk? To ingest a substance so that you can feel better? To belong to a union? To refuse to grant mortgages to Catholics? To charge high interest rates? To steal your employees' wages? To drill for oil? To release toxic liquids into the water? To seize land from Indigenous people? To participate in a lynch mob? To enslave people? To fire someone from a job based on their sexual orientation? To evict someone from their home for complaining about mold? To sexually harass someone at work? To hoard wealth? To decide not to vote? To abuse a family dog? To abuse thousands of pigs to make higher profits from their flesh? To donate money to a politician with the expectation that they will approve a real estate deal? To refuse to identify oneself to a police officer? To expose secret government misdeeds in the media? To hit one's child? To boycott apartheid? To design voting boundaries based on race? To charge someone overdraft fees and change the order of their transactions to rack up more overdraft fees? To run a bank for profit? To raise the price on a life-saving medication after purchasing a monopoly on it? To force sex upon a spouse? To search a person without probable cause? To grow tobacco? To have oral sex with another consenting adult? To hold profits offshore? To sag your pants? To possess a gun? To possess a hunting rifle ten years after a marijuana conviction?

The powerful define crime to suit their interests, making some things legal and others punishable. They also decide how what is criminalized gets punished. Should the government execute or cage or whip people who break a law? Should the government mandate a public apology, permit survivors to initiate restorative processes, seize assets, require volunteer work, revoke a business or driver's license, confine someone to their home, banish them? Should society show them love and give them help? Should society instead invest more in preventing certain harms from happening in the first place?

Having defined crime and punishment, the government also determines *which crimes* to enforce against *which people*. "Law enforcement" rarely responds to most violations of the law. It only enforces *some* criminal laws against *some* people *some* of the time.

These decisions, too, follow patterns of power, not safety. That is why U.S. police chose for many years to arrest more people for marijuana possession than for all "violent crime" *combined*. That is why police prioritize budgets for SWAT teams to search for drugs in poor communities over testing rape kits. That is why the Los Angeles Sheriff's Office responded to proposed county budget cuts by threatening to cut the divisions that handle white-collar crimes and sexual abuse. That is why about 90 percent of people prosecuted for crimes are very poor. That is why no senior figures were prosecuted for the 2008 financial crisis or the U.S. torture program after 9/11. That is why police tolerate widespread drug use in dorms at Ivy League universities. That is why most of the undercover police operations in hundreds of U.S. cities target disproportionately Black, Hispanic, and immigrant people instead of other police officers, prosecutors, real estate developers, fraternities with histories of drug distribution and rape, or corporate board rooms with histories of tax evasion, fraud, and insider trading. That is why a playground fight at a low-income school results in a child being taken away from their parents and jailed with a criminal record, while the same fight at a prep school may result in a call to parents for an early pickup that afternoon.[18]

In an unequal society where a few have more money and power than the many, the punishment bureaucracy is a tool for preserving inequalities. It maintains the social order by using government violence to manage the unrest that comes from unfairness, desperation, and alienation, and it crushes organized opposition against the political system. These functions explain why the punishment bureaucracy expands during times of growing inequality and social agitation. Throughout history, those who are comfortable with how society looks tend to preserve and expand the punishment bureaucracy, even though—and largely because—it operates as an anti-democratic force. Those who have wanted to change certain aspects of our society—such as movements for workers, racial justice, women's suffrage, economic equality, peace, ecological sustainability, immigrant rights, LGBTQ+ rights, and so on—have tended throughout history to combat the size, power, and discretion of the punishment bureaucracy. Why? Because it is almost always wielded against them.

A lot of punishment bureaucrats are involved in the system: police, prosecutors, prison and jail guards, probation and parole officers, judges, and other government employees who design and carry out the system's policies. But the punishment bureaucracy has also been commercialized. Many people know about privatized prisons, but even bigger industries profit from nearly every aspect of the administration of public human-caging facilities, including medical care, food, telephone calls, digitized mail, cash transfer systems, "education," tablets for entertainment, so-called "treatment" programs, and prison industries that make products for the world's largest corporations with modern-day slave labor.

This commercial sector reaches far beyond the walls of our privatized prisons and jails. Companies profit from manufacturing guns, jail cells, detention centers, handcuffs, tasers, batons, uniforms, body armor, tanks, license plate readers, body cameras, facial recognition software, chemical weapons, and military equipment used by police. A multibillion-dollar industry profits from discretionary arrest and pretrial release decisions by selling bail bonds. Companies make even larger profits from surveillance equipment, software, training programs, drug tests, electronic monitors, car towing schemes, police auctions of seized property, private halfway houses, forensic consultants, big-data databases, debt-collection contracts, and case management systems for courts, prosecutors, police, probation and parole departments, and prisons. On top of all that, the police public relations industry rakes in money while police unions, probation and parole officer unions, prison guard unions, and prosecutor unions maximize their members' wages, overtime, pensions, and benefits worth tens of billions of dollars. Most broadly, there is a growing web of multinational consulting corporations who contract with police, prisons, border patrol, and military bureaucracies to help procure and market these commodities and services.[19]

The fact that many people benefit from mass incarceration does not necessarily mean that all punishment bureaucrats are cynical profiteers—although many of them are. The range of people who depend on the punishment bureaucracy for their livelihoods has created an ideological foundation that enables many of them to believe that their role in the bureaucracy makes our society safer. Professional bureaucrats themselves consume and believe copaganda, and they make some of its best ambassadors.

So, how does copaganda work? It has three main roles.

Job #1: Narrowing Our Understanding of Threat

The first job of copaganda is to narrow our conception of threat. Rather than the bigger threats to our safety caused by people with power, we narrow our conception to crimes committed by the poorest, most vulnerable people in our society. For example, wage theft by employers dwarfs all other property crime combined—such as burglaries, retail theft, and robberies—costing an estimated $50 billion every year. Tax evasion steals about $1 trillion each year. That's over sixty times the wealth lost in all police-reported property crime. There are hundreds of thousands of known Clean Water Act violations each year, causing cancer, kidney failure, rotting teeth, damage to the nervous system, and death. Over 100,000 people in the United States die every year from air pollution, about *five times* the number of homicides. At the same time, most sexual assaults, domestic violence crimes, and sex offenses against children go unreported, unrecorded, and ignored by the legal system.[20]

Punishment bureaucrats feed reporters stories that measure "safety" as any short-term increase or decrease in, say, official homicide or robbery rates, rather than by how many people died from lack of health care, how many children suffered lead poisoning, how many families were rendered homeless by eviction or foreclosure, how many people couldn't pay utility bills because of various white-collar crimes, how many thousands of illegal assaults police and jail guards committed, and so on. Sometimes the rates of various crimes go up and down, and we should all be concerned about any form of violence against any human being. But the first job of copaganda is getting us focused *almost exclusively* on a narrow range of the threats we face, mostly the officially-recorded crimes of poor people, rather than the large-scale devastation wrought by people with power and money.

Job #2: Manufacturing Fear

The second job of copaganda is to manufacture crises and panics about this narrow category of threats. After the 2020 George Floyd uprisings, for example, the news bombarded the public with a series of "crime waves" concerning various forms of crime committed by the poor even though government data showed that, despite some categories of police-reported crime rising and others falling at the beginning of the pandemic, overall property and violent crime continued to be at near-historic fifty-year lows the entire time.[21] As a result of continual news-generated panics, nearly every year of this century, public opinion polls showed people believing that police-reported crime was rising, even when it was generally falling.[22]

Copaganda leaves the public in a vague state of fear. It manufactures suspicion against poor people, immigrants, and racial minorities rather than, say, bankers, pharmaceutical executives, fraternity brothers, landlords, employers, and polluters. Copaganda also engenders fear of strangers while obscuring the oppressive forces that lead to interpersonal violence between acquaintances, friends, and family members. (Police themselves commit one-third of all stranger-homicides in the U.S., but these figures are generally excluded from reported crime rates.)[23] This matters because when people are in a perpetual state of fear for their physical safety, they are more likely to support the punishment bureaucracy and authoritarian reactions against those they fear.

Job #3: Promoting Punishment as the Solution

The third job of copaganda is to convince the public to spend more money on the punishment bureaucracy by framing police, prosecutors, probation, parole, and prisons as effective solutions to interpersonal harm. Copaganda links safety to things the punishment bureaucracy does, while downplaying the connection between safety and the material, structural conditions of people's lives. So, for example, a rise in homeless people sleeping in the street might be framed as an economic problem requiring more affordable housing, but copaganda frames it as "disorder" solvable with more arrests for trespassing. Instead of linking sexual assault to toxic masculinity or a lack of resources and vibrant social connections to escape high-risk situations, copaganda links it to an under-resourced punishment system. Like a media-induced Stockholm syndrome, copaganda sells us the illusion that the violent abuser is somehow the liberator, the protector, our best and only option.

If police, prosecutions, and prisons made us safe, we would be living in the safest society in world history. But, as I discuss later, greater investment in the punishment bureaucracy actually increases a number of social harms, including physical violence, sexual harm, disease, trauma, drug abuse, mental illness, isolation, and even, in the long term, police-recorded crime.[24] Instead, overwhelming evidence supports addressing the controllable things that determine the levels of interpersonal harm in our society, including: poverty; lack of affordable housing; inadequate healthcare and mental wellness resources; nutrition; access to recreation and exercise; pollution; human and social connection; design of cities, buildings, and physical environments; and early-childhood education.[25] Addressing root causes like these would lower police-reported crime and also prevent the other harms that flow from inequality that never make it into the legal system for punishment, including millions of avoidable deaths and unnecessary suffering that exceed the narrow category of harm that police record as "crime."

The obsessive focus by news outlets on the punishment bureaucracy as a solution to interpersonal harm draws away resources from investment in the things that work better, along with a sense of urgency for those priorities. It also promotes the surveillance and repression of social movements that are *trying to solve those root structural problems* by fighting for a more equal and sustainable society.[26] Copaganda thus contributes to a cycle in which the root causes of our safety problems never get solved even though people in power constantly claim to be trying.

As you read the examples collected in this book with the above three themes in mind, ask yourself: what kind of *public* is created by consuming such news? If we see one of these articles once, we may not notice anything odd, or we may shake our heads at how silly, uninformed, and nefarious it is. But if we see thousands of them over the course of years, and we hardly see anything else, we become different people. It is the ubiquity of copaganda that requires us to set up daily practices of individual and collective vigilance.

This book focuses on copaganda in the news. I'm not going to analyze other common types of copaganda, including fictional copaganda in television, movies, and music. Cultural copaganda is all around us—from the CIA, starting in the 1950s, funding projects like the Iowa Writers' Workshop or fronting literary magazines to influence modern journalism and fiction writing, to the DEA paying Hollywood in the 1990s to insert drug war propaganda into popular television shows, to the vast array of police and military consultants who shape every fictional TV series, podcast, or movie that touches on crime.[27] Shows like *COPS* and *Law & Order* have done a lot to distort society's understanding of what the punishment bureaucracy does. The creator of the latter, for example, explained that his goal was to help people understand that prosecutors were doing "God's work." The NYPD even signed Spike Lee to a $219,113 marketing contract before he made his movie *BlackKkKlansman*—perhaps the most flagrant copaganda that I have ever seen because of its simplistic good cop/bad cop depictions and erasure of the systemic functions of the punishment bureaucracy.[28] (It's also a very bad movie.)

The entire genre of police procedurals mythologizes punishment bureaucrats and the allegedly sophisticated technologies they wield. And it's not just Hollywood—fictional copaganda planned and paid for by the police and their industry allies is on TikTok and YouTube, and it's behind many community groups, online posts, neighborhood list-serv emails, and charitable campaigns that seem genuine to the unassuming public. But all of that is beyond the scope of this book, which is about news coverage of crime and safety. Many of the lessons explored here, however, enable a more critical consumption of other kinds of copaganda too.

I also largely avoid self-consciously partisan right-wing media. The *New York Post*, Fox News, and a prodigious right-wing propaganda ecosystem are enormously influential, and they must be studied. But if I reference them, I will simply note similarities in ideology to what many people perceive to be more objective and trusted news. Although more "mainstream" news uses different words and methods, the ideologies and effects of its coverage are similar to a lot of right-wing media. The modest goal of this book is to reach people who do *not* have the goal of pushing society toward greater inequality and authoritarianism and are instead open to understanding the world more honestly and working for a better one.

I focus on the most prestigious corporate news outlets because their copaganda is often the most subtle and insidious, and because it is targeted at people who think of themselves as informed. These news outlets, such as the *New York Times*, also tend to set the agenda, to reflect the vibes and zeitgeist of people in power, and to play an important role in legitimating authoritarian repression among liberal elites. This should not be read as a judgment that crime stories in lo-cal TV news are not copaganda. To the contrary, the daily and nightly volume of crude local crime stories is perhaps the single most im-portant feature of contemporary news copaganda. But my focus will mostly be on teasing out lessons from more sophisticated news sources that are also applicable to less sophisticated ones. And every exam-ple I discuss represents something pervasive that infects the larger world of media—it is chosen precisely because of its prevalence in the copaganda ecosystem.

Finally, this book is a creature of a particular moment. I ana-lyze examples from the news about crime and safety from 2020 to 2024. This is not a comprehensive historical account of copaganda or a scholarly work with new theories on the media. I attempt only to apply replicable methods of critical thinking to news stories at a time when the punishment bureaucracy faced the greatest threat to its power in modern history and at a time of rising domestic and global authoritarianism.

I took a second picture that day in front of the jail in downtown Flint. The second picture shows how the punishment bureaucracy

responded to children's messages of love for their parents, who were jailed by the sheriff because their families could not make cash payments and who were now forbidden to have family visits because of a telecom-profit scheme. Employees emerged from the sheriff's office and hosed down the sidewalk. The vibrant chalk drawings of flowers and hearts were reduced to splotches of muted color, like an abstract expressionist's representation of bureaucratic cruelty. Police had mangled the messages of love from children to their parents—a distortion of human truth that made me think about George Orwell's warning of an authoritarian propaganda apparatus so pervasive that it could challenge the notion that two and two make four. But the children of Flint, who would come back again and again to redraw their messages, understood something important: the forceful denial of honest communication is the forceful denial of a meaningful life.

1

What Is Crime News?

St. Augustine tells the story of a pirate captured by Alexander the Great, who asked him "how he dares molest the sea." "How dare you molest the whole world?" the pirate replied: "Because I do it with a little ship only, I am called a thief; you, doing it with a great navy, are called an Emperor."

-Noam Chomsky[1]

It is said that the camera cannot lie, but rarely do we allow it to do anything else, since the camera sees what you point it at: the camera sees what you want it to see. The language of the camera is the language of our dreams.

-James Baldwin[2]

In 2022, I appeared on a Sunday morning news show in Los Angeles amid an increase in local news stories about theft. I pointed out patterns in which news stations devoted more coverage to low-level theft than to other behavior that causes more suffering, including larger forms of theft. The anchor incredulously asked me why the news should not be covering it when a man in a Ferrari is robbed and has his Rolex taken in Beverly Hills, which he explained was "one of the most affluent areas." Referencing that anecdote and retail theft by groups of teenagers in clothing stores, he said, "I think we have an obligation to cover that, don't you think?"[3] How we think about his question depends on what one thinks to be the purpose of news.

Air pollution kills 10 million people each year and causes untold additional illness and suffering.[4] It kills at least 100,000 people in the United States alone annually—about five times the number of police-reported

homicides. But it rarely features in daily news stories. Police and prosecutors ignore pollution, much of which is *criminal*, and so do most
journalists. For example, federal prosecutors charged twenty-three people with environmental offenses in 2020, and they charged more than
23,000 people with drug offenses in the same period.[5] Daily news stories
focus on the kinds of legal violations publicized by police and prosecutor
press releases, usually involving poor people.

Why is this important? Because what the news treats as urgent affects what we *think* is urgent. It shapes what (and who) we are afraid of. It
helps dictate what we demand from our political system, and from each
other. Imagine if, every day for the last four years, every newspaper and
TV station had "breaking news" stories and graphics about the thousands of deaths the night before from water pollution, eviction, lack of
access to medication and health care, or poverty.[6] Or debilitating inju-
ries caused by workplace safety violations? Or tens of thousands of child
labor violations? What about the death, destruction, cancer, infertility,
and other harms to humans, animals, and ecosystems from criminal acts
of industrial littering in cities across the U.S. every day?

Imagine a daily news segment on your local TV station called
"Bad Landlord of the Day," where the anchor reported on the worst
building code violations that government regulators document each
day. Imagine a "Bad Employer of the Week" segment for wage-theft
violations that local, state, and national regulators find every day.[7] Or
a "Bad Insurer of the Week" story about fraudulent denials of health
care benefits that lead people to suffer and die. Imagine if reporters
reported stories every day from people who could not pay for diapers
or food because of illegal lending practices? Or stories from nurses,
doctors, or teachers about threats to well-being they see every day
through lack of investment in health and education infrastructure? If
we were bombarded with daily and nightly stories and press conferences about harmful legal violations and broader threats that cause
far more harm than the kinds of legal violations reported in the daily

news, how would that change political discourse and how would it change what investments we prioritize as a society?

Consider, for example, the frenzy over "retail theft" that took over local and national news after the uprisings over police violence in 2020. The same editors and reporters who wrote thousands of stories about low-level shoplifting from chain stores chose for years *not* to cover the estimated $137 million in corporate wage theft that happens *every day*, including by the same companies whose press releases about shoplifting they quoted. The news media's obsession with shoplifting led to emergency actions by politicians across the U.S. to address the "crisis" of retail theft through hundreds of millions of dollars in new punishment investments. Politicians felt intense political pressure to pass laws, hire and assign thousands more police officers, and increase "enforcement" budgets to tackle a supposed "wave" of retail theft, even as police-recorded theft crimes were going *down*. These politicians and journalists nonetheless projected an urgency they have *never* shown for wage theft.[8]

Measured in dollars lost, total estimated wage theft is more devastating than all other police-reported property crime combined.[9] And, unlike theft from big retail stores, wage theft is a crime committed by people with a lot of money against workers, many of whom struggle to meet their basic needs.[10] In a society in which access to health care depends on having the means to pay for it, wage theft can mean not having enough money to buy insulin or asthma medication. It is among the most significant and common crimes in our society.

What about the 28,260 to 412,000 deaths caused every year in the U.S. because of toxic lead exposure? When a bombshell investigation by *The Guardian* revealed in 2022 that a huge percentage of pipes in Chicago, the third largest city in the U.S., contained unsafe levels of lead for children, the story was not covered at all by CNN, the *New York Times*, *Wall Street Journal*, *USA Today*, the *Washington Post*, ABC News, CBS News, or NBC News. Intentional action, incompetence, and corruption leading to delays in lead abatement is almost *never* covered in the news, local or national. As a result, cities like Chicago have exhibited little urgency to fix the problem: the current pace of lead abatement in Chicago would not finish the project for a thousand years.[11]

Or, to take another example, in many years fraudulent overdraft fees charged by banks total about the same as all burglary, larceny, car theft, and shoplifting combined.[12] But the news doesn't report on anecdotes of overdraft fraud crimes by bankers every day. Similarly, it is hard to grasp the scope of the news's daily silence on the estimated $1 trillion in yearly tax evasion—this is 1,672 times the value of all U.S. robberies combined.[13] What about the estimated $830 billion in other forms of corporate fraud each year?[14] Addressing financial crimes could significantly alter the distribution of wealth, the array of life opportunities, and physical safety for hundreds of millions of human beings. But neither the police nor the media pay much attention to them, and they certainly don't foment panic about them.

The same principle applies across public health, banking, manufacturing, employment, consumer protection, taxation, and the environment: the things that cause the greatest suffering and threaten safety for the largest number of people—many of which are crimes—receive a fraction of the attention that reporters devote to the things police press releases publicize as crimes. Most people don't know, because the "news" didn't tell them the night before, that bankers' fraud crimes likely killed tens of thousands of people during the 2008 financial crisis.[15] Hundreds of thousands of people become homeless each year because of illegal evictions by landlords.[16] Almost none of this is reported each day even though there could easily be a housing-court beat reporter the same way many outlets assign a reporter to talk to police every day.

The same absence of urgently reported, daily anecdotal coverage applies to the great criminal littering epidemic: several trillion pieces of plastic are thrown illegally into our waterways each year, and they make their way into the bodies and bloodstreams of every living organism on the planet, with profound consequences for all of us. Are there local news anecdotes each day covering the "crime wave" of the intentional insertion of lead, mercury, cyanide, and cadmium into the ground? Or the tens of billions of dollars in fraud crimes committed by entities that are supposed to be providing hospice care for terminally ill seniors? At most, each of these issues is covered in an occasional, hard-hitting piece of investigative journalism, and then the news cycle moves on. They are not considered *daily* news of continuing alarm over public safety.[17]

None of this is to say that violent crime and property crime recorded by police doesn't matter, or that we shouldn't care about it. To the contrary, we should care about anything that harms people. But it is vital to be cognizant of what kinds of harm—by whom, against whom, in which moments, and to what end—are treated as "news." The news about public safety is a social and political creation that contains judgment calls at every turn, one that creates winners and losers and that could look different if we wanted it to.

So, who is deciding to cover each subsequent example of shoplifting with hourly, "breaking news" urgency, but not other legal violations that leave adults and children dying, sick, and in poverty? Who is shaping what makes us feel scared? Why are they doing it, and who benefits? Identifying the gap between the reality of holistic safety and "the news" is the first step in understanding how so many people who care about creating a society that expands our collective safety end up prioritizing investments in a punishment bureaucracy that ignores the things that threaten us the most.

2

The Volume of Crime News

When they stopped killing witches, witches ceased to exist.
                                                -Clarence Darrow[1]

How do you defend yourself from a fantasy? A fantasy that shoots real bullets?
                                                -Fred Moten[2]

An issue related to what counts as "news" is how intensely the news focuses on what it chooses to cover. The volume, timing, frequency, and delivery method of news stories shape how we think about safety and crime.

About ten years ago, when I was first investigating the rise of modern debtors' prisons, I asked a news editor if they could do a story on the thousands of human beings forcibly detained in jail cells each day solely because they owed debts. This seemed to be a big story for many reasons, including because it was illegal, because it was separating families and killing people who died because of our country's terrible jail conditions, and because it revealed widespread predatory behavior by police, prosecutors, judges, and private debt-collection and probation companies in several thousand cities, affecting hundreds of thousands of people. In fact, I had successfully pitched the story to another outlet before. But this editor declined. Why? Another reporter at a major news outlet had *"already covered the debtors' prison story* a few months ago."

That was the first time in my career I had really thought about what is considered "newsworthy" and what isn't. But it's now something I encounter a lot. In late 2022, I got a similar response from a different editor when I asked a major news outlet to cover the more than 400,000 human beings jailed across the U.S. for the holidays because their families could not pay cash bail. Every night, new people are jailed in violation of the Constitution, and new families suffer the corresponding loss of housing, jobs, medical care, and intimate relationships. The story is an interesting and important one because courts have concluded, after evaluating the available evidence, that these constitutional violations cost tens of billions of dollars in economic damage, spread infectious disease, make our society less safe by increasing future crime, and harm millions of families for generations. But the editor told me: "There have been other good stories on the bail system over the last few years."

In each of these two instances, the editor's explanations to me raise important questions about the *volume* of news. What does it mean to have "already covered" a social problem that continues happening unabated to new people each day? News editors do not decline to cover today's plane crash because they covered a previous one. Why is "the debtors' prison story" or "the bail story" conceptualized as a single one-off news story while stories about kidnapping and ransom—the criminalized parallel to debtors' prison—are seen as always new and newsworthy each time they happen?

If one were primarily focused on objective harm, one might expect thousands of new stories when so many parents are being illegally separated from their children solely because of their poverty in the wealthiest country in the world. What does the editor's use of the phrase "a few months ago" suggest about how journalists evaluate the urgency and importance of illegal incarceration of the poor versus the theft of another Rolex in Beverly Hills?

By contrast, during a two-week period in December 2022, the *New York Times* published three long articles about a supposed "shortage" of police officers in the U.S. One article, headlined "As Applications Fall, Police Departments Lure Recruits with New Tactics," regurgitated police union talking points, including that more police means more safety, that police need more money, and that this "shortage" is a crisis. The second article, "NYPD Officers Leave in Droves for Better Pay in Smaller

Towns," repeated these talking points by interviewing the reporter who wrote the first article. And the third article, "Why Police Officers Are Leaving: Low Pay, Overwork and High Costs," was written by a different reporter who used similar sources and therefore gave the same talking points.[3] What is the purpose and effect of editors approving three articles on this subject in a matter of days in the same news publication?

One of the most overlooked aspects of contemporary news analysis is how the volume of certain news stories distorts our understanding of what is important and reflects the priorities of those in power.[4] Most issues have no hope of penetrating a public discourse in a world of limited attention spans unless they become sustained news *themes* as opposed to single-coverage novelties. You can tell which stories people in power care about by their volume. The charts below show how the volume of "crime" segments on Fox News, CNN, and MSNBC ballooned as the U.S. neared the 2022 election:[5]

Mentions of topic relative to first six months of 2022

The figures below compare the average percentage of 15-second segments in a given day during a 10-day chunk of a month with the average percentage for 10-day chunks over the first six months of the year.

—— CNN —— Fox News ---- MSNBC

Source: GDELT Analysis of Internet Archive data   *The Washington Post*

Look at what happened on Fox News as soon as the 2022 midterm election was over:[6]

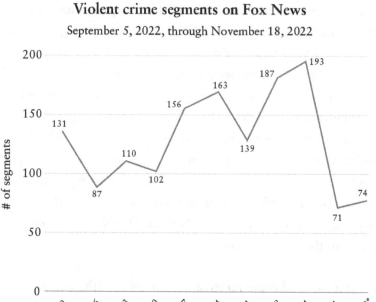

Violent crime segments on Fox News
September 5, 2022, through November 18, 2022

Source: Media Matters

Fox News is a sophisticated propaganda operation that understands the importance of news volume. The volume of its coverage is *not* linked to any objective reality concerning public safety. This point is crucial: the increased number of "violent crime" stories does not coincide with any increase of police-reported violent crime. But it *is* linked to a political event—an election—and Fox News understands that the number of times a story is told affects how many people hear it and how urgent people think the subject matter is. And this analysis applies equally to all mainstream, corporate-owned news outlets.

In another example, look at what happened to the volume of "violent crime" news stories in New York City when Eric Adams launched his campaign and then, dramatically, after he became mayor:[7]

Sounding Alarms

Digital and print media mentions of violent crime surged after Mayor Adams was elected

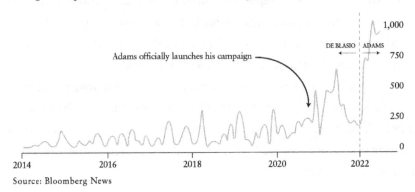

Source: Bloomberg News

The volume of news references to "shootings" was not connected to the number of shootings. It spiked after Adams came to office and made *talking to the news about shootings* a focus of his public relations strategy:

Media Mismatch

Coverage about shootings outweigh the number of incidents

☐ Number of shootings   ▨ Number of times shootings were mentioned in the media

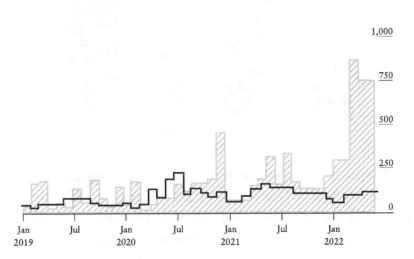

Note: Monthly media mentions of shootings are localized to NYC print and digital media headlines.
Sources: New York City Police Department, Media Cloud

These graphs show an enduring, decades-long trend: fluctuations in news coverage of police-reported crimes are not determined primarily by police-reported crime rates. Instead, they are more responsive to political occurrences, campaigns, and agendas. Public safety "news" surges when someone *wants police-reported crime to be news.*

This same thing that happens during elections happens in the context of contested legislation. For example, stories connecting bail reform in New York to crime increased when politicians deliberated over rolling back bail reforms in 2022—even though the evidence shows that bail reform *reduces* crime: [8]

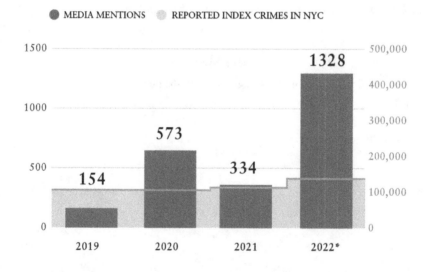

Media Mentions of Crime vs. Actual Rise in Crime in New York City

Perhaps the most famous instance of this phenomenon is the case of William "Willie" Horton, a Black man whose image and story were thrust into the 1988 presidential campaign through the sheer force of news volume. The *Lawrence Eagle-Tribune* alone published over 175 stories about Horton's release from prison, his subsequent rape of a white woman and assault of her white husband, and the Massachusetts prison furlough system. The governor of Massachusetts was running for president, and he reacted to the high-volume coverage by reducing eligibility for a routine prison furlough program, even though more than 99 percent of people released through the program returned to prison without incident.

The coverage was later credited, including by the *Lawrence Eagle-Tribune* itself, with helping George H.W. Bush win the election. The paper ran a post-election headline, "Horton Strategy Pays Off for Bush." More generally, the coverage contributed to an increase in public and political support for harsher sentencing laws and fewer release opportunities for people in prison all over the United States. Based on the social science evidence, these changes resulted in a net *harm* to public safety and had devastating consequences for Black people and poor people. The *Lawrence Eagle-Tribune* won the 1988 Pulitzer Prize.[9]

Many political, economic, and cultural forces distort the volume of news on public safety. The last several years have seen revealing examples. In the summer of 2021, a right-wing media personality posted a twenty-one-second video of a shoplifting incident at Walgreens in San Francisco with the hashtag #noconsequences and tagging the local district attorney.[10] The video was posted amid a public relations push by Walgreens to spin the news about its pre-planned store closures, as well as a political campaign by police unions, far-right media, and billionaires trying to recall the progressive district attorney in San Francisco.[11] Each of these groups sought to drive fear around retail theft for their own reasons, and mainstream news quickly adopted their viewpoint, running thousands of stories about shoplifting. These stories, with their message about the need for more policing and imprisonment, fueled the reactionary backlash against racial and social justice campaigns seeking to reduce the size and power of the police bureaucracy. And the news coverage also served the interests of real estate investors and commercial retail companies eager to use police to clear out neighborhoods for gentrification and to socialize corporate security costs.

Journalists at Fairness & Accuracy in Reporting (FAIR) did an analysis and found that, within twenty-eight days of being posted, this single shoplifting video spawned *309 separate articles* about the Walgreens incident. It was difficult to consume news in the U.S. without confronting this story in some format. At the same time, the researchers found not a single article about a multi-million-dollar wage-theft settlement that Walgreens paid to its California employees.[12]

In 2023, Walgreens admitted that the company had overblown its prior claims about retail theft, and investigative reporting debunked the hysteria by showing that reported shoplifting was *decreasing* and that the company had planned the store closures for unrelated business reasons. More broadly, the "shoplifting wave" narrative fell apart nationally after investigative reporters looked into the data and internal industry documents. In addition to the political campaigns by police, the reporters discovered another motive driving the timing of the stories: the retailers were lobbying for bills that would hurt their online competitors. Incredibly, by December 2023, it emerged that shoplifting had *not* actually increased from 2019 to 2023, and the leading retail trade group formally retracted its claims about the scope of U.S. shoplifting.[13]

But the damage had been done. As demonstrated by the following screenshot of five stories, all appearing on the *San Francisco Chronicle*'s web page on November 22, 2021, anecdotal news coverage had created a moral panic about retail theft.[14]

It wasn't just the *Chronicle*. During a six-day period, CNN assigned three reporters to do different stories about shoplifting in San Francisco, repeating false statements by Walgreens and calling for bigger police budgets.[15]

The trend spread across the country. The NYPD public relations department announced a coordinated takedown of a dozen shoplifters using twenty-three arrest and search warrants, and then tweeted out the kind of photo usually reserved for multi-million-dollar drug cartel busts. This time, the arrests yielded a lot of diapers. During the highly touted shoplifting bust, police seized basic necessities worth an average of $150 from twelve people, some of whom were living in homeless shelters.[16]

Packs of thieves hit stores in Walnut Creek, Hayward, S.J. Any ties to Union Square...

Bay Area retailers were on alert after groups of thieves rushed a Nordstrom in Walnut Creek on Saturday night and then hit stores in Hayward and San Jose on Sunday, stealing merchandise in the wake of Friday's ransacking of San Francisco high-end retailers in Union Square.

- S.F. leaders promise crackdown after night of Union Square looting

- Looters hit Union Square luxury stores in wild rampage

- S.F.'s Castro Safeway closing early because of 'out of control' shoplifting

- Is shoplifting forcing Walgreens to cut back in S.F.?

NYPD NEWS
@NYPDnews

After receiving numerous larceny complaints in the Bronx, officers from the @NYPD44Pct recently arrested 12 individuals following an enforcement initiative targeting shoplifters. The arrests made led to the closure of 23 warrants & the recovery of $1800 worth of merchandise.

Anatole France remarked in 1894 that "the law, in its majestic equality, forbids rich and poor alike to sleep under bridges." [17] One might now say that the news, in its majestic impartiality, covers the shoplifting of diapers by the rich and the poor with equal fervor.

Amid this barrage of stories about the manufactured "retail theft" panic, I noticed something weird while reading the *Chicago Tribune*. Many of the articles looked eerily similar. They started using the same words and phrases that appeared in industry and police press releases— "brazen," "organized crime," "flash mobs," and "smash and grab." During a period of nine days the *Chicago Tribune*, the Associated Press, and the *New York Times* each published a feature news article on retail theft becoming more "brazen," with punishment bureaucrats calling for more money. Look at the sources cited in each article:[18]

The *Chicago Tribune*:

- CEO of a local retail lobby
- National Retail Federation
- Chicago Police
- CEO of Magnificent Mile, a Chicago retail business association
- CEO of Illinois's Retail Merchants Association
- CEO of World Business Chicago
- President of the Illinois Restaurant Association
- CEO of the Illinois Hotel & Lodging Association
- CEO of a new luxury hotel
- Retail association CEO, again

The Associated Press:

- President of the conservative California District Attorneys Association
- "Authorities"

- President and CEO of the California Retailers Association
- "National retail groups"
- Director of California's chapter of the National Federation of Independent Businesses
- San Mateo County Sheriff
- California Governor
- California Attorney General
- San Francisco District Attorney
- Pro-establishment non-profit
- Attorney for the California District Attorneys Association
- California Retailers Association, again

Finally, the *New York Times*:

- President of the California Retailers Association
- Vice President of Asset Protection at Home Depot
- "Retail executives and security experts"
- "Industry veterans"
- President of the Coalition of Law Enforcement and Retail
- "Some industry experts"
- Head of the California Retail Trade Group
- California Governor
- Coalition of Law Enforcement and Retail (twice)
- Sergeant from the Broward County Sheriff's Office

The *Tribune* article on "organized" retail theft painted a picture of a city in chaos, calling for more investment in police and more felony prosecutions. Alarming phrases in the article included:

- "Organized crime and seemingly random assaults"
- "There's nowhere that's immune."
- "Increasingly brazen retail thefts and assaults"

- "Growing fear of crime among travelers"
- "Criminal activity plaguing the city"
- "We hear about all these murders and shootings, and we're afraid. We're afraid to come there."
- "The rise in crime may discourage new tenants."
- "But getting crime under control . . . will require more than increased security by the retailers" (by a business leader blaming shoplifting on lenient criminal sentences).

This article was written in one of the premier news outlets in one of the largest cities in the U.S., at a time when property crime—specifically theft—was *down* from the prior year and near historic lows. The Chicago Police Department publishes the data:[19]

Property Crime	2020	2021	% CHANGE
Burglary	8,752	6,655	-24.0%
Larceny - Theft	41,268	40,583	-1.7%
Motor Vehicle Theft	9,951	10,566	6.2%
Arson	585	516	-11.8%
Property Crime Subtotal	60,556	58,320	-3.7%
Index Crime Total	85,197	84,316	-1.0%

During the late 2021 news media panic over retail theft, there were almost no stories run in major news outlets on far larger property crimes like wage theft, tax evasion, antitrust violations, and securities fraud. In the following chart, the Center for Just Journalism looked at several years of data on the number of stories about various crimes in the top ten newspapers in the U.S. compared with the economic harm done by those crimes.

To see this play out in real time, look at something that happened in January 2022. All of a sudden, in news outlets across the country, a new crisis emerged: a supposed wave of thefts from cargo trains in Los Angeles operated by a multi-billion-dollar monopoly company.[20] The articles usually cited only police and railroad industry public relations

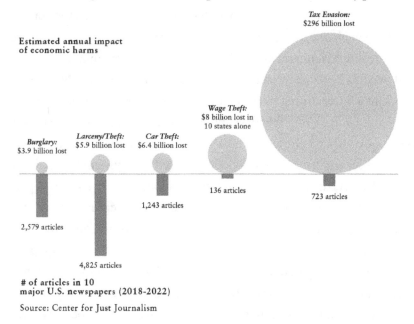

Media coverage of economic harm prioritizes crimes tracked by police

Estimated annual impact
of economic harms

Tax Evasion:
$296 billion lost

Wage Theft:
$8 billion lost in
10 states alone

Burglary:
$3.9 billion lost

Larceny/Theft:
$5.9 billion lost

Car Theft:
$6.4 billion lost

136 articles

723 articles

1,243 articles

2,579 articles

4,825 articles

# of articles in 10
major U.S. newspapers (2018-2022)

Source: Center for Just Journalism

executives, asserting that the crisis necessitated bigger police budgets to provide security for private companies.

It later emerged that the avalanche of stories began with a letter from a railroad company lobbyist complaining about reduced punishment for theft from trains by the supposedly progressive district attorney in Los Angeles. Not coincidentally, that prosecutor was then the subject of a nascent right-wing recall campaign. The story went viral after it was picked up by CBS, ABC, Fox News, the *New York Times*, and others. Many of the stories contained the same quotes, sources, turns of phrase, and suggestions of more surveillance, more money for police, and longer prison sentences. A powerful corporate monopoly was portrayed as a hapless victim of "organized" bands of "homeless" people stealing from trains. Each new story gave the impression that the emergency was expanding.

The high-volume news pressure worked: almost immediately, the governor of California was videotaped standing on train tracks

promising new expenditures on police to help the railroad monopoly—
urgent action he had never taken with respect to wage theft, for example.
With no evidence, the governor compared train thefts to the supposed
wave of shoplifting and said, "The train thieves are equally organized
and need to be prosecuted as such." Then, a group of Republican sena-
tors sent a letter urging a national federal crackdown on train theft.[21]

In the course of a few days, police, lobbyists, and journalists combined to concoct a panic around a truly minor problem relative to, say,
the cost-cutting by train monopolies that led to a systemic lack of train
safety. In fact, the railroad hub at issue had long been the scene of petty
thefts and littering, and not much had changed, except now news organizations had decided it was a *news* story. Other train companies were
not experiencing the same supposed problem, and it later emerged that
the train monopoly in question had been negligent by doing "little to secure or lock trains" and by decreasing its security staffing.[22] By the time
these facts became public, however, the panic had already occurred, taking its place in the series of similar panics about one petty crime after
another, all of which came with suggestions that the solution was more
police and prison funding. Only a tiny fraction of the people exposed to
the high volume of panic-inducing stories about "organized" train theft
ever learned the true context, because the investigation uncovering it
received a tiny fraction of the news volume.

Hot on the heels of this panic, California news media was onto a
new one: "burglary tourism" from wealthy homes near San Francisco.[23]

The scant evidence offered by the *San Francisco Chronicle* to

BAY AREA // CRIME

Is an international crime operation targeting the Bay Area's wealthiest cities with 'burglary tourism'?

Source: *San Francisco Chronicle*

substantiate the claim of an "international crime ring" was that "burglars in one instance were heard 'speaking Spanish' "; "three years ago, one burglary had ties to a car rented by someone visiting from Chile"; and "two other police departments in the U.S. said some burglaries were connected to 'South America.' " In reality, as the article admits, the number of burglaries in the town being profiled had grown from twenty-seven in 2018 to thirty-six in 2021. An increase of *nine burglaries* in three years. Strong evidence of an international crime syndicate run by Dr. Evil?

The point is not that no one ever steals from trains or commits burglary. But the volume of news stories on police-reported crimes dwarfs their relative importance on any conceivable metric of objective global and domestic harm. Such a barrage of reporting affects which harmful things we feel emotionally terrified of and which harmful things we rarely think about.

As with all news-driven panics, we must ask several questions about these panics: Why did police, politicians, and a multi-billion-dollar monopoly want us to think there was an imminent crisis at *that* moment? Why were the train thefts and burglaries portrayed as some sort of "organized crime" threat from vague but sophisticated bands of criminals? Why were the thefts linked to insufficient police funding and lenient prosecution? Why did the news treat it with more urgency than other issues that cause more harm? Why was it a national news story? Why, among all potential news stories, was it singled out for high-volume saturation?

The volume of public safety news is not driven by transparent, accountable, objective principles. News outlets make judgment calls using processes that are not made public to news consumers and that are often not written down, let alone audited after the fact. Most news outlets do not evaluate how many stories of certain kinds featuring certain sources get published. It's remarkable that a field so important to our lives has not developed more rigorous practices for evaluating potential biases in how it selects which things the public should know. The result is that things affecting hundreds of millions of people's safety and well-being, that kill millions of people, and that cause billions of dollars in harm are not even identified by casual news consumers as problems, while a small range of harms comes to dominate the public's imagination.

The volume of news about police-reported crime is instead driven by factors that most people agree should not determine newsworthiness: who owns media outlets and what serves their interests; police PR spending; relationships between reporters and sources that are culti-vated through for-profit consultants and elite social networks; racial bias about whose suffering matters and who is perceived as dangerous; the timing of political events; pending police union negotiations; the cultural or political interests of journalists and their social circles, and so on. More specifically, the amount of coverage is driven by political agendas of powerful people who can use their positions to get the media to keep covering an issue. Editors have, in my conversations with them, justified covering these powerful people's priorities by saying that they are simply covering what the CEOs and politicians are *talking about*. But here's the bottom line: in any of these situations, coverage volume choices are not driven by an objective analysis of well-being, safety, or human life.

There is a neverending battle to get news media to focus on particu-lar stories and not others. Given who is funding and who stands to ben-efit from these choices in this war, it is not surprising that a bad thing is deemed worthy of high-volume coverage if poor people are doing it, especially if poor people are doing the bad thing to rich people and if the poor people are not white. But when rich people are doing something bad to poor people, it's viewed as a niche story for boutique investigative pieces, not daily breaking news that the outlet must make sure everyone is aware of as a *trend*.

In my experience, reporters and editors nonetheless tell themselves that these public safety decisions are "objective." Reporters tend to use little tricks to rationalize why *this* shoplifting of a Rolex is different from last week's shoplifting of a deodorant by a different person. But when

writing about systemic constitutional violations in the money bail system, for example, reporters have often told me that when a judge violates
the constitutional rights of the alleged Rolex thief in the same way that a
different judge violated the rights of the alleged deodorant thief, it's the
"same story" that doesn't need to be reported twice.

There are many ways to make a low-level crime appear novel. In
this story it's a theft from Macy's, in that story it's a theft from CVS.
Now it's Walgreens! But wait, have you heard of train theft? We see
the contrast, for example, with the almost complete blackout on stories
about child labor violations, which are only covered every now and
then in an isolated investigative piece. If you consumed news in 2023,
I bet you did not know that the federal government found thousands
of child labor violations that year, the most documented violations in
two decades.[24] But individual stories about vulnerable children are not
told in high volume, unless it is a story about police arresting them
for something.

What determines this differential treatment is whether powerful
people benefit from something saturating the news or not. When trying to get news coverage about all the work that seeks to make our society more equal and just, those of us who talk to the media a lot know
that the onus is always on us to come up with a new angle to make the
story seem *different*. This is a bad situation if the story you really need
to tell is that our society continues to do a lot of the same things—in
the same ways—that harm the world's vulnerable people, animals, and
ecosystems every day.

Amplification

News volume isn't just about the number of stories. It's also about how
the news gets those stories to us. In the 1980s, the executive editor of the
New York Times explained: "Every journalist knows that a story on the
front page or its television equivalent can interest the whole country,
but that the same story, inside, often has no impact at all."[25] Journalists

understand that this principle extends beyond an article's physical placement on a website or the printed page.

For example, dedicated teams at most big media outlets decide which
of their stories to promote and which details to emphasize in marketing
the story. These include spreading some stories on social media with
sensationalizing captions and sending push notifications to our phones
to convey urgency, as the *Los Angeles Times* did in the heat of a misinformation campaign by the Los Angeles County Sheriff's Department
to oppose an ultimately successful local effort to reduce the sheriff's
fraudulent contract with the City of West Hollywood:[26]

News outlets and their marketing teams also make editorial decisions about which stories get sent to the news outlet's other platforms
such as its daily podcast, web show, and weekly roundup newsletter;
which get the "Live Blog" treatment with multiple reporters assigned
and automatic page refreshing for each new update every few minutes;
which get promoted on social media, and which aspects of each story are
pulled out for promotion through summarized captions that may be the
only thing most people ever see; which get selected for crossover stories
on the nightly TV news partnerships; and which stories are so important that they get day-after-day follow-up coverage, with new stories
about what people are saying about the initial story.

In 2015, the *New York Times* created an eleven-person team to focus on push alerts. "We used to be standing on a hill and shouting messages at people," the team leader said. "Now, by comparison, there's a growing number of users who only engage with us when we send a push."[27] Think about the potential urgency if local news sent a push notification every time a police officer illegally stopped, searched, and arrested someone. Or a push notification for every illegal eviction in your neighborhood. Or a push notification for every toxic dumping of chemicals that threatens the water that our families drink. Or for every time a local polluter exceeded emissions rules for toxic gas near a kindergarten. Or every time a general committed a war crime. Our political priorities as news consumers might look different.

The threat suggested by volume is not isolated to formal "news." Neighborhood news apps like NextDoor and the dystopian Citizen have tens of millions of users who receive push notifications about police-reported crime around them all the time, including phone alerts like "Man with gun reported near playground" and "Suspect seen heading west" and "Officers are in pursuit."[28] In this profit-driven culture of surveillance and dread, news organizations use push notifications about crime to compete for fear-based attention.

Whether made by news outlets or surveillance companies, decisions about what information to bombard the public with are not made based on an editorial analysis of which stories are most important for the well-being of our world.

3

Moral Panics and the Selective Curation of Anecdote

WHAT ARE the British people most concerned about today? Wages? Prices? Immigration? Pornography? People are talking about all these things. But the Sun believes there is another issue which has everyone deeply worried and angry: VIOLENCE IN OUR STREETS. . . .

Nothing could be more utterly against our way of life, based on a commonsense regard for law and order. . . . If punitive jail sentences help to stop the violence—and nothing else has done—then they will not only prove to be the only way. They will, regrettably, be the RIGHT way. And the judges will have the backing of the public.
                                                    -Editorial, *The Sun*, October 13, 1972[1]

By manipulating the volume of stories *at particular times*, the news media creates a society-wide frenzy concerning particular kinds of behavior by particular groups of people. Scholars call them "moral panics."

When a moral panic is created, it almost always leads to the expansion of government repression. That's what happened during the "crime waves" reported by the press in Victorian England, and in more recent U.S. moral panics like the 1980s panic about "crack babies," the 1990s panic about "super predators," the 2021–23 panic about "retail theft," and the ongoing multiyear panic about "fare evasion" by poor people on public transit.[2] Moral panics can also be acute creations of a particular news moment, such as the fabricated "Summer of Violence" in Denver, in which violent crime went down but increase in media stories about juvenile crime in 1993 led to expansion in the

incarceration of children;[3] the viral "train theft" story; the scientifically debunked panic about police officers overdosing on fentanyl by
touching or being near it;[4] and the 2023 panic about "carjacking" in
Washington, DC.

In each case, there were almost immediate policy responses that
increased the budgets of punishment bureaucrats, passed more punitive laws, and diverted the system's resources from other priorities. For
example, the shoplifting panic led California state lawmakers to furnish
$300 million more to police and prosecutors so they could punish retail
theft more aggressively. A few months later, the California governor
announced yet another measure, the "largest-ever single investment to
combat organized retail theft," adding another $267 million to fifty-five
police agencies. Justifying the move, the governor said: "When shame-
less criminals walk out of stores with stolen goods, they'll walk straight
into jail cells."[5]

Similarly, while news outlets were focused on the supposed crisis
of shoplifting in New York City, prosecutions for building code violations for fire safety went down 98 percent, after which seventeen
people died from a preventable fire in the Bronx.[6] When the *New York
Times* covered the fire, it didn't mention a pattern of code violations.
It didn't mention the criminal law at all. The news didn't connect
the fire to systemic conditions, or even mention the identity of the
landlord.[7] It wasn't the *kind* of crime about which the news foments
moral panics.

So, how do moral panics happen?

The seminal work on moral panics is the 1978 study *Policing the Crisis* by a group of British scholars led by legendary Jamaican-British sociologist Stuart Hall.[8] In the book, leading social theorists asked whether
it could be possible "that a societal reaction to crime could precede the
appearance of a pattern of crimes."[9] They dissected how the British police, courts, and news media manufactured panic about "mugging" that
resulted in more punishment and prosecution of Black immigrant youth

from former British colonies. Indeed, the concept and terminology of "mugging" as opposed to, say, "robbery" was *created* as part of the panic, even though there was no evidence that this ill-defined criminal activity was increasing. This is similar to the creation of the term "carjacking" in Detroit in the early 1990s. The book is profound, and I constantly recommend it to journalists.

During the 1960s and 1970s in England and the U.S., the news focused on Black people, poor people, and immigrants as the source of uncontrollable "crime waves." Their stories were nearly identical to what we see today: media panic about "crime waves" and quotes from police, prosecutors, and judges about the need to roll back so-called reforms framed as too lenient. The rhetoric of current punishment bureaucrats and pundits echoes almost verbatim the opinions voiced by conservative white business and police groups of the 1970s, although now there is more of an effort, as I'll discuss later, to portray such views as "progressive" and demanded by marginalized people themselves. In each case, minor tweaks in bureaucratic policy or marginal reforms that could not, as a matter of empirical reality, have a significant impact on society-wide violence are vehemently debated. The evidence of the root causes of interpersonal harm—like that marshaled by the Kerner Commission, which studied U.S. crime in 1968 and recommended massive social investment to reduce inequality—is ignored.[11] And the cycle continues: moral panic is followed by calls for more police surveillance, militarization, higher budgets for prosecutors and prisons, and harsher sentencing. Because none of these things affect violence too much, the problems continue.

Another important account is Mark Fishman's book *Manufacturing the News*. Fishman describes his first-hand account of how a newsroom can conjure a "crime wave" out of thin air. In 1976, reporters in New York suddenly started reporting on crimes by young Black and Brown suspects against older white victims in neighborhoods undergoing demographic transitions. A single reporter (later followed by many more)

ignored statistics showing a *decrease* in crime against the elderly and
wrote a story falsely suggesting that true anecdotes of individual incidents were part of a broader *pattern*. Like bad scientists cherry-picking
hypothesis-confirming evidence, reporters then looked for stories to
fit the pattern, and a special police unit happily provided them with a
stream of fresh daily anecdotes.

Fishman noted that "each story on the elderly seen independently
might not have merited attention. Seen together, however, all of them
were made newsworthy by the perception of a common theme." Local
news broadcasts began with multiple stories about crimes against the
elderly, provided by police. Fishman explained:

> As journalists notice each other reporting the same news
> theme, it becomes established within a community of media
> organizations. Journalists who are not yet reporting a theme
> learn to use it by watching their competition. And when jour-
> nalists who first report a theme see others beginning to use it,
> they feel their original news judgment is confirmed. Within
> the space of a week a crime theme can become so "hot," so
> entrenched in a community of news organizations, that even
> journalists skeptical of the crime wave cannot ignore reporting
> each new incident that comes along. Crime waves have a life of
> their own.[12]

As with moral panics generally, the reactionary backlash in Fishman's example was swift. The mayor denounced the juvenile punishment system as too lenient and increased funding for a specialized
NYPD force called the Senior Citizens Robbery Unit. State legislators
introduced bills to increase incarceration of children, and national polls
showed widespread anger and fear about juveniles targeting the elderly.
Fishman, who happened to be embedded in a newsroom as part of a
different project, began seeing that "the entire news production process

was *creating* the crime wave it was reporting." Even though many journalists privately had doubts about the existence of the trend, "no one could resist reporting it." So, how did the panic finally end? According to Fishman:

> The police policy of closely monitoring and reporting crimes against the elderly was only designed for a three-month period. About the time that the special monitoring stopped, coverage died down and the crime wave was over.

How to Tell a Lie with the Truth

The false story—about a new wave of crimes against the elderly by non-white youth for a few months in 1976—was made up of true anecdotes about individual incidents. It was the *categorization and presentation* of these true events into themes with particular causes and effects that distorted reality. It would be like making Michael Jordan appear to be a bad basketball player by compiling a highlight reel that consists entirely of every missed shot in his career. The selective curation of anecdote is an essential mechanism of copaganda.

Imagine two scenarios. A city had ten thousand shoplifting incidents in 2023, down from fifteen thousand shoplifting incidents in 2022. But in 2023, a local news outlet ran a story every day about a different shoplifting incident, while in 2022, the news ran only fifteen stories all year on shoplifting incidents. In which city do you think the public is more likely to believe shoplifting is a greater problem, even a crisis? In the city with more shoplifting, or the city with twenty-five times more *stories* about shoplifting?

A few examples illustrate the point. First, after months of crime coverage that downplayed overall decreases in police-reported crime but spotlighted short-term increases in murder in 2021, the *New York Times* pulled the old switcheroo when murders started to go down in

2022.[13] Now, according to the paper, it was time to start worrying about "property offenses."[14]

A Shift in Crime

Murders are declining, but other crimes
are still disrupting American life.

It is pervasive in local journalism to lead with whatever police-reported crime statistic happens to be up and to ignore or downplay other statistics that are down, or to publish news stories when police-reported crime is up but not when it is down, or to select particular time periods within which to suggest a trend when choosing a slightly longer or shorter period could reflect a different trend. For example, a North Carolina headline stated: "Police in Charlotte Investigating 13 Homicides So Far This Month, Making October Deadliest Month This Year." What fact is left out? Murders in Charlotte were down 14 percent overall that year.[15]

By cherry-picking anecdotes—indeed, even by using isolated individual pieces of data as misleading anecdotes—news reports can distort our interpretation of the world. Using a similar process, they can also distort our understanding of what other people—particularly people with whom we don't interact—*think* about the world. Because one can find anyone to say essentially anything, reporters have leeway to select which "true" views of "ordinary people" to share and which to ignore. For example, amid news emphasis on a "crime wave" and as the governor of California was vetoing a popular bill named after Nelson Mandela to limit solitary confinement in California prisons, a news outlet influential with state officials, *CalMatters*, published a story in which the reporter managed to find one "former inmate" who "spent decades alone in 8-by-10 cells" and was opposed to the Mandela bill. The reporter granted the person anonymity to tell the public why "eliminating solitary confinement is a bad idea."[16] The anonymous person happened to mirror prison guard union talking points, omitted overwhelming evidence of pervasive abuse and ineffectiveness of solitary confinement tactics, and questioned the global scientific consesus that solitary confinement hurts people's health. The person suggested solitary confinement was a necessary evil because "they have to have bad places for bad people."

Because this person was anonymous, we don't know whether they had connections to unions or lobbyists or how the reporter got connected with them. But the person's views were used to distort public perception of how incarcerated people feel about long-term solitary confinement. None of the thousands of incarcerated people who hold opposing views were quoted. None of their families who organized for the legislation—and who convinced the California legislature to pass such a law—were quoted. Evidently, "true" voices matter only if they support punishment. The anonymous person was quoted to *give people a reason to feel okay* with an outcome that should engender outrage: a Democratic governor in a liberal state vetoing a bill that would place some limits on a practice the United Nations defines as "torture."[17]

Finding the aberrational individual who may truthfully support the oppression to which the rest of their marginalized group is subjected is a staple of news reporting during moral panics. There is no more effective voice to validate how powerful people shape and respond to a moral panic.

One of my favorite examples comes from Copaganda Hall of Famer Martin Kaste, who for some reason National Public Radio still permits to cover the police.[18] (I awarded Kaste this honor in absentia during a private ceremony attended by two cats and my research assistants in my basement.) In 2022, Kaste published an article and widely disseminated radio piece about a rise in shootings and murders during the pandemic.[19] Murders were down nationally in 2022 when he published the stories,

but they had increased in 2020 and 2021.[20] As with much of Kaste's police reporting, the article is a buffet for the copaganda gourmand.

Under the bolded heading "Less Risk of Getting Caught," Kaste
asserts that there is now "less risk of getting caught" for shooting someone in the United States. The support for that assertion was an ordinary
person in Seattle:

> Anthony Branch, 26, got into trouble for carrying a gun when
> he was a teen. Watching the gun culture in his neighborhood,
> he thinks more minors and felons are carrying guns illegally
> now for one simple reason: "Defund the police," as he puts it.

Kaste reports as national news—without context or skepticism—a
single person blaming "defund the police" for more shootings. Without presenting any contrary views, NPR delivers Branch's views, accurately conveyed though they may be, as implicitly representative of
other people who've been prosecuted and incarcerated and who live in
poor neighborhoods.

In fact, police budgets were (and are) at all-time highs nationally.
And a review of hundreds of police budgets showed that they received
the same share of overall city budgets in 2021 as in 2019.[21] So, the police
were not defunded after the 2020 George Floyd protests. Their budgets
have increased overall each year, including the year George Floyd was
murdered.[22] Thus, reduced police budgets could not have led to it being easier to get away with shooting someone in 2021 than 2019. The
article's thesis is impossible.

Knowing this national causal connection is unsupported, Kaste
nonetheless boosts the claim by immediately noting that Seattle has "lost
hundreds of officers after the protests that followed the 2020 murder of
George Floyd." But even in Seattle, which was an outlier in slightly reducing its police budget by about 10 percent, the reduction didn't affect
relevant police operations, and police executives themselves in internal

memos identified non-essential duties that armed officers could cut without affecting enforcement of violent crime (such as parking meter ticketing). Indeed, as the local NPR station reported, debunking the "myth" that Seattle police were defunded, "not a single sworn officer has lost their job or pay due to budget constraints."[23]

Even if we ignore that the NPR piece purported to draw *national* lessons and if we focus only on Seattle, there is no evidence that the kind of small reduction to unrelated categories in Seattle's police budget in 2021 *could have* led to widespread changes in murder. Most damning to Kaste's thesis, though, is that murders *decreased* in Seattle in 2021 even though the police budget decreased, which undermines the article's thesis.[24] Indeed, the police budget was *larger* in 2020 when murder increased the *most*. No person with a contrary view is quoted, nor is anyone included to explain the actual empirical evidence.

In both the *CalMatters* and NPR examples, I do not doubt that sources gave these quotes to the reporter. But by selectively choosing which people's views to represent and which people's views to exclude, the news can distort our perceptions. This is one of the pernicious functions of NPR here: to give liberal news consumers intellectual permission to support more funding for more police because, although it is baselessly connected to less murder, even marginalized people targeted by police supposedly want it.

This is how the curation of *true anecdotes* leads to *false interpretations* of the world. How the biased dissemination of real facts is the essence of the best propaganda. As French philosopher, sociologist, theologian, and World War II resistance hero Jacques Ellul explained in his landmark 1962 study of propaganda:

> For a long time, propagandists have recognized that lying must be avoided. . . . It seems that in propaganda we must make a radical distinction between a fact on the one hand and intentions or interpretations on the other. . . . The truth that pays off is in

the realm of *facts*. The necessary falsehoods, which also pay off, are in the realm of *intentions* and *interpretations*. This is a fundamental rule for propaganda analysis.[25]

The Most Panicked Are the Most "Informed"

I have a lot of conversations with people from different backgrounds about crime. Many of my conversations are with my clients, community organizers we work with, public defenders, and survivors of violence. But I also have conversations with elites who are positioned to shape how the punishment bureaucracy functions, including journalists, lawyers, judges, prosecutors, politicians, philanthropists, researchers, lobbyists, nonprofit employees, and professors.

One of many notable things from these conversations is how focused many privileged people are, at any given moment, on their belief that there is a "crime wave." They are routinely in a state of panic about some crime or another—specifically, the narrow range of crimes for which police arrest mostly poor people—and they are often the people who consume the most daily news. Staying "informed" is part of their identity.

The reasons for panic are so self-evident to these plugged-in news consumers that they cannot fathom that the news is being organized into misleading themes for them, or that, at any given moment with enough resources, a sophisticated propagandist could make them believe that some *other* set of criminal events in the world (which are always happening and number in the millions) *was also an urgent trend*. It happened to be train thefts, but it could have been toxic train derailments due to corporate cost-cutting. They think each panic is real—not just in the sense that it describes true events, but that it describes a *trend* that is unique (i.e., that something *different* is happening *now* with respect to *this* crime as compared with before and as compared with other crimes) and important (i.e., that paying attention to it is a vital part of being—and being seen as—an engaged, caring person in our society).

I have noticed two themes in these conversations. First, the subjective view that there is a "crime wave" is accompanied by a contrary-to-the-evidence assertion, confidently made, that tweaking some kind of policy within the punishment bureaucracy will address the problem. These news super-consumers are particularly susceptible to connections the news media makes, without evidence, between a moral panic and something like bail reform, defunding police, lower prison sentences, or slightly different prosecutorial charging policies.

Offering such policy tweaks to remedy allegedly huge shifts in "crime" is reminiscent of the petrochemical industry pushing plastic recycling for decades as a solution to its prodigious global pollution, even though it knew that almost no plastic is recycled, that trillions of pieces of plastic will spew into the environment each year, and that the only way to stop it would be to reduce needless production of plastic.[26] In many areas of public life, many proposed solutions serve the same interests that create the problem. Tweaks in punishment policy do nothing to remedy the root causes of criminal violence and pervasive "non-criminal" violence: inequality; poverty; trauma; lack of access to care, housing, early childhood education, and community programs; toxic masculinity; the number of guns manufactured; demographic shifts; lack of resources for restorative conflict resolution; and the general alienation and disconnection of people in contemporary society. But manufactured "panic" creates an environment in which anyone talking about "long-term" solutions is dismissed as unserious, even uncaring, about imminent harm.

Second, professional-class news consumers rarely feel personally threatened by crimes like wage theft, foreclosure fraud, tax evasion, building safety code violations, pollution, prison guard brutality, illegal police spying, political corruption, sexual assault of incarcerated people, or other widespread crimes that cause objectively greater degrees of harm in terms of physical bodily injury and illness, financial loss, decreased well-being, and death. They obsess about *some* crimes committed by *some* people *some* of the time, and this obsession is usually not correlated with a rational assessment of overall threat.

Professional-class news consumers regularly accuse any skeptic of the moral panic du jour of being an "elitist" who is "out of touch" with the most marginalized communities. I have been accused more than once by reporters at major corporate news outlets of disrespecting vulnerable people because I question the overall messages embedded in the latest crime headlines. This is a vital part of moral panics: you are treated as an obtuse, unfeeling person if you do not swim in the "irresistible sociological current," to use Ellul's phrase.

The role that the far right plays in this area is obvious, but it's important to highlight the role of liberal and establishment pundits in creating moral panics, in claiming that the government must meet "out of control" crime with more repression, and in maligning the critics of repression as elitist cranks who lack compassion for the vulnerable.[27] This view ignores the possibility that someone can care deeply about violence or marginalized communities *and* be skeptical about the moral panics that have historically been used to expand police, prosecution, and prisons.

We can hold these two views simultaneously because the evidence shows that the frenzied curation of crime anecdotes makes the public dizzyingly uninformed and, therefore, less capable of addressing the root causes of interpersonal harm. As Gallup polls—such as the one following—document, people consistently believe that crime is rising.[28]

Every year for the two decades preceding the publication of this book, most people believed crime was up from the year before. But, in that multi-decade period, *property, violent, and total police-recorded crime went down the vast majority of years*. So, most people believed something that was untrue. Moreover, the polls reveal something else interesting: people's perceptions of crime are different when asked about *their own neighborhoods*. For example, according to Gallup's Crime survey released

Is there more crime in the U.S. than there was a year ago, or less?

	More %	Less %
2022 Oct 3-20	78	13
2021 Oct 1-19	74	17
2020 Sep 30-Oct 15	78	14
2019 Oct 1-13	64	24
2018 Oct 1-10	60	25
2017 Oct 5-11	68	19
2016 Oct 5-9	70	20
2015 Oct 7-11	70	18
2014 Oct 12-15	63	21
2013 Oct 3-6	64	19
2011 Oct 6-9	68	17
2010 Oct 7-10	66	17
2009 Oct 1-4	74	15

in 2023, 63 percent of Americans said that "the crime problem" was "extremely or very serious." However, only 17 percent of people said that "the crime problem" was "extremely or very serious" in their own local area.[29] This reveals a pervasive effect of news media copaganda: people's perceptions are more accurate and less fearful the more they are based on their own experience and the less they are mediated through the mass media's coverage decisions. Another wrinkle is that people's perceptions of crime are significantly affected by their political party, and whether the party they oppose is in power, as demonstrated in the following graphic.

It is remarkable that professional-class news consumers feel so confident about their erroneous and highly manipulated perceptions about

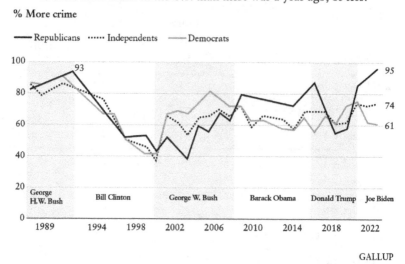

Partisans' Perceptions of National Crime, 1989-2022
Is there more crime in the U.S. than there was a year ago, or less?

% More crime

——Republicans　······ Independents　——Democrats

GALLUP

crime. The introduction to the English translation of Ellul's *Propaganda* explains that professional-class "intellectuals" are

> virtually the most vulnerable of all to modern propaganda, for three reasons: (1) they absorb the largest amount of secondhand, unverifiable information; (2) they feel a compelling need to have an opinion on every important question of our time, and thus easily succumb to opinions offered to them by propaganda on all such indigestible pieces of information; (3) they consider themselves capable of "judging for themselves." They literally need propaganda.[30]

More than sixty years later, this remains one of the most prescient observations about copaganda.

4

Policing Public Relations

Liberal democracies in the West were generally run for the benefit of the top, say, 20 percent of the wealth and income distribution. The trick . . . to keeping this scheme running smoothly has been to convince, especially at election time, the next 30 to 35 percent of the income distribution to fear the poorest half more than they envy the richest 20 percent.

-James C. Scott[1]

On the day Chicago police murdered Laquan McDonald, a seventeen-year-old Black teenager, in 2014, Chicago cops had six full-time public relations employees. As the city fought in court to keep evidence of the child's murder secret and then later to control the uproar when a judge ordered it to release a video of the shooting, Chicago increased its police budget to pay for twenty-five full-time public relations positions. As of early 2023, Chicago cops had forty-eight full-time positions devoted to manipulating public information. The 2024 budget funded fifty-five.[2]

Chicago is not alone. Cities across the country spend enormous amounts on police PR, and even elected officials are often kept in the dark about it. In 2022, for example, I was asked to testify at a San Francisco Board of Supervisors hearing because something weird was happening: the elected leaders of San Francisco were struggling to find out from secretive police officials exactly how much money they spent on PR.[3]

In most cities, there is little information about such funding, including for elected officials who supposedly oversee police budgets. After the 2020 racial justice protests, a *Los Angeles Times* investigation found that the Los Angeles County Sheriff's Department alone had forty-two full-time employees dedicated to shaping public information. The LAPD had another twenty-five full-time PR employees. Some of them made more than $200,000 a year. That's sixty-seven cops doing public relations manipulation across just two departments in one county—and Los Angeles has almost fifty other municipal and state police forces that don't report this information and that weren't included in the *Times*'s investigation.[4] A similar 2024 investigation in New York City uncovered at least eighty-six full-time employees in the NYPD public relations department, which *doubled* in size from 2022 to 2024 and includes many officers making tens of thousands of dollars in overtime pay.[5]

Police PR Is Bigger Than You Think

Just before my testimony in San Francisco, newly uncovered documents showed that the SFPD had nine full-time employee positions dedicated to "strategic communications" and "media relations." These cops were "supplemented" by an undisclosed number of non-full-time cops who do PR work for the department but not as their primary job. Then, in a bombshell revelation, previously unreleased documents showed that SFPD employs a "full-time videographer" to make videos glorifying SFPD at a public cost of $120,941. Moreover, it was uncovered that the SFPD was quietly trying to get funding to hire a *second* videographer. Police employing video propagandists has become more common after the murder of George Floyd. For example, when a criminal gang of sheriff deputies was accused of murdering people and extorting other police officers, the Los Angeles Sheriff's Department used public money to rehabilitate their image with a *Star Wars*–themed promotional video that included droids, lasers, and military weapons.[6]

As the San Francisco hearings went on, the revelations kept coming. One document revealed that a sergeant had ordered that "all members of the Media Relations team should closely monitor social media for posts, video, etc. related to the [killing]." The board also

 **LA County Sheriffs** ✔
@LASDHQ

Wishing everyone a #HappyStarWarsDay and #MayThe4thBeWithYou .

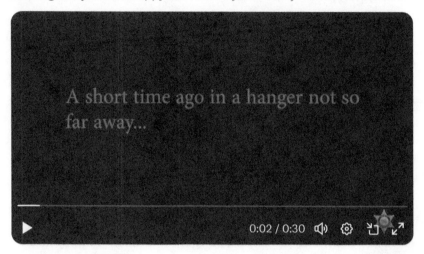

12:05 PM · May 4, 2022

 **LA County Sheriffs** ✔
@LASDHQ

Wishing everyone a #HappyStarWarsDay and #MayThe4thBeWithYou .

12:05 PM · May 4, 2022

LA County Sheriffs ✓
@LASDHQ   ...

Wishing everyone a #HappyStarWarsDay and #MayThe4thBeWithYou .

▶   0:20 / 0:30 🔊 ⚙ ⤴ ⤢

12:05 PM · May 4, 2022

LA County Sheriffs ✓
@LASDHQ   ...

Wishing everyone a #HappyStarWarsDay and #MayThe4thBeWithYou .

12:05 PM · May 4, 2022

learned that the SFPD has another secretive unit called the "Community Engagement Division," which works closely to "plan messaging priorities." Among other things, the unit does focus-group style "surveys" to help the police department manipulate public opinion. It also manages potential public outrage through strategic intervention with families of people killed by cops. To help prevent incidents from going viral, police try to get to these families as soon as possible to influence their reactions.

Police PR budgets do not include the cash spent on branding, logos, slogans designed and printed on cop cars, swag, gear, and public events. Think of how every police car in your city is emblazoned with a slogan like "Courtesy, Professionalism, Respect." Do an internet search for specialty police cars glorifying the commitment of police to solidarity with various groups that they have disproportionately targeted with violence, such as LGBTQ people and those with autism. You'll find a wide range of rainbow-painted cop cars in city after city.[7]

In Chicago and hundreds of other cities, police PR units also invite the media to activities like basketball tournaments for kids or food giveaways for poor families. Chicago police PR officials even produced a video showing armed Chicago cops giving away food in neighborhoods most harmed by the city's economic, environmental, and policing policies.[8]

Official PR expenditures, to the extent they are ever publicly available, significantly undercount the time and money devoted to the PR operations of the approximately 18,000 local, state, and federal police agencies in the U.S. For example, they do not count the separate public relations staff and consultants used by prosecutors.[9] Police in most cities also coordinate with PR staff in mayors' offices. In a particularly silly case, for example, staff of Mayor London Breed in San Francisco collaborated with cops to stage a press conference in front of Louis Vuitton because, a trove of police text messages argued, "that's the visual for where the rule of law needs to make its stand" against the retail theft panic.[10]

The few attempts that have been made to quantify police public relations did not count similar programs run by police unions using dues funded by public money. Most major police unions have their own independent public relations teams and strategies, and they are supplemented by a network of multi-million-dollar private police foundations, non-profits, and political action committees that use a vast operation of publicly subsidized funding and professional relationships to affect news coverage.[11] Finally, there is an industry of for-profit media consulting firms that cater to police departments for damage control after police kill people.[12]

Compare these enormous operations with most public agencies, which have either minuscule or no public relations teams at all. Police are secretive about this vast ecosystem because they want news coverage to appear spontaneous and not carefully cultivated.

Cultivating Friends in the News

In 2021, a national investigative journalist did a story debunking claims spread by a local TV news reporter to carjacking victims—telling them, wrongly, that charges had been dropped against the perpetrators by the progressive DA—based on false information that San Francisco police fed the reporter. In the aftermath, text messages were uncovered between the director of the SFPD propaganda unit, Matt Dorsey, and the reporter. In the exchange, Dorsey told the reporter, "Thank God for you." The reporter then asked for cops to "protect" her. Dorsey responded that she had "a lot of fans" in "our department." He ended: "Keep up the great work." At the time, this director of the PR unit cost San Francisco $289,423 annually. And after this scandal, the mayor appointed him to fill a vacant spot on the Board of Supervisors, which controls the police budget.[13]

This image from police department files uncovered by San Francisco elected officials in the budget hearings captures the collaborative relationship between the police and media, with a police officer smiling on either side of two local TV news anchors seated at their studio desk:

Photos of reporters smiling with police is one of my favorite sub-genres of copaganda. I've covered the bathroom of the Copaganda Hall of Fame with photos from various cities, and I created a visual poem in three stanzas, which I'll reproduce on the following page, showing reporters in New Orleans coordinating blue outfits to show their "love" and "support" for police along with special blue heart emojis on social media.[14]

To see how this web of relationships operates, let's look at what happened in Seattle after the 2020 protests against police violence. Seattle police conducted internal surveys of police commanders and determined that the *police themselves* thought that at least twelve of their service functions would be better handled by unarmed civilian employees instead of police—things including crisis intervention and homelessness outreach. These functions amounted to a huge percentage of police time, and an internal assessment concluded that "up to 45% of SPD patrol service hours do not require an officer." But the department's public-facing

Sheba Turk
@ShebaTurk

The @WWLTV morning crew wearing blue for Geaux Blue NOLA today to support the NOPD @NOPDNews

Sheba Turk
@ShebaTurk

🩶🩶🩶🩶 We love you guys! Thanks for all you do to keep our community safe

New Orleans Police Department   @NOPDNews

Love it! 💨🩶😎👮 #GeauxBlueNola

New Orleans Police Department
@NOPDNews

Love it! 👏🩶😎👮
#GeauxBlueNola

narrative was almost the opposite of its internal assessment. An investigative journalist unearthed a trove of emails that explained why: "Top-level communications and strategy staff within the department privately ridicul[ed] the idea of civilianizing certain police functions, all while working to clandestinely reshape the public conversation around police reform."[15]

In addition to producing misleading social media, the Seattle Police Department's chief strategy officer used textbook copaganda tactics. For example, he provided research assistance to a former cop and current deputy mayor to write an op-ed opposing the changes endorsed by the department's own private internal surveys. A local journalist found that the chief strategy officer also appeared to ghostwrite a first draft of another op-ed for a Harvard scholar and business consultant named Antonio Oftelie, who later published the piece under his own name during the 2020 uprisings.[16]

According to internal emails, the chief strategy officer shared the draft op-ed ostensibly by the Harvard scholar with several police staff, saying, "Do you two want to play around with this a little and then I will send to Antonio." Upon seeing the Seattle police edits, the scholar responded: "Wow! This is fantastic at first read through. I'd like to work for you when you run for Governor! I'll dig into this soon and get back to you. Stay strong . . ."

At that point, the team reached out to the police department's "director of strategic communications," to find the best outlet to run the op-ed: "I like this a lot—how do we help him [Oftelie] get it placed. *Times* would be ideal." Neither Oftelie nor the news outlet disclosed the Seattle police official's role in the published piece. A month later, with additional behind-the-scenes help from police, Oftelie was appointed to oversee the Seattle Police Department as the federal court monitor in charge of the civil rights consent decree against it.

I have seen firsthand this dynamic play out in city after city in which our civil rights work takes us. There is a complex, and often hidden, web of relationships—funded by public money—that manufactures and places police propaganda in the news. The result is "strategic" messaging laundered for public consumption—either as objective stories or opinion pieces by seemingly neutral observers compelled to share their expertise with the public out of a yearning for a better world and nothing more. If you're an amateur, professional, or aspiring journalist in any city in the U.S., a good next story for you would be to dig into the budget and number of employees that your local police department devotes to all forms of public relations. There's a reason they try to hide it.

The Reality of News Production

I was contacted in 2022 by several national TV news producers and an anchor for a local television station who read my copaganda newsletter. I learned a lot from conversations with them. Local television producers face pressure to fill twenty to twenty-four minutes of programming several times per day for each thirty-minute newscast. Depending on the station, this can include a morning show, a dinner-time show, and multiple late-evening shows. Mid-market news stations often produce even more content than that each day. National network and cable news producers face a different kind of crunch with different levels of resources, but some of the pressures operate in similar ways with respect to their coverage of public safety. One of the chief functions of the thousands of public relations employees in police departments and prosecutor offices across the U.S. is to provide content for news outlets desperate for stories to fill their shows in real time.

It is not just a matter of having a budget that enables police to pitch dozens of stories to news outlets about police saving baby ducklings—amazingly, "police-duckling" stories happen a lot and someone has even counted them.[17] It is deeper. Police PR employees do not just call reporters and tell them about a story. They build long-term relationships of mutual benefit. When police PR teams prepare stories for the media, they often contain video, audio, screenshots of documents, charts, and other easy visuals that require less work for the journalists. Police and prosecutors pay spokespeople to be briefed and prepared for soundbite interviews, or otherwise make available employees who are prepared to be on camera, give quotes, or spend time with the reporter "on background" to shape the reporter's understanding of the story. They also suggest "experts" they have vetted and connect reporters to those experts.

I talk "on background" with dozens of reporters every month, trying to provide accurate information about public safety and the punishment bureaucracy, so I know how time-consuming it is to provide context to reporters who are not specialists in criminal law. The amount of time and public money spent by police to do this with thousands of journalists across thousands of cities and counties every day shapes how our society sees the world. Police PR units literally produce content for the news, in a format that allows reporters, editors, and producers to exert as little work as possible. The replication and replacement by police PR officials of traditional journalist functions is particularly important given the prolonged and steep decline in the number of reporters and budgets in local newsrooms.[18] Busy reporters, including those who aren't necessarily punishment bureaucracy zealots, thus fall into place, generating daily streams of copaganda because it is the path of least resistance.

The Police PR Ecosystem

Police public relations has another function: *creating an ecosystem of validation.* On top of their message testing, focus groups, and cultivated relationships with reporters, police PR teams build relationships with ideological allies in academic institutions and opinion punditry. They build lists of experts, selectively provide them data, fund and cherry-pick research, and spend time working with researchers on talking points for journalists with whom they help the experts connect. These police officials—and their coordinated surrogates—routinely have calls with editorial boards and opinion columnists, who rarely seek public safety experts outside such networks. One of my favorite questions to ask journalists and pundits is who they have spoken to about a story and how they were put in touch with them.

A trove of emails obtained by community organizers at the Stop LAPD Spying Coalition in 2021 documents the way that the public comments of academic "experts" are often drafted, revised, and coordinated with police, and then the "experts" are either directly offered or indirectly suggested to reporters as *independent* validators of the police perspective.[19] Over time, this process becomes more and more informal in a local ecosystem, with reporters coming to build their own relationships with experts originally introduced to them by police.

What develops is a sort of groupthink, and reporters and news organizations end up being exposed to only a small slice of opinion from a narrow social group with particular interests. Many of them come to view contrary perspectives as unserious because no one in their bubble shares them.

Your local government is spending a lot of money building an ecosystem of "conventional wisdom" that legitimizes the punishment bureaucracy as the primary solution to myriad social problems. The content of daily news would be different if the bureaucrats who test lead levels in water or who inspect safety code violations or who teach children had the same PR budgets and connections to shape the conventional wisdom about a concept like "safety." Shifting public resources from police PR to other government agencies that care for people would change whether and how the public thinks about the issues these other agencies address and could demonstrate the role that institutions other than the punishment bureaucracy play in improving community well-being.[20] So, pay attention to police PR budgets.

5

Whose Perspective? How Sources Shape the News

Thanks to the mass media, the individual finds himself outside the battle. . . . Freedom to express ideas is no longer at stake in the debate. . . . What we have is master and domination by the State or by some powerful groups over the whole of the technical media of opinion formation. . . . The individual has no access to them. . . . He is no longer a participant in this battle for the free expression of ideas: he is the stake. What matters for him is which voice he will be permitted to hear, and which words will have the power to obsess him.

-Jean Rivero[1]

Few of the things we see in the news are events we experience firsthand, or things we know a lot about. We rely on the sources presented to us to make sense of the world. Whose voices are included in the news to explain things to us and whose voices are ignored?

There's a bustling world underneath the stories that we see. In crime coverage, many reporters rely on repeat sources to decide which events to report, describe what happened, choose which facts to include or exclude, explain why it matters, and suggest what can be done about it.

In December 2021, a CBS Los Angeles story warned tourists not to come to LA because "rampant crime continues," evoking the dystopia of the film *The Purge*. Despite LA's reported crime being near historic lows, the article was titled " 'We Can't Guarantee Your Safety': Head of LAPD's Police Officers' Union Warns Tourists Away." The sources included in the article were:

- The police union president (who had shot six people; he was quoted twice)
- A woman who moved to LA six months ago
- A police chief (quoted three times)
- An anonymous tourist
- Unidentified "people out in Hollywood"
- A press release from the district attorney[2]

Here are the sources in a similar 2022 *New York Times* article about a short-term rise in shootings and "perceptions" of safety. No source mentions the concepts of poverty, inequality, medical care, housing, education, or the prevalence of guns:

- The NYPD police commissioner (quoted three times)
- A professor who is a member of the New York State Probation Commission (twice)
- "The police department" (twice)
- Anonymous police "officials"
- The chief of detectives[3]

And in a different *Los Angeles Times* article on the theft of a luxury watch:

- "Sheriff's Department said in a statement"
- "The Sheriff's statement"
- "Authorities said"[4]

Remember the train theft articles? Here are the sources in the main *New York Times* story:

- "The authorities"
- An LAPD captain
- "The police"

- The LAPD captain (twice more)
- Union Pacific Railroad (four times)
- UPS and FedEx (added to the article later)
- "A spokeswoman for the Association of American Railroads"
- The LAPD captain (again)
- An assistant professor of marketing at the Fowler College of Business (twice)
- Union Pacific Railroad (twice more)
- A spokesman for the district attorney
- The LAPD captain (four more times)[5]

What do these stories have in common? They select punishment bureaucrats and corporate representatives to tell us what is happening in the world that is supposedly relevant to our safety, why those things are happening, what and whom we should be afraid of, and what we can do about it. These people share certain characteristics, including that they are invested in emphasizing certain social harms over others and in advocating government surveillance and individualized punishment as a solution to those social harms.

In article after article, hundreds of times a month and tens of thousands of times during our adult lives, we are bombarded with a curated selection of facts about the world that depends on who is telling us the story. In ways large and small, this deluge makes us think more like the people we are exposed to.

Who tells the story often determines what is considered a problem, which problems are surfaced, how problems are characterized, and which solutions are proposed. For example, a story told by sources who are special education teachers about kids fighting at school will be different from the same story told by sources who are cops. The story of drug addiction will be different when told by public health sources than by prosecutor sources.

A good illustration is the story told about the 2020 police killing of Breonna Taylor during an illegal home raid. The story of how and why police killed her as told by community members opposing gentrification and scholars of urban planning highlighted that Louisville was using increased policing in her neighborhood to support a lucrative real estate development project. The same story was told differently by police, who emphasized the supposed urgency of fighting the drug war with a no-knock warrant.[6]

Punishment bureaucrats also have professional and financial stakes in sustaining the punishment bureaucracy. They have a long history of manipulating crime statistics, lying, hiding the truth, making misleading claims based on true anecdotes, and covering up violence and corruption.[7] Because most stories about crime and public safety are sourced from the punishment bureaucracy, they tend to narrow our conception of safety, generate feelings of fear, sustain the illusion that the punishment bureaucracy provides safety, and minimize the violent and ineffective nature of the punishment bureaucracy. The ultimate effect is to persuade news consumers—not just rationally, but emotionally—that systems of social control need more power and resources or else we will never feel safe. The dominance of these voices distracts people from thinking about other approaches and investments that would better address the root causes of harm.

A Reader's Guide to Sources

When you see a news story about public safety, look at the sources reporters have chosen to tell the story. Ask yourself some questions:

- Whose voices are included?
- Who benefits from this point of view being presented as news?
- *What harms* to *which people* in *which places* at *which times* do the sources emphasize?
- Was anyone with a viewpoint critical of the punishment bureaucracy included? If included, where in the article were views

challenging the narrative put forward by punishment bureaucrats placed? Whose voices were prioritized?

- How did the reporter choose which voices to quote and which to ignore?
- How might this source have gotten to the reporter?
- Which sources were granted anonymity and why?
- Did the reporter include skepticism for claims made by punishment bureaucrats, or note whether the source has a history of dishonesty or conflicts of interest? Did the reporter include skepticism for claims made by any critics of the punishment bureaucracy?
- How, if at all, would this story have been told by different groups of sources with different perspectives?
- What role do the ownership, consolidation, and business models of media companies play in determining which sources with what views are presented?

How "Expert" Sources Shape News

Journalists need to explain complex concepts by offering context and background, and one way they do this is by using sources who are "experts." There's nothing wrong with using experts; all of us, including reporters, lack the time or ability to master every issue that affects our lives. So, it's helpful to turn to people who have accumulated knowledge through study and experience. But the selection of experts can also be a tool for manipulation, and the news media's curation of experts exhibits patterns that promote the interests of the punishment bureaucracy.

A few examples from the *New York Times* illustrate these patterns. In September 2021, the paper published an article on an increase in the national murder rate.[8] The article put forward several unfounded hypotheses about the short-term rise in homicides, which occurred at the same time as a *decline* in overall major police-recorded crime. According to the *Times*, among the reasons for the rise in murders were racial justice protests:

> The protests that erupted after the police killing of George Floyd in Minneapolis were also an important factor, in 2020, although experts differ about why. Some argue that the police, under intense scrutiny and demoralized, pulled back from some aspects of crime prevention. Others put the emphasis on the public, suggesting that diminished respect for the police prompted more people to try to take the law into their own hands.

There is no meaningful evidence to support the idea that racial justice protests were "an important factor" in increased murder in 2020. So, how can a newspaper assert something when it lacks actual evidence? Experts. According to the paper, "experts" have a consensus that "protests" increased murder, and the only thing "experts" dispute is whether it is because police "pulled back" or because the public had "diminished respect for the police." Notice a common copaganda tactic: asserting without evidence that a controversial opinion is uncontested, and subtly shifting the terrain of focus for readers to debating the *reasons* for the supposedly uncontested opinion. The message is: "No reasonable person disputes that racial justice protests cause murder; the only question among experts is why."

As to the "why," no evidence is provided—indeed, none exists—to support the notion that police were "pulling back" anywhere; that such "pullbacks" correlated with differences in murder in different places; that such changes in police behavior, even if they did occur, *could* affect society-wide murder rates; or that the "pullbacks" would have *reverse* effects on murder versus all other forms of violent crime, which *decreased*. Moreover, no evidence is offered to support the idea that "diminished respect" for police led more people to "take the law into their own hands" or that such a development would increase murder while reducing all other violence. And yet, this unexplained speculation is the entire universe of hypotheses offered by the reporter. He presented none of the many experts who had other opinions.

In the critical moment when the supposed consensus blaming racial justice protests for murder is introduced to readers, notice that the names of the "experts" are not revealed. It's impossible to evaluate the biases in or bases for their opinions without knowing who the experts are, why they believe the things they are saying, and what evidence supports them. Moreover, if the opinion is later proven wrong, it's impossible to hold anyone accountable for it or prevent them from being quoted anonymously again for millions of readers to consume. This is a recurring feature of expert anonymity—and a reason so many people who are so wrong so much of the time keep getting the platform to do it again.

The only expert named for the claim that police "pulled back" is Peter N. Winograd, a retired law professor and consultant for the Albuquerque Police Department, which between 2015 to 2021 had one of the highest per-capita rates of police shooting people dead in the country, six times that of NYPD.[9] Winograd is no newcomer to misinformation. He had previously argued that reductions in local jail populations (for example by detaining fewer people who cannot pay cash bail) caused more crime, a debunked claim.[10] Despite this track record, he is offered as an expert in a national news story. Without evidence, Winograd contends that police are "legitimately worried about being backed up by their superiors," which contributes to "low morale among police [and] the fact that the police are being less proactive," which in turn *may* be causing a rise in homicides across the United States.

Winograd provides no definition for or metric of "low morale" and no evidence of that supposed phenomenon. No proof is presented that "less proactive" policing causes more murder, let alone that it could conceivably cause the specific murder trends seen in the first months of the COVID-19 pandemic and lockdowns. Winograd does not even offer an explanation of what police "being less proactive" means. The newspaper does not ask him to substantiate the claim or provide evidence that *anything* had meaningfully changed with U.S. policing. In reality, the police were actually *more* aggressive, killing *more* people across the country in 2020 than they did in 2019 and more people in 2021 than they did in 2020.[11] And total major crime collectively declined during the same period—hardly what one would expect under his theory if a police "pullback" had actually taken place and if such "pullbacks" affect criminal behavior.

Another individual in the article—offered as an expert on homicides—is Jeff Asher.[12] The paper calls Asher a "crime analyst based in New Orleans." The *Times* does not tell readers that Asher previously worked for the CIA, and then for the New Orleans police. While at NOPD, Asher worked with multi-billion-dollar surveillance technology corporation Palantir to deploy a "predictive policing" system that disproportionately surveilled and targeted Black people.[13] None of Asher's biases or conflicts of interest are disclosed. Interestingly, just days before the *Times* printed this article promoting the notion of "pullbacks," Asher himself had written a similar piece in the *Times*, again with no disclosure of his professional and financial ties.[14] In that article published in the paper's section called "The Upshot," which features "analytical journalism," Asher linked the increase in homicides to, among other things, an alleged "pullback by the police." The paper ignored his vested interests in the punishment bureaucracy and told readers only that Asher was "a crime analyst based in New Orleans and co-founder of AH Datalytics," providing him a free ad for his business.

At the time, I wrote two criticisms about these articles and Asher's undisclosed conflicts of interests that were viewed almost 10 million times.[15] According to what I was told by a source inside the *Times*, the paper afterward decided that Asher would no longer write articles with a byline suggesting he was an analytical journalist. So, what happened next? Asher has been repeatedly featured as a seemingly neutral *expert* in stories written by other reporters. Readers were told that he was merely a learned person who "analyzes" these issues, perhaps out of the goodness of his heart or a lifelong commitment to intellectual curiosity, rather than at the behest of police and as part of a business.

If this "expert" were instead presented as a policing insider and profiteer with past connections to the CIA, his credibility as an expert among liberal readers would decrease. The *Times* lends credibility to Asher's claims by omitting his ties to the punishment bureaucracy and suggesting that he is some sort of magnanimous public resource interested only in the neutral pursuit of knowledge.[16]

What evidence does Asher cite to support his claim about a "pullback" causing murder, a claim that repeatedly appeared in the news after he first made it? Like Winograd several days later, he provides none. In fact, he doesn't even describe what a "pullback" is or provide any evidence that it happened at all. He merely relies on anonymous "analysts" to say they "pointed to" a "pullback" to explain the murder rate. Perhaps no one reputable would associate their name publicly with an evidence-free claim. But why did *Times* editors publish it? Will we ever know who these phantom "analysts" are? Is it the same two people referred to anonymously in article after article? Whoever it is, they managed to achieve copaganda Valhalla: repeated citation in the most widely read newspaper in the United States making a causal claim with no evidence—but treated as unquestioned consensus—blaming nationwide murder fluctuations on a concept they never explain or define but that vaguely suggests we need more policing.

A couple of months after these episodes, in November 2021, the paper published another article pushing the expansion of policing to combat murder, this time focusing on homicides in the Bronx. The article led with a false but alarming headline, claiming that murders had "doubled overnight" in the Bronx.[17] The paper later quietly deleted the false claim in the headline after I noted its falsity publicly in a social media thread viewed more than 4 million times. But where did the misinformation come from? An "expert" named Peter Moskos, whom the *Times* presented to readers as "a professor at John Jay College of Criminal Justice." Although the paper later altered the headline, it left in a quote by Moskos, which claimed that police "caseloads" were what "literally doubled overnight." That was also false: detective caseloads did not "double overnight." Not even in its "corrected" article did the

Times tell readers something important: Moskos is a former cop.[18] Current and former police officers regularly appear in the news offering the "expert" opinion that a given incident of police violence was justified or that police need more money and that police bureaucracies, which are at their highest level of funding ever, are short of cash.

A few months later, in January 2022, the *Times* published another article again promoting the idea that the U.S. needed more policing to stop rising murder, this time by Copaganda Lifetime Achievement Award winner German Lopez.[19] Relying on data from Asher, the article again referred to an anonymous gaggle of "experts" who declared that there were only "three broad explanations" for rising murders in the United States. (Is "gaggle" the appropriate English-language term for a group of experts anonymously assembled to peddle copaganda? Perhaps "murder of experts" might be more appropriate.)

One of the "three" explanations for more murder was "changes in policing" resulting from "fallout from the 2020 racial justice protests and riots," which the article says "could have" increased murders. The other two explanations were the pandemic, which the reporter largely dismissed for reasons that make no sense,[20] and the presence of more guns.[21] Here's what the article said about "changes in policing":

> **Changes in policing.** The fallout from the 2020 racial justice protests and riots could have contributed to the murder spike. Police officers, scared of being caught in the next viral video, may have pulled back on proactive anti-violence practices. More of the public lost confidence in the police, possibly reducing the kind of cooperation needed to prevent murders. In extreme circumstances, the lack of confidence in the police could have led some people to take the law into their own hands—in acts of street or vigilante violence.

The nonprofit Fairness & Accuracy in Reporting debunked the article and, as I discuss later, there is no meaningful evidence that such "changes in policing" even could cause society-wide increases in murder.[22] But, here, I want to examine how the article used experts.

First, the reference to anonymous experts enables the reporter to say things that would have otherwise been considered wild conjecture. The following claims by Lopez entail several layers of evidence-free speculation: (1) that widespread "protests and riots" "could have" made police "scared" of doing legally valid policing; (2) that cops "may have pulled back" on unspecified tactics because of this fear; (3) that this problem could be exacerbated by people "possibly" losing confidence in police; (4) that this loss of confidence made people more likely to be vigilantes; (5) and that something called "proactive" policing would otherwise interrupt this vigilante cycle to reduce murder. And neither does Lopez address the logical implication of his argument: that these effects of policing on *murder* would be directly the reverse of the effects of police on *all other violent crime*, which went down. Each of these claims is without support.

Second, most of the article's claims contain no citation or evidence. The excerpted paragraph above is supported only by a prefatory assertion that, "while experts are also divided on why murders spiked in 2020 and 2021, there are three broad explanations they typically point to [the pandemic, changes to policing, and more guns]," and the following statement by a controversial pro-police expert: " 'All three played a role,' Richard Rosenfeld, a criminologist at the University of Missouri–St. Louis, told me. 'What's difficult is to assign priority to one compared to the others.' "

Let's pause and marvel at the hubris of this so-called expert. He confidently makes an assertion about the "three" causes of short-term increases in murder—a social phenomenon about which many learned people who study the issue for their entire careers disagree in good faith—even though he concedes he has no idea which of these causes has the greatest bearing on the trend or how they interact. He neglects other structural features of our society and other potential causes more grounded in evidence. But then again, this is the same person who once argued to the news media without evidence that reducing mass incarceration might increase murder and who peddled to the news media former FBI director James Comey's famous "Ferguson Effect" theory that civil rights protests cause more murder.[23] Shortly after the article was published, I awarded Rosenfeld the prestigious Walter Cronkite Award for Innovation in Baseless Speculation, which is not named after the famous news anchor, but after a one-eyed cat I used to live with whom we all called Wally for short. Like the *Times*, we often speculated increasingly outlandish scenarios to explain how he lost his eye—perhaps it was a police "pull back."

What's most remarkable, though, is that the article hid from readers that there are *other experts* who contest these assertions, who have different theories, who think that it is imprudent to explain short-term fluctuations in murder in this manner, and who believe it is implausible that unexplained changes in police officer morale supposedly caused by protests even happened, let alone that they could meaningfully alter national murder rates while having a reverse impact on recorded violent crime.

Lurking in the background of this portrayal of a simplistic and nonexistent consensus by the leading newspaper in the U.S was a significant question of public concern: will more people be murdered if police are made to feel bad about their unaccountable violence against the most vulnerable people? Instead of addressing important questions about murder with seriousness, the paper chose to make it seem like every knowledgeable person agreed. Something nefarious is going on when a reporter knows that an assertion is controversial and that experts across a number of fields of scholarly study dispute it, but nonetheless declines to tell readers about these debates. News consumers are denied the knowledge that something is contested. They are not alerted that the subject is even a domain for critical thinking. This is a quintessential form of "expert" copaganda: what the news tells us knowledgeable people dispute versus what the news *assumes as true without indicating that anyone knowledgeable might disagree.*

By contrast, when an article signals that something is contested, it invites people to learn more about an issue, and primes us to use our brain to think about who might be right and what interests each side might have in its respective conclusions. It encourages active mental engagement. But when an assertion is made without a hint that it could be contested, it becomes passively absorbed as conventional wisdom. The casual reader has no reason to suspect that anyone does, or even *could*, think differently.

Copaganda's Small Team of "Experts"

The experts quoted in an article often play a role behind the scenes. Reporters who are not scholars of a subject rely on specialists to help frame their stories, decide when something is important enough to rise to the level of "news," and suggest a list of other people to speak with to write the story. In this way, experts can steer reporters to ideological allies and manipulate how stories are told. The people regularly quoted in the *New York Times* as experts play this role, and there is a social and professional network of such experts consistently recommending each other to reporters. It is not a coincidence, for example, that Asher appears in most of the news stories in this chapter.

In March 2022, *New York Times* editors not only cited Asher yet again but also let German Lopez claim that "experts said" that "policing stops violence in the short term."[24] Since these experts are anonymous, it's possible that *all of these separate articles* are repeating the same talking points of the same small group of people with ties to police. Unless there are strong, overriding reasons for anonymity, the news should name experts and require evidence of their claims.

Predictably, the article again does not tell readers that these "expert" opinions are contested. For instance, it claims: "Policing, in general, reduces crime and violence." An anonymous group of "experts" is again referenced as if there is a consensus on this controversial point. And it evades questions that real experts explore, such as "What kinds of 'crime' do you mean?" and "By whom and against whom is the crime committed?" and "Which kinds of 'violence' do you mean?" and "Does policing work *better* than other kinds of interventions?" The attempt to hide from readers an important and interesting debate is a failure of journalism and a hallmark of copaganda.

It is noteworthy that, even after the widespread criticism the paper received for its late 2021 articles on this point from the watchdog Fairness and Accuracy in Reporting, such a dubious position like "policing reduces crime and violence" was still being passed off as a consensus in a news article months later. It calls to mind the fossil fuel companies' decades-long public relations effort that included paying academic "experts" to tell news organizations that fossil fuels did not contribute to climate change. Such vague claims about policing reducing crime are disputed in almost every detail—for example, as I discuss later, none of the major studies I've seen pro-police experts rely on even include estimates of the crimes committed *by* police. Regardless, the largest meta-study of the sixty-two available studies published from 1972 to 2013 concluded that "the effect on crime of adding or subtracting police is miniscule and not statistically significant."[25] Can you imagine publishing an article claiming that "experts" share the opposite conclusion without telling readers about the most prominent meta-study on the topic?

The article's selective use of experts is revealing in another way. In the March 2022 article, Lopez drops a quiet bombshell: he admits that even his cherry-picked subset of flawed pro-police research shows that policing has only limited "short-term" effects, and the *positive effects evaporate over time*. This proposition is dubious in its own right because, as I explain later, none of the studies establish that more police reduce short-term crime. But that is not my point here. Lopez *concedes* that even his anonymous experts agree policing doesn't reduce crime in the medium or long term and that the key to medium- and long-term safety are social investments. And yet, he continues to argue for more money for more cops on top of the globally unprecedented amount the U.S.

already spends. Even worse, Lopez neglects to share a different expert consensus: historians, sociologists, anthropologists, economists, and political scientists have shown that the police are a significant regressive *political* force. Not only do police and police unions openly support right-wing causes, but they also have used their influence, power, and budgets for over 125 years to block progressive policies like investment in housing, education, and redistribution of wealth. As I explain later, throughout U.S. history, police have turned to surveillance, violence, infiltration, SWAT raids, false-flag operations, lobbying, threats, assassinations, political advocacy, public relations, and intimidation to oppose progressive social movements. Therefore, it makes little sense to gesture at reducing inequality while advocating more money and power for cops, because the more money and power police get, the more they have used it to block that agenda.[26]

In April 2022, news editors invited Lopez and his band of experts back for yet another performance. The *Times* published an article about a mass shooting on the Brooklyn subway that quoted Asher, Rosenfeld, and a merry murder of anonymous experts reiterating the same unfounded contention about the "three" causes of murder.[27]

A Violent Crisis
The Brooklyn shooting and other headline-making violence are part of a broader trend.

The article cynically exploits the acute news emergency of a mass subway shooting to suggest that neutral experts are calling for more police. Lopez writes that "studies broadly suggest that more support for policing" "could help" in combating "crime and violence." Again, this vague claim is controversial on many levels, but note for now its timing. Why are we talking about such studies after a mass shooting? There is no study showing that more money for cops reduces mass shootings— and there is a good reason for that. Remember, police departments spend 96 percent of their time on what they call "non-violent" crimes.[28]

So, what exactly is being advocated to stop mass subway shootings? That police should get more money, 96 percent of which will go to the policing of drugs, homelessness, and petty theft; mental health arrests; minor traffic stops; evictions; surveillance, infiltration, and targeting of progressive protests; municipal debt collection; and seizure of more people's property through civil forfeiture? That doubling down on current policing priorities will stop events like the mass subway shooting? It is difficult to know what Lopez is saying because the conversation is so superficial, and the embedded links in the article that are supposed to support its assertions are often citations to prior posts by Lopez himself.[29]

Lopez cites himself a lot because the *Times* lets him publish a lot of stuff. Eight days after the article about the subway shooting, the paper published another one by Lopez, this time about the "perils of legalization" of drugs.[30] Fighting legalization is an issue of monumental importance for police and police unions, because policing drug use by poor people has been one of the major, and most lucrative, focuses of police for almost fifty years. (Setting aside the trillions in public spending that filters to public and private actors in the punishment bureaucracy, police use drug laws to take billions of dollars in private property through civil forfeiture each year, much of which they get to keep as a sort of incentive payment.) Again, editors allow Lopez to assert a vague consensus of anonymous "experts" who oppose drug legalization. As in his other articles, he then mentions only what *some* pro-police experts think while pretending that there are not others who disagree. In the April 2022 legalization article, he primarily features a "drug policy expert" who has been publishing anti-legalization material for years but is cited as a neutral expert, representative of a consensus.[31]

In a classic straw-person argument, Lopez's "drug policy expert" says that the people who want to legalize drugs argue that we can "legalize and all the problems will go away." What does this mean? Who says that? We don't know, because there is no reasonable attempt to present the actual arguments of experts whose research has concluded that our society should stop caging people for consuming criminalized drugs. We are left with the impression that their unexplained views are naive. Framed by Lopez, drug legalization sounds silly and poorly considered. But he is presenting a caricature of what pro-legalization experts argue. They argue many things, including that policing, prosecution, and imprisonment fail to reduce drug addiction and cause massive collateral damage.[32] And they present an evidence-based case for other means for redressing the social roots of unhealthy drug consumption. None of the experts is given meaningful space in the *Times* to explain their views to readers. Lopez does briefly quote Kassandra Frederique of the Drug Policy Alliance, a leading authority on the public health consequences of the drug war.[33] But rather than calling her an "expert," he questions the objectivity of her position by stating that she leads an "advocacy group." And he does not give Frederique any space to *explain* her arguments.

So, on the one side are "experts" who are dispassionate, learned, scholarly, realistic, and unanimous. On the other side, readers are presented with silly "advocates" who are portrayed as believing that the world will all be peaches and cream if only we could legalize drugs. Readers might even infer from Lopez's failure to include substantial arguments for legalization that these advocates must not be able to articulate explanations, reasons, or evidence to support their views. This is another feature of "expert" copaganda: in the rare instances that it refers to critics of the punishment bureaucracy, it often does not explain the substance of their arguments or the evidence on which they are based, leaving news consumers with the impression that critics' positions are nonexistent or not credible when compared with dispassionate "experts."

Once concocted and hammered into us through repetition, this conventional news consensus is nearly impossible to combat with accurate information. In August 2023, Lopez published an article with the same "experts" and talking points criticizing Oregon's decriminalization of drugs and suggesting that it caused a "surge" in overdoses.[34] A flood of similar reporting appeared in many outlets. A few weeks later, the Centers for Disease Control published a study debunking that claim, saying that scientists found no evidence linking decriminalization of drugs in Oregon to an increase in overdoses.[35] But the false consensus peddled by Lopez and punishment bureaucrats desperate to keep the drug war alive was too powerful for the evidence: the Oregon legislature significantly rolled back the decriminalization ballot measures overwhelmingly approved by the voters.[36]

A Footnote to the Lopez Affair

These examples are only a tiny fraction of the problematic news articles editors at the *Times* permitted Lopez to publish based on a selective and deceptive weaponization of "expert" sources. Indeed, years later, as I began turning parts of my archive into this book, Lopez was still using "experts" to suggest that "fallout" from protests after the police killings of Michael Brown, George Floyd, and Tyre Nichols "likely" caused murders and that more spending on the punishment bureaucracy will save lives.[37]

But by June 2023, one thing caught my eye. The newspaper inserted a two-paragraph qualification at the end of Lopez's article, essentially undercutting his claims that the brief spike in murder in 2020 was caused by a reduction in police funding or morale:

What we don't know

Experts caution that these three explanations are not proven. And it is possible that the rest of the year will be more violent than the first half. "I do think it's a little premature to be making any strong conclusions about what it all means just yet," Jeff Asher, a crime analyst who tracks the big-city murder data, told me.

The lack of certainty is typical in discussions about crime. Starting in the 1990s, crime rate plummeted. Yet decades later, after much scholarship, no consensus has emerged for why violence subsided. Crime is an incredibly complicated topic, involving personal disputes, the economy, social services, the political system and more. A few decades, much less a couple of years, is typically too little time to explain a trend definitively.

This is extraordinary. Suddenly we are told that, according to "experts," the causes invoked by Lopez in article after article are speculation. Contrast Lopez's use of the term "likely" to describe racial justice protests causing more murder with what the addendum says about the theory being "not proven."

A Reader's Guide to Experts

As we have seen, there are several common ways reporters and editors use experts to further copaganda. Here are a few overarching techniques to look out for:

- Reporters cite "experts" without providing background on who they are or conflicts of interest they have, including their connection to police. That can disguise bias, imply neutrality, and make people less prone to skepticism when evaluating an expert's claims.
- "Experts" are referred to as a group, generating a kind of unaccountable anonymity that suggests a consensus even when one doesn't exist. For example, many articles support otherwise unsubstantiated claims by prefacing them with "experts say . . ." or "analysts say . . ."
- Reporters use "experts" to offer opinions that have no basis in fact or that are false as a way of avoiding having to provide evidence.
- In articles about safety and crime, the most well-resourced news outlets tilt their "expert" roster toward those from the punishment bureaucracy and away from those in public health, education, poverty reduction, housing, urban planning, environmental justice, medicine, and other similar fields. The latter are often referred to as "advocates" or "activists."

- News outlets also tilt their "expert" roster toward those with pro-incarceration ideologies. These "experts" justify and normalize state violence, and they almost always suggest more resources for the punishment bureaucracy in response to social problems.
- Experts are used to constrain the range of reasonable explanations, solutions, and policies on crime. Anyone with a view outside this range is explicitly or implicitly defined as too extreme to be credible.

The above examples from the *New York Times* demonstrate that the people held out as "experts" in the news aren't necessarily the wisest thinkers with the greatest values speaking to you out of love for humanity. The thing they are an "expert" in is repeating talking points that powerful people want absorbed. The path to becoming an "expert" in the news is not through some kind of lofty intellectual trial—it is cultivating and using connections, and then collectively agreeing with everyone involved that there is mutual benefit in some things being said and other things being left unsaid." So, when you read a news article that quotes an expert, ask yourself a few questions. Consider this a sort of Reader's Guide to Experts:

- Who chose this expert?
- How did this expert make their way to this journalist?
- Who benefits from this expert opinion?
- Does anything about the expert's background suggest a conflict of interest?
- Does the expert or the article offer a sound basis for their conclusions?
- Is this expert frequently chosen by news outlets to present this view?
- Does the article suggest that different experts have a difference of opinion on the issue?
- Does the article offer critics of the expert's view a chance to explain the basis of and reasons for their disagreement?

6

Academic Copaganda

Outflanked on its student left, intellectual liberalism threw in the sponge without a fight, and many of its outstanding stalwarts, eloquent about academic freedom in general only up to the point where some actual, particular freedom was threatened, emigrated speedily to the extreme right, and made themselves over into the range-riders of discipline.

-Stuart Hall[1]

Intellectual activity . . . must be disinterested—the truth is a two-edged sword—and if one is not willing to be pierced by that sword, even to the extreme of dying on it, then all of one's intellectual activity is a masturbatory delusion and a wicked and dangerous fraud.

-James Baldwin[2]

Two Harvard professors, Christopher Lewis and Adaner Usmani, published an article in 2022 titled "The Injustice of Under-Policing in America" in the *American Journal of Law and Equality*.[3] The professors, who refer to themselves as "socialists" and "progressives," call for "almost half a million" more armed cops, who they say will arrest 7.8 million more people per year, in what would be the greatest expansion of militarized police and surveillance in modern world history.

In this chapter, I analyze the proposal for 500,000 more armed police officers, as well as the strange responses from the professors to my questions. These two Harvard professors are not outliers; in fact, I focus on them because their bad arguments illustrate a pervasive lack of rigor among criminologists who appear frequently in the news.

What Do the Harvard Professors Say, and What Do They Hide?

The proposal by the Harvard professors argues that (1) the U.S. has way more prisoners than other comparable countries, and (2) that it has way fewer cops. This is bad, they say, because: (3) prisons bring little benefit for their costs, and (4) cops bring big benefits for their costs. As a result, they argue, we should add a lot more cops to achieve what they call the "First World Balance."

Before I get into the main flaws with the proposal, I want to describe my brief interaction with the professors over email. I was immediately skeptical about the second claim above, and I worried that news outlets might mindlessly repeat the claim that the U.S. has below-median numbers of police officers. So I emailed the professors to better understand the origin of that claim. It's notoriously fraught to count cops across countries with different local/national approaches to classifying civilian and criminal enforcement bureaucrats (including, in some countries, the identification of unarmed officers as police), so I asked for their data.

I noted to the professors that their U.S. data source appeared to exclude federal policing agencies (e.g., border patrol, ICE, FBI, DEA, ATF, Capitol Police, Park Police, military police, deputized national guard, etc.), potentially many non-local state agencies, and *all* private police forces.[4] These exclusions were striking given revelations, for example, about the covert and illegal role border agents played across the country in helping local police crush the 2020 protests that the Harvard professors opened their article discussing.[5]

One of the professors responded that they chose to use the number 697,195 from an FBI survey, even though they knew many local police departments were excluded from it. So, he admitted, the number of police may be much higher, perhaps 900,000 if you include those and federal police officers. (Wikipedia, for example, at the time reported 900,000 based on a major police nonprofit source.) The professor then told me that the U.S. Census count was actually 1,227,788 police (a number they later corrected to 1,088,027). That's 56 percent higher than the number they chose to publish. Using this number, he conceded, would mean the U.S. police presence truthfully is "1.1 times the median rate in rich countries."

Recall that the published proposal had begun with the sexy assertion that the U.S. has *fewer* cops per capita than the median developed country. This was the key premise in Figure 1 of the article, the very first chart presented to readers. Nowhere in the article did the professors explain that they had intentionally excluded hundreds of thousands of cops that might undermine their glossy premise that the U.S. is significantly below its "First World" peers in per capita police.[6] Instead of disclosing competing estimates and explaining their choices to readers, the Harvard professors used a knowingly wrong estimate that enabled them to suggest, falsely, that the U.S. falls below the median developed country in per capita police. This is the kind of assertion by "experts" that gets picked up by journalists, spread through the news in a circular web of citations, and turned into conventional wisdom because the reasons to be skeptical about it are hidden from the audience.

Relatedly, the professors also chose to omit from their discussion the higher police *budgets* in the U.S., owing in part to more advanced surveillance and weaponry, longer work weeks, and overtime hours, which make the policing *footprint* in the U.S. different than what their comparison suggested. Incredibly, the Harvard professors also did not tell readers that they excluded privately operated police forces. This omission would be puzzling to residents of Detroit, for example, who see private police forces taking over downtown, or to people familiar with many private universities and wealthy neighborhoods with armed, deputized police across the country.[7] Many people do not even know whether a given police force is private or public. Indeed, as I was heading to my office to revise this chapter in the summer of 2024, I saw an interaction between an armed police officer and a rider on public transit, and I only realized after several minutes of internet searching that the cop was part of the privatized police force contracted to police the D.C. metro—which refers to itself as "a private law enforcement agency."[8] As of 2021, there were 1.1 million private police officers in the U.S. This figure alone, if it had been included, would have almost tripled the total number of police officers the professors reported.[9]

When I confronted them with these omissions, they switched course. They claimed that they were not interested in privately deputized armed police and that per capita police comparisons don't actually matter much, even though it had been the starting point for their published proposal. They said they instead care about *ratios* of police to prisoners and police to homicides. Even a moment's thought reveals that this focus on ratios is strange. Such ratios might merely show that the U.S. has way more prisoners than other countries and that the U.S. is also a violent society with lots of guns. The denominators in these ratios, prisoners and homicides, do not say anything necessarily about the numerator in terms of whether there should be *more police*—i.e., the main point of their article.

These manipulations in counting the number of police officers are not central to the argument about whether the U.S. needs more police, but they are revealing and representative of the way sloppiness can slip into public discourse about police. The two professors knew they had available data that would refute the headline-grabbing point on international per-capita police comparisons, and they chose to omit it. It's perhaps less persuasive to start a proposal for 500,000 more cops with "the U.S. probably already has more police than most comparable countries and it is less safe than those countries, but we think it needs way more police!"

The "Core" Problem

In fairness, although the Harvard professors name their proposal for "almost half a million more police officers" the "First World Balance" and say in the article that the international comparisons "anchor this piece," they correctly admitted to me that none of these international comparisons are important to their "core" points. Their "core" points relate only to the U.S. and are captured in argument #4 above about the supposedly big benefits of police. I agree that this is the core of the article, but this is also where the article goes off the copaganda rails.

The most glaring flaw is that the professors ignore the social costs of adding more police. They present the main social cost of their proposal as 7.8 million more arrests. They call this the "main downside," and it is the only one they credit. They then conclude that the benefits of more police far outweigh the costs of 7.8 million more people arrested.

But more arrests are *not* the only social cost of "almost half a million" more armed cops. To start, the professors don't mention that they are excluding *millions* of police assaults as a social cost of policing. They similarly exclude all pretextual and abusive police stops. Philando Castile, a school cafeteria worker who frequently paid for the lunches of kids who couldn't afford to eat, was stopped for minor traffic issues fifty-two times before he was stopped for a broken taillight and shot to death by police with his girlfriend filming.[10] They also exclude forcible searches, home raids, beatings, taserings, handcuffings, strip searches, sexual assaults, and property seizures. They exclude all the jail deaths, like that of Sandra Bland, caused by police arrests, and all the lost jobs, lost homes, dead pets, billions in bail bond and other jail fees transferred from the poorest people in our society to large corporations, the increased spread of infectious disease, lost medical care, and family separations attendant in 7.8 million more *legal* arrests. They further omit the robust research showing that more low-level arrests and prosecutions lead to *more* crime in the future.[11] They also omit the downstream consequences from arming hundreds of thousands more people with guns in general, including the sale of police-issued guns. A CBS news investigation found that because police sell so many of their guns, between 2006 and 2024, "at least 52,529 guns once owned by police" were "later used in crimes."[12] Instead of accounting for all (or any) of this, Lewis and Usmani merely "guess" (their word) that adding more armed cops

might "cause" there to be "less police violence," which they measure
only by police homicides. So, if cops engage in legal or illegal violence
of the kind I mentioned above but don't kill anyone, the professors don't
count it at all. And when they try to explain their "guess" on the antici-
pated decrease in police homicides, they do not support their contention
with *any evidence*. They offer only "speculative reasons" that more police
would make society safer, which they say might make policing less dangerous, which, in turn, might end in police killing fewer people. They
therefore conclude that "it is not at all clear" that fewer police would
reduce police homicides. This kind of armchair guesswork about police
homicides, extrapolated to all forms of legal and illegal police violence,
is unfounded at every level of inference.

The issue of domestic violence underlines a related category of social cost that the professors ignore. For decades, studies have found that
families of police officers experience domestic violence at astronomical
rates: between 24 and 40 percent of all families with a police officer report criminal domestic violence. That is a rate of domestic violence up
to 400 percent that of the general population.[13] Given how frequently
domestic conflict turns violent, and that more police officers will have
more guns, one might "speculate," to borrow a term from the professors, that more cops could mean more murdered domestic partners.
Already nearly half of all murders of women in the U.S. are committed
by a current or former partner.[14] The complete refusal to acknowledge,
much less explore the implications of, these kinds of secondary effects
for a society with more armed police officers is not unique to the Harvard professors—it is a feature of most summaries of the criminological
literature purporting to balance the social costs and benefits of police.

More broadly, though, the professors ignore the social costs of the
massive expansion in other bureaucracies that would result from the
7.8 million more arrests they call for, including: prosecutors, judges,
probation officers, drug testing, stay-away orders, fines and fees, debt
collectors, GPS monitoring, bail bond companies, the jail telecom industry, and consulting firms that, among others, would be involved with

pretrial and posttrial supervision of millions more people. All of this leads to an unprecedented involvement of government penal institutions and corporate profiteers in the lives of tens of millions of additional arrested individuals and their families. Once these profitable bureaucratic institutions grow, it is nearly impossible for a society later to shrink them, because of the political power and inertia that they accumulate.

More fundamentally, many scholars have studied deeper social costs when a society increases the number of centrally controlled, armed government bureaucrats. These non-financial costs include, among others: the deterioration of privacy across society; expanded capacity for organized schemes of municipal political retaliation, reprisal, and censorship; greater ability of police to distort the news and public knowledge acquisition with hundreds of thousands more officers and tens of billions more in budgets, union dues, and consultant contracts; the international linkages and consequences for democracy in other countries of expanding the global policing industry by tens of billions of dollars; increases in overall masculine violence and aggression; increased power of the government to surveil, investigate, and interfere in people's lives; and reduced infrastructure and capacity of people and communities to resolve interpersonal conflict.[15]

The professors casually dismiss such concerns without seriously considering them. They claim that, after adding 500,000 more police, "the United States could hardly be considered a police state." To justify this conclusion, they assert (based on their earlier inaccurate numbers and exclusion of private police) that the addition of 500,000 police would make the U.S. look like "today's Spain." That is the entirety of the argument by two Harvard scholars for the claim that a historic expansion of armed surveillance agents would have little impact on private life in the United States.

But it gets worse. Perhaps the most profound social cost the professors ignore is the role police play in preserving inequality. A primary function of police for 150 years has been to surveil, infiltrate, and crush progressive social movements seeking to reduce inequality. It's why police spied on, infiltrated, brutally repressed, and continue to crush labor, feminist, civil rights, anti-war, LGBTQ, environmental, reproductive rights, indigenous, and economic justice movements.[16] To take one of thousands of examples, as I was completing a final edit of this chapter, the chief of patrol of the NYPD made a public announcement from his official social media account in the wake of the police violence against students calling for peace and justice in Palestine. He wrote:

> Who is funding this? What is happening? There is an unknown entity who is radicalizing our vulnerable students. Taking advantage of their young minds. As parents and Americans we must demand some answers! I can't speak for the rest of America, but in NYC we won't rest until we find out! We will broadcast what we see and find. We will use the might of our Intelligence Bureau and our Federal partners to quite simply connect the dots. Follow the money!!!!!![17]

I encourage you to peruse the archive of this repression collected by scholars that I have made available in the corresponding endnote.[18] To take one vivid example that inspired me to study the issue further, the NYPD assaulted and arrested fruit and vegetable workers, who were deemed essential workers during the pandemic, for the "crime" of organizing for a $1 raise after the 2020 lockdowns.[19]

Apart from their role in destroying those organizing for progressive social change, the police are and have always been central to protecting private concentrations of wealth through selective enforcement of the law; gentrification; unlawful redlining; evictions; immigration enforcement and the management of migrants fleeing the effects of global U.S. policy; civil forfeiture; and many other forms of exclusion and predation.[20] And they are preparing to play a central role in the enforcement of anti-democratic voter restriction laws sweeping the country, as well as laws banning books from libraries and anti-trans laws.[21] How can two scholars write confidently about the social costs of police but not mention, for example, the prospect that, in about half the United States, police will now be tracking the communications of and arresting women and providers of reproductive medical care?

In addition to the authoritarian role that U.S. police play by selectively enforcing rules made by those with power in an unequal society, they also have a long history of both overtly supporting and actively being infiltrated by the far right. As professor Naomi Murakawa has documented, for example, during and after the 2020 protests that the two Harvard professors express sympathy for, police across the country helped far-right and white nationalist groups terrorize protesters, even calling fascists who showed up to civil rights protests as "armed friendlies."[22]

In addition to what they do as police on the job, police are also *political* actors. In recent years, for example, police unions have used their financial and political capital to endorse far-right politicians like Donald Trump, Marjorie Taylor Greene, Ron DeSantis, Nicole Malliotakis, Elise Stefanik, and almost every contemporary prominent election-denier running for major office.[23] And they have called on these politicians to increase border militarization; end the Deferred Action for Childhood Arrivals, or DACA, program; support private prisons; and even roll back the Affordable Care Act.

Police unions are even more active in pushing right-wing agendas at the local level. They intervene in elections and privately pressure local officials such as judges, budget auditors, district attorneys, city councilmembers, and county executives. Over the years, numerous local officials have told me they cannot support reducing police budgets because they are terrified of retaliation by police, including of cops raiding their homes or stopping and harassing their loved ones.[24] Such intimidation is a pervasive fact of daily life for local progressive politicians—and even of numerous judges who have confided to me about their fear of retaliation against their families by police. The Harvard professors don't address *any* of these political ramifications when they talk about the effects on society of more—and more powerful—police.

The professors also ignore a related point: because police are both the front door and a crucial driver of the punishment bureaucracy, they use their political power to lobby for the large prison populations that the professors concede are harmful. This happens in many obvious ways both overt and covert, including through many of the same overlapping punishment-bureaucrat organized labor formations. The self-proclaimed "rigorous" academic article about what the professors call the political "feasibility" of reducing prison populations by two million to pay for 500,000 more cops therefore does not ask the question about what bad things, *including more imprisonment*, might come from a more powerful police lobby.[25] The professors are essentially asking, "Imagine a fantasy world where everyone agrees to massively reduce prisoners by two million; what should we do with the resulting budget surplus?" Their answer is police. But if we could save money by freeing two million people from prison—which we cannot do in part because police drive mass incarceration through lobbying, pressure, and propaganda—why would we spend it on cops instead of on approaches addressing the root causes of violence that even the professors agree are better at producing safety and that don't carry these costs? Their lip service to reducing prison populations is just that—it's an attempt to feign "progressive" credentials and insulate themselves from attacks about the authoritarian nature of their proposal.

Ironically, the professors admit that greater social equality would be the best way of reducing violence. But the power of armed surveillance bureaucracies within local, state, and federal governments is one major reason we can't fund many of the things that the professors admit lead to real safety—like the various social equality programs that police help block. And police threaten society whenever their funding is at risk—through organized work stoppages, misinformation, violence, or simple political campaign expenditures—so once you add all these police, there is no realistic chance of going back.[26] The expansion and militarization of the police is one of the biggest political barriers to the "egalitarian" society the professors say they want.

I have seen this firsthand. In every place I have worked on civil rights and economic justice issues, police have organized to oppose us. They have lied in court and in the news; they have made threats to me, my family, and my friends; they have intimidated vulnerable allies of mine seeking progressive change for their communities, and they have spent huge sums lobbying against even modest changes that are backed by evidence. To take one example, a police chief I had publicly criticized once grabbed the back of my neck in a public hallway, looked at his hand, smiled, and commented that he now had my DNA before telling me the make and model of my rental car and wishing me a good day. To take another of many personal examples, a Harvard Law School student intern and I (traveling with a *New York Times* reporter doing a profile of our civil rights work) were illegally detained inside a small room at a courthouse by armed sheriffs after I asked a clerk at a public desk for public case records that could expose police and judicial corruption. That crime committed by the sheriffs against us met the elements of kidnapping. Millions of police assaults, kidnappings, and illegal searches and detentions like the one visited on me and my intern happen—mostly to vulnerable people or people advocating for social change—and they are rarely recorded. Professors Lewis and Usmani excluded illegal actions like this from their analysis, even though these actions collectively shape, at its very core, the kind of society we have and how safe many people feel fighting for a better one.

Finally, the social costs of police expansion are global. The rise of the policing-industrial complex in the U.S. has been a key driver of global authoritarianism through a web of lucrative and strategic training partnerships; task forces; shared infrastructure; and multinational intelligence, surveillance, weapons, and policing technology companies that promote authoritarian control to manage and preserve inequality across the world.[27]

It's one thing to weigh all these social costs against supposed benefits, but it's something different to pretend that the costs do not exist. I have gone into detail about what the Harvard professors omit because it helps reveal the purpose and effect of such scholarship. As with copaganda in the news, the selective erasure of profound harm committed by the punishment bureaucracy is a ubiquitous feature of pro-police scholarship. Incredibly, despite their refusal to consider most of the social costs, the professors are confident, proclaiming that the costs "pale in comparison to the benefits." They call an alternative view on the social costs of police "implausible on almost any accounting."

Copaganda's Cynicism

This brings me to another of the proposal's copaganda themes: its incoherent cynicism. The professors claim to acknowledge that a primary underlying root cause of violence is "concentrated disadvantage"—that is, the very inequality and maldistribution of social investments that cops protect.[28]

The professors admit that inequality is the biggest factor leading to violence, but they declare that increasing social investment to reduce inequality through programs like early childhood education is "infeasible." So, two Harvard scholars conclude that they have no choice but to base an entire academic project on the assumption that it is impossible to make the world more equal:

> We think that in the long run, a significant expansion of social policy would reduce crime by addressing its root causes and in turn reduce the need and demand for both policing and imprisonment. In other work, we argue that *any* coherent conception of distributive justice or economic efficiency entails that the United States *should* expand social policy. But a significant expansion of social policy requires significant redistribution from rich to poor. Redistribution of this magnitude would require the poor to wield some kind of leverage over the rich. Given the collapse of the American labor movement and the electoral fracturing of the American working class, we doubt we will see anything like this soon.[29]

In our email correspondence, the professors reiterated their "pessimism about what kind of social policy alternatives to policing are feasible." I couldn't believe what I was reading: two Harvard professors agree that violence is caused by structural inequality, but since they don't think we can reduce inequality because the poor have little power, they advocate the only solution they think feasible: authoritarianism. Of course, 500,000 more cops to control oppressed people isn't a surprising—or intellectually interesting—proposal if you start from the premise that social change and a more equal society are impossible!

As with a lot of the best copaganda that I analyze later, what makes this cynicism more pernicious is that Lewis and Usmani claimed to be "coming from the left" and that they "hated" their own conclusion. They wrote to me:

> But we are, like you, coming from the left. . . . The conclusion Adaner and I have reached in this particular project is one we tried our hardest to avoid for a long time. But we have come to think it's the only way to be consistent with our fundamental egalitarian and progressive commitments. We didn't come into this project hoping to vindicate the under-policing thesis. We both hated the idea from the start and it is still uncomfortable to us.[30]

Elite criminology is awash in this kind of de-politicizing drivel dressed up as scholarship. Any solution—especially those that would require organizing, building power, political education, changing hearts and minds, reshaping institutions, and mobilizing marginalized people to shift the balance of power in our society—is treated as so inconceivable that it does not even merit discussion. Even immediately implementable alternatives that are currently working well in many places are not mentioned. *Copaganda requires this sense of hopelessness to thrive.* Two scholars at one of the most elite institutions in the country celebrate their own article as "rigorous normative argument," which it is not. But it does serve powerful institutions, which benefit from more people sharing the authors' cynicism about the possibility of progressive social change and ignorance of other potential alternatives—and which benefit from the call for increased investment in bureaucracies of social control. And so, like many political elites before them for over a century, they conclude, after a lot of fancy words in a prestigious journal whose title includes the word "equality," that the response to inequality can only be . . . more government agents with guns.

A Circular Loop

The real core of the proposal is an empirical assertion that more police will reduce "serious crime"—which the professors define to exclude white-collar crime, environmental crime, police crime, and public corruption, to name a few. Thus, at bottom, the professors are merely arguing that police are better than anything else at reducing "serious crime," so we should have a lot more of them. If this claim is incorrect, all their other conclusions would be invalidated. To make this claim, the professors offer no original research.

The core thesis, on which the entire argument rests, repeats a controversial claim by a few pro-police professors, whose 2017 article on this point the Harvard professors cite in a footnote. They do not cite the contradictory research that has for decades found that an increase in police officers does *not* reduce police-recorded crime, or other research showing that non-police alternatives are more cost-effective.[31] A casual reader would have no idea that these other bodies of research exist.

Ignoring other research on whether police are effective at all and whether other alternatives are more effective, they "guess," based on work by other pro-police professors, that adding 500,000 cops would lead to four thousand fewer homicides. It's important to pause here to note that, even according to Lewis and Usmani, this is *the main benefit of their proposal*. Amazingly, even if this linear relationship between more police and fewer homicides were true, it would mean that, under their plan, the U.S. would still have about 80 percent of its current homicides.

Unsurprisingly, when discussing homicides, they ignore findings that policing increases *non-homicide* deaths in the short term and increases homicide in the long term by maintaining inequality. For example, police violence has been shown to increase infant mortality in Black children and to "substantially decrease the birth weight and gestational age of black infants residing nearby."[32] A few other examples demonstrate how 500,000 more cops could lead to more death. Recall that air pollution kills 100,000 people in the U.S. every year—about five times the number of homicides—and that cops crush environmental organizing and threaten even modest local protests about pollution, such as demonstrations against local point-source dumping and emissions that cause cancer.[33] To take one widely reported example, a pipeline company paid Minnesota cops millions of dollars to target climate protesters.[34] Adding more police will lead to more repression of people organizing to stop environmental destruction. The same can be said about police repression of organizing against foreclosures, evictions, lack of access to health care, poisoned drinking water, and labor exploitation, all of which lead to more social harm and death.

This approach is the scholarly equivalent of citing a big oil–funded study of climate change that contradicts other independent studies, and presenting the former as scientific consensus while not even mentioning the existence of the latter. As we saw when discussing the news media's use of experts, one of the routine practices across the copaganda universe is permitting claims to be made without acknowledging the extent to which they are disputed. And often, having ignored most of the available evidence and making it seem like no one else disagrees with them, copagandists can then claim that they only came to their authoritarian conclusions reluctantly, as a last resort. These are not clerical errors or little boo-boos by meticulous scholars. They are omissions and distortions that undermine the integrity of scholarly discourse. An article arguing for *reducing* police by 500,000 officers resting on similarly weak and misleading claims would have put the career of non-tenured scholars in jeopardy.

The Harvard Professors Respond

After I published a version of this analysis and coauthored a similar critique with the sociology professor Alex Vitale, the two professors posted a link to a PDF document on a Dropbox account entitled "Reply to Alec Karakatsanis."[35] I do not know to whom this "reply" was selectively sent, but I was alerted to its existence by another Harvard professor a few months later. The reply accuses me of trying to censor the Harvard professors, and it illustrates how scholars in fancy institutions become adept at using a lot of flowery rhetoric but operate without the transparency, curiosity, humility, meticulousness, and accountability that people who care about the advancement of knowledge should aspire to. I discuss the reply here because it is representative of how difficult it can be to get prominent academics to have a genuine conversation about the flaws that plague the field of pro-police criminology.

First, and most importantly, Lewis and Usmani's reply does not address *any* of my main criticisms. Without explanation, they say in one sentence that most of my critiques are "unserious":

> In a recent Substack newsletter and Twitter thread, the lawyer Alec Karakatsanis has raised a number of objections. Most of these are unserious, and so we would have preferred to ignore them. But because his accusations of scholarly malpractice have garnered some attention, it has seemed necessary to set the record straight.[36]

I do not think it was "unserious" for me to point out—to take just a few examples discussed above—that professors recommending the greatest expansion of police in modern history did not consider the social costs of or alternatives to policing, the effects of the increased political power of 500,000 more cops, the impact on the criminalization of reproductive rights, or the research on increased infant mortality and reduced birth weight of Black babies. It is not a response to numerous careful criticisms to say they are all "unserious" but decline to explain why.

Second, almost the entirety of their reply is devoted to a distraction: the issue of how they count existing police officers, which all of us had agreed was not central to their argument. Despite my statement that their misleading assertion about the number of cops in the U.S. was *not* the "core" problem with their article, their reply calls it my "main accusation." They conclude that our disagreement regarding the numbers of police across countries "has nothing to do with" their conclusion. I concur. But we are only talking about it because *they decided to begin their paper with it* as a public relations strategy and to name their police-expansion plan the "First World Balance."

Third, their reply makes no effort to respond to anything Professor Vitale and I said about the social costs of policing, the political power of police, the role of police in disrupting progressive movements, the research they ignored showing the ineffectiveness of police in reducing "serious crime," or any of our other points about the flaws and internal contradictions in their article. They only repeat the point that "serious crime" causes a lot of harm, so *if* they are right that more police are the best possible way to reduce "serious crime" without negative consequences, then yes, the U.S. should add 500,000 police. But that's one of the big "ifs" we used evidence to dispute!

Finally, they conclude: "Karakatsanis has done nothing to sway us from our position." That is hardly a rebuttal. One standard of scholarly discourse is to explain *why* one comes to one's views, including the logical and evidentiary steps that would allow someone to follow one's reasoning. The Harvard professors failed to do that in either the original article or their reply. And this is a feature of academic copaganda—it is difficult to get pro-police professors to respond to specific criticisms with any rigor. In this way, an entire bubble of scholarship can develop without anyone asking the most basic questions or holding each other intellectually accountable.

In classic copaganda fashion, the professors instead assure us again that they are "progressives" who care a lot about marginalized people. But a vow of compassion is no substitute for good scholarly work. Their reply opens with the assertion that they are "socialists" who care about inequality, especially racism. This is like the mayor of San Francisco saying that she cares deeply about solving homelessness while proposing armed police sweeps to put homeless people in jail because real estate developers announced they would object to any policy that involves more affordable housing. As I explain later in the book, doing authoritarian stuff while claiming to be "progressive" is a copaganda *strategy* designed to dissuade well-meaning people from asking hard questions.

Lewis and Usmani continue by asserting that any redistribution of wealth will require "the mobilization of the poor and the working class," but since this is "a distant prospect," the best we can do for now is more police. Their reply thus repeats the argument that social change, such as reducing inequality and investing in early childhood education, is not possible. Ignoring recent evidence, scholarship, and real-world examples being implemented across the U.S., they even double down, saying "there are no feasible social policy alternatives" to reduce crime.[37] And, yet again, they ignore the scholarship, which I cited, that documents how increasing the power of police would *hinder* the very progressive movements and social policy campaigns they claim to support. Eugene Debs, the most prominent socialist leader in American history, imprisoned by police and prosecutors for his opposition to World War I, must be rolling over in his grave. (Then again, his grave would probably need to be dug up to make room for one of the several dozen new $100 million training facilities for 500,000 new cops.)

The professors were savvy to combine their call for an unprecedented expansion of police with a half-hearted assertion that they wanted to reduce imprisonment, something they know, but didn't tell readers, is inconsistent with increased police political power. Unsurprisingly, the *Washington Post* later used the professor's bad scholarship the way I predicted: it embraced their call for more police but said that the reducing imprisonment part isn't politically feasible at this point.[38] It argued, therefore, that we should dramatically expand police and then promised that, later, wink-wink, perhaps the reduction of mass imprisonment could be explored. I can find no attempt by the professors to criticize this use of their work.

The political right also embraced the professors. The San Francisco Deputy Sheriffs' Association began urging people to read the article "in its entirety," through a social media account paid for by its political action committee. The police union explained that the "study" showed "exactly what is going on in San Francisco. Little to no consequences and lack of police." The police union then said that the article by the Harvard professors is proof that "the civilianization of police will go down in history as the biggest mistake any city can make." In what can only be understood as a fascist warning, the police union then said: "Only a new leader that will make drastic changes can correct the course."[39]

Similarly, employees of the far-right Manhattan Institute published an article, in the "Ideas" section of *The Atlantic*, called "We're Underfunding the Police," which cites the Harvard professors as a key piece of evidence.[40] The right-wing weaponization of their arguments should not be surprising. It is to the advantage of the far right to use an article by self-proclaimed "progressives" to further entrench the punishment bureaucracy, justify authoritarian policies, and block social change.

Accusations of Censorship

After avoiding my arguments, the professors suggest that I tried to "censor" them:

> The real shame of Karakatsanis's reply is that he has pandered to our intellectual culture's worst features. Students today too

often graduate from college and graduate schools unable to engage people who disagree with them in good faith, or even to make the relevant counterarguments. Instead, they look to institutions to censor views which make them uncomfortable. This anti-intellectual tendency is a lamentable feature of our times. It undermines the integrity of scholarly discourse and, therefore, the research necessary for informed public policy.

The Harvard professors portray themselves as interested in debate and the "integrity" of scholarship, suggest that I am not engaging in "good faith" or making "relevant counterarguments," and charge me with having a corrupting influence on impressionable students. In reality, I set forth counterarguments clearly relevant to the question of whether to add 500,000 armed police, which they entirely ignored. As for their aspersions about my fostering an "anti-intellectual tendency" and even advocating censorship, they do not and cannot cite a single word, clause, sentence, or paragraph as evidence. (This mistreatment also did not go over well with my grandmother, who doesn't like when people are mean to me.)

More seriously, the accusation of censorship cheapens what is an important problem, and is an insult to the scholars around the world who are *actually being* threatened with the loss of their jobs based on the content of their syllabi or the bravery of scholarship that challenges powerful institutions. And, most profoundly, it is a perversion of the concept of "scholarly discourse." Pointing out sloppy scholarship, debunking poorly constructed arguments that help powerful institutions maintain inequality, and calling out the manipulation of facts is not "censorship."

The professors' attempt to cast a critique of how criminology scholars support their arguments as "censorship" is perhaps the most alarming part of this episode. These are two powerful people. I have no doubt that their pro-police views will help their scholarship escape the scrutiny that would otherwise accompany an anti-police scholar in the tenure review process at Harvard. They will probably teach thousands of students at Harvard and have huge platforms to influence the most powerful people in our society, as evidenced by the *Washington Post* and *The Atlantic* quickly parroting their conclusions. They will become even more prominent public figures as the right-wing and corporate media embrace their plan for 500,000 more cops precisely because it comes from self-styled "socialists" and "progressives."

I tried my best to marshal my experience and my safe position outside academia to explain why their proposal lacked rigor and honesty. I tried to explain why this kind of scholarship poses a danger to our society, particularly at a time of rising authoritarianism, because of the effect it can have on students and journalists, and because stuff like this adds a veneer of legitimacy to the proposals of a growing fascist movement. I didn't do this because their opinions made me "uncomfortable"; I did it because there are consequences to Harvard professors making public proposals for 500,000 more police as right-wing mobs take over school boards, as university professors are fired for discussing race (*actual* "censorship"); as women, pregnant people, and healers are arrested for receiving or providing reproductive health care; as poor people are arrested for voting; as people forced from their homes are arrested for sleeping on the streets; as police beat striking union workers; as students and faculty calling for an end to militarism, apartheid, and genocide are violently arrested; and as people seeking to draw attention to ecological calamity are surveilled, shot, and imprisoned.

Writing an op-ed that criticizes the professors is not "censorship," but by invoking that specter, they turn their own failure to address criticism into a moral crusade to protect the integrity of the academy. It is a scenario where, as Orwell would say, "two plus two equals five." For these reasons, I offer the two Harvard professors, Adaner Usmani and Christopher Lewis, tenured chairs at Copaganda University—new positions made possible by a donation from an anonymous company that makes ecofriendly handcuffs. If things don't work out for them at Harvard, they now have a home more suited to their work.

Harvard Students Contact Me

My critique of the 500,000 cops proposal became widely shared and referenced by scholars and in classroom discussions across the country. It appears that the "Reply to Alec Karakatsanis" may have been written as a form of damage control for their reputations among other Harvard professors, preparing them to make the argument that any critiques they face from students or other faculty are the inventions of a "woke" mob who cannot handle arguments that make them "uncomfortable."[41]

After my critique was published and around the time of their "reply" (addressed to me but not shared with me), private armed cops employed by Harvard surveilled and crushed a student protest at Harvard Law School calling for more reproductive rights staff, more professors of color with tenure, and racial justice on campus.[42] Harvard's private police action was part of a long history of armed campus policing by privately deputized police.[43] According to these two professors, though, these aren't "police" worth counting and what happened isn't a social cost worth considering. Shortly afterward, some Harvard Law School students contacted me and exposed how one of the two professors, Christopher Lewis, had used the stressful first-year final exams to get law students to do intellectual labor in furtherance of his scholarship. The students sent me the final exam question, which asked students to brainstorm potential counterarguments to his personal scholarship on police. I posted the exam questions on social media with some reflections about the ethics of an instructor forcing students to give free intellectual labor for pro-police scholarship on a final exam that is supposed to be assessing their proficiency in first-year criminal law.[44] The students also told me that they had raised critiques similar to mine in class before I had published my article, confirming that at least one of the professors was aware of the omissions in his arguments but chose not to engage with them. Finally, the students informed me that the journal that published the "progressive" call for 500,000 more police by "socialists" was a recently created journal about "equality" that had been presented as one of Harvard's major responses to racial justice uprisings and student protests on campus against police brutality in 2020. Just two years later, it was publishing shoddy articles with no meaningful original research, including one proposing the greatest expansion of police in modern history.

Academic Copaganda and Its Incentives

Many people within elite institutions know that the ticket to stardom—the key to tenure, lucrative grants, appointments to institutes, chairs, awards, fancy invitations, and access to op-ed pages—is to serve power. There is an academic wing of the copaganda ecosystem that churns out scholarship as simplistic as the work of the two Harvard professors featured in this chapter.[45] As recent research has found, almost none of the punishment bureaucracy's interventions have significant effects on interpersonal harm even when the most rigorous experimental techniques are used, and for good reason: the root causes of big problems in our society—like violence committed by human beings against each other—are deeper.[46] But this reality of what actually influences social harm doesn't stop an endless stream of studies, quotes, and op-eds focusing the public on tweaks to the machinery of punishment that won't significantly reduce interpersonal harm but will enhance profit, control, and bureaucratic power. In this way, enormous effort is spent figuring out how to *manage* the chaos and suffering caused by poor material living conditions, rather than directing intellectual energy toward *ameliorating those conditions*. Some of it is well-funded and corrupt, but much of it is a more complex result of the culture and political economy of universities, as well as the systemic incentives in how to choose, get funding for, and publicly present one's work. The whole enterprise is an elaborate effort at losing the forest through the trees.

An academic article by "progressives" proposing the greatest expansion of the militarized police surveillance bureaucracy in Western history is a moment of reckoning for well-meaning people in the academy. What standards should we expect from a "social scientist" and a "philosopher" at the most prominent university in the United States? What role should intellectuals play on the precipice of authoritarianism? How can well-meaning people in academic work with each other to preserve the integrity of the knowledge-production process? How can we instill in a new generation of students and scholars the ability to dream bigger, but also the obligation to be humble, accountable, critical, and thorough?

7

How Bad Academic Research
Becomes News

The lower-class individual lives from moment to moment. . . . Impulse governs his behavior. . . . He is therefore radically improvident: whatever he cannot consume immediately he considers valueless. His bodily needs (especially for sex) and his taste for "action" take precedence over everything else. . . . [He] has a feeble, attenuated sense of self.
-Harvard professor Edward Banfield,
proposing more policing in 1968[1]

Let's look at an example of how bad academic work makes its way into the news as conventional wisdom. A few weeks after Minneapolis police murdered George Floyd, the writer and 2020 Copaganda Newcomer of the Year Matthew Yglesias announced in a now-deleted social media post that he had developed "some thoughts on police."[2] He published a *Vox* article ostensibly using academic research to oppose the calls by a growing mass protest movement to curb the size and power of the policing bureaucracy.[3]

Yglesias was one of many. In that moment of mass consciousness in 2020, defenders of the way things are burst into action. Pundits in every corporate-owned outlet I tracked suggested that the social movement's demands were naive and dangerous rather than an evidence-based call to curb an expensive, corrupt, discriminatory, unsafe, and ineffective punishment bureaucracy. Yglesias auditioned for a leading role in this journalistic chorus, contending simply that "police reduce crime."

To make this argument, Yglesias and many other journalists made it seem like there was some sort of consensus on this controversial question by sprinkling hyperlinks to the research of the same cabal of pro-police professors relied on by the two "socialist" Harvard professors in their call for 500,000 more police officers. Because this "police reduce crime" argument from a few professors spread like wildfire throughout mainstream news, it's important to unpack it.

There Is No "Consensus"

As a preliminary matter, the data available about the punishment bureaucracy is terrible.[4] Scientifically determining causal inferences for complex social phenomena is inherently difficult, but one of the scandals of mass criminalization for over fifty years is that politicians have cared so little about whether the bureaucracy *actually* serves its stated goals that they have not invested in collecting sufficient data or studying it.

Journalists like Yglesias and German Lopez nevertheless used several studies based on police-reported data by pro-police professors to assert a consensus that more police and certain policing tactics—such as flooding "high crime" areas with armed officers—will reduce police-reported crime. You would not know from reading these mainstream news stories that other academic studies dispute the pro-police ones even on their own flawed terms.

Most broadly, for example, when pushing the "police reduce crime" mantra, mainstream news outlets ignore the comprehensive 2017 meta-study—a study of all other studies—that I mentioned earlier. It reviewed forty years of studies and concluded: "The effect on crime of adding or subtracting police is miniscule and not statistically significant."[5] Yglesias did not mention it, and I have never seen it referenced in the *New York Times* articles claiming that "experts" agree more police will reduce crime. More specifically, for example, several recent randomized controlled trials, the most robust form of testing the effectiveness of specific policing strategies, found that the short-term high-intensity policing tactics emphasized by Yglesias and other journalists have *no effect on crime*, even in the short term.[6] Put simply, there is no "consensus" that doing more of what U.S. police do reduces even the narrow range of crimes police focus on. Anyone claiming that such a consensus exists is not trustworthy, and it is a red flag that journalism's "police reduce crime" cult members don't acknowledge that a lot of research exists finding that contemporary policing does *not* reduce crime,[7] or even tell readers that other scholars contest the studies they rely on.[8]

Pro-police research is a closed loop of self-referential confusion and conflicts of interest, but my goal here is not to nitpick the many technical errors in pro-police research.[9] I have read the studies on both sides of the narrow debate about whether police data shows that "police reduce crime," and they are of almost no use in answering the most relevant policy questions about how society should improve overall safety. When promoters of the punishment bureaucracy invoke (one side of) this questionable police data and research in the news, they are having the wrong conversation.

Reducing "Crime" Misses That We Care About Overall Safety

Yglesias and many pundits in the news, like the Harvard professors, propose a trump card to begin and end debates about investments in police: "police reduce crime."[10] There is a lot wrong with that approach. First, there is a glaring problem: the studies they cite deliberately exclude estimates of crimes *committed by police*. Police do not record their own assaults or illegal stops and searches as crimes, even though counting these would add thousands of violent assaults in every major U.S. city each year.[11] By declining to include estimates of such violence, these studies cited by Yglesias and others leave out millions of illegal police assaults each year,[12] and hundreds of thousands of sexual and physical assaults in jails and prisons (including the sexual assuault of almost 10 percent of all children who are arrested and detained).[13] Concluding that more police might reduce police-reported crime is an impossible proposition to maintain if you accurately counted, for example, every additional un-lawful stop-and-frisk, home raid, arrest, or strip search as a physical or sexual assault—after all, such incidents meet the legal elements of various violent crimes. Thus, even if one imprudently focuses only on the question of whether increases in contemporary policing expenditures would reduce official "index crimes," the news media consensus on that question relies on a body of research that selectively ignores crime committed by the police and prison bureaucracy itself.

On a deeper and more important level, limiting public discussion to police-recorded "index crimes" (which most of the research does) misses most of what matters for public safety. Over the last eighteen years, I have worked with many crime survivors, community organizers, and scholars, and no one I know is primarily concerned with asking the stand-alone question, *do police reduce police-recorded crime?* Most people I come across are more concerned with reducing violence in all its forms. They care about overall levels of harm, well-being, and the social costs and benefits of various approaches to safety.[14] That is why critics of the punishment bureaucracy emphasize how narrowly "law enforcement" bureaucrats focus on enforcing only *certain* crimes committed by *certain* people, and how they largely ignore most social violence and harm. For them, crime isn't the question and police aren't the answer.

Many people I know who work in, study, and critique the punishment bureaucracy point out that the central function of the punishment bureaucracy has never been to "reduce crime" but to preserve whatever social, political, and economic order exists at any given time on behalf of those who benefit from that order, particularly people who own things.[15] This is not a fact unique to the U.S.—the same applies to police, prosecutors, and prisons in England, Russia, France, China, and any other modern nation state, particularly those with greater inequality. As I noted when discussing the Harvard professors, in the context of the contemporary and historical United States, this has meant preserving class, race, religious, ethnicity, gender and sexuality, environmental, and other inequalities, and to prevent social movements from organizing for deeper change. Historians have demonstrated that the rise of modern U.S. police forces in the nineteenth and early twentieth centuries had little to do with "violent crime," and far more to do with organizing and funding efforts to catch enslaved people who had liberated themselves and building government-funded squads to crush striking workers.[16]

And today, most of what police do has nothing to do with even what they themselves call serious crime: "violent crime" amounts to only about 4 percent of their time, and only 5 percent of all police arrests are for what the FBI considers serious "violent crime."[17] On top of sprawling politicized intelligence divisions, surveillance, and protest control, the vast bulk of what police do is arrest marginalized people for low-level offenses such as driving with a suspended license (11 million people have suspended licenses because of unpaid debts, and it is one of the leading police arrests in many places),[18] trespassing, "disorderly" behavior (particularly that of unhoused people and people with mental illness), technical probation violations, and owing debts. Tens of millions of people have been caged and separated from their families for drug possession—by 2015, four decades into the War on Drugs, more people every year were handcuffed and put in a jail cell by police for marijuana offenses than for all "violent crimes" combined.[19]

So, for a lot of police-recorded crimes, police actually *create* their own police-reported crime through *policy choices* about where and when to look for it and then documenting the results of those choices. These choices about which behaviors and incidents to record as "crime" also erase the vast bulk of criminal activity from the public record by choosing not to look for or to document it. This is why, to take just one example, police-recorded "index crime" does not include most white-collar property crime, which by conservative estimates dwarfs by orders of magnitude the harm caused by all the property crimes recorded by police.

There is an even more profound problem for pro-punishment bureaucracy pundits and the studies they rely on. Remember, the vast majority of sexual assaults, child molestation, and violent incidents are *never reported to police at all*.[20] This is true for many reasons, from survivors

fearing punishment bureaucrats, to the legal system not offering appropriate resources to survivors, to the fact that most serious crimes happen
between people who know each other. As a result, most people choose
not to record harm with punishment bureaucrats. These facts show that
the punishment bureaucracy undercounts social violence, because people deem the system to be ineffective in confronting or preventing most
harm. For this reason, measuring public safety with police-recorded
crime is an especially bad proxy for interpersonal *harm*.

Ignoring Alternatives

Let's be blunt: the police do not even attempt to address all this social
harm, which explains why most research consistently shows that the best
way to reduce interpersonal harm is through other social investments.[21]
In fact, even a survey of leading pro-police researchers shows that,
though they produce work used by police to secure higher budgets, these
researchers concede when asked by other researchers that the overall research gives them more confidence that investments in housing, health
care, and education will reduce crime more than increases in police.[22]
The obvious solution, based on the evidence—and the one news coverage largely ignores—is to prioritize spending public money on policies,
programs, and systems that provide the highest marginal return on investment. This means interventions that best reduce social violence and
harm, including *unreported* and *unrecorded* violence and harm.[23]

When arguing for a particular policy over other policies, it is incumbent on serious analysts not just to evaluate one method of achieving a
stated goal, but to *consider the other options*. Instead of flooding neighborhoods with expensive armed police earning overtime cash, for example,
what would happen if the neighborhood were flooded with members of
the community paid living wages and trained to help each other and
to de-escalate conflict? Or with well-paid poets, priests, and painters?
Or Black Panthers?[24] Or nurses, preschool teachers, basketball coaches,
and dancers? Yglesias's article reveals a remarkable theme of pro-police

punditry that mirrors the errors of the Harvard professors: at no point in his article or in any of the studies he linked to does anyone compare the effectiveness of policing with that of alternative social investments, even short-term ones.

Many pro-police professors and pundits nonetheless take relatively narrow research findings about the marginal, short-term effects of police on police-reported crime and carelessly make public assertions that suggest this research supports paying for more armed police, which is not a responsible policy conclusion from a piece of research that does not evaluate alternatives.

There are many places where such alternatives have been implemented. In Chicago, for example, researchers found that simply placing unarmed civilian employees with neon jackets in areas of concern for a few hours each day was more cost-effective at reducing police-reported crime.[25] One of my favorite examples is an initiative in Bogotá, Columbia, where officials disbanded their corrupt police traffic units and replaced them with mimes, who mocked or applauded people for breaking or following traffic laws. That led to huge reductions in traffic fatalities.[26] Other researchers have found that expanding non-police alternative first responders can improve neighborhood safety.[27] And cities across the U.S. are beginning to spend relatively small amounts of money on highly effective mental-health first responders.[28]

At best, a punditry consensus based on a few pro-police studies that don't consider alternatives is like a salesperson selling you a gas heater for your house without telling you that the model they are peddling also leaks carbon monoxide and that other higher-efficiency heaters on the market create more heat without killing your kids.

The Costs of Police

Even if one believed that more armed government agents would marginally reduce a small category of police-reported crimes more than any other public intervention—and by that logic, we should consider hiring enough police to station one officer with a gun inside every person's bedroom and outside every person's home—one might still conclude that the *costs* of living in such a society would make it undesirable. George Orwell wrote a book called *1984* about that dystopia. So, what about the inequality, violence, and misery police preserve and create?

It is here that we can see the ripple effects of irresponsible academic practices like those practiced by the Harvard professors. Because of how pro-police scholars distort their academic work, when copaganda translates academic research for popular consumption, it likewise ignores wide swaths of research on the social costs of policing. Some pundits like Yglesias acknowledge "excessive force" like the police murder of George Floyd as a cost of policing. But none of the survivors of police violence I know are concerned *only* about "excessive force" that is *already nominally illegal*. They are just as concerned about what the "good cops" are doing every day, because law-abiding non-newsworthy policing has costs to public health, families, democratic participation, the economy, and more.[29]

Consider the well-publicized research of Aaron Chalfin, after whom the Aaron J. Chalfin wing in the Copaganda Hall of Fame is named. In a study promoted by Yglesias and later in the *New York Times*, Chalfin and co-author Justin McCrary claimed that every $1 spent on police brings $1.63 in "social return,"[30] as if every additional armed officer adds linear and perpetual marginal net value to society. Setting aside that this study shares the data and design problems I describe above, note that this calculation is premised on particular monetary valuations of *certain* social harms but not others. For example, Chalfin's study estimated that every sexual assault caused exactly $142,020 in damage.

More importantly, the study does not calculate almost any of the social costs of policing, including the most obvious: the cost of violent crimes committed by police or prison guards. Using the study's own numbers, the cost of the one thousand police homicides every year plus

100,000 yearly sexual assaults committed mostly by government agents against people they arrest every year (a low-end estimate that is half the number of custodial sexual assaults federal researchers estimate) would be an additional $20 billion, altering the study's results completely.[31] And this does not count the hundreds of thousands of premature deaths caused by confinement in government-run cells resulting from arrests. These deaths alone amount to tens of billions of dollars in additional social costs under Chalfin's own estimates.

What follows is not a comprehensive accounting but just a few examples of the social costs of policing *not including* rape and death, all of which the pro-police studies generally leave out:

- Millions of stops, car searches, home searches, strip searches, property seizures, arrests (both legal and illegal), beatings, chokeholds, and taserings. (It is important to emphasize that even such incidents ultimately ruled lawful still incur social costs, and recent groundbreaking research suggests that ordinary people view these costs as far higher than had been understood, including that they would rather be victimized by a violent crime than endure, for example, standard periods of *lawful* post-arrest detention.)[32]
- Hundreds of thousands of lost jobs, lost homes, starved pets with nobody to feed them, separated families, and children traumatized in group homes and foster care.
- Interrupted or completely severed medical and mental health care for hundreds of thousands of people.
- Expanded ability of the government to track and punish abortions and reproductive health care, to arrest and prosecute marginalized or unpopular people seeking to vote, to obtain gender-affirming care, to protest, or to engage in any other activity that a local, state, or federal government entity opposes.
- The spread of infectious disease inside and then beyond jails and prisons with enormous effects on public health more broadly.[33]

- Interference with community-based efforts to combat violence by political targeting of non-police violence workers.[34]
- Increased crime in the future caused by police performing more low-level arrests, which research I discuss later shows is criminogenic.
- Increased deportations.
- Massively reduced voting and civic engagement caused by police interactions.[35]
- Harder-to-quantify effects of widespread Orwellian surveillance on human relationships, progressive social movements, and privacy.
- Long-term effects of expanded policing established in the literature, such as intergenerational trauma and the negative effects of policing in terms of low birth-weights of Black infants, diabetes, obesity, the longitudinal impacts on children growing up with an incarcerated parent, and the cumulative loss of intergenerational wealth that contributes to the racialized wealth gap.

An estimate of these social costs is intentionally excluded in studies like Chalfin's that make their way into mainstream news, because virtually any one of them, if quantified using conservative estimates, would reverse their marginal findings and invalidate the policy prescription of more policing.

Calling for a policy based on its supposed benefits without counting its costs is not objective science. It is also a form of academic deception to conclude, based only on counting the supposed benefits of police, that "U.S. cities are almost surely underpoliced."[36] To give the illusion of scientific status to this claim and similar claims like "U.S. cities are substantially underpoliced," Chalfin and McCrary, the authors of the study cited by Yglesias and the two "progressive" Harvard professors, include equations like this one:

$$0 = V'(S)\frac{S}{C} = y'(S)\frac{S}{C} - C'(S)\frac{S}{C} \equiv -\frac{wS}{nC} - \varepsilon,$$

Do you see how this proves we need more police? If you don't, look a little harder at it, and I'm sure you'll figure it out. Here's the thing: no matter how beautiful an equation, a researcher can mislead a journalist and the public when they make broad statements ostensibly based on the equation *that are not supported by it.* And a study can include pages of complex—and sometimes unimpeachable—math by the smartest people in the world, but if it asks and answers the wrong questions, then its conclusions on whether we need more armed police are useless.

In his popular article, Chalfin concluded that "increases in police in medium to large U.S. cities in recent years would have substantially improved social welfare."[37] Statements like this—in which pro-police researchers make claims that are not supported by their own data analysis—are among the most common forms of academic copaganda that seep into the news.

In another study based on other similarly flawed and limited research, Chalfin and a different co-author concluded that "the benefits of hiring police officers likely exceeds [sic] the cost of doing so."[38] I want you to pause for a moment and think about how unserious a piece of scholarship has to be in order to draw such a conclusion *without counting the social costs of the thing being studied.* This is what passes for research among pro-police professors who make public comments in leading news outlets about important issues of human well-being.

Chalfin is not just anybody; he is the "Graduate Chair of Criminology" at the University of Pennsylvania. Chalfin and other pro-police researchers cite each other repeatedly, establishing a self-referential "consensus" that more police would make society better overall that is entirely premised on ignoring the costs of policing. Many of them are funded by the same sources and some, like five-time Copaganda Conflict of Interest Award winner NYU professor Barry Friedman, lead non-profits who get funding from the police surveillance industry.[39] As cringy internal emails obtained through the Freedom of Information Act reveal, many of these professors also rely on cozy relationships with police leaders to maintain access to the police-controlled data without which they could not get funding for their research—part of a smorgasbord of systemic conflicts of interest about which leading economists have started to sound the alarm.[40]

To be sure, there is pressure for researchers and journalists to take narrow research findings and make them seem relevant to complex public policy debates—which sometimes morphs their statements in the news into a sort of blending of research and personal political opinions. All of this is then thrust into the hands of police PR officials and their media networks.

In short, pro-police researchers will use funding from a small number of sources to design a study that looks at the (usually short-term) effects of police on police-recorded "index crimes," obtain and manipulate police datasets in proprietary ways, produce a result based on dozens of biased assumptions and omissions, and spit out a result that they claim shows a general, indefinite marginal linear effect of police on police-recorded "index crime." Most alarming, they will then falsely portray these findings as suggesting that more police are a good investment *overall* without having weighed the alternatives or counted the costs.

Unqualified pundits like Matt Yglesias and German Lopez then simplify and distort pro-police research even further for popular consumption in the most prestigious news outlets. It's like a game of telephone, although one played with a megaphone and gone horribly awry on matters of great import. By the time it gets to us news consumers, what started as a few claims by a few pro-police researchers that are not supported by their own research becomes a "consensus" among "experts" about social policy questions that none of the experts had studied.[41]

Speaking openly about this cycle presents an important opportunity for people of good will in academia and journalism. Because it suggests a failure to grasp how to approach life-and-death questions with critical thinking, it is natural, when looking at the work of someone like Chalfin, Yglesias, Lewis, Lopez, or Usmani to ask: how can we trust anything that a person who would do *this* says or does? But we must also ask something more important: what are we to make of the *institutions* in which these individuals operate successfully—institutions supposedly about the advancement and dissemination of knowledge—who fail to help them become more serious? What do we make of their colleagues, who take unserious work seriously, who have not developed internal mechanisms of accountability, or who lack the courage to use those mechansims? It is remarkable that this kind of deception about costs, benefits, and overall "social welfare" is carried out in the corners of our society supposedly most committed to intellectual pursuit of knowledge. Would we tolerate such bumbling misrepresentation of empirical results in *any* other context? It would be career-ending for a doctor treating our child, an electrician wiring our house, or an engineer building a bridge to mislead us about their supposed weighing of costs, benefits, and alternative options. We expect people in every other area of our lives who make recommendations about the best course of action to weigh the costs of that course of action and of alternative courses of action. Why has such profound intellectual sloppiness been acceptable in the field of criminology? Because scholarship like this—and the ways that research is later characterized for popular consumption—undermines the rigor and reputation of knowledge-producing institutions generally, it will be up to the people who study and work in academia and journalism to organize together to correct profound flaws in our society's organs of elite and mass popular education. A lot depends on whether we come together to do it.

8

Keywords of Copaganda: Smuggling Ideology into the News

"The newspapers all say the same thing, that is true," said the old prince, "but then so do all the frogs croak before a storm."

-Leo Tolstoy[1]

But no, they appear to glory in their chains; now, more than ever, they appear to measure their safety in chains and corpses.

-James Baldwin[2]

People who produce the news smuggle political, ideological, and moral judgments into reporting through ordinary words and phrases. Using case studies of certain keywords, I illustrate how this happens and why it matters.

"Major" Reforms

A 2021 *New York Times* article touted the Queens district attorney's new "conviction integrity unit" as a "major" improvement to a notoriously corrupt institution.[3]

However, many prosecutors have created such units. They typically review and remedy an infinitesimal share of the office's problematic convictions in recent decades and, with a few exceptions, they rarely do anything significant relative to the office's volume of illegal convictions. Conviction integrity units are thus used largely for public relations, to give the impression that prosecutors care about redressing injustice.[4] The *New York Times* obliged, calling Melinda Katz a "major" reformer even though her office has not materially changed what it does every day. As it has for decades, it is still almost exclusively prosecuting poor people—disproportionately people of color and immigrants—for the same offenses in similar rates using the same laws, discretionary prosecution priorities, and theories of criminal liability. It is seeking similar sentences, engaging in the same widespread practice of coercing guilty pleas by threatening longer imprisonment, and exploiting the same police investigative priorities and tactics. It is a mass-incarceration machine. And, it is still *not* prosecuting police, prosecutors, judges, jail guards, landlords, employers, or wealthy people in similar rates. If an alien from a utopian world without the *New York Times* or a person from virtually any other legal system on earth were to observe the Queens DA office before and after her "major" reforms, they would have trouble telling the difference.

The article nonetheless makes a normative claim, reported as a fact in the reporter's voice, that what Katz is doing is "major." This characterization helps regulate the boundaries of the reader's imagination about what kinds of changes are possible, let alone desirable.

Actual major reforms are inconceivable for the *Times*, including, for example: firing and charging the prosecutors in the office who violated people's rights and intentionally withheld evidence; paying reparations to the office's past victims; reviewing and reducing all prior sentences so that they are in line with those in the rest of the world; refusing to support illegal pretrial detention in thousands of cases; ceasing the prosecution of drug cases; and prosecuting wealthy people who violate New York criminal laws at the same rates as poor people. Neither the Queens DA nor the *Times* contemplates such policies. Instead, the list of supposed changes the article highlights are almost comically insignificant. They include: charging a single cop out of the thousands of police-committed crimes in Queens; hiring slightly more women and people of color to enforce largely the same prosecution policies as before; and ceasing prosecution of some low-level misdemeanor marijuana offenses.

The idea that this Queens DA is a "major" reformer on the issue of prosecutor misconduct is especially jarring for me. In the spirit of disclosure, my nonprofit organization, Civil Rights Corps, had to sue this DA after she violated our First Amendment rights and threatened us and the law professors working with us to publicize misconduct in her office.[5] She threatened the law professors with the claim that the mere act of posting ethics complaints against Queens prosecutors (based on public court rulings of misconduct) on a website we created was unlawful. She and New York City's Corporation Counsel, its top lawyer, then warned us that even *telling the public about their threats against us* was illegal. A federal judge ruled in our favor that she violated our First Amendment rights. In a scathing editorial supportive of our lawsuit, the *New York Times* editorial board called her threats a "prosecutor protection racket," targeting people who are trying to inform the public about misconduct in her office.[6] The *Times* declared, "This isn't just shooting the messenger; it's tossing the gun into the East River and threatening anyone who tries to fish it out."

The Queens DA won her initial election by mimicking the "reform" rhetoric of her opponent, a progressive from the public defender's office, while quietly signaling to rank-and-file cops and prosecutors that little would change. So, it's obvious why she would want to convince New Yorkers that she was enacting "major" reforms while she maintained the wretched status quo. But why would the *news* be an accomplice in this propaganda?

A similar phenomenon pervaded the coverage of the Manhattan DA's race in 2022. A *Times* article asserted that the new DA "campaigned on lenient policies aimed at making the justice system fairer."[7] By any objective comparison to other countries or the U.S. in earlier times, the policies he campaigned on were harsh, not "lenient." That's why public defenders in New York pointed out that his election would have little effect on the cases they handled. Portraying the policies as "lenient" has implications: it makes proposals that *do* significantly reduce harsh punishment seem *radical* and *beyond acceptable boundaries.* A person hearing about some of those more significant policies might exclaim, "Gosh, that's too far. Not even the 'fairer, lenient reformer' went that far!" Characterizing minor tweaks to extremely harsh policies as objectively lenient decreases the public's ability to conceive of more profound change and depresses its appetite to support it. Such lowering of expectations for radical change is a key feature of copaganda.

As I explained in *Usual Cruelty,* "reform" discourse often makes well-meaning people feel like those in power are working in good faith to improve society. This discourse can disguise the fact that people in power, the punishment bureaucracy, and the owners of media companies oppose changes to the legal system that would materially improve the lives of most people.

Announcing reforms as "major" and "important" is clickbait.[8] Nonexperts, or people who cultivate their knowledge by reading mainstream media outlets, will have little grounding in the punishment bureaucracy's history of using the concept of "reform" to legitimize and further entrench mass incarceration. So, they accept reform discourse as genuine.

"Sweeping" and "Overhaul"

Another *Times* article, published in 2021, states that the U.S. House of Representatives "passed a sweeping police bill designed to address racial discrimination and excessive use of force."[9] The journalist uses the word "sweeping" three times and "overhaul" twice to describe three different proposed federal laws, none of which would have had any significant impact. In another article entitled "Can Policing Change?" the *Times* calls similarly inconsequential proposals pushed by police that include many of the same things on the local level "meaningful" and "substantial."[10]

None of these laws, if passed, had any chance of causing measurable change in police behavior, and in reality none of them were even "designed," to borrow the paper's copaganda term about the intentions of punishment bureaucrats, in good faith to do that. But describing them with words like "sweeping" and "overhaul" makes it seem like there is no debate to be had about whether these would be "historic" changes. Wouldn't the "paper of record," which prints "all the news that's fit to print," tell me if knowledgeable people thought these bills wouldn't do much?

"Overhaul" means to "take apart [something] . . . in order to examine it and repair it if necessary." None of these initiatives "takes apart" any aspect of U.S. policing. "Sweeping" means "wide in range or effect," but the article concedes that the vast majority of the U.S. didn't see *any changes at all* to policing laws or policies, and years of data have confirmed my point: not only have various similar reformist tweaks at the federal, state, and local level not measurably changed what police do or who they target where they have been implemented, but as I discuss later, police killed more people each successive year between George Floyd's murder and the publication of this book in 2025.[11]

The "overhaul" article above cites a *different* "overhaul"-themed article that describes a police reform bill, the George Floyd Justice in Policing Act, as a "sweeping" bill "aimed at combating racial discrimination and excessive use of force in law enforcement."[12] Of course, that could not be further from the truth. Lawmakers and congressional staff privately agreed with many civil rights and public safety experts in my professional circles that the bill was mostly symbolic: it would leave U.S. policing virtually unchanged. This was an open secret on Capitol Hill. Indeed, *that was the point.* There is not political support in either party to significantly change U.S. policing, hold police accountable, or reduce their power. But they want to look like they are doing something in moments of public outrage, and news outlets oblige them by making their charade look serious, even monumental.

The *Times* portrays the legislative debate over these bills as a partisan dispute, with Democrats "aiming" to "overhaul" the system against Republican opposition.[13] In this way, consumers of news think that the entire range of possible or reasonable political positions lies between these two poles of calls for minor tweaks by Democrats and more "law and order" by Republicans. Left undiscussed is the substance of these tweaks, how little they change the punishment bureaucracy, and that most of them give it more power and make it more dangerous. No matter. The news assures us that there are serious politicians working on serious problems in a serious way, even if other politicians are blocking their efforts.

In another article on "police reform," the *Times* portrays the outer boundary of "progressive" viewpoints with this framing: "We need police on the streets, well equipped, but we need them to have the cooperation and trust of the community."[14] No voice critical of the police is presented or portrayed as conceivable. The article repeatedly refers to police interests as "centrist" and politicians giving into police union demands as "moving to the center." To the contrary, police unions are openly far-right political formations, and the news is normalizing them as a fictional "center" between the Democrats and Republicans. All those with more far-reaching criticisms of the punishment bureaucracy are ignored. No one is quoted to offer the perspective that the hyped-up tweaks were minuscule and would not change policing. The two perspectives presented are people fearmongering about the meaningless "reforms" and self-interested officials with an incentive to inflate the significance of their proposals. This framing makes readers think that serious change is being contemplated because it presents these two positions as in deep—even existential—conflict instead of being part of a symbiotic *performance* that keeps everything mostly the same.

Such copaganda invokes Noam Chomsky's observation about how to control a population:

The smart way to keep people passive and obedient is to strictly limit the spectrum of acceptable opinion but allow very lively debate within that spectrum—even encourage the more critical and dissident views. That gives people the sense that there's free thinking going on, while all the time the presuppositions of the system are being reinforced by the limits put on the range of the debate.[15]

Chomsky's observation helps us understand why it is so pervasive for news outlets to characterize reforms to the punishment bureaucracy with language that inflates their significance. It's useful to those who want to preserve things if people's imaginations about the kinds of changes that are possible are constrained, and also useful if people come to believe that the individuals in power and in control over these bureaucracies are constantly doing the laudable work of making "significant overhauls."

In this spirit, I recently undertook sweeping renovations to overhaul the Copaganda Hall of Fame, moving it from one wall of my basement to another.

"Quality of Life"

A 1994 *New York Times* article entitled "Police Announce Crackdown on Quality-of-Life Offenses" describes intensified policing of poor people as "pursuing Mayor Rudolph W. Giuliani's theme of improving the quality of life in the city."[16] Almost thirty years later, in 2023, news articles described Eric Adams's policy to increase stops, searches, putting metal chains on people's bodies, and putting people in cages for minor violations as "focusing on quality-of-life offenses."[17] What does the news mean when it says "quality-of-life offenses" and what does this phrase reveal about its unstated goals? Whose "quality of life" is imagined and whose is ignored?

Recent "quality of life" articles describe police arresting poor people for things like "public drinking, public urination, dice games" and forms of "disorder" such as "fare evasion" and "trespassing." News outlets are not talking here about the "quality of life" for people who are unhoused as a result of real estate development and urban planning policies, people unable to access medical treatment, people forced to work in jobs or live in apartments where safety codes are not enforced, or people severed from library programming that New York is cutting. The "quality of life" contemplated here is for those who benefit from our society's inequalities but don't want the fleeting discomfort of seeing the suffering of those around them.

By presenting the policing of poverty or mental illness as improving "quality of life," the news puts a benevolent veneer on some of the most ruthless and empirically discredited policies of modern government.

"Officer-Involved Shooting"

Copaganda obscures the active role police play in doing bad things. Many people have criticized the police-invented term "officer-involved shooting" because it obscures who is responsible.[18] It was first adopted by the LAPD in the 1970s, and the news now uses it widely. In a remarkable recent study, researchers demonstrated that "the media is significantly more likely to use several language structures—e.g., passive voice, nominalization, intransitive verbs—that obfuscate responsibility for police killings compared to civilian homicides," and that news consumers "are less likely to hold a police officer morally responsible for a killing, and to demand penalties, after reading a story that uses obfuscatory language."[19]

The news uses related tricks to obscure police culpability. For example, a New Mexico news channel described a police murder with the headline, "SWAT Standoff Ends with House Fire, 14-Year-Old Killed." Another channel outdid that one, saying, "APD Standoff Ends in House Fire, 1 Dead."[20] What really happened? The cops brought a SWAT team to a house owned by a family who were not the target of the raid. With guns drawn, the cops deployed a drone and robots and launched gas grenades into the house that caught fire. They handcuffed the family outside, broke the doors and windows. A teenage boy—also not the target of the raid—was left in the house and died in the fire. The police initially claimed that the target, who had been visiting the house, was wanted for robbery and other violent crimes, but it turned out the warrants were for "unlawful taking of a vehicle out of Santa Fe" and a probation violation.[21]

A "Shortage" of Punishment Bureaucrats

After massive protests and calls in 2020 to reduce police and prison budgets, a series of news stories decried a supposed "shortage" of police and prison guards. For example, a *New York Times* article declared: "The shortage has prompted agencies . . . to broaden and intensify their searches for talent."[22]

The article appeared in the news section, not in the opinion section, and was written by a reporter who "covers breaking news and criminal justice." It frames the supposed "shortage" as a crisis: "the single most daunting challenge that policing has faced in decades."

By taking the "shortage" as a given and focusing on recruiting efforts, news articles signal to readers that the factuality of a "shortage" is so obvious that no reasonable person questions it. This is drive-by copaganda—it carelessly shoots out as fact what should be presented as a controversial opinion on a debatable proposition. After reading something like this, a casual news reader might mindlessly mention to coworkers over lunch that there is a shortage of police, and this is how innocent bystanders become victims of copaganda.

News articles about "shortages" and "understaffing" do not appear out of nowhere; they are an effort by punishment bureaucrats, pro-police politicians, corporate profiteers, and a small group of academics to build a consensus that the U.S. needs more investment in the punishment bureaucracy. As with the articles about the mysterious police "pullbacks," the "shortage" articles also tend to use pro-police sources to blame the "shortage" problem (hyped as an "exodus" by the *New York Times*) on civil rights "unrest."[23] Here are the sources in that *Times* article quoted above, in the order they appear:

- Police chief in Colorado;
- NYC police union president
- NYPD
- Head of a police policy organization who is a former cop
- Same police chief in Colorado along with his portrait
- Former Miami cop who works for a Florida police union
- Professor whom the reporter quotes as an expert without disclosing that she had been an Israeli police officer and sergeant in the Israeli Defense Forces
- NYC police union president (again)

The paper does not hint that anyone—let alone experts, crime survivors, directly affected individuals, and scholars—thinks that there are *too many* armed cops.

The article gives a prominent position to Patrick Lynch, the president of a local police union, presenting this purveyor of far-right misinformation as a credible source. His comments about the need for higher pay to combat "shortages" not only treat the shortages as a given fact but also elide the NYPD's overtime bonanza and the sick-leave fraud epidemic.[24] After printing the claim that New York does not pay a "market" wage for police officers, the reporter includes Lynch's assertion about "the staffing shortage" as if "*the* shortage" is a fact:

Lower pay is exacerbated by other grievances, Mr. Lynch said. Many officers must work longer hours to make up for the staffing shortage to meet extra demands like patrolling the subway system, he said. Some officers feel frustrated when the people they have arrested are quickly released, he added.

There is a lot wrong here. Lynch is referring to the NYPD's baseless criticisms of changes to the state's bail laws and claiming that because criminals are running free, good police officers cannot take it any longer and leave. Inserting this (incorrect) grievance without correction, context, or explication bolsters the article's controversial assumption that there is a "shortage" because *offering an explanation for a phenomenon* solidifies the impression that the phenomenon exists.

Lynch's explanation for "the staffing shortage" and the "grievance" of "some officers" is also darkly amusing. It should feature on some sort of Rosetta Stone so that people of the future can piece together the role of copaganda in the fall of our civilization. It is essentially a complaint that the U.S. has a Constitution and that New York, like every other state, has laws that limit indefinite detention without trial. The inclusion of this statement normalizes an authoritarian mentality: the newspaper informs its readers that, if they want cops to keep their jobs during a crisis-level "shortage," they need to allow police to indefinitely detain those they arrest. Otherwise, no one will want to keep us all safe.

One of the most consequential and vibrant debates in the contemporary U.S. is whether our society needs armed government bureaucrats equipped with military surveillance and weaponry at anywhere near the level that it currently employs them. This debate was thrust into the spotlight in 2020, when a nationwide mass protest movement coalesced on a simple demand: to reduce police funding. Tens of millions of people believe reducing overall violence requires reducing investments in the punishment bureaucracy and increasing investments in systems of care. Journalists reporting a "shortage" of police as objective fact assume that the protesting millions are so naive, so marginal, so irrelevant, that their perspective merits not even a nod recognizing it as a reasonable position, let alone detailed treatment of the evidence and arguments supporting it. The pro-police frame is offered as the only reasonable position.

The "police shortage" articles assuming the need to preserve or increase the current number of armed police officers are really about something else: the question of whether our society wants to reduce key forms of inequality or not. If we do not, then we may have a "shortage" of police and prisons, because the amount of repression it takes to manage and enforce extant levels of inequality and predation is significant. This is what the specter of a "shortage" means to many of the sophisticated people invoking it.

Portraying a "shortage" in the midst of already world-record spending on police, prosecutors, and prisons is therefore ideological and political. (It was also comically incorrect on basic empirical facts. It later emerged, in the largest-ever study of the police labor market, that the total impact of the supposed "retention crisis" on the police labor force was only 1 percent, , and that it did not align with the 2020 civil rights protests.)[25] Some journalists reporting coordinated police and prison guard campaigns about "shortages" and "understaffing" as objective fact may not even be aware that they are playing a role in a well-funded public relations campaign designed to influence policy at *particular* moments of political relevance. Campaigns like this—ultimately yielding billions in government funds—are coordinated at the highest levels, both formally in that many aspects of the PR offensive are planned and paid for, and informally in that people in politics, media, consulting, the nonprofit sector, and academia understand what their role should be; what opinions they should have; how, where, and when they should express their opinions; how they will be rewarded professionally for expressing the *right* opinions (pun intended); and how they will be harmed professionally if they speak differently. One job of journalism is to help people see these things, not obscure them further by repeating campaign positions as objective fact.

Instead, the *Times* published three articles in two weeks asserting a "shortage" of police—relying on the same set of sources, including the same police industry leaders—just as Democratic lawmakers in Congress were considering President Joe Biden's plan for the biggest increase in police in more than a generation.[26]

The Enduring "Shortage" of Prison Guards

A few days before the barrage of police "shortage" articles, the *Times* published another article, this one about the sexual abuse of women detained in federal prisons.[27] In an article that makes otherwise important facts known to the public, the reporter inserted the following paragraph:

> The issue of sexual assault at the 160,000-inmate Bureau of Prisons, an agency hamstrung by labor shortages, budget shortfalls and mismanagement, has become increasingly evident in recent years. The perpetrators have included male employees at every level of the prison hierarchy: warden pastor, guard.

It is hard to convey how strange it sounds to anyone who has studied sexual violence in prisons to assume that the problem could be solved with *more* guards, who are themselves the greatest source of sexual violence, or *larger* budgets for a federal prison bureaucracy that has been violent, lawless, and unaccountable since before Eugene Debs wrote his indictment of federal prisons while running for President from behind bars in the 1920s.[28] The article, like most in its genre, makes no reference to the fact that the U.S. cages six times more people per capita than its own pre-1980 historical average and five to ten times more than other countries, with a prison system that is one of the government's most bloated bureaucracies. The paper could easily have presented the problem as one of *over*incarceration rather than *under*staffing. And, it is profoundly manipulative to use the issue of systemic sexual assault of incarcerated women to enlarge the very bureaucracy that victimizes them—a special kind of copaganda that gets well-meaning people to feel bad before inundating them with solutions that exacerbate the problem, with no indication that anyone with knowledge even thinks differently.

A defining theme in coverage of unspeakable conditions and abuse in U.S. prisons is that they are caused by not spending enough money on the punishment bureaucracy.[29] To take one representative example, a story in the *Texas Tribune* about decades-long conditions of criminal torture in child jails in Texas frames the problem as follows:

- "The agency is so understaffed that teens have reported spending up to 23 hours locked in their cells, using water bottles to go to the bathroom. A staggering number have hurt themselves."
- "Dangerously understaffed."
- "The Agency has never escaped its problem of chronic understaffing."
- "The short-staffing impacts every piece of the youths' prison lives."
- "And more and more, children are hurting themselves—sometimes severely—out of distress . . . in their isolation."
- "In the last year, teens have forced springs from pens into their necks or pieces of metal into their urethras. . . . Many have used ligatures to strangle themselves."
- "The staffing crisis only worsened following the pandemic and the subsequent wave of resignations throughout the country."
- "Ultimately, the answer comes down to money."
- "But while the governor and lawmakers have denounced agency failures, replaced leadership and demanded change after abuse reports in recent years, their outcries are not typically reflected in the budget."
- "TJJD leaders were able to implement emergency 15% raises for staff earlier this year by postponing reentry programs and using savings from unfilled positions. But they said salaries are still too low."
- " 'The first step in addressing these shortages and moving us out of survival mode is to provide a competitive salary.' "
- "The state of crisis has led the agency to scrap planned programs to help teens avoid being arrested again when they are released, and it canceled therapeutic programming targeting violent behavior."[30]

You will find nearly identical articles and stories across the U.S. It is a feature of contemporary news, even from reporters who care enough to bring what's happening in our dungeons into public view.[31]

Another way of framing the problem plaguing Texas and other parts of the country would be that there are *too many children in cages* or that there is something inherent in the project of jailing children itself that cannot be made humane through more jailers. But the news almost always ignores the elephant in the room: increases in human caging are a primary driver of the suffering behind bars. Moreover, news about horrific prison conditions almost always excludes discussion of several points: (1) much of the violence is intentionally perpetrated by guards; (2) chronic torture, brutality, isolation, and death are inherent to the construction, design, and management of U.S. prisons; (3) the punishment bureaucracy disproportionately cages people with physical and mental illness, often *because of* those illnesses, instead of treating them; (4) the institutions are managed to be democratically unaccountable and prioritize secrecy; (5) many aspects of the system are run for profit, including medical care, food, and communication with the outside world; and (6) many intentional policies unrelated to staffing contribute to violence behind bars.

Instead of reckoning with the role mass incarceration plays in our society, almost the entire body of news coverage about the scandalous state of prisons and jails focuses on getting them more money.

I want to end this discussion about the ostensible "shortage" of punishment bureaucrats with one of my favorite stories about U.S. prisons. After guards went on strike for two months at a prison in Walpole, Massachusetts, in 1973, prisoners took over the institution. Here's a short account of what happened:

> In protest of their loss of control, the guards walked off the job. They thought this act would prove how necessary they were, but . . . it had the exact opposite effect. For two months, the prisoners ran the prison themselves. . . . One observer recounted:

"The atmosphere was so relaxed—not at all what I expected. I find that my own thinking has been so conditioned by society and the media. These men are not animals, they are not dangerous maniacs. I found my own fears were really groundless."

Another observer insisted, "It is imperative that none of the personnel formerly in Block 9 [a segregation block] ever return. It's worth paying them to retire. The guards are the security problem."

Walpole had been one of the most violent prisons in the country, but while the prisoners were in control, recidivism dropped dramatically, and murders and rapes fell to zero. . . .

Many of the civilian observers and the corrections commissioner, who was soon forced out of his job, ultimately came to favor prison abolition. The prisoners who took over Walpole continued to fight for their freedom and dignity, but the guards' union ended up with greater power than before, the media ceased talking about prison reform, and as of this writing Walpole prison, now MCI Cedar Junction, still warehouses, tortures, and kills people.[32]

The point of this example is not to argue that everyone should support immediate prison abolition or to deny the complexity of addressing mass incarceration. Precisely the opposite: because these are difficult issues, news consumers deserve to be presented with assessments of problems and solutions in their full complexity so they can engage in critical thinking and informed debate.

"Tough on Crime"

"Tough on crime" terminology normalizes the idea that the punishment bureaucracy is essential for our safety. Associating punishment with safety is so commonplace in the news that even those featured in articles who oppose aspects of the punishment bureaucracy on *other* grounds, such as its infringement of civil liberties or its disproportionate impact, often are not quoted questioning its connection to *safety*.

The news constantly links the problem, "crime," with the solution, the punishment bureaucracy.[33] This ironclad link is not supported by social science, which points to systemic causes of interpersonal harm. Police and prisons do not address those systemic causes, and in fact protect them. Nevertheless, it is a foundational myth of copaganda to pair *being against violence* with increased punishment.

Since the early 1970s, when Richard Nixon postured as "tough on crime" and attacked liberals as "soft" on crime, both Democratic and Republican politicians have used this rhetoric. Ronald Reagan weaponized the phrase "tough on crime" to expand punishment for drugs after the 1986 death of basketball star Len Bias. Bill Clinton employed it to promote his infamous 1994 crime bill that led to a prison construction boom and added 100,000 more armed bureaucrats to the public payroll. Democratic political strategists made a decision to operationalize the phrase to change the party's political platform in the 1990s. Here is a Democratic consultant reflecting back on his role:

Mandatory minimums were originally a Democratic idea.... We produced crime attacks for both primary and general elections, targeting other Democrats and Republicans alike. In 1994, it reached an absolute fever pitch. My firm had about 30 clients, all Democrats, and we did tough-on-crime pieces for every single one. In many cases, we'd make ten or so different mail pieces for a client, and eight of them would be about crime. In other words, in every last race we worked on, every candidate was accusing every other candidate of being soft on crime. The highlight of my consulting career was when I lay down on a sidewalk so our photographer could trace around my body with chalk for a murder aftermath scene we staged.[34]

A lawyer for the House Judiciary Committee described the logic of Democrats who enacted mandatory minimum sentences for drugs:

> They were told, look, you've got one month to put together your anti-drug agenda and then you're . . . going to campaign the hell out of that agenda. . . . We had no hearings. We did not consult with the Bureau of Prisons, or with the federal judiciary, or with DEA, or with the Justice Department, to at least find out from those folks what would be the effect of mandatory minimums.[35]

This process was driven by electoral calculations, not an assessment of what would reduce violence.

Many people now view such political strategies as abhorrent. They also recognize them as pure *politics*. But everyday news discourse preserves some of their worst vestiges under the guise of objective journalism. While some of the most grotesque flourishes of the Nixon, Reagan, and Clinton rhetoric are gone, the association of "crime" with the need for "tough" punishment remains a news staple. Here are a few recent representative examples:[36]

The New York Times

They Wanted to Roll Back Tough-on-Crime Policies. Then Violent Crime Surged.

The New York Times

As Adams Toughens on Crime, Some Fear a Return to '90s Era Policing

With violent crime surging, Mayor Eric Adams is testing how much policing a changed New York City will tolerate.

This association mirrors tabloid press strategy. The editorial board of the right-wing *New York Post*, for instance, described President Biden's plan to spend billions of dollars to add 100,000 cops as insufficiently "tough on crime" because some of the funding was also going to "public health" measures.[37] It also wrote: "Biden's plan wouldn't do anything to address soft-on-crime district attorneys like Manhattan DA Alvin Bragg." The right-wing *Washington Examiner* put it even more bluntly: "Soft-on-crime policy emboldens criminals to commit more dangerous crimes."[38]

There are a lot of problems with the news portraying punitive policies as "tough on crime" and approaches that address the root causes of interpersonal harm as "soft on crime." To start, the claim that more imprisonment would make us safer is wrong. The Justice Department adopted a highly regarded review of the 116 existing studies about whether incarceration makes people less likely to commit police-recorded crime in the future. The study concluded, "Compared with noncustodial sanctions, incarceration appears to have a null or mildly criminogenic effect on future criminal behavior."[39] Other studies have found that even a few days in jail after an arrest and before being convicted makes people more likely to commit police-recorded crime in the future.[40] Why? Because it destabilizes their lives. The Center for Just Journalism has also produced a helpful summary of the research for journalists showing why both deterrence and incapacitation, lynchpins of the "tough on crime" approach, do not support increasing current punishment levels.[41]

By contrast, addressing root causes of violence with various social investments is more effective at reducing interpersonal harm.[42] To take just one example, research shows that simply expanding Medicaid reduces arrests for violence by 19–29 percent over the following three years, and all police arrests by 20–32 percent. Another of the most widely accepted empirical findings is the impact of early childhood investments on crime. Children excluded from publicly funded preschool programs are 70 percent more likely to be arrested for a violent crime by age eighteen, and at-risk children are five times more likely to commit crimes repeatedly as adults if they do not have access to preschool programming.[43]

Given the evidence, suggesting that mass-incarceration advocates are being "tough on crime" when they push for policies that do not make people safer is like praising fossil fuel profiteers for mitigating global warming. It is one of the great achievements of modern copaganda that police, prosecutors, prison guard unions, bail bond companies, private equity firms, surveillance corporations, for-profit prisons, and politicians have convinced news outlets to call the policies that benefit them "tough on crime." But it gets worse, because "tough on crime" groups are among the biggest proponents of shifting "law enforcement" resources away from investigating and prosecuting millions of much more threatening crimes by powerful people.[44]

"Real Public Safety Problems"

Every now and then, someone with power says the quiet part out loud and enables us to better see how ideology is smuggled into the news. Sometimes they expose malicious intentions, such as when a sheriff and county commissioner were caught on tape in 2023 discussing "hanging Black people by a creek."[45] Or when prosecutors in Chicago played what they called "The Two-Ton Contest" or "Ni**ers by the Pound," which involved looking at the weights of the Black people charged with crimes and competing to see who could be the first to convict a combined total of 4,000 pounds of Black people, which often meant offering lenient plea deals for more serious crimes if the person was heavy enough in order to score big points for the game.[46] The most infamous of these instances was when one of Nixon's advisers discussed the real reasons the government began the fifty-year war on drugs: to target Black people and the political left.[47] But only infrequently is someone caught saying something overtly nefarious like these examples. More often, they say something to a journalist that they believe to be fit for public consumption but that is unintentionally revealing.

An example is what happened after a high-profile murder of a tech executive in San Francisco in 2023. At first, when a homeless person was suspected, the news delivered hysterical wall-to-wall coverage about declining public safety. But it was soon revealed that the accused killer was another tech entrepreneur. In the aftermath of this revelation, a California state senator told the news that the stabbing murder "does not appear to have anything to do with" the "real public safety problems" in San Francisco.[48]

These moments of unintentional truth offer a chance for people to see how distorted and ideological the media's depiction of safety is.[49] As had been true for years, violent crime in San Francisco was near historic lows, and it was one of the safest big cities in the U.S. when the incident occurred. But the local media, tech industry leaders, and right-wing politicians used the murder to cast the city as a dystopian hellscape of homeless drug users engaging in so much random violence that "normal" people could not function.

It was in this context that the politician quoted in the news separated the horrific murder from the city's "real public safety problems." A human being stabbed another human being to death. But it somehow didn't count as a "real" problem once we learned that it wasn't committed by a homeless person. Because another affluent person was arrested for the crime, it was no longer a "real public safety problem." I urge you to spend a few minutes thinking about what this quotation reveals about how people with power understand the concept of "crime" and how they use "crime" discourse in the daily news as a tool for ends other than the safety and well-being of everyone in our society.

It is one thing to know intellectually that police spend only 4 percent of their time on what they call "violent crime." It is one thing to know intellectually that, for decades, police chose to arrest more poor people for marijuana possession than for *all violent crime combined*. It is one thing to know intellectually that the punishment bureaucracy chooses not to prosecute violations of drug laws, fraud, bribery, tax evasion, wage theft, environmental pollution, police brutality, and prosecutorial misconduct by elites, even though such crimes dwarf the harm of crimes they do prosecute. But it is quite another thing to see the ideology laid bare: harm committed by wealthy people *isn't what we mean by "public safety."* Or, to use his words, harm by elites isn't "real" crime.

As we see here, copaganda also promotes the idea that interpersonal harms are committed by strangers. In reality, most violence is perpetrated by *people who know the victim.*[50] Thus, it should come as no surprise that the tech entrepreneur knew the executive he was accused of killing in San Francisco. This fact alone, if more widely understood, would be damaging for the punishment bureaucracy because it suggests a different set of theories about what might reduce violence. Taking seriously why people hurt each other, especially people who know each other, would mean taking seriously problems in our culture and political economy. It would mean addressing things like toxic masculinity, trauma, access to medical care and therapy, and various material deprivations as "public safety" issues.

If all harms and who perpetrates them were reported more objectively, the picture would change. A more complex story would emerge: the line between perpetrator and victim blurs. We are all perpetrators and victims at different times. The survivor of an armed robbery may also be a person who shoplifts deodorant. A society with extreme levels of poverty, desperation, and isolation creates cycles of trauma and produces situations in which friends, families, and acquaintances hurt each other.

Because of the fearmongering about poor people and unhoused people through around-the-clock coverage of anecdotal stranger crimes, the news has conditioned people to misunderstand the nature of risk and vulnerability. To take just one local example, during the panic about supposed threats posed by homeless people, the San Francisco mayor shut down a community health clinic that had prevented 330 overdoses in favor of more spending on police surveillance and arrests of drug users.[51] After its closure, there was a 41 percent increase in overdose deaths in the first three months of 2023. We are talking about hundreds of people dying preventable deaths, and yet investing in such a clinic was not portrayed as an urgent matter of "public safety."

In general, we are far more likely to be harmed by wealthy people, the institutions that serve them, and people we know. But people in power suggest that the "real" threats come from bad poor people whose mode of living normal people cannot possibly understand or address other than through punishment. And the news uses the moral panic du jour—from violent crime to shoplifting, carjacking, public drug use, and juvenile super-predators; to car theft, fentanyl, and crack dealers; to people released on bail or people released on parole; to Central American migrants, etc.—to win support for increased funding for the punishment bureaucracy instead of providing care and safety for all human beings.

Stuart Hall describes how this ideological manipulation works:

> The "moral panic" appears to us to be one of the principal forms of ideological consciousness by means of which a "silent majority" is won over to the support of increasingly coercive measures on the part of the state and lends its legitimacy to a "more than usual" exercise of control. . . .
>
> Their typical form is that of a dramatic event which focuses and triggers a local response and public disquiet. . . . The wider powers of the control culture are both alerted (the media play a crucial role here) and mobilized (the police, the courts). The issue is then seen as "symptomatic" of wider, more troubling but less concrete themes. . . . In the later 1960s, these panics follow faster on the heels of one another than earlier; and an increasingly amplified general "threat to society" is imputed to them (drugs, hippies, the underground, pornography, long-haired students, layabouts, vandalism, football hooliganism). . . .

There is indeed in the later stages a "mapping together" of moral panics into a general panic about social order; and such a spiral has tended, not only in Britain, to culminate in what we call a "law and order" campaign, of the kind which . . . powered Nixon and Agnew into the White House in 1968.[52]

The same week as the San Francisco story, the *Times* ran a series of stories about serious problems in our society, including: the danger posed by the transportation of toxic chemicals on trains because of the risk of (often-criminal) derailments;[53] thousands of child labor violations that federal "law enforcement" chose to ignore;[54] and state and local courts engaging in millions of intentional constitutional violations by charging people excessive fees/fines and jailing people who can't pay them (the article failed to mention that prosecutors, judges, and debt collectors were engaging in widespread federal crimes through this extortion).[55]

Stories like these are not treated as "real public safety" problems. They are not, as with street crimes by poor people, presented individually, one after another, as urgent illustrations of a crisis of "law and order" in the daily news. None of these stories described the repeated law violations as a "crime wave" or even labeled them "crimes" at all.[56] This is because they are not considered "real" crimes or issues to be dealt with through surveillance and punishment of the people who commit them. Even when these threats are discussed as bad things or sometimes civil violations, their *criminal* component is rarely mentioned. The news doesn't portray the criminal law as a place where we deal with the harms caused by the powerful.[57]

Using "tough on crime" or "public safety–minded" or "real threats" to describe the selective imprisonment of marginalized people has consequences. Although harsher sentences don't reduce crime, they do kill people. The U.S. had a total life expectancy for *the entire population* of almost two years lower than if it imprisoned people at the rate it used to prior to the early 1980s—i.e. rates closer to other comparable countries.[58] "Tough on crime" policies are destroying hundreds of millions of years of human life, yet the news allows proponents of these policies to present themselves as concerned with well-being.

All of this makes people think that if we care about the safety of the people we love—and who doesn't?—then we must support more imprisonment. When it is *assumed* that authoritarian policies are required for safety, and the only tolerated debate is whether the tradeoffs with regard to discrimination and liberty are worth being less safe, then people fighting authoritarianism will probably lose. People will support authoritarian reaction when they are afraid.

The association between the punishment bureaucracy and "real safety" is not caused solely by language. Stock images also make this connection. Take the following example from the *Washington Post*.[59]

The *Washington Post* could have used a variety of images, including

 **Post Crime**
@postcrime

Man fatally shot in Fort Totten area of Northeast Washington

washingtonpost.com
Man fatally shot in Fort Totten area of Northeast Washington

a photograph of the Fort Totten neighborhood. Or, imagine if instead of the stock photo of a police car standing in for incidents of
daily violence, the paper featured a graph of local poverty rates, the
photo of a gun manufacturer's headquarters, charts showing levels
of lead poisoning by neighborhood, a graph of divestment from affordable housing and public schools, or a chart comparing crime in
places where politicians refused to expand Medicaid. These images
would help illustrate more scientifically accurate links to violence;
on a subconscious level, they would conjure in readers different sas-
sociations, and on a conscious one, they would cultivate different
political discussions.

People are conditioned automatically to associate repressive bureaucracy with safety. Among all the deadly features of copaganda, the
intuitive connection between increased repression and safety is one of
the most important. No matter how good the logic or evidence supporting challenges to the punishment bureaucracy, they are likely to fail if,
at an intuitive level, people connect safety to more police, prosecutors,
and prisons.

The "Wave" and the "Surge"

The news relies on metaphors from nature to describe increases in
police-reported crimes, calling them "crime waves" or "surges." The
daily news uses the terms to describe the collective behavior of marginalized groups, but almost never to describe crimes of powerful people.
How often do you see a news story about a "surge" in tax evasion or a
"crime wave" by bankers?

The choice of when and when not to use such metaphors is ideological. For example, although every day there are cases highlighting
the widespread problem of domestic violence committed by police officers, when the news covers one of these examples, it does not aggregate the incidents into a coherent phenomenon like a "wave" or "surge."
The same reporters choose to use different conceptual frameworks for

reporting on crimes depending on who commits them. Here are a few representative examples in headlines:

- *Minneapolis Star Tribune*: "Twin Cities Area Sees Surge in Carjackings, Putting Drivers on Edge"[60]
- *New York Times*: "San Francisco's Shoplifting Surge."[61]
- CNN: "New York City Crime Wave Continues into 2022 as City Rolls Out Safety Plan."[62]
- NBC New York: "Surge in NYC Subway Crime Sets City on Edge." The article begins: "Every day it seems there's another violent attack on a subway or bus in New York City, a crime wave that has set many residents on edge—and one that has occurred despite Mayor Eric Adams' pledge to crack down and flood transit with police officers."[63]

"Crime wave" and "crime surge" convey powerful, uncontrollable natural phenomena.[64] Each metaphor is an inaccurate way to describe the narrow range of police-reported crimes for which police arrest marginalized people, but they make people falsely believe that such crimes are increasing when they aren't, as the following graph shows.[65]

And when people are scared, punitive policy becomes more popular.[66] Journalists who use hyperbolic metaphors about crime are thus helping to fuel historic rates of punitiveness.

Most importantly, by focusing so much on *changes* in "crime," the metaphors elide the relatively high levels of violence in U.S. society compared with other societies that have less inequality. The relentless focus in U.S. media on short-term *fluctuations* distracts people from examining the root causes of the *consistently* high levels of harm relative to those that would exist in an achievable society. Instead of looking to explain high levels of social violence generally, news stories speculate about what has changed, say, 4–6 percent from the month or year before.

Next, the news reports rotating policy tweaks suggested by some politician or police department to address these "surges" and "waves."

Perceptions of Crime in the United States
Is there more crime in the U.S. than there was a year ago, or less?
& Reported violent crime rate in the United States from 1990 to 2020 [per 100,000 of the population]

■ More crime   ■ Less crime   ▒ Same amount   ▓ Reported violent crime rate

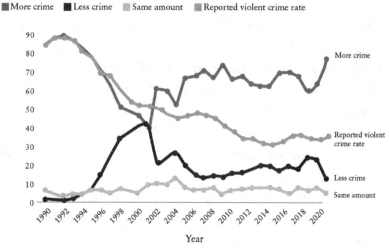

Source: Gallup Poll Social Series
Combined chart assembled by Sean Laney

Ignored in the process are the features of our society that determine overall levels of harm. To play on the analogy, we should not be asking, "Are the waves slightly higher today than yesterday?" We should be asking, "Where is all this water coming from?"

A specter thus haunts crime reporting: the punishment bureaucracy looked *very* similar in 2022 to what it looked like in 2021. It still looked similar in 2023. Same in 2024. There have not been meaningful changes to the system that, as a matter of physical reality, *could have caused* significant changes in overall aggregate amounts of interpersonal harm under any prevailing understanding of the evidence, and any fluctuations pale in comparison to the level of total harm. Juxtaposing "waves" and "surges" with one or another policy tweak obscures this reality.

Moreover, one of the most harmful impacts of the "wave" and "surge" metaphors is that they suggest we shouldn't or can't grasp the root structural causes of violence and harm, just as people can't really grasp big natural phenomena in our physical world. We are just mortals at their mercy. Obscuring the structural causes and ways to address them leaves people predisposed to accept police, prosecutors, and prisons, because those interventions thrive when people don't care about or don't believe we can tackle the root causes and instead are resigned to demand short-term protection from the ineffable dangers of life.

So, beneath these metaphors is an assumption about the *natural* violence of humanity. This was brought home to me when a student from the Federalist Society approached me after a lecture I gave at Harvard Law School. He told me that he hadn't thought about many of the things I said and that, on reflection, he agreed with nearly everything I said about the punishment bureaucracy. However, he said, the difference between us was that he believed human beings are inherently evil and dangerous, and that I believed human beings are inherently loving and kind. As a result, he said, he tended to favor government spending on police and prisons because we will never be able to stop people harming each other and that the primary role of the government should be protecting people from the violence inherent in human nature.

But different human societies have had radically different levels of interpersonal coercion, violence, and harm. Not every society is as violent and alienating as every other one. The key decisions we make as a society—the institutions and culture we create, and the investments we make—*matter.*

9

Copaganda Against Change

For a century and a half, the prison has always been offered as its own remedy: the reactivation of the penitentiary techniques as the only means of overcoming their perpetual failure.

-Michel Foucault[1]

Copaganda goes into overdrive when the punishment bureaucracy encounters threats to its size, power, and profit. The punishment bureaucracy crafts stories about its own violence and ineffectiveness to get people to support "reforms" that do not challenge and—even worse—often increase its size and power. A few representative examples demonstrate how the news gets well-intentioned people to support this cycle.

Copaganda Against the 2020 Uprisings

The coverage of the 2020 racial justice uprisings, and the subsequent murders of Tyre Nichols and Keenan Anderson in 2023 that threatened to reignite them, offers a case study in the perpetual cycle of police failure, protest, "reform," and bureaucratic expansion.[2]

The two main *New York Times* articles covering the police response to the 2020 protests are among the best examples of how police and their allies shape public opinion about causes and solutions and how they leverage their own violence to acquire more money and power. The first article is about a report concluding that the LAPD "mishandled" the protests.[3]

The second article, which appeared nine days later, is about the

L.A.P.D Severely Mishandled George Floyd Protests, Report Finds

An independent report commissioned by the Los Angeles City Council faulted the department for its lack of planning and chaotic response.

In City After City, Police Mishandled Black Lives Matter Protests

Inquiries into law enforcement's handling of the George Floyd protests last summer found insufficient training and militarized responses — a widespread failure in policing nationwide.

release of similar reports criticizing the police response to racial justice protests in "city after city."[4]

These articles were not about police misconduct. They were about what official government reports *said* about police misconduct. As we will see, this distinction matters.

The articles, and the reports on which they were based, reinforced the misleading view that police who brutalized people in 2020 were not *intentionally* trying to repress protests for equality, but instead were hampered by a lack of money, "training," "preparation," and surveillance technology.

Both articles characterized the police response to protests as a series of "mistakes" and "missteps" that resulted from insufficient resources. Here is how the first article describes the factors underlying police violence against protesters:

- "Ill-prepared"
- "Mishandled"
- "Botched their handling"
- "Untrained officers"
- "There was a lack of preparation, a lack of planning."
- "They lacked experience in managing peaceful protests and said they did not receive enough training to maintain order."

- "Police department should prioritize the training [in crowd control] going forward."
- "Their confidence resulted in them failing to plan."

The second article uses similar language:

- "Poorly trained"
- "Stunningly unprepared"
- "Mistakes"
- "Police officers nationwide were unprepared to calm the summer's unrest."
- "Almost uniformly, the reports said departments need more training in how to handle large protests."
- "Not planning for protests"
- "The lack of adequate planning and preparation"
- "They lacked resources devoted to intelligence and outreach."
- "American police simply were not prepared for the challenge that they faced in terms of planning, logistics, training and police command-and-control supervision."
- "Failing to train officers to de-escalate conflict, control crowds and arrest large numbers of people"
- "Kits were sometimes outdated," "police . . . did not have enough computers," "police did not have enough buses."
- "Did not plan appropriately for field jails"
- "Planning anti-racism training for all officers"
- "Missteps"

This language is a politicized way to disguise violent repression.[5] If any other group went around illegally beating, shooting, kidnapping, running over, chemically poisoning, torturing, mocking, taunting, tasering, and caging their political opponents before lying about it in written reports contradicted by video, would the *New York Times* say they "mishandled" things and made some "missteps"? What about if that group did those things in hundreds of cities at once?

The *Times* fed millions of readers the premise that police were try-ing to keep everyone safe during the protests and that, in doing so, they made some unintentional whoopsies. On this view, it's not that powerful institutions *benefit* from repression of social movements seeking more equality or that the policing bureaucracy was *designed* to repress social movements that challenge inequality. Instead, the news is telling well-meaning readers that the police violence we all witnessed on video was a problem of insufficient "training," "intelligence," "preparation," and funding. Framed this way, the solution to a problem isn't to reduce the power of the police, but to give them more stuff.

In fact, tens of thousands of brazen acts of criminality were *inten-tionally* committed by thousands of police officers of all ranks. Many of them were coordinated and planned at all levels of the policing bureau-cracy.[6] Police leaders in city after city then chose not to discipline offi-cers for their brutality or for lying about it. The police were doing what they were trained to do. The widespread training, planning, and coordi-nation of police officers is one reason video archives compiled from tens of thousands of ordinary people in the streets show *eerily similar* inten-tional acts. All these officers and all these commanders across all these departments were *well prepared* and following time-honored strategies to crush a popular movement against injustice.

None of this is new. It resembles the tactics presented in counter-insurgency manuals and the colonial repression of protests across the world by police forces trained by U.S., British, and French military counterinsurgency specialists.[7] And it bears a striking resemblance to archival videos, audio recordings, oral histories, whistleblower testimo-nies, and written witness accounts of police violence and repression of social justice movements from the 1920s, 1930s, 1940s, 1950s, 1960s, 1970s, 1980s, 1990s, 2000s, and 2010s.

When I hear about calling for more police training as a re-sponse to brutality, I often think back to one of the most remarkable moments in U.S. police history. On March 7, 1965, white police in Alabama beat hundreds of civil rights marchers—including fracturing the skull of civil rights icon John Lewis—as they walked across the Edmund Pettus Bridge in Selma on "Bloody Sunday." The very next day, President Lyndon Johnson announced an unprecedented expansion of funding for U.S. police departments, including for "improved training of policemen."[8]

In his history of U.S. policing, scholar Kristian Williams analyzed newspaper articles from the nineteenth and twentieth centuries and found that, whether it was violence against enslaved people or striking workers or European immigrants or civil rights advocates, the violence was organized and intentional. It was so systematic and pervasive that it defined everyone's understanding of "law enforcement" itself. And as with today, police were happy to look the other way with respect to the enforcement of most laws:

> Contrary to the conventional wisdom, the police did not suppress vice; they licensed it. From New York's Tenderloin to San Francisco's Barbary Coast and from Chicago's Levee to New Orleans' French Quarter, they permitted gamblers, prostitutes, and saloon keepers to do business under certain well-understood conditions. These entrepreneurs were required to make regular payoffs. . . .
>
> In this way vice laws, and the liquor laws especially, proved a useful tool for political machines to enhance their power. . . . Selective enforcement allowed political bosses to discipline their supporters and put their competitors out of business.[9]

Back then, the government pacified an uneasy public with assurances that police would receive better "training" and funding so that organized politicized violence wouldn't keep happening. They poured money into "training" to combat pervasive law-breaking by police, prison guards, prosecutors, and judges.

But police training *instills* misconduct. Many people don't know that the police training industry is one of the most corrupt, violent, and authoritarian corners of our society. For example, a 2023 investigation by the state comptroller of New Jersey found that a popular police training company "taught unconstitutional policing tactics, glorified violence, denigrated women and minorities, and likely violated a myriad of state laws and policies."[10] At least fifty-four government agencies in New Jersey spent public money on the training, and the company that provided it also trains police in forty-six other states. One of this profitable industry's focus areas is to train police in how to be more violent, disrupt public protest, and spy on dissidents more effectively, including through popular trainings in which police are taught to be "warriors" with "a plan to kill everyone." Other lucrative programs send officers from hundreds of U.S. police departments to train with the Israeli military to master tactics used in its occupation of Palestinian territory—an occupation that violates international law.[11] The historian Stuart Schrader has documented how, in the wake of prominent public inquiries into state violence against racial justice protesters in the 1960s, police got funding to adopt numerous "reforms," including what was billed as new "nonlethal weapons" and "riot-control training." The result? Police killed more people than ever in the following years. Schrader exposed the vast international network of police and military training programs set up by the U.S. government during the Cold War. This network and funding for training enabled the U.S. and repressive puppet regimes to exchange ideas, strategies, and methods, which their soldiers and police used to crush progressive social movements throughout the world.[12]

Think for a moment about what it would look like if the news adopted a historically accurate framing of police violence rather than dismissing it as accidental or incidental. If the *New York Times* had framed the 2020 police violence as the impressive execution of a strategy to crush racial justice protests, then readers might conceive of different public policy responses to it. If the widespread police violence in the U.S. is instead framed as the product of counterinsurgency training, the coordination of tactical units in similar ways across hundreds of cities, and the expert use of surveillance and weaponry developed by Western militaries to crush liberation struggle in the Global South, then readers might reach different conclusions about whether the solution is to buy more of that stuff.

If one views police as sophisticated agents who have effectively infiltrated and repressed progressive social movements for 150 years, then their violence and spying on 2020 protesters cannot be mystified as anomalous or the result of a lack of "preparation," "training," or "resources." And you can see this obfuscation in one of the most glaring omissions in the articles: they make no acknowledgment that police committed many thousands of intentional crimes. If the news acknowledged those acts as *crimes*, it would have had to turn a piece about a lack of "training" into one about why police, prosecutors, and federal authorities in virtually every city *largely chose to ignore those crimes*.[13] And what would *that* story get people thinking about?

In sum, whatever your level of familiarity with this history, how the news talks about what went wrong shapes how people think we should fix it. During and after the 2020 uprisings, the news obscured what should have been a central question of public debate: should we spend billions more building larger garrisons of armed bureaucrats that consistently crush the poorest people in our society and smash people who organize for progressive social change? It's the same question posed by the Church Committee, a congressional body empaneled in the 1970s to investigate repression and spying conducted by the CIA, FBI, and other intelligence agencies together with local police to repress the civil rights movement in the 1960s and 1970s.[14] News outlets evade this question by presenting police violence as isolated and unintentional.

In response to my question of whether the police violence in the coverage of the 2020 uprisings should be described as unintentional, one reporter wrote, "I don't write editorials or opinion pieces. This story was really about what these [government] reports said." Two things in this statement stand out. First, the reporter was asserting the following: coverage that includes accurate historical context and is cognizant of the propagandistic connotation of words like "mistakes" and "missteps" would be considered an *opinion* piece. This is a standard journalistic dodge: in the eyes of reporters, challenges to conventional wisdom lack "objectivity," while reporting based on pro-punishment bureaucracy premises, however contrary to evidence, is "objective." Second, the reporter told me that the story their editors assigned was not about the police violence, its historical context, causes, and solutions to it, but about *what official reports said* about it. Here, a newspaper ceded its own editorial judgment to disseminate the talking points of officials. Parroting what those officials *wanted* to tell the public is typical protocol for state-run media that the *Times* might decry in other countries.

The reporter's response brings me to another problem common to reporting on police reform: obscuring the background of sources they cite. For example, both articles portray the report about the LAPD violence—the subject of the article—as "independent."

In reality, the "independent" report about the LAPD was written by *six former LAPD officials*.[15] Every member of the "review team" was a former high-ranking LAPD official. It is journalistic malpractice to tell millions of readers that a "scathing" report was "independent" when it was written by former cops with decades of experience at the LAPD. One of the two *Times* articles didn't acknowledge this issue at all, thus hiding the report's origins from readers. The other, after calling the report "independent" in the subheading, waited fifteen paragraphs into the story to tell readers that the report was "completed by a panel of former police commanders and led by Gerald Chaleff, who has served on police oversight panels in Los Angeles dating back to the city's 1992 riots."[16] Even this explanation, which stretches the meaning of the word "independent" beyond anything recognizable to dictionary owners, did not inform readers that Chaleff himself was a former LAPD official or that he had overseen "constitutional policing" at the LAPD and therefore had a vested interest in how systemic constitutional failures were described.[17] Indeed, the efficacy of efforts he had led for the LAPD was the subject matter of the report! Here is another way to describe the "independent" report: the people who wrote it are among the individuals most responsible for, beholden to, and invested in how the LAPD (and police in general) appears to the public.

The punishment bureaucracy uses such "independent" panels and commissions to churn out reports that serve its copaganda interests. It's something I hear government officials joke about in private. When some potentially uncomfortable thing becomes public or when they want to get buy-in for changes that might be unpopular, they'll "appoint a commission" to study it. They know that either the urgency of the situation will dissipate while a commission prepares a report for release in two years, or, through controlling the composition of the commission, they can manufacture support for policies that would otherwise have caused concern. Their own policy preferences are then laundered as "independent" recommendations by experts. Journalists should expose the compromised nature of such reports, not help officials pass all this off as objective. Instead, the news routinely participates in this charade.

It benefits the LAPD to have the *news* describe recommendations for lavish new police spending as the judgment of neutral experts. Imagine what it would look like if an "internal" LAPD report or a report by the company selling police spyware had been the one to recommend more money for more spying on protesters in the wake of the LAPD's widespread crimes. The *news*'s portrayal of the commission report about the LAPD as "independent" is an example of how *reporting on* police violence becomes a stage in the cycle of police violence.

Shakeer Rahman, an organizer, civil rights lawyer, and community-based scholar of the LAPD, describes this cycle well: "There's a long history of this cycle (cops violently crush dissent, a police commission proposes reforms, police get more resources), going back to the disastrous Safe Streets Act of 1968 enacting the Katzenbach Commission's police 'modernization' proposals after [the] Watts [uprising]." [18] Not surprisingly, given who wrote it, the "independent" report that the *Times* called "scathing" also reads like a wish list of police fantasies: huge budget increases for new technology, weapons, and military counterinsurgency training. Better pay and "wellness" benefits for cops. And so on.

The *Times* also justified one of the report's most disturbing recommendations for increased surveillance through the creation of a new bureau focused on "public order," noting that "the department's intelligence operations have become less effective as positions in that field were cut."[19] This is chilling. The report recommends strengthening the LAPD's capacity to spy on Black people and civil rights leaders—through "intelligence" focusing on internet surveillance and operationalizing the monitoring of political activity—despite the department's notorious record of violence and abuse of those communities, and the *Times* presents the analysis as objectively true.

So, under the guise of "reform," the country's leading newspaper helped former high-level LAPD officials use a moment of public consciousness to present what would otherwise be seen as extremist proposals for more LAPD spying by portraying such repression as a sober, serious, "independent" analysis.[20]

Rahman and other surveillance experts also noticed something else: the report says LAPD "shadow teams" infiltrated peaceful protest groups in 2020. But rather than analyzing the dangers of entrapment, First Amendment violations, or instigation of crimes, the report calls for better *coordination* of such infiltration.[21] What's remarkable about this is the utter lack of historical context; specifically, the LAPD used to have a public order division until it was disbanded in disgrace after a lawsuit found that it infiltrated civil rights organizations after the Watts uprising, blackmailed critics of the LAPD, and illegally shared surveillance information with right-wing extremist groups in a way that encouraged vigilante violence against progressives.

The LAPD is not alone—across the country, police forces have for years created large intelligence squads with the goal of suppressing movements for racial justice, social justice, labor organizing, LGBTQ rights, peace, and environmental sustainability. These squads carried out extortion and murder, alongside more routine violent felonies, surveillance, infiltration, false-flag operations, and wiretapping. During the peak of the civil rights era, for example, Chicago alone assigned over five hundred officers to spy on and infiltrate the civil rights movement.[22]

If people are to make reasoned judgments about police reform, journalists should inform them if the policing bureaucracy responded to previous instances of similar misconduct with similar reports and proposals, if those proposals were implemented, and if similar police misconduct still occurred after those similar steps were taken. Instead, the cycle of profitable bureaucratic "reforms" is left out of news coverage, making a lot of people think that our society is doing something helpful each time in response. And the choice to do a story only about what "independent" reports *said* about police violence gives readers who want to see *something* done about the problems they saw on video the illusion that the system is working well. *Serious* people are doing *serious* things to implement a system of checks and balances, transparency, after-the-fact evaluation, and oversight. The *Times* paints a fraudulent picture of an accountable punishment bureaucracy.

The news can thus obscure relevant history to present the system as fundamentally sound and capable of overcoming its problems once they are identified. This coverage of police violence would be like telling the story of the Trojan Horse but leaving out the part where hidden soldiers appear and conquer the unsuspecting recipients of the gift. Because the articles exclude sources who could provide that information, readers are led to believe that the widespread misconduct in 2020 was aberrational, that independent experts have identified the causes, that those were mishaps caused by insufficient resources for police, that once supplied with money and training those missteps will be eliminated, and that we have a functioning system that does rigorous good-faith audits of the punishment bureaucracy when it messes up so that it can become better.

We never learn from this cycle, because the next time attention is focused on the next police scandal, the news does not report what had previously happened, and the history that would enable people to make sense of what is happening vanishes into Orwell's "memory hole."[23]

Suggesting that certain systemic features of the punishment bureaucracy are accidents is part of a broader pattern in the news. Some
bad things are painted as the intentional conduct of bad people, while
certain systemic harms are treated as randomly materializing out of the
ether. Look, for example, at how the news covered a series of decisions
made by Kroger, a large grocery store corporation, to steal money from
hundreds of workers across five states: "payroll mistakes that made their
checks too small."[24]

This is like saying mistakes were made at racial justice protests, resulting in some protesters having too much electricity in their bodies.
Or take what happened in late 2022, when a woman died and babies
and adults were taken to the hospital in Akron, Ohio, after a carbon
monoxide leak at an apartment building.[25] The corporate landlord had
not installed carbon monoxide detectors. Many more people would have
died had a paramedic not realized what was happening and evacuated
people. A news article quoted the property management company as
feeling bad about the death and offering to pay for hotel rooms for the
sick survivors. But the reporters didn't inform the public that the company *had broken the law*, which in Ohio requires landlords to pay for
and install detectors.[26] Instead, it was allowed to present itself as caring
and responsive through a spokesperson, saying, "We feel terrible for the
situation. It's a terrible tragedy." Not once does the news article suggest
that a crime had occurred, that it was a systemic problem, that the police
could treat it as a criminal matter if they chose, that police and government lawyers in Akron were not enforcing building safety laws, or that
companies make intentional decisions about whether to comply with
building codes based on profit.[27]

All of this is part of a pattern of the news describing as "accidents"
things that are predictable, preventable, and the result of intentional decisions by powerful institutions.[28] It is a form of propaganda used across
related contexts. For example, when drones from the U.S. or its allies
kill civilians, the murders are often portrayed as "mistakes" despite the
deliberate military policy to, for example, classify all young men in a

geographic area as military targets for assassination, or to bomb medical personnel who attempt to rescue people after a drone attack.[29] These actions meet the legal definition of intentional murder under U.S. law.

By contrast, consider the language the news uses when *other* governments attack civil rights protesters. When a disfavored foreign government assaults crowds, it is often deemed a *strategic response planned at the highest levels to curb dissent*, not a series of isolated failures to properly "train" security forces or to give them sufficient technology. For example, it would never occur to U.S. journalists to describe the 2023 police violence against women's liberation protesters by Iran's "morality police" as a series of "mistakes" by an "unprepared" policing bureaucracy that could be fixed with more funding, surveillance technology, and training. In fact, in an ironic copaganda twist, the Iranian government seems to have studied the PR response of U.S. police, because it now recycles many of the same lines they use.[30] In each country, the goal of the government in its public statements about its police violence, which media in each country parrot, is to spread the view that a particular institution is well-meaning and working to figure out what happened and how to make it better.

There is a similar dissonance in how the *Times* covered police violence against protesters in Cuba during the same summer as the George Floyd protests. The *Times* treated police violence and surveillance in Cuba as an intentional and coordinated government effort to "send a chilling message" to dissidents by "making an example out of people."[31] Characterizing the state's response as intentionally "draconian," the *Times* complained, without irony, about Cuban copaganda because Cuban "media outlets denounce demonstrators as vandals and looters." Yet the news almost never describes police repression in the U.S. as consciously planned and carried out by police leaders, and it constantly demonizes demonstrators in broad brush strokes in the same way.

Similarly, in 2022, the *Times* published a deep dive into Chinese police surveillance.[32] The paper says things about the breathtaking scope of policing in China that the *Times* does not permit its reporters to write about the U.S., including accurately describing the technological ability and desire of the government bureaucrats to track and control dissent. What the paper calls the "techno-authoritarian" capabilities of Chinese police are similar to U.S. policing, and total surveillance is one of the primary goals of the policing bureaucracies in both countries, as well as the consulting companies who develop those same systems for use by governments across the world. But in the U.S., the news promotes similar domestic surveillance as "data-driven policing" that is a well-meaning "reform" to make policing *smarter* and less unintentionally hapless—it can even be a suggested salve to a well-meaning public in the wake of police violence and corruption. Buried fourteen paragraphs into the article on China, the *Times* reveals a crucial detail: the technological infrastructure enabling authoritarian practices around the globe was a "police reform" invented in and produced by the U.S. and European policing industries.

Case Study: The Body Camera

The framing of the police body camera as a means of "reform" is one of the most significant achievements of copaganda in contemporary history.[33] In the wake of the police shooting of Michael Brown in Ferguson, Missouri, in 2014, punishment bureaucrats and the news media widely called for body cameras as a solution to police violence that would make police more "accountable" and "transparent."

What many people don't know is that internal documents, public statements, and industry materials reveal that police officials and for-profit manufacturers of body cameras and related software had been clamoring for the technology for years. However, prior to Michael Brown's murder, police and prosecutors had been unable to get local governments to spend the *billions* of dollars needed to outfit every cop with a mobile surveillance camera that the cops themselves control and that prosecutors would use almost exclusively against marginalized people accused of minor crimes. Several large companies—who were eyeing body cameras as a multi-billion-dollar industry—had unsuccessfully lobbied for years for government funding to help police procure the money needed to integrate body-camera data into cloud-based computing systems and artificial intelligence algorithms that operationalize facial and voice-recognition. In the absence of government funding, they had even turned to the vast world of private police foundations, raising millions in donations from people like Stephen Spielberg to privately fund body cameras because police wanted them so badly.[34]

After police shot Michael Brown in 2014, the cops, prosecutors, and companies seized their opportunity, taking advantage of public outrage and a willing news media to convince local government officials to pay for the most expensive expansion of police surveillance technology in modern history. They reframed cameras as a "reform" to control police violence, almost always excluding from media coverage the views of experts, social movement leaders, and directly affected people who were warning that the technology, in the hands of the police and prosecutors, would not only fail to stop police violence, but usher in a new era of state surveillance and big data–fueled repression.

In my 2024 study of body cameras, *Body Cameras: The Language of Our Dreams*, I show how police and their allies used the news to dispense talking points that police lacked funding for crucial technology to hold themselves accountable. In reality, in addition to new surveillance technology useful in intelligence gathering at protests and to protect against civil liability for individual officers, police and prosecutors wanted body cameras because the technology gave them a powerful new form of evidence: an outward-looking camera that government agents control in terms of what it captures, from whose perspective, when video is publicly released, and how videos are edited. Body-camera videos are now routinely used in every courtroom in the U.S. to convict people of things like drug possession and trespassing and are almost never used against police. They help the punishment bureaucracy process more arrests because police, prosecutors, and judges use the videos to pressure people to plead guilty more quickly and to secure harsher punishment with that increased leverage. This is precisely the future police chiefs and corporate sales representatives envisioned over a decade earlier. The leading manufacturers of the cameras and purveyors of the software, like Axon (renamed from TASER), grew by billions in net worth, and many of the largest companies in the world—including Microsoft and Amazon—are making a lot of money from the perpetual surveillance technology contracts for software, databases, storage, and training.[35]

The news media collaborated every step of the way in this charade. In the nine years of media coverage I examined for my study, nearly every article characterized body cameras as a "reform" offered to promote police "accountability" and "transparency." I demonstrate that the news used buzzwords and carefully chosen "experts" to disseminate police talking points with little critical perspective, and never mentioned the actual history about the long-standing desire that punishment bureaucrats and surveillance companies had for them or why. A common police refrain parroted by cherry-picked "experts" was that the cameras were a "win-win." Even the growing number of detailed news investigations in recent years that accurately discuss the evidence from the government's own studies concluding that body cameras do *not* make police less violent or more accountable nonetheless erase the true history that body cameras were not intended as a well-meaning police accountability measure. Copaganda manufactures both consensus for dangerous policies and powerful mythologies about the *intentions* of the punishment bureaucracy.

Provided with the illusion that body cameras could protect marginalized people from police violence—the opposite of why they were created and how they were marketed to police and prosecutors internally—it is no wonder that huge percentages of people supported the technology despite knowing very little about it. Meanwhile, the news's focus on individual police body-camera videos after each new incident of police violence steered conversations away from deeper systemic questions about the purpose and function of policing, why police violence was still increasing, and the nature of policing reform.

In the wake of the 2023 murder of Tyre Nichols, New York City mayor Eric Adams went on national television to explain his decision to resurrect a controversial police unit similar to the SCORPION Unit that killed Nichols in Memphis. He argued that the NYC squad would be trained to "keep your body cameras on," and he used Nichols's murder to celebrate body cameras (even though they had neither prevented the murder nor provided the definitive footage of it).[36] The mere *existence* of the body-camera technology was now used as an excuse to engage in the practices that had been protested. The dots had all been connected, the circle completed.

The police, prosecutors, courts, prisons, and probation and parole officers, along with the multi-billion-dollar industries that evolve in symbiosis with them, use their own violence, waste, and ineffectiveness to justify securing ever more power in a perpetual cycle of "reform." Each failure becomes a reason to hoard more money doing the same things.[37]

Case Study: Bail Reform

A significant part of my career for the last decade has been bringing and winning civil rights cases to challenge the cash bail system. In much of the U.S., when a person is arrested, they are free to go home if their family pays a form of conditional release called cash bail. If the families can't pay, their loved one remains in jail. For much of U.S. history, most people were released without requiring any upfront cash payment, but the rise of mass incarceration over the last forty years saw an explosion of cash bail.[38] If a person is wealthy enough to pay the amount required, they can get the money back when their case is over. If the person's family cannot afford the full amount, they can pay a non-refundable premium, usually 10 percent but sometimes offered for less upfront with installments, to a for-profit bail bond company. If the person is too poor to pay even a substantial fraction of the amount required, they languish in jail. The for-profit bail industry has become a multi-billion-dollar industry, which exists only in the U.S. and the Philippines.[39] Every night, hundreds of thousands of families cannot afford even the small non-refundable payment. Can you imagine what it feels like to be a mother whose child is trapped in a jail cell, and you cannot bring them home because you don't have $350? I have watched families go door to door in some of the poorest neighborhoods in the country asking neighbors for $5 or $10 just to help bring a child or a pregnant spouse home. The bail industry worries that any exposure of its corrupt and ineffective practices would threaten this profitable operation with extinction.

Dozens of judges have privately told me that they agreed the cash bail system was unfair, unsafe, and ineffective. As one judge put it to me, they didn't *want* to separate presumed innocent people from their families just because they lacked cash but, they said, every judge knows that if they release someone and they are one of the few people who commits a serious crime, "the media will blame me, and no judge wants to be in the news." As a result, the judge said, it's in their interest to keep people in jail before trial even if it's bad for overall safety. In contrast, every judge knows that when a person dies or is sexually assaulted in jail because they lack cash to pay for their release, the news will not mention the judge's name. Judges understand whose misery—and whose role in that misery—is deemed newsworthy. If, however, police feed reporters a story about one of the rare instances in which a released person commits a serious crime, local news will devote sensational coverage to it. The inverse is true regarding positive outcomes: if a judge releases a thousand people and they keep their jobs such that their children don't become homeless, no one will tell the public about it on the nightly news. Bad curation of anecdote leads to bad policy.

As energy grew across the U.S. in recent years to join other countries in moving away from the notion that who is in jail and who is free depends on who has money, police, prosecutors, and bail industry lobbyists embarked on a campaign of false information about "bail reform." They were successful in getting the news to spread disinformation that demanding people pay cash to get out of jail makes society safer.[40]

Why did they do this? Cops, prosecutors, and judges like cash bail for a different reason: they depend on pretrial detention of low-level cases to coerce guilty pleas, and to do it quickly. In a civil rights case that my organization brought in Houston, the chief judge of the federal court made several important findings applicable across the U.S.:

- Of the roughly fifty thousand people arrested for misdemeanors in Harris County each year before our lawsuit, about twenty thousand of them were detained, even though they were presumed innocent, solely because they couldn't pay what was usually a few hundred dollars or less. These individuals pled guilty 84 percent of the time. The median time before conviction? 3.2 days.
- However, people who could pay a few hundred dollars for release were likely *never* to be convicted. And their cases lasted a median of four months while a lawyer worked on their behalf. Because so many arrests are bogus and don't have the evidence required for conviction, and because courts can't process so many cases, most low-level charges are dismissed if people fight them.
- After our lawsuit ended the practice of jailing people in the most minor cases solely because of poverty, about 19,000 fewer people are detained every year on misdemeanors in Houston alone, and there are about 24,000 fewer misdemeanor convictions each year. Now, most misdemeanor cases never result in convictions because, if forced to prove them, police and prosecutors can't.[41]

Seven years after our 2017 success in reducing misdemeanor pretrial detention in Houston, the data collected from hundreds of thousands of cases shows that the decreased number of people jailed resulted in *more* public safety and huge economic benefits.[42] These findings have been confirmed time and again. For instance, the court in Los Angeles County came to the same conclusion when reviewing all the available empirical evidence after we brought another case that struck down the cash bail system there in 2023.[43]

These are among the most important facts you will ever need if you want to understand the punishment bureaucracy: the U.S. arrests so many people for so many low-level things that it could never provide adequate defense lawyers, investigation services, prosecutors, judges, or jury trials for them all even though the Constitution requires it. The Constitution wasn't designed for mass incarceration. If all people could exercise their constitutional right to a fair trial and a zealous lawyer, the assembly line would grind to a halt because no society in modern history has attempted to arrest and prosecute so many people per capita. The crushing volume of cases is what the for-profit bail industry exploits. The industry didn't exist when the Constitution was drafted or in the century that followed it, and before the 1990s, release without requiring cash was more common than release requiring cash. But as court dockets became overwhelming, cash became an efficient point of leverage for bureaucrats to coerce more people to plead guilty quickly. Most of these people are released with time served if they plead guilty, and are almost always charged fines and fees that police, prosecutors, and courts then collect as revenue. Thus, the system profits from its own injustice, and tens of millions of poor people are trapped in a cycle of debt collection and jailing for years.

Even on its own terms, this system has nothing to do with "safety" because most people are released *immediately* if they either pay money, which they don't lose even if they commit a crime, or if they agree to plead guilty and accrue debt. They are typically put on probation for additional fees, and many have their driver's license suspended for unpaid fees, incurring yet more fees. As of this writing, the licenses of 11 million people are suspended solely because of these coerced debts.[44] Police, prosecutors, and judges understand that business as usual would end if people couldn't be quickly jailed. The machine on which their jobs, overtime, and consulting contracts depend would crash to a halt.

Every court to look at the evidence has made an additional crucial finding: empirical studies of millions of cases demonstrate that *cash bail does nothing to protect the community or encourage court appearance.*[45] In fact, it makes people *more* likely to commit crime in the future because short periods of detention destabilize people's lives—they lose their shelter, jobs, and kids. Their medication for physical and psychiatric care is disrupted, and they contract infectious diseases that spread through society. They are often physically traumatized and sexually assaulted in jail. It costs taxpayers billions in public money and local economies even more.

In the face of a system that is unconstitutional, unfair, and that makes everyone less safe, a small number of jurisdictions tried modest but meaningful changes. Take New York, for example. In 2019, the state legislature passed a law to reduce the number of people jailed before trial solely because of poverty.[46] People charged with misdemeanors and nonviolent felonies were to be released without having to pay cash, but cash could still be demanded for more serious offenses. By eliminating the use of cash to secure detention in lower-level cases, the state's pretrial detention population was predicted to shrink 40 percent, saving hundreds of millions of dollars and reducing crime.

The media backlash was swift. Over and over again, reporters cherry-picked anecdotes to whip up public frenzy on the false premise that "bail reform" caused various crimes. A comprehensive study of New York coverage found:

> Many news outlets printed irresponsible articles that falsely portrayed bail reform as harming public safety, stirring up public fears. This onslaught of bad press began before the reforms were even implemented and only ramped up after bail reform took effect on January 1, 2020.[47]

The volume of fearmongering stories was unlike anything I've tracked. Journalists even started inserting criticisms of bail reform into articles about *other* topics. For example, in the middle of an article about mental illness and adding cops to the subway, the *New York Times* quoted a politician falsely suggesting that "bail reform" caused crime, without correction.[48] The NYPD commissioner led the police counter-offensive against bail reform. He spent months making baseless claims blaming bail changes for various crimes, which the news media printed. Finally, at a hearing before the legislature, he admitted that he had no basis for the claims the news had spread.[49]

Support for bail reform had been popular after the death of teenager Kalief Browder, who spent three years enduring beatings and solitary confinement on Rikers Island after being falsely accused of taking another child's backpack.[50] But after the police counter-offensive, support dropped precipitously. In April 2020, just months after the reforms went into effect, New York rolled back some of them.[51]

I have documented backlash to local bail reforms in many cities such as Houston and San Jose, as well as in many states considering modest changes, such as Wisconsin, Illinois, New Jersey, and California, to name just a few.[52] The media typically includes a deluge of stories in which police blame "reforms" for anecdotal crimes while ignoring actual data. Ironically, upon inspection, the crime anecdote chosen by police usually isn't even related to bail changes.

Although "bail reform" was blamed for crime across the country between 2020 and 2022, there had been few meaningful changes to bail policies in many places. The pretrial punishment bureaucracy in 2022 was *very* similar to what it was in 2020. Even in the places that implemented substantial bail reforms, the pretrial assembly line still looked similar in court rooms each day, especially in more serious cases. All of the available evidence shows that, where attempted, reforms to reduce the use of cash bail reduce crime.

Case Study: Overturning Local Democratic Change

The punishment bureaucracy uses the news to relentlessly target progressive reforms, however small. A tweet by Ashley Parker, a senior *Washington Post* reporter, is an example of a fake frenzy about a minuscule reform:[53]

Ashley Parker ✓
@AshleyRParker

Crime in DC is out of control. It's depressing the @washingtonpost Ed Board even needed to write this: "Washingtonians have a right to feel and be safe. At the moment, it would be hard to say this is the case."

> 🌐 **James Hohmann** @jameshohmann · Mar 3, 2023
> New Washington Post Editorial: Feeling forced to choose, President Biden picked public safety over home rule for the capital city. Despite our grave concerns about the law, it shouldn't have come to this. Washington's leaders should have acted on their own.

Parker's tweet referred to a law, passed the previous November by the local city council, that would have modernized DC's criminal code, adding new crimes while also slightly reducing the maximum possible prison sentences for certain serious crimes. The new code would still have maintained sentences that were longer than most of the rest of the world's and *longer than what people are actually sentenced to in practice* in DC. So, this part of the law would have had no discernable effect.

When Parker made her comments, police-recorded crime in DC was at half-century lows, lower than at any point in the entire span of her life, as evidenced in the following graphic.[54]

Yet Parker wrote that she was so distraught by crime that it was "depressing" her. As a journalist with more than 400,000 Twitter followers and who regularly appears on TV and in the pages of one of the world's most influential newspapers, posting a statement like that weaponizes Parker's feelings in place of facts. She added that the newspaper's editorial board needed to intervene because people in DC have a right not just to "be safe" but—and she listed this *first*—to "feel" safe. A lot of the post-2020 copaganda backlash boiled down to this sentiment: "Yes it's true that the statistics don't back up our claims about safety, but we 'feel' more afraid of strangers and poor people."

By the time Parker made her public statement, the news had coalesced around the "conventional wisdom" that the city's majority-Black

Washington, DC Crime Incident Dashboard

3/7/2023

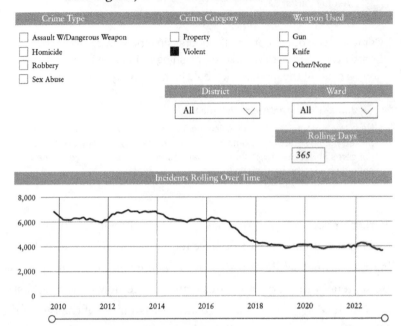

Crime Type	Crime Category	Weapon Used
☐ Assault W/Dangerous Weapon	☐ Property	☐ Gun
☐ Homicide	■ Violent	☐ Knife
☐ Robbery		☐ Other/None
☐ Sex Abuse		

District	Ward
All ∨	All ∨

Rolling Days
365

Incidents Rolling Over Time

YTD Crime Incidents

Crime Type	This YTD	Last YTD	2 Years YTD	3 Years YTD	4 Years YTD
Assault W/ Dangerous Weapon	232	240	248	263	253
Homicide	38	29	31	29	30
Robbery	422	507	349	328	319
Sex Abuse	33	15	28	36	31
Total	725	791	656	655	633

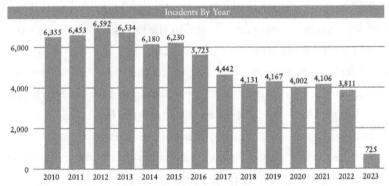

Incidents By Year

6,355 — 6,453 — 6,592 — 6,534 — 6,180 — 6,230 — 5,725 — 4,442 — 4,131 — 4,167 — 4,002 — 4,106 — 3,811 — 725

2010 2011 2012 2013 2014 2015 2016 2017 2018 2019 2020 2021 2022 2023

This dashboard measures incident totals as reported by the District of Columbia Metropolitan Police Department (MPD). Figures may differ slightly from MPD's formal crime statistics reported on the department's website.

elected officials should not be permitted to pass the reform. Parker shared a post by James Hohmann—a member of the *Post*'s editorial board with no business writing about these issues but who nonetheless parlayed his access to the internet into a Copaganda Rookie of the Year Award. Hohmann produced an editorial and social media post in which he suggested: (1) increased "sentences for violent crimes" are necessary for safety, contrary to overwhelming evidence; (2) DC residents "want" increased sentences despite a veto-proof body of elected representatives approving the law, which was also supported by federal prosecutors; and (3) safety and democracy are mutually exclusive because safety requires more imprisonment, so if democracy produces less imprisonment, it must be overruled.[55]

The social media posts and editorial were timed to influence deliberations of Democrats in Congress, who were considering whether to overrule the local DC democratic process—something Congress (in which DC has no voting representation) can do because DC is not a state. The *Post*—whose masthead declares "Because Democracy Dies in Darkness"—used its platform to call, based on misinformation, for authoritarian intervention to overturn the local law.

After similar interventions from a horde of journalists, President Biden announced on social media that he would sign a repeal of the law, supposedly because it reduced the maximum penalty for carjacking from forty years (a sentence no one got in practice) to twenty-four years (about nine years longer than the typical carjacking sentence).[56] Based on this single articulated reason, a supermajority of Democrats in the Senate and dozens of Democrats in the House voted with Republicans to overturn the democratic process in the District of Columbia.

The episode was based on copaganda, including: a distortion of what the new law did;[57] misinformation about crime rates; and lies about longer sentences reducing violent crime. Bipartisan acceptance of this effort to overturn a democratically produced law is one of the

President Biden ✔   •••
@POTUS

I support D.C. Statehood and home-rule – but I don't support some of
the changes D.C. Council put forward over the Mayor's objections – such
as lowering penalties for carjackings.

If the Senate votes to overturn what D.C. Council did – I'll sign it.

3:33 PM · Mar 2, 2023 · **14.5M** Views

most significant instances of copaganda I have witnessed during my
time working against the punishment bureaucracy. DC imprisons Black
people at nineteen times the rate of white people.[58] Faced with the most
minor prospect that people would hypothetically (but not in reality) face
reduced punishment after decades in prison, news outlets urged national
politicians to appease authoritarians, while also *adopting their lies and
their framing of the problem.* Among them was Arkansas senator Tom
Cotton, who stated, "I'm glad President Biden agrees that Washington,
D.C. is unfit to govern itself. D.C. must never become a state."[59]

Mainstream news and right-wing authoritarians had agreed: there
can be no safety without preserving the greatest levels of imprisonment
in world history, and if there is a conflict between democracy and a
slightly reduced number of human beings in prison cells, which the
Washington Post now asserts that there is, then democracy itself must
give way.

10

Progressives Want a Pro-Crime Hellscape

I have almost reached the regrettable conclusion that the Negro's great stumbling block in his stride toward freedom is not the White Citizen's Counciler or the Ku Klux Klanner, but the white moderate. . . . Shallow understanding from people of good will is more frustrating than absolute misunderstanding from people of ill will.
                                        -Martin Luther King Jr.[1]

On June 8, 2022, the day after national primary elections, the *New York Times* published a story announcing what it called "the shifting winds on criminal justice."[2]

California Sends Democrats and the Nation a Message on Crime

The recall of a progressive prosecutor in San Francisco and the strong showing by a former Republican in the mayor's race in Los Angeles showed the shifting winds on criminal justice.

The article reported that voters had rebuked progressive policies on crime and "delivered a stark warning about the potency of law and order as a political message in 2022." This conclusion was based on two individual races, the primary for mayor of Los Angeles and the recall of the district attorney in San Francisco. Using only these examples, the newspaper declared a *national* reckoning on progressive public safety policy. The message: Democrats must move right on crime.

Virtually every paragraph of the article is a case study in misinformation, beginning with the inaccurate reporting of the results themselves. Because the article purported to analyze the meaning of the election before many of the votes in Los Angeles were counted, the paper told readers that the more "law and order" candidate (a luxury real-estate developer who had switched from the Republican Party to become a Democrat) had a "strong showing." The newspaper told its audience that "he is currently the top vote-getter," hinging the article's thesis about the message being sent to national Democrats on this fact. But throughout the day and the following days, as votes were counted, the election turned into a landslide victory for the *other* candidate, who was running on a more progressive platform. Not only was the "law and order" candidate not the "top vote-getter," but he ended up losing the primary by a wide margin, with 64 percent of the voters rejecting him. He had outspent the winning candidate ten to one, using $80 million of his own money and boasting endorsements from celebrities like Elon Musk, Kim Kardashian, Gwyneth Paltrow, Katy Perry, and Snoop Dogg.[3] (He later spent even more money in the general election on a "law and order" platform and lost by even more—about 10 percent.) But the news had already told the public what the election results meant without waiting for the election results.

More broadly, there were progressive *victories* throughout California on that election night on "criminal justice" issues, and the *Times* chose not to cover them. The paradigmatic candidate for "tough on crime" politics, who ran a campaign against the more progressive California attorney general, got trounced 54 percent to 8 percent in a *statewide* election that *Politico* had called, prior to the election, a "bellwether" that "could be the most consequential contest" to "gauge the public's commitment to criminal justice reform."[4] The *Times* article ignored it. Very near San Francisco, in Contra Costa County, home to 1.2 million people, another progressive district attorney targeted by police unions and "tough on crime" Democrats won easily.[5] The *Times* article ignored it. As a local journalist pointed out, just one subway stop away from San Francisco, in Oakland, a progressive reformer won the district attorney primary.[6] The *Times* ignored it. In Los Angeles itself, an insurgent candidate for city controller, who ran on a campaign of auditing and defunding the LAPD, walloped a longtime city councilmember and machine politician running on a pro-police "law and order" platform by a margin of 19 percent. The controller ran on one of the most progressive platforms in the country focused on public safety issues, with billboards and wildly popular TikTok videos explaining wasteful spending by police. (In the general election a few months later, the progressive accountant beat his pro-police opponent by almost 27 percent, receiving more votes than the winning mayoral candidate. The *Times* also ignored that.)

So how did the article ignore election results all over California to declare the electoral death knell of progressive policy on "criminal justice"? Here's how the article began:

> LOS ANGELES—Progressive Democrats were knocked on the defensive in their own party over crime and homelessness on Wednesday after voters in two high-profile California races delivered a stark warning about the potency of law and order as a political message in 2022.

Notice that the phrases "voters . . . delivered" and "results" were false statements at the time of publication. But the selective "results" were nonetheless portrayed as a "vivid" warning that even "progressives" were "frustrated" with progressive policies: "The two results made vivid the depths of voter frustration over rising crime and rampant homelessness in even the most progressive corners of the country."

After a flood of criticism, including my own, the newspaper eventually made changes to the article, including: changing the headline, changing the sub-headline, adding sources, deleting paragraphs, changing words, and inserting a reference opaquely suggesting that the original article's thesis about crime was misleading. One later insertion was a paragraph that undermined the thesis of the article by acknowledging, with no specificity, explanation, or retraction, that "two elections in two cities, of course, do not fully capture the dynamics of an issue as complex as crime politics. And even on Tuesday, the left did not only suffer losses in prosecutor contests but scored a few victories." None of these corrections were noted as corrections, and they were seen by a fraction of the people who saw the original article. For example, the paper quietly altered the above sentence to replace the phrase "rising crime and rampant homelessness" with the phrase "quality-of-life issues." This was a key alteration because the misleading statement that crime was rising was critical to the article's thesis that this (nonexistent thing) was the cause of a putative (but nonexistent) electoral rejection of progressive policy.

Even more bizarre was the *Times*'s attempt to portray California's results as a "stark warning" for *an entire nation*. Aside from the progressive California victories that the *Times* ignored, candidates running elsewhere on a platform to challenge the punishment bureaucracy did well in the June 2022 primary elections, continuing a multiyear trend.[7] The *Times* didn't mention *any* of the victories from around the U.S. in its post-election coverage of what it said was a national trend.

But there was another important distortion in the article. It neglected to tell readers that the progressive policies of the San Francisco district attorney were popular. He championed reducing the prosecution of children, reducing the use of cash bail, creating a unit to investigate wrongful convictions, empowering a unit to investigate companies for worker protection offenses, and prosecuting more corrupt cops. In detailed polling, his policies received overwhelming support from constituents.[8]

Imagine if the *Times* article had told readers that the "law and order" candidate in Los Angeles had *lost decisively* and that the policies that differentiated the San Francisco prosecutor from his opponents were widely *popular*. It would have been forced to explore other explanations for why a *single* politician pursuing popular policies had lost a *particular* recall race. These explanations might have included that the lavish spending disparity fueled by Republican billionaires[9] and police union organizing had made people dislike the incumbent even though they liked his progressive policies;[10] that the news coverage and a flood of attack ads had confused people about *who* supported *which* policies; that once wealthy interests spend enough money on signature gathering for a recall, many sitting politicians would lose in up-or-down recall votes, as the San Francisco school board had found out four months earlier; that something specific to the economic, media, political, and racial environment was going on in San Francisco that might not be broadly applicable to progressives *ideas* across the U.S. The list goes on. There are many theories that do not involve the notion that progressive voters across the country now favor more authoritarian policies. And, given that the Los Angeles results turned out to be the opposite of what the paper reported, the thesis that a national *trend* existed was now predicated on one recall election in one city. Had the *Times* included these facts, the newspaper could not have concocted its narrative for tens of millions of liberal-leaning readers about voters rejecting progressive policies.

Fifteen paragraphs into the *Times* election-night story, the paper provides a disclaimer that "turnout was low" and that "there is always a risk of over-interpreting local races." After that brief flirtation with reality, it gets back to the main message: *Democrats need to get tough on crime.* Then, twenty-three paragraphs into the piece, readers are treated to a copaganda gem, which was also later deleted by the *Times* with no explanation:

> The extent to which crime is actually up depends on the category being measured and the particular jurisdiction. But strategists in both parties said that whatever the data shows, there is a widespread sense that daily life in big-city America is no longer as safe as it once was.[11]

This is a striking paragraph. First, it contradicts the article's original (now deleted) claim that "rising crime" was motivating Democrats. Second, it dismisses concern for facts with the phrase "whatever the data shows." In reality, according to the evidence available to the reporter when the paper published the story, both "violent crime" and "property crime" as measured by police were near historic lows. Here are the national crime statistics reported by the FBI from 1985 to 2022:[12]

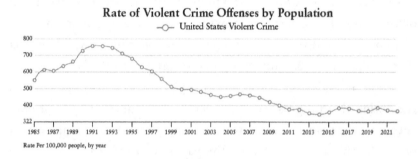

Rate of Violent Crime Offenses by Population
—◯— United States Violent Crime

Rate Per 100,000 people, by year

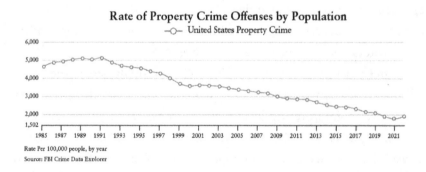

Rate of Property Crime Offenses by Population
—◯— United States Property Crime

Rate Per 100,000 people, by year
Source: FBI Crime Data Explorer

A good rule of thumb is that, when a news article contains the phrase "whatever the data shows," it is about to say something silly. A fun game at dinner parties is prefacing almost any outlandish statement with these ten words: *"Whatever the data shows, there is a widespread sense that . . ."* You can complete the sentence with almost anything and people will laugh and invite you back to their next party. Like, for example, ". . . a circus clown named Rick played a role in the early development of antibiotics" or ". . . no one who has had a pet cat has ever started a war." If anyone questions you, just tell them that you read it in the *New York Times* (but the paper later deleted it.)

Third, this paragraph isn't coverage that cares about accurately reporting evidence about public safety. Instead, it reports what hand-picked "strategists" *say* many people "sense" at a time when progressive policies were gaining traction against the punishment bureaucracy. The broader function of such reporting is to create and deepen the "widespread sense" of evidence-free fear that it identifies. Such reporting sits at the apex of a predatory copaganda feedback foodchain: once the news churns out a barrage of similar stories, those stories themselves help create a "widespread sense" that we are not as safe as we were. Having generated that "widespread sense," the news publishes stories about that *feeling* itself. Then, more articles are written with "strategists" speculating about what impact this feeling must be having on various political races. This is followed by yet more stories about how people seeking to reduce the size and power of the punishment bureaucracy are out of step and must abandon their goals if they want to compete in those races given what "strategists" are saying about the apparent zeitgeist.

Most news stories targeting progressive policies critical of the punishment bureaucracy never tell readers either the specifics of the policy being criticized or the empirical evidence on safety. "Strategists" say progressive candidates must promote authoritarian policies, even though the available evidence supports progressive safety interventions. "Strategists" say progressives must be more authoritarian, even if the evidence shows it has not been a winning strategy for progressives in the past.[13] "Strategists" say progressives must adopt authoritarian narratives and policies, even if victory on those terms creates a fearful electorate and political commitments that render progressive change difficult or impossible even if they prevail. The role of news becomes to report what establishment strategists are saying about vaguely reported feelings, not to help us understand what might create a safer world.

The starting point for understanding an article is to identify its sources. In the *Times* election-night story, we have:

- Political consultant and former adviser to conservative Democrat Joe Lieberman, known for criticizing progressives
- Anonymous "strategists and leaders in both parties"
- Pro-police former mayor (three times)
- Pollster for the former Republican who switched parties to run for Los Angeles mayor and then lost in a landslide (twice)
- A real estate developer, adviser to former Republican mayor, currently a Los Angeles police commissioner
- The pollster for the former Republican (again)
- Pro-police chief of staff to New York mayor Eric Adams
- Anonymous "strategists in both parties"
- Head of a super PAC for House Republicans (twice)
- Pro-police, pro–drug war mayor of San Francisco who was caught lying about seeking to have homeless people removed from nearby her at lunch.
- San Francisco DA
- Jesse Jackson (I know, this is a weird article)
- Anonymous Democratic strategist
- Sean Patrick Maloney (a "law and order" politician who is not an expert in winning 2022 elections, having lost his own)

These sources have political and business interests in promoting the punishment bureaucracy. The article surgically excludes any other perspective, including the many progressive strategists and candidates who won on the opposite message. Many of those people believe, based on evidence, that attacking the root causes of inequality and violence by giving people better housing, schools, care, and working conditions and safe water/food/air is a more popular political strategy for Democrats than authoritarian fearmongering to promote the interests of police unions and real estate developers. Instead of explaining these other perspectives, the *Times* mocks them without describing the substance of their views. The article dismisses them as the "activist left" and the "activist class," and it even gives space to eighty-eight-year-old male former San Francisco mayor Willie Brown to make a joke about a progressive leader, this time about "A.O.S. or A.O.C. or whatever that woman's name is." He was not quoted ironically to show how out of touch powerful people are. It was an attempt to suggest through ridicule that progressive approaches are beyond the pale while the authoritarian perspective is the only position serious people consider, and the one popular with voters.

The article is not an attempt to educate people based on evidence about different potential electoral strategies for Democrats, and it does not feature experts who disagree so that readers can decide what they think is the most well-founded approach for progressives to win elections—or, having won, how different ways of campaigning can shape a political climate in which progressive change can actually be enacted afterward. This highlights something essential about copaganda: it is hard for a consumer of daily news in the U.S. to get an explanation of the views held by critics of the punishment bureaucracy or the evidence supporting those views. As a result, many people have misconceptions about what critics of the bureaucracy believe, what they are proposing, and how effective and popular a lot of those views are.

The paper instead misleads the public with straw-person caricatures of progressive positions. According to the article:

> For Democrats, the issue of crime and disorder threatens to drive a wedge between some of the party's core constituencies, as some voters demand action on racial and systemic disparities while others are focused on their own sense of safety in their homes and neighborhoods.

The implication is that it's an "either/or" situation. Experts and politicians with more progressive views on "racial and systemic disparities" cannot, at the same time, care about "safety in their homes and neighbor-hoods." The election results say that people either want justice *or* safety. And it goes further, implying that the two are conflicting values split-ting the Democratic Party because "voters" cannot be "focused on" the safety of their neighborhood if they also care about systemic injustice.

Does anyone seriously believe that the tens of millions of poor peo-ple, Black people, young people, immigrants, teachers, nurses, public health experts, faith leaders, crime survivors, public interest lawyers, scholars, and so on who have been fighting against systemic injustices and inequality don't care about "safety in their homes and neighbor-hoods"? In fact, researchers showed, for example, that it is exactly the neighborhoods with the most gun violence that most support more pro-gressive prosecutors.[14] But copaganda routinely counterposes progres-sive policies like fairness and justice against safety.

The morning after Larry Krasner won a landslide reelection vic-tory on a progressive platform against his "tough on crime" opponents in Philadelphia, the national media did not have an article ready to go by 5:00 a.m. with anonymous quoted experts and political strategists celebrating a national progressive trend. To be clear, I've been one of the most vocal critics of "progressive prosecutors"; no set of prosecutors has the tools to solve the deep-seated inequality that the punishment bureaucracy both thrives on and preserves. Local prosecutors cannot enact sweeping environmental policy or universal health care or build worker power or fund early childhood education or cancel predatory debt or build more housing. But it is not difficult to observe the differ-ences in how more progressive candidates are covered. By contrast, the recall of DA Chesa Boudin in San Francisco was used in dozens of major outlets to suggest that progressive approaches to safety don't work, are unpopular, and should be abandoned. This is all the more bizarre be-cause "tough on crime" prosecutors do not lower crime, and more right-wing states with harsher sentencing policies have *higher* murder rates.[15] This differential treatment between stories that confirm punishment bureaucracy narratives and those that complicate them is particularly pronounced in news coverage in the context of contested elections.[16]

The other election-night front-page article by the *Times* in its summer 2022 election coverage, titled "6 Takeaways from Tuesday's Elections," was filled with similar misinformation. The paper wrote:

> And in San Francisco, where voters once were moved by Chesa Boudin's plans as district attorney to end cash bail and reduce the number of people sent to prison, they ran out of patience with seemingly unchecked property crime, violent attacks on elderly residents and open drug use.[17]

Property crime was *down* in San Francisco under Boudin, but the election-night article told readers that it was "seemingly unchecked." I don't know what "unchecked" means, and neither does the *Times*. But it sounds scary. Words like "unchecked" are copaganda because they create a sense of vague panic that is hard to combat. The connotation it means to conjure is false; property crime was both lower than in the past and not "unchecked" in that it was still very much prosecuted in San Francisco.

The second article nevertheless had the same message to readers, placed in a large bold font: voters want Democrats to move right on crime.

California called for order.

Wracked by pandemic, littered with tent camps, frightened by smash-and-grab robberies and anti-Asian-American hate crimes, voters in two of the most progressive cities sent a message on Tuesday: Restore stability.

Let's take these claims apart step by step. First, the premise is false. Voters in Los Angeles did *not* send the message the paper is asserting because they *rejected* the candidate that the paper says was for "order."

Second, voters in San Francisco disapproved of many standard "law and order" *policies* in polling even as they recalled the district attorney. Third, other election results in California that were not recall elections were contrary to the San Francisco result, electing candidates who ran on progressive public safety platforms. Fourth, one cannot make a claim about national trends based on one local result while ignoring contrary local results. That makes a mockery of the concept of a trend. The paper's use of the word "California" in the second article is thus fraudulent because, in many of the elections in California, voters sent the *opposite* message. Fifth, what are highly charged words like "littered," "frightened," and "smash and-grab" doing in election coverage? What does it mean to "restore stability?" Is the paper suggesting a return to some prior time in history when things were more "stable" despite reported crime being near historic fifty-year lows? Sixth, whose "stability" is the newspaper invoking?

The *Times*'s election-day spin was part of a pre-planned narrative. Days before the recall vote, another article gave San Francisco's pro-police mayor a platform to claim that her increases to police funding supposedly to crack down on drug addiction and homelessness were borne of a genuine desire to "counter rampant street crimes" attributed to the progressive district attorney, as opposed to, for example, criminalizing homelessness to help the real estate interests who donated to her.[18] In printing her claims about who bore the blame for "rampant street crime" in the city and specifically in the Tenderloin neighborhood, the *Times* did not tell readers that crime was down in San Francisco generally and in the Tenderloin specifically since the district attorney had taken office. (As I explain later, Boudin took office in January 2020. Compared with pre-Boudin numbers from 2019, violent crime in San Francisco was down 19 percent and property crime down 11 percent in 2021, the last full year Boudin was in office.)

Then, setting the tone for its two election-night articles, the pre-election article claimed that the district attorney's "policies have taken much of the blame for what critics say is San Francisco's passive response to rising crime." This sentence belongs on the marble facade of the National Copaganda Museum and Gift Shop. It foists one false premise (crime is rising) on top of another false and incoherent premise (there has been a "passive response"). It does this not by asserting facts, but by quoting "critics" who are "saying" something. The article then declares, obliquely, that progressive policies "have taken the blame." What a house of cards. Crime was not rising under the progressive district attorney, the policies he implemented have been shown in rigorous studies to reduce crime elsewhere, a response to something that was not happening cannot be called "passive," and unnamed policies cannot be anonymously blamed for an occurrence that never occurs.

A sentence like this offers a window into how copagandistic the 2022 election reporting climate became in response to any candidate pushing policies opposed by the punishment bureaucracy. For example, even a news article about the lack of data transparency from local judges, which is a genuine problem the district attorney and others were combatting, became occasions for a local newspaper to muse in a headline, "Think Chesa Boudin Is Letting Criminals Roam Free? You Have No Idea, Because SF's Court Records Are a Mess."[19] Phrasing a headline that way is like asking: "Think the *San Francisco Chronicle* is a CIA front? You have no idea because the CIA won't tell us who its collaborators are."

The pre-election *Times* article nationalized this local propaganda war against progressives. It included a gratuitous joke from Willie Brown, the same former mayor who mocked Representative Alexandria Ocasio-Cortez during the *Times*'s election-night coverage, about the district attorney being so soft on "nonviolent" crime that he wouldn't want to jail Donald Trump for his financial crimes.[20] When it came time to market the article, the reporter shared the article by quoting the former mayor's joke mocking the progressive district attorney for being lenient. The official *New York Times* Twitter account reposted the reporter's quotation of the joke to its tens of millions of followers, with neither the paper nor its reporter informing readers that crime had gone down in San Francisco or that empirical evidence showed the district attorney's policies reduce crime.

Such journalistic malfeasance is unsurprising from this reporter, who previously retweeted a plea on Twitter that "I don't want another story giving NYC crime stats, telling me it's not as bad as 1989."[21] Let that sink in. A reporter is amplifying pleas to news organizations to withhold crime statistics if the data show that crime is—contrary to people's feelings—down, so that people are free to draw authoritarian conclusions based on vibes. Of course, as Noam Chomsky pointed out decades ago, if this reporter were sharing positions that threatened people in power, such violations of journalistic standards would not be tolerated.[22]

News stories in key moments of political contention tend to serve the interests of those who benefit from the punishment bureaucracy. Journalistic practices that would not be tolerated in reporting critical of powerful institutions are weaponized against people who are proposing change. In the period following the 2020 racial justice uprisings and leading up to the 2022 elections, U.S. society exhibited unprecedented energy for challenging mass incarceration. Thousands of local officials, although still in the significant minority nearly everywhere, began at least proposing reduced funding, less discretion and power for police, changed prosecution priorities, greater scrutiny of bloated contracts, fewer military weapons and technology, curbing civil forfeiture, transparency, and accountability for corruption. This occurred while the federal government was allocating hundreds of billions of dollars to local governments for COVID-19 relief. Cities, mostly controlled by Democrats, faced a choice between spending that money on programs like medical care, housing, urban and suburban ecological transformation, and schools, or diverting it to police, prosecutors, and prisons. In addition to reconstituting the mass-incarceration zeitgeist after it came under threat, diverting massive streams of pandemic relief money to the punishment bureaucracy was seen by punishment bureaucrats as one of the primary stakes of defeating people critical of the punishment bureaucracy in the 2022 elections. Indeed, although data on the question of local expenditures is deliberately opaque, investigative journalists were able to uncover that, of the pandemic "rescue" money sent to local governments prior to the 2022 midterm elections, only 10 percent seems to have gone to "public health" and over half—more than $25 billion—appears to have gone to the punishment bureaucracy.[23]

The reporters who wrote these various *Times* election articles—Shane Goldmacher, Alexander Burns, Shawn Hubler, and Jonathan Weisman—bombarded tens of millions of people with the message that political experts agree progressives need to become more authoritarian and invest more in the punishment bureaucracy, a conclusion based on nonexistent patterns in uncounted election "results." In recognition of their achievement, each reporter received a prestigious Academy Award for Copaganda at a small private ceremony that I conducted in my living room in front of an elderly black cat with one tooth.[24]

Targeting Politicians Who Pose a Threat to the Punishment Bureaucracy

Several months after the 2022 primary elections, another group of punishment-bureaucrat unions, profiteers, and right-wing donors launched a campaign to recall District Attorney George Gascón in Los Angeles, attacking him for policies that were not authoritarian enough.

A recall would have been a major boon to police unions, the prosecutor union, the $3.6 billion budget of the Sheriff Department (who wanted to sign lucrative contracts to expand the jail), real estate developers (who wanted to coordinate on harsher prosecution of unhoused people), the for-profit bail bond industry (which saw Los Angeles as its most lucrative U.S. county),[25] and private equity firms investing in surveillance, incarceration, and supervision technology such as GPS electronic monitoring.[26]

With only a few days left to collect signatures, it was uncertain whether the recall campaign would get on the ballot. Enter the *Los Angeles Times*. At this crucial moment, the paper wrote about the murder of an elderly Asian immigrant, which had occurred two months earlier.[27] The paper told the story of the tragedy from the perspective of his daughter, who shared haunting family photos and recounted her father's murder as an example of the American Dream destroyed. The emotional and political conclusion of the story was her plea for the recall of DA George Gascón.

If copaganda were an Italian opera, this article would be one of the last dramatic arias before society's slide into authoritarian dystopia. In a classic example of the Willie Horton effect, the article uses a terrible tragedy to stoke outrage and suggest that replacing the local prosecutor with a more authoritarian one would prevent these kinds of tragedies. This suggestion has no basis in evidence. Nevertheless, the *LA Times* promoted the article about "a Korean man's shocking killing on the streets of LA" through social media posts highlighting its most sensational aspects and purported connection to Gascón's policies:[28]

 **Los Angeles Times** ☑   ...
@latimes

Detectives presented a case for felony assault with a deadly weapon, but prosecutors rejected the filing.

Instead, they passed it on to the city attorney's office for misdemeanor consideration on May 4.

Lee was killed the next day.

A Korean man's shocking killing on streets of L.A. sends his daughter searching for answ...

From latimes.com

3:28 PM · Jun 30, 2022

Like a ventriloquist, the *LA Times* uses a person of color to suggest: if you care about this person of color, his family, and people like them, you should support the recall just like his daughter does.

The article has a number of flaws. First, it admits its own thesis is bogus, acknowledging that nothing would likely have been different under the previous, more authoritarian prosecutor: the assistant prosecutors on the case, who used to work for the harsher predecessor, handled the case in the same manner they would have under their previous boss. And the article cites no evidence to support the assertion that any different policy of the new district attorney would have either caused or prevented this murder, nor does it offer any evidence that tweaks in a local prosecutor's policies *could* cause or prevent racially motivated hate crimes. And there is none. Such hate crimes have little to do with the policies practiced by local prosecutors. Neither the article nor its sources identify *a single policy of the new prosecutor that played any role in the tragic murder.*

When reading an article that criticizes a more progressive approach to the punishment bureaucracy, you should always ask: Is the person being quoted arguing for something different? What, in *specific* terms, is that different thing? Is there any evidence offered to believe that doing this different thing would affect the problem that the person has identified? Much news coverage about public safety is merely vague innuendo that *something*—we are not told what or how—might be better or different or safer about the world if we just did *something else* more punitively.

Second, the article suppresses evidence that supports the policy changes the new prosecutor implemented, like reducing cash bail, charging fewer people with low-level crimes, and reducing prosecution of children as adults. The journalist chose not to report the studies, evidence, or experts explaining that these policies reduce crime and the harmful impact of the punishment bureaucracy.

Instead, the article used a sympathetic victim to present right-wing campaign misinformation that contradicts this evidence. The reporter didn't ask the woman featured in the story to support the factual claims she was making and didn't provide readers the evidence they would need to evaluate them. It merely used her personal pain to make the recall campaign's policy arguments, making it harder for would-be critics to respond without appearing callous.

In doing so, the article omitted an obvious fact: if this prosecutor's policies are supposedly increasing hate crimes, why were reported anti-Asian hate crimes increasing across the country, including in places with harsh prosecutors? In reality, anti-Asian racism and hate crime are the products of broader political, economic, social, and racial factors. And tragically, the article ignores how its proposals for harsher policies would disproportionately incarcerate people of color, including Asian and Pacific Islander (AAPI) immigrants. Nonetheless, it presents as fact the daughter's *opinion* that the Los Angeles prosecutor was at fault for hate crimes, and portrays his status among the daughter and other "hardworking" immigrants as "embattled." This is particularly odd reporting because the district attorney himself is an immigrant, former Republican, and former police officer. (After many decades in the punishment bureaucracy, he adopted slightly more progressive policies to win his election as a reformer in a landslide.)

Third, the article excludes dissenting voices, including from AAPI leaders and experts in Los Angeles, which is troubling because the story claims to be reporting views that represent "L.A.'s diverse Asian and Pacific Islander communities." These dissenting voices could have offered different views about how to reduce anti-Asian racism and hate crimes. For example, the article could have quoted AAPI crime survivors in Los Angeles who are campaigning to address hate crimes with investments in systems of care. Many of those people have challenged the district attorney because he has failed to go far enough in changing his authoritarian predecessor's policies. But editors routinely exclude opponents of the carceral state.

Like so much copaganda claiming to express concern about survivors, the article does a disservice to many of them, especially those working to address the root causes of hate-based violence: white supremacy, inequality, poverty, systemic trauma, profitable hate-spewing algorithms on social media, toxic masculinity, and mental illness. This damage is more severe because the article claims to be a *news* story, not an opinion piece. That gives it the appearance of reporting *objectively* and *comprehensively* about reasonable policies to redress hate crimes.

Finally, in classic copaganda fashion, the reporter disguises the paper's service to authoritarian principles by portraying the daughter as progressive. He quotes her as saying she "supports criminal justice reform" and believes there are "systemic injustices" that "need correcting." The article fails to identify those policies or injustices, and it does not call attention to the contradiction that her support for the recall and its reimposition of old unjust policies would make the problems she mentions worse. In fact, the recall's public relations operatives themselves packaged its campaign as "progressive." To be successful in a city like Los Angeles, they knew that they had to disguise the right-wing forces behind the campaign. So, they presented their plot to restore racist, cruel, and authoritarian policies as one supported by people calling themselves "progressives."[29] As we explore later, the articulation of progressive sentiment while proposing regressive policy is one of the main features of copaganda in the contemporary era.

Manufacturing Confusion About Progressives

Rendering the public unable to distinguish between change and the status quo is one of the main goals of copaganda. In an iconic example of this trickery, New York City mayor Eric Adams, who has an online masters from Copaganda University, announced the appointment of a new NYPD commissioner in front of a mural of mostly Black social movement leaders whom police once tried to (and sometimes did) imprison and kill:[30]

Source: *The Daily Mail*

One of the most interesting features of copaganda is how brutal, senseless things are laundered with progressive language in order to be marketed under a new label. This is what one of my clients once called "covering a turd with M&Ms." This propaganda strategy creates a state of confusion and chaos about who and what to believe and trust that makes the public too disoriented to engage in the informed debate that a tolerant, democratic, participatory society requires.[31]

The prosecutor recall efforts are a case in point. The progressive district attorney in San Francisco was elected at the end of 2019 on a detailed platform, including using diversion (i.e. steering people away from criminal punishment and toward other interventions) more frequently because it can reduce recidivism and other harms; prosecuting police misconduct; and going after corporations for wage theft and consumer violations. Police unions, corporations, and the real estate lobby mobilized against him *before his policies went into effect*, and the campaign was funded in large part by a Republican billionaire. But even though the point of the campaign was to preserve regressive and authoritarian policies, its public relations strategy was to portray itself as "progressive." One of the key players in this charade was a pro-police *San*

Francisco Chronicle journalist who produced a series of significant cop-aganda articles leading up to the campaign. She was later rewarded by being named San Francisco bureau chief of the *New York Times*. In one memorable instance, she called Brooke Jenkins—a Black woman and the media star of the recall campaign who was eventually installed by the mayor to replace Boudin after the right-wing recall—a "progressive prosecutor." It was journalism designed to deceive:[32]

BAY AREA // HEATHER KNIGHT

Why a progressive prosecutor just left D.A. Chesa Boudin's office and joined the recall effort

Jenkins was anything but progressive. She was a former corporate lawyer who had represented big business before she became a prosecutor. While the *Chronicle* was calling her "progressive," she was busy hiring a talent agent and appearing on TV news shows like *Real Time with Bill Maher*, spewing right-wing misinformation.[33] A local news outlet exposed that she committed egregious prosecutorial misconduct while prosecuting poor people. After a scandal in which she tried to violate California law by sending a legally insane person to prison against the wishes of the crime victim's family and medical experts, she resigned from the prosecutor's office before being found by an appeals court to have committed prosecutorial misconduct. In another instance, she publicly admitted to engaging in criminal conduct by illegally sharing confidential information about a teenager. As of late 2024, she still faces numerous pending ethics complaints filed against her by retired judges and prominent law professors. They set forth a litany of violations of her sworn duties, including instances alleging various crimes.[34]

Around the time that the *Chronicle* published the article holding her up as "progressive," she was signaling to police unions and Republican donors (who it turned out were paying her, a fact hidden in disclosures and the subject of one of the ethics complaints) that she supported regressive crime policies.[35] She made clear that she would seek longer prison sentences for the predominantly poor people her office prosecutes, cage more people whose families cannot pay cash bail before trial, use "gang conspiracy" laws to target young people of color and poor people, charge more children as adults, and prosecute more homeless people and people with mental illness. She later received praise from Fox News, Sean Hannity, and other far-right figures.[36] By every metric, she was planning to be not just more regressive than Boudin, but more regressive than previous authoritarian prosecutors in the city. And here's the key: she was being platformed *specifically because she portended regressive actions*. She would not have been newsworthy otherwise. Words have lost all meaning when *Brooke Jenkins* is called "progressive."

But it was precisely this label that the *Chronicle* chose for its headline, not as something up for dispute but as a *fact*. The journalist could easily have told Jenkins's story with the headline "Why This Prosecutor Just Left D.A. Chesa Boudin's Office and Joined the Recall." When you realize that adding the word "progressive" was unnecessary, you see that the point was to *mislead people* about how to interpret Jenkins's political intervention. It is designed to get readers to exclaim: "Oh, wow, even a progressive Black woman now opposes the DA!" *That* framing gives people who don't know much about prosecutorial policy and the punishment bureaucracy the rationale to support the recall campaign while still believing themselves to have progressive values. This is an important copaganda tactic in disorienting and winning over the large block of well-meaning people who may not know a lot about the details but who want to support changes to things that are ineffective and unjust.

The political class in San Francisco engaged in a similar campaign for Matt Dorsey, the former head of public relations at the San Francisco Police Department. I noted earlier that Dorsey was caught sending scandalous texts to journalists encouraging copaganda. Shortly after the mayor appointed him to a vacant seat on the Board of Supervisors (without an election, as with Jenkins), a prominent Democratic Party political organization called him a "progressive activist."[37] His paid job had been to manipulate public perception of police to expand the war on drugs, increase surveillance, and minimize accountability for police violence, and he was now installed into the city's governing body as a "progressive."

After both Jenkins and Dorsey were in office, they spearheaded a reinvestment in the war on drugs in San Francisco. The city shut down a treatment center and saw huge increases in overdoses, and the Board of Supervisors approved new spending on incarceration and cops. The jail population rose over 30 percent after Jenkins's first thirteen months in office. In her first year, she dismissed every single prosecution begun by Boudin of a shooting by a police officer, and also began blocking future investigations.[38] At the same time, violent crime went up.[39] But there was a dearth of news stories blaming the rise in violence on the district attorney and the increased investment in punishment.

When it comes to designing the special copaganda recipe of authoritarian policy cake with progressive icing on top, San Francisco is a Michelin-star chef. But it is far from alone. One of my all-time favorite examples is when the *Detroit Free Press* profiled a Black woman assistant Detroit prosecutor.[40] In the article, the prosecutor claims that Angela Davis—the Black radical and one of the recognized founders of the modern prison-abolition movement—inspired her to become a *prosecutor.* The article goes on to portray the prosecutor as a racial justice activist, whose mass human-caging policies are so benevolent that even the parents of children she sends to prison thank her for convicting their children because prison saves lives. Ignoring rampant police brutality in Detroit, she told the newspaper, which did not correct her statement, that "the type of police brutality that we have seen in other places has not been tolerated in Wayne County."

Finding and profiling Black women prosecutors and portraying them as progressives in the tradition of Angela Davis is copaganda. It allows punishment bureaucrats to rebrand toxic policies with organic artisan labels.

Copaganda that portrays authoritarian policies as "progressive" invokes George Orwell's "Ministry of Truth." The function is to disorient people who think of themselves as wanting a more equal and just world so that they support a wretched status quo. Oil companies paint their websites green; the bail industry calls cash bail a "civil rights issue" because it supports small, Black-owned bail-bond businesses; real estate developers that demolish homes talk about "building community with our neighbors"; corporate landlords frame eviction moratoriums during a global pandemic as hurting "immigrant landlords of color."[41] Up is down, left is right. Prison abolition is the same thing as sending more people to prison. Only by confusing a lot of people can a small group of people get enough support for policies that destroy our connection to each other and our natural world while not making us safer.

We must develop defense mechanisms against these attempts to befuddle us. When evaluating what a punishment bureaucrat says, pay less attention to labels they use for themselves or to labels the news puts on them. Ask yourself: How have they chosen to spend their life's work? Who is funding them? Who do they associate with in their social circles? Who are they accountable to, powerful or working-class people? Do their proposals give more money and power to the punishment bureaucracy or to themselves? Have they been fighting for the most vulnerable people in our society or exploiting them?

Editorials Against Change

Opinion writing plays an important copaganda role at key political moments by reinforcing pro-punishment perspectives as conventional wisdom. Let's look at how some of the same progressive challenges to the punishment bureaucracy were covered in editorials as opposed to news reporting.

The Washington Post

Several days after the 2022 primary elections, the *Washington Post* editorial board covered the San Francisco recall election.[42] The *Post's* editorial copaganda is similar to the efforts I have tracked across the country against officials who propose reducing the power of the punishment bureaucracy.[43]

The editorial is entitled: "The San Francisco District Attorney Saga Set Back Criminal Justice Reform." Like the *Times* election-night stories, the *Post* attempts to use the San Francisco recall to create a consensus that "criminal justice reform" has gone too far. But the *Post* editorial board takes spreading misinformation to the extreme.

The thesis is that the progressive district attorney didn't serve the public "carefully" and that, therefore, his "tenure served to discredit . . . more effective and humane approaches to public safety." This is a bold claim: that "humane" and "effective" approaches were "discredited." We would be in trouble as a civilization if treating people humanely had been discredited!

Nearly every factual assertion in the *Post* editorial either lacks a citation to support it or links to a citation that doesn't support the assertion. The leading claim that Boudin didn't give "attention to people's safety and quality of life" is striking for three reasons. First, at the time the article was written in mid-2022, total property crime (down 19.4 percent) and total violent crime (down 21.4 percent) had decreased under Boudin compared to before he took office at the beginning of 2020.[44] Second, as noted earlier, Boudin's major policy changes were popular, not discredited. His *personal* popularity did decrease after Republican billionaires and police unions spent $6 million on personal attacks, and the media spewed out a wave of misinformation.[45] But his popular policies reduced local incarceration, released wrongfully convicted people, saved tens of millions of dollars for families, saved a lot of children from adult prosecution, prosecuted more police misconduct, and pursued major wage theft and consumer protection cases. Third, as noted earlier, the scholarly evidence backs these progressive policies.

So, how does the *Post* support its thesis that the person implementing more humane and evidence-based policies had "discredited" those popular policies? Let's dismantle the charges line by line because they are revealing and somewhat funny.

"Mr. Boudin failed to address the fentanyl trade in his city." First, the article omits that Boudin proposed a multi-agency fentanyl task force that would have included prosecutors and public health officials. But the mayor refused to fund it. The omission of that fact invalidates the *Post*'s charge. Second, and more importantly, the editorial board suggests a lone prosecutor could fix the opioid epidemic. It omits that other, non-progressive prosecutors had likewise not ended the fentanyl trade with more authoritarian policies. As always with copaganda, pay attention to whether the news identifies a *different* policy that *could* have been implemented. The *Post* does not offer any suggestions. Third, if the answer to addiction were more prosecution and prison—as it seems the *Post* is implying—then that means every prosecutor for the last fifty years failed.[46] Despite spending trillions on policing and punishment of drugs, overdoses are higher than ever, and dangerous drugs are more available than ever. The editorial board omits the consensus among public health experts that the government can't reduce drug abuse through criminal punishment.

"Burglaries climbed 45 percent during his tenure." This is a good old-fashioned lie. I rarely discuss lies because I focus on more sophisticated copaganda, which is more effective than obvious falsehoods. But, as the data reporter for the *San Francisco Chronicle* reported using actual information, burglaries were at "their pre-pandemic rates" (i.e., the same as the period before Boudin took office).[47] So, how did the *Post* come up with the figure of burglaries going up by 45 percent? It cited another *Post* opinion piece from the day after the election that made the same claim with no support.[48] This self-referential loop is the kind of Trumpian performance art that one finds in major news editorials when it comes time to discredit critics of the punishment bureaucracy. As

Hannah Arendt said in her last public interview, "If everybody always lies to you, the consequence is not that you believe the lies, but rather that nobody believes anything any longer."[49]

"Businesses closed rather than face petty crime." The editorial board appears to have fallen for a right-wing conspiracy theory promoted by recall campaign election ads. Although its citation for the business-closure claim was a May 2021 *Yahoo!* article, the claims were later debunked.[50] In the most prominent example of these false viral election ads funded by right-wing dark money, a local businessowner claiming to have closed his store because of Boudin had actually shut it down in 2019, before Boudin was either elected or took office.[51]

"Mr. Boudin oversaw an exodus of prosecutors from his office, some of whom left because they say they were pressured to relax charges on major crimes." This assertion is, to use a technical term from propaganda analysis, gobbledygook. First, offices see staff turnover when a new elected official with a different political vision takes over, whether conservative or progressive. Second, the *Post* doesn't explain its terms—"exodus" or "pressured"—and neither of them is supported by evidence. One of Boudin's campaign promises was to reduce unnecessary severity in sentencing and to end the use of certain racially biased sentencing enhancements. The single citation for the article's claim is not firsthand accounts from anyone with knowledge of the issue, but an *opinion* essay by Nellie Bowles, an heiress from one of the wealthiest families in California history, which, as I show later, is riddled with false claims and embarrassing errors.[52] Although the *Post* does not state why it links to this piece to support *this* factual claim, it appears to be referencing Bowles's anecdote about a single prosecutor, Brooke Jenkins, leaving the office. Remember, Jenkins resigned after Boudin refused to let her violate ethical rules in a case where she was later found to have violated the law. She went on to be a paid operative for the recall campaign, without disclosing it. This would be like me claiming that the *Washington Post* is widely considered the worst news publication in the world and supporting that assertion by linking to a blog post where someone explained that they had heard someone talk about a bad editorial the *Washington Post* published.

"San Francisco writer Nellie Bowles in a Wednesday article in the Atlantic [said] 'the D.A. said from the beginning that he would not prioritize the prosecution of lower-level offenses.' " The board's final reason for its thesis about "humane" and "effective" policies being "discredited" is that a random wealthy writer with no expertise on these issues *said* something in *The Atlantic*. But all prosecutors in the U.S. claim to "prioritize" the most serious cases. That's what everyone *wants* them to do. Imagine what would have happened if Boudin had said that he was going to prioritize the *least important crimes*? And Boudin's policy of not prioritizing some low-level offenses has been shown to *reduce* crime, as the *Post*'s own reporters previously reported.[53]

Overall, the editorial board is vaguely suggesting that expanding prison and prosecution is the way to solve drug abuse, homelessness, and petty crime without coming out and making that claim so explicitly that it could be accused of doing so or forced to back it up with evidence. This is like pretending to care about climate change while backing more fossil fuel extraction without noting the evidence linking the two. And the *Post* portrays brutal, discredited policy as enlightened, beginning by listing the progressive things it supports in *theory*:

> Those suffering from drug addiction should be treated rather than incarcerated first. Early mistakes should not ruin the rest of a person's life. Fewer human beings should be warehoused uselessly in prisons on sentences that are too steep for their crimes. Police should no longer be the nation's default front-line mental health responders. De-escalation should be every officer's routine first response. Authorities should not use efforts to police petty crime and quality-of-life matters as cover to harass minority Americans. There would be less crime if

the government better addressed root causes—poverty, poor civic services, substandard education and a lack of decent, affordable housing.

This is a common move by elites who want readers to support something terrible: they tell us up front they share our desire for equality and human flourishing. This is the moment M&Ms are placed delicately with tweezers onto the turd.

As the editorial board was assuring us what it likes in theory, it was common knowledge that the mayor, Republicans, police unions, bail companies, and profiteers behind the recall would pursue policies that frustrate each of those progressive values. Many more people would be jailed for mental illness, drug addiction, and being unhoused—which would do nothing for public safety. Then, as we saw with recall activists in California and the Harvard professors claiming to be progressive socialists, the *Post* assures us that it cares:

> As longtime advocates for criminal justice reform, we are as frustrated as anyone at the seemingly slow pace of change in the face of police misconduct, racial disparities in the justice system and worsening mental health and addiction crises that call for innovative public safety solutions.

I cannot stress enough how important this tactic is for contemporary copaganda. Before promoting something with indefensible and authoritarian consequences, pundits preface it with, "Look, what I'm saying can't be bad because I'm a well-meaning person and I care about making things better too." Everyone knows these policies wouldn't be supported if they were portrayed with clarity for what they are: expansions of a profitable status quo. Pundits and institutions portray themselves as progressive while cynically opposing *every attempt* to implement progressive policies in *practice*. It's like when someone says every time you meet them at a dinner party that they'd love to hang out with you, but it turns out that they pretend to be busy every time you propose concrete plans.

The Houston Chronicle

The editorial board of the *Houston Chronicle* took copaganda to another level during the 2022 elections. In a bewildering piece, it endorsed a far-right Republican candidate for Harris County judge, the county's highest elected position, against the progressive Democratic incumbent.[54] The election was one of the most significant local government elections in the U.S., as the office wields unique power over executive and legislative affairs across the third largest county in the country.[55]

In its editorial, the board agrees with the progressive candidate on virtually every issue, and throughout the article it lays out the case for rejecting the far-right candidate:

> We have always appreciated the dynamic mix of wonkishness and progressive optimism of Harris county's first Latina [executive]. She's an inspiration to many and, if given the choice, we'd rather live in Hidalgo's vision of Harris County, where government is inclusive, transparent and ethical, policy isn't tainted by politics, the air is cleaner, the streets are safer, more children can attend pre-K, and climate change is treated with the urgency it deserves.

The piece also conveys how troubled the *Chronicle*'s board is by the far-right candidate's policies, including the defunding of early childhood education (the board singles out for criticism her proposal to defund early childhood education in order to hire a thousand new cops), ignoring preventable environmental pollution catastrophes near Houston, rolling back reproductive rights, denying equality for LGBTQ people, and blocking gun control. The piece also notes that the far-right candidate lied in campaign ads, and that her campaign's website featured statements of support from fascists.

The editorial board then goes on to override its own values, arguments, and evidence to endorse the far-right candidate. It cites concerns about "crime," even though the board's chosen candidate has never worked on crime issues, holds positions on crime that the board opposes, and lacks, in its words, "experience in government." In defense of its choice, the board cites the views of a crime victim's family member:

> "If I have cancer and I've been stabbed and I'm overweight, I'm going to handle those in a certain order," he said.
> He's right. Some call it triage. . . . Harris County must treat the stab wound: the murders and violent crimes being committed by repeat, violent offenders who are enabled by an underfunded criminal justice system that's paralyzed by severe backlogs.

The editorial is a smorgasbord of copaganda—a kind of incomprehensible manifesto of journalistic mediocrity and cowardice in the face of authoritarianism. Let's start with a remarkable aspect: the board endorses the candidate it disagrees with on almost every issue because of fears about "crime," even though the editorial admits that statistics show crime is *down* in Harris County.

But reason, evidence, and civics are secondary to anecdotes about "feelings" on crime. In a cavalier dismissal of evidence, the editorial weaponizes the person it found whose family member was a victim of crime, stating: "Statistics, of course, mean little to those such as Paul Castro." This is like saying it felt colder one day last week to someone the board spoke to, so statistics on global temperature increases don't matter. The board continues with the observation that "the seemingly infinite ticker tape of suspect mug shots on the 10 o'clock news has us looking over our shoulders and praying."

Having established that data doesn't matter, and that everyone is afraid because of incessant media stories about crime, the paper zeros in on the reason for its endorsement, which is the far-right candidate's supposed compassion for crime survivors. It explains that "her heart for victims and their families will guide her budgeting priorities." Based on this vague sentiment, the board hopes that she will address the *one* specific problem it identifies: a court backlog. It is *this* issue on which the endorsement hinges. Indeed, there was a yearslong backlog of cases in Harris County, but the elected office that was the subject of the endorsement is *not responsible for the court backlog.* To the contrary, police, prosecutors, and judges have control over the backlog, and they refused to implement independent recommendations for clearing it that were commissioned by the county government because those punishment bureaucrats sought to use the backlog as pretext to obtain more money.

The *Chronicle* then claims that the court backlog is responsible for increasing people's fear of crime, even as it acknowledges that actual crime is going down (violent crime was down about 10 percent in Houston in 2022).[56] The editors merely go on to assure readers that pre-K programs "aren't essential," so it's not that bad that the Republican they are endorsing to clear the court backlog wants to cut early childhood education to hire more cops, even though such programs are one of the most proven strategies to reduce crime.[57] (The board doesn't explain how the Republican candidate's planned expansion of police, which would increase the number of low-level arrests, would not *exacerbate* the court backlog.)

Finally, the editorial states that it would be a "deal breaker" if the far-right candidate tried to reinstate the old misdemeanor cash-bail system (which my organization's civil rights litigation showed to be unconstitutional, bad for public safety, and terrible for the local economy), even though this is exactly what the candidate promised to do.[58] (It was a particularly silly campaign position because a federal court order in our case required changes to the bail system that the politician could not change.)

It is alarming to see a newspaper reject evidence and reason so openly. It is the editorial coda to a symphony of coverage whose movements are performed by news article after news article covering anecdotal crimes. In this collective mystification, the social brain shrivels on the drug of fear. The editorial board concludes that, while we all might want a better world, our only option is to promote authoritarianism. The conclusion is based on a nihilistic rejection of logic and evidence. It is the human spirit fully surrendered to copaganda.

After hard work by a lot of dedicated advocates, the far-right candidate lost the election.

Thoughtless Think Pieces

As these editorials popped up in the 2022 election cycle, fancy magazines ran opinion pieces criticizing would-be reformers. In particular, they attacked so-called progressive prosecutors, claiming that attempts to shrink the punishment bureaucracy were destroying our society. Here are a few examples about San Francisco:[59]

THE POLITICAL SCENE

WHY SAN FRANCISCO FIRED CHESA BOUDIN

Does the district attorney's recall reveal the limitations of progressive criminal-justice reform?

 By Benjamin Wallace-Wells
June 8, 2022

IDEAS

The People vs. Chesa Boudin

San Franciscans do not feel safe and secure.

By Annie Lowrey

Newsletters   *The Atlantic*

IDEAS

HOW SAN FRANCISCO BECAME A FAILED CITY

And how it could recover

By Nellie Bowles
Photographs by Austin Leong

Like a lot of writing about crime in liberal magazines, the articles use flowery writing as an aesthetic façade to mask a lack of intellectual rigor. Each of these "think pieces" has the same problematic features as the election cycle's news coverage: misleading assertions, one-sided sourcing, misrepresentation of empirical evidence and law, and omission of necessary context. But the think pieces share one special fraudulent theme: Various progressive ideas and tweaks in punishment policy have made San Francisco a "failed city"—as demonstrated by "disorder," homelessness, tents, filthiness, mentally ill people in the streets, low-level theft, and open-air drug use.

Several of the articles express a facade of compassion for drug users and homeless people. For example, *The Atlantic* laments:

A couple years ago, one of my friends saw a man staggering down the street, bleeding. She recognized him as someone who regularly slept outside in the neighborhood, and called

911. Paramedics and police arrived and began treating him, but members of a homeless advocacy group noticed and intervened. They told the man that he didn't have to get into the ambulance, that he had the right to refuse treatment. So that's what he did. The paramedics left; the activists left. The man sat on the sidewalk alone, still bleeding. A few months later, he died about a block away.

The writer relies on anonymous sourcing for a dubious anecdote to support a claim that progressive policies have been a holistic failure in U.S. society. Notice how she insinuates that progressive policies with "the very best of intentions" are "cruel" because it was *their* fault that this homeless person died:

> Petty crime was rampant. I used to tell myself that San Francisco's politics were wacky but the city was trying—really trying—to be good. But the reality is that with the smartest minds and so much money and the very best of intentions, San Francisco became a cruel city. It became so dogmatically progressive that maintaining the purity of the politics required accepting—or at least ignoring—devastating results.

There are several problems here. First, these claims have nothing to do with reality. The premise that major cities have *actually implemented* "dogmatically" progressive social and economic policies on crime, punishment, and public safety is false. San Francisco did nothing of the sort. Its urban planning policy remained in the control of real estate developers, tech industry billionaires, the political establishment they bankroll, and the punishment bureaucracy that protects them. It is ludicrous to claim that progressives with the "smartest minds" and "best intentions" have been in control of policing, incarceration, housing, and economic or social policy there. The city never abandoned mass incarceration, ended the war on drugs, addressed racial disparities, provided universal health care, reinvested in mental health care, created sufficient affordable housing, or mitigated widening economic inequality.

Instead, the overlapping constellation of state police, federal agents, sheriffs, local cops, and privately deputized security have grown enormously during the period *The Atlantic* is discussing. At all times, the city has been subject to the same California and federal criminal laws as every other city, which are separately enforced by a range of federal and state agencies. So, it is incorrect to imply that abolitionists and socialists took over San Francisco and implemented their program. And, since that has not happened, there is no basis for the claim that the radical left program has failed and is responsible for the city's condition. The "cruelty" of a person dying on the street has *nothing* to do with the "purity" of "progressive" rule under any conceivable understanding of recent San Francisco political history.

What *was* occurring under the new district attorney was a modest but meaningful reduction in the severity and reach of the local incarceration system. He couldn't implement reforms that would bring the city in line with practices in other liberal democracies, but he began to point the city back toward where the U.S. was prior to its fifty-year period of mass incarceration. For example, at the start of the COVID-19 pandemic, when jails threatened to become sites of incubation for the coronavirus, local officials reduced the jail population by about 50 percent. Fewer children were being prosecuted, bail industry profits were down, more police officers were being prosecuted, fewer people were being sent to state prison, more cases were being rejected because of improper police behavior, several more companies were being investigated for violations that hurt workers, and more old cases of people in prison were being reexamined for errors. In the culture and economics of the local punishment bureaucracy, these were just nascent seedlings of change.

Second, many of the think pieces before the recall election portray San Francisco as some sort of criminal dystopia. In fact, San Francisco is one of the safest big cities by police metrics. At the time, crime was *decreasing* according to traditional metrics. Property and violent crime went *down* under the new district attorney. As public defender Peter Calloway explained using police data:

> Rape, robbery, and assault *decreased* by 47% (-191), 27% (-851), and 6% (-160). So, violent crime (which the SFPD categorizes as homicide, rape, robbery, and assault) decreased by 19% (-1187). Property crime . . . is down by 11% (-6083).[60]

The articles maneuver around these facts with the skill of Olympic breakdancers. Like many of the news articles about the 2022 election, they both assert and manufacture a general feeling of "disorder." And so, despite the facts, a record number of people *believed* crime was increasing prior to the 2022 election.[61]

Third, the think pieces all make a similar move: each article's central theme is that the removal of the "progressive" prosecutor is a *natural* response to inequality, homelessness, drug abuse, and mental illness. They all imply that the blame for those social and economic issues lies with the prosecutor for not punishing people enough. None of the articles explains how this could be. None explains which specific *prosecutorial* policies are responsible for specific harms. Which policy increased homelessness? Which policy caused the fentanyl epidemic? Which policy caused mental illness to spiral in public? Which prosecutor policy would fix them, based on what evidence?

At a time of historically low crime, the news was blaming anecdotal manifestations of the city's growing inequality and lack of public health infrastructure on a prosecutor with almost no power to affect the root causes of crime one way or another. This is like blaming an earthquake on a group of schoolchildren jumping up and down too much after there having not been an earthquake.

Notably, none of the think pieces contains a statement of what the authors are specifically advocating. Life in prison for drugs? A mandatory ten-year sentence for a homeless person for sleeping in public?

Detention camps and involuntary electroshock for the mentally ill? Caging more people who can't afford to pay cash bail? Prosecuting all children as adults? Detaining children in places where they will continue to be sexually abused? Whipping people in the public square if they urinate because they couldn't find a public bathroom? Because none of the think pieces contains *analysis of concrete policies*, one question becomes unavoidable for the copaganda aficionado: Why are none of these smart people discussing the actual policies at stake in the recall? They all know what the right-wing proponents want: more criminal prosecution (except for police who kill people, who will never be prosecuted); more prison for poor people (but not for company executives under investigation by Boudin's worker protection unit); and more profits for consultants with punishment bureaucracy contracts. They all know that the consequence of a recall will be jailing more poor people and separating more poor families. But none of them mention these consequences to their liberal readers. They do not come out and say that they are advocating for more imprisonment or that such a policy will have disparate consequences.

Why? I think there are two main reasons. First, these pundits know that a new pro-punishment prosecutor won't solve the problems. Little policy tweaks of the kind a prosecutor has power over are not that consequential a factor in huge social phenomena such as the extent to which people harm each other and the extent to which people are seen suffering in public. A new pro-punishment prosecutor would not solve these problems, just as the progressive one didn't create them. Indeed, police-recorded crime and overdoses got *worse* after the recall. No one could pen a coherent article that links the prosecutorial policies at stake in the San Francisco recall to creating a safer society.

So, one consistent theme of this book is that many people writing for elite publications do not want to talk about safety if it means discussing the social changes necessary to address the root causes of interpersonal harm. Solving these problems is not what such punditry seeks. This probably explains why typical standards for journalistic ethics—fact-checking, a pretense of neutrality, knowledge of the subject matter, respect for evidence, the inclusion of contrary perspectives—are dispensed with. Creating a shroud of innuendo around a poorly curated anecdote is the only way to blame San Francisco's material problems on a recently elected prosecutor.

Second, these writers know that—at least in their current political environment—they could not pass themselves off as liberals at dinner parties and write for fancy publications if they openly stated their support for more authoritarian policies, such as disbanding prosecutorial units that find wrongful convictions and illegal sentences; caging people for being homeless, being mentally ill, or using drugs; closing cases against police and corporate offenders; expanding indefinite detention of children; increasing racial disparities; and enlarging the number of people detained solely because they cannot pay cash. That's what *right-wingers* want, and they are supposed to (pretend to) disagree with those people. That's the discredited position Hillary Clinton took against "super predators" in 1996. They can't say *those* things *openly* anymore, largely because social movements made them unacceptable in public debate. So, they must obfuscate. They lament "disorder," blow the dog whistles, and attack reformer after reformer seriatim without stating out loud the consequence of this whack-a-mole strategy: no one ever changes what the punishment bureaucracy does. The function of "think pieces" like this is to achieve the same outcomes without saying the quiet part out loud.

These articles are copaganda catnip for liberals. They sedate readers with the illusion that they can be progressives while opposing the people who would implement progressive policies in practice. Elite magazines and newspapers commission and publish these pieces during election season to corral people otherwise attracted to more progressive positions back into the carceral status quo. They trick them into thinking their communities' problems don't have root causes that need social and economic investment, but are instead problems that can be solved by slightly tweaking punishment policy and giving more money to the bureaucrats who enforce it.

The fancy think piece, then, is perhaps more like fentanyl than catnip. It's like pumping a drug into the veins of liberals to give them the momentary bliss of thinking that we don't need structural changes to make our society more equal. Consuming stuff like this is killing us fast, and it's often laced with fake ingredients.

11

What We Don't Know
Can Hurt Us

A really efficient totalitarian state would be one in which the all-powerful executive of political bosses and their army of managers control a population of slaves who do not have to be coerced, because they love their servitude. To make them love it is the task assigned.

-Aldous Huxley[1]

In September 2022, as Congress debated police reform, the *New York Times* dropped a bombshell. Buried in an article about "drama" between Democrats over whether to authorize more funding for militarized police, the paper told millions of readers that "civil rights groups including the NAACP" were "pressing" for more police funding:

> Civil rights groups including the N.A.A.C.P. are also pressing for passage of the legislation, making the case that additional police funding should be paired with accountability measures.[2]

This statement is false. Let's unpack how and why misinformation like this routinely characterizes reporting on efforts to curb the size and power of the punishment bureaucracy.

First, neither the NAACP nor any "civil rights group" of which I am aware supported the police-funding bills, and none was "pressing" to pass them. The letter from civil rights groups (which the organization I founded, Civil Rights Corps, was involved with drafting) that the article quotes in the next paragraph to support its assertion says *nothing* of the kind. The letter says the opposite: it calls for investments in non-police alternatives to public safety instead of more funding for police.[3] The letter said, repeatedly: "We request that the House not advance these bills" and "we stand together to urge the House of Representatives not to advance" the legislation. The error is glaring in the context of our letter, which *criticizes* the police-funding bills and promotes *different* legislation to increase investments in public safety programs that *aren't* police-based.

Second, can you imagine how big this revelation would be if it were true? The paper is telling millions of liberal readers that the "civil rights" community, including the most famous Black civil rights group in the U.S., now supports more militarized police funding. A reader may reasonably think: "If the *civil rights groups* want more police funding, who could possibly oppose it?" That impression helps punishment bureaucrats marginalize the view that the U.S. spends too much on an ineffective and violent militarized bureaucracy.

Third, the misinformation in the article is elaborate. The paper bolsters the core falsity with the claim that the Congressional Black Caucus "pressed successfully for the package to include measures to strengthen accountability for police misconduct." On that basis, it asserts that civil rights organizations are also "pressing" to pass the legislation because it is "paired with accountability." This is nonsense. The text of the bills did not include anything that could be characterized as "accountability" measures. The article does not explain what it means by that term. But the reader, without being able to mention let alone evaluate a single example of an "accountability" measure, may now infect others with whom they converse with the idea that new "accountability" policies were proposed. After all, they read in the *New York Times* that this was the reason people who care about civil rights wanted expanded police funding to pass.

Fourth, the paper uses the phrase "civil right groups" to suggest that the entire civil rights community supported more police funding.

Even if the NAACP did support more police funding, which the letter in the reporter's possession made clear it did not, nowhere are the many organizations that opposed more funding for police, prosecutors, and prisons acknowledged. The coverage makes no attempt to educate readers about why experts, survivors of violence, and millions of people oppose more surveillance, armed police, and incarceration—or even the fact that they oppose those things.

So, how did this happen? It likely stems from the fact that there were *other* pending bills that civil rights groups *did* support. Those other bills included the Mental Health Justice Act, which proposed more non-carceral responses to people suffering mental health crises, and the Break the Cycle of Violence Act, which proposed non-police methods to handle community violence.[4] The Democratic leadership had strategically packaged these bills that the civil rights community supported with controversial bills that increase militarized police funding, which the civil rights community opposed. As for how the *Times* article came together, the most charitable scenario I can speculate is that none of the three reporters credited as having contributed to the story nor any of their editors had sufficient background knowledge, critical thinking habits, or contacts in the civil rights community to know the difference, and that none of them bothered to make a phone call before publishing a story on what would be a major pro-police shift in the civil rights community.

Together, these reporting blunders represent a systemic flaw in news coverage of public safety. It stems directly from the ideological and economic incentives of corporate-owned news—which affect everything from who works at the outlets to what stories are told—and the endemic problem of journalists misrepresenting the views of people who seek to reduce the size, power, and profit of the punishment bureaucracy. There is a persistent lack of interest in deeply understanding the issues, lack of skepticism of government sources, lack of pressure to be thorough, and lack of time spent cultivating connections to sources critical of the status quo. Because the *Times* excludes sources who could explain what is important and what is not, it focuses on a supposed "drama" among Democrats about vague "accountability" measures rather than the deeper point: a debate about unexplained measures masks the fact that most Democrats were not proposing consequential reforms. To the contrary, several powerful Democrats, including President Biden, were trying to quietly provide funding for 100,000 more police. Democratic leaders were using rhetoric about "accountability" to obscure what most of them agreed on: more policing. *That's* what the civil rights groups opposed. But what is treated as "news" is not the vital concern raised by the civil rights groups of whether our society should make the biggest investment in militarized policing in a generation, but a manufactured horse race between "progressives" and "moderates" within the Democratic Party fighting about something meaningless that is never explained. The mere illusion of fighting over "accountability" measures thus serves as diversion for the larger project of dramatically expanding policing.

This framing—that politicians are fighting without telling people exactly what they are fighting about—is an important form of copaganda. Countless stories report political conflicts without explaining the differences between the various positions or the reasons for those positions—or, importantly, that many of the positions are often quite similar. Those omissions prevent the public from learning about the substance of the views of people challenging the way things are. Manufactured ignorance enables the punishment bureaucrats to maintain, and even expand, destructive policies.

The article made several other omissions that exemplify the worst aspects of how copaganda makes people ignorant. First, it omits information that a reasonable reader would need to understand the debate. The article caricatures the "progressive" position as leaving Democrats "without an answer" to Republican attacks that they are "soft on crime." The only way to make this claim is by ignoring the answers progressives are proposing, *including the other bills pending before the House.* By omitting progressive policies from the article, the *Times* can portray progressives as without any ideas at all on crime and safety:

House Speaker Nancy Pelosi has pledged for weeks to bring up a package of bills that would provide funding for hiring more police officers, increasing salaries, investing in officer safety and training and body cameras, as well as mental health resources for officers.

But the measures . . . have become mired in a yearslong internal feud about the politics of crime, leaving the party without an answer to Republican attacks and some of its members livid.

The omission suggesting progressives have no "answers" is especially harmful because it validates the long-standing narrative that they are "soft on crime." Progressives have a lot of proposals for improving safety, and those ideas are detailed and well supported, but the relentless refrain in the news is that progressives don't care about the issue and have therefore not developed specific policy proposals that would make people safer.

Second, the article tells readers that bills funding police have support from progressives because they include "accountability" measures that are neither identified nor explained. This is false. When police violence reemerges as a sustained news theme every few years, the words "accountability" and "transparency" are sprinkled into story after story and used as a substitute for informed discussion about the terrible track record of *specific* policies and broader discussions about how and whether it's even possible to make armed police forces less violent and corrupt as they are currently constituted. After vague calls for "accountability" in 2020, police killed more people in 2021 than in 2020. Then police killed even more people than that in 2022. And even more people than that in 2023, and even more in 2024.[5] To my knowledge, there has not been a specific "accountability measure" implemented in contemporary U.S. history that has made U.S. police meaningfully less violent and more responsive to democratic oversight. Readers are nonetheless given the impression that there are good "accountability" measures written into a pending federal bill and that conscientious congresspersons are tirelessly pushing for them. So, there's no reason to worry about more funding for a bloated bureaucracy because it will be "paired" with "accountability" measures.

Third, the article quotes a former CIA employee and sitting U.S. representative falsely claiming that she isn't aware of evidence-based objections to her police-funding bill. She refers to any opposition to billions of dollars on more militarized cops as "generalized excuses" that amount to nothing more than opposing policy based on random weather events:

> "I haven't heard a whole host of reasons for people wanting to excuse inaction," said Representative Abigail Spanberger . . . who is in a difficult re-election race in a competitive district . . . and is a lead proponent of the legislation. "The sort of generalized excuses—I've heard it a lot. Tomorrow it will be, 'It's raining.'"

Publishing this quote while omitting the context that would enable readers to evaluate its falsity makes a mockery of journalism. The article chose not to quote civil rights leaders and scholars explaining the reasons they oppose her bill. This is like publishing an article on global warming that doesn't quote any climate scientists, argues that the solution to global warming is more coal mines, and quotes West Virginia senator and coal-industry tycoon Joe Manchin saying he's never heard any reason to oppose fossil fuels.

Fourth, the assertion that more funding for cops is necessary for Democrats to win reelection is unchallenged. Eric Adams, the poster politician for "tough on crime" policy—portrayed by the national press in the 2022 election cycle as some sort of crusading visionary for other Democrats to emulate—was wildly unpopular in New York when the article was written. According to a *Times* poll taken around that time, he had a 29 percent approval rating, with only 21 percent of respondents saying he was doing a good job on "fighting crime."[6]

Fifth, the article also omits the harm done by increased police funding. For instance, amid widespread criminalization of abortion, Spanberger's proposal to dramatically expand police threatened to surveil, arrest, and jail more people seeking reproductive care and their medical providers. As demonstrated by the Republicans' targeting of funding for the IRS to reduce enforcement of the tax code, the level of enforcement for something across society is not fixed. This principle applies to the number of police and level of technology targeting abortion care. Laws become real in their enforcement—and many people in Democratic circles were talking about sending more police to right-wing states at the same time those states were criminalizing reproductive health care. The *Times* made an editorial choice to omit the potential impact on abortion enforcement and other examples of the known, immediate consequences of Spanberger's police funding. As the electorate—and liberal *Times* readers—supported measure after measure to protect abortion rights across the U.S., imagine how differently it would have responded to calls for expanding the punishment bureaucracy in 2022 if the news told them it would empower police to track and arrest more people for violating laws that criminalize abortion?

As often happens, the paper issued a correction to the article after I and others publicly documented these falsities.[7] It edited the paragraph describing the position of civil rights groups to state: "Civil rights groups including the N.A.A.C.P. are making the case that additional police funding must be paired with accountability measures." This "correction," however, again misstates the position of the civil rights groups, who were not in favor of the increases in police funding *at all*, and who instead were supporting *different* legislation. The "correction" actually doubles down on the article's central falsehood, suggesting that the groups *supported* the increased police funding so long as it contained "accountability measures." Thankfully, dedicated people across the country countered this wave of misinformation and made it clear to Democrats that the civil rights community would not tolerate Spanberger and Biden's police expansion plan, and together we successfully prevented it from passing.

Erase and Distort

As the police-funding coverage demonstrates, the news either ignores or distorts the ideas of those challenging the punishment bureaucracy. As a result, many people have almost no understanding of what critics of the punishment bureaucracy are proposing or why. And when people are informed about such proposals, they tend to agree with them. For example, I have found in my career that the more someone knows about police budgets or the research on alternative social investments, the more likely they are to support significant change. Even police leaders I've spoken to privately almost universally believe that their budgets are full of waste, overtime fraud, and misplaced priorities—and that large portions should instead be transferred to civilian alternatives.[8] Perhaps that's why the news keeps people ignorant of such alternatives.

For example, in 2023, journalist Glenn Greenwald interviewed reporter Lee Fang about policing.[9] Fang claimed that the people who oppose expanding the punishment bureaucracy are wealthy elitists who don't care about poor people's safety. Fang unleashed a tirade of cartoonish falsehoods and conspiracy theories about racial justice protesters.[10] Then he made a key point, on which Greenwald concurred, that mirrors the messaging of corporate news generally. According to Fang:

> There's another faction of Black Lives Matter that's just kind of this catchall liberal bandwagon that's angry at, you know, 40 different issues that just wants to abolish policing altogether but *has no solutions for how to keep a community safe.*

Greenwald agreed that critics of the punishment bureaucracy have no vision about alternatives to policing and that anyone seeking to reduce policing was "born into this privilege bubble" and "spewing hatred at whatever institutions they can find only to kind of elevate their own image without any concern with results because they don't actually care because none of these problems affect them."

These are not good-faith arguments. I share their skepticism of many non-profit and academic elites, but both Fang and Greenwald know that there are detailed, evidence-based policies being proposed, and that they are widely proposed by working-class people and survivors of violence.[11] This is a common copaganda tactic throughout contemporary corporate news: avoid dealing with the substantial arguments of a social movement to improve safety—led by people who are the most harmed by the punishment bureaucracy—by erasing those arguments.

The news consistently fails to explain the substance of legitimate critiques of police, prosecutors, and prisons. Instead, it recycles far-right police union arguments, fails to mention evidence or counterarguments, and questions the motivations of anyone who might oppose authoritarian policies as "privileged" "outside agitators" seeking only to "elevate their own image." Because news articles do not tell people what critics of the punishment bureaucracy believe and why, those Trumpian talking points are absorbed into conventional wisdom.

Such coverage validates the idea that people fighting for a safer society must have self-serving intentions because they offer nothing of substance, which leaves news consumers uninformed about solutions that knowledgeable and passionate people are building. And this ignorance makes news consumers cynical about anyone trying to both increase liberty and safety.

As silly as Greenwald and Fang sound to the survivors and experts who have devoted their lives to coming up with inspiring, workable solutions to problems of social violence but who lack the power and money to get our society to adopt them, they are typical of mainstream news. One representative example is a *New York Times* hit piece on New York City councilmember Kristin Richardson Jordan.[12] Describing her as "a revolutionary activist and poet" who wants to abolish the police, the article claimed that Jordan's views on police were out of touch, especially after someone killed two cops in her district. Ignoring her election victory as evidence that a lot of voters *liked her positions*, the journalists quoted one person on the street to prove her unpopularity. The random person stated that police were "underpaid," that they were necessary to "keep order," and that he was opposed to their abolition. Where did the intrepid *Times* reporters unearth this supposedly ordinary person? Outside a memorial for the two police officers at a police station.

The article quoted a series of political figures bashing Jordan: "Asked to assess her performance so far in office, Keith L.T. Wright, the chairman of the Manhattan Democratic Party, replied, 'I've never had a conversation with her, and I don't know what she does.' " The paper then gives space to Patrick J. Lynch, the leader of the pro-Trump Police Benevolent Association: "We are aware of her public statements about police officers and public safety," he said. "They don't reflect what police officers hear from her constituents."

I want to highlight something: the profile of the councilmember never explains her views. Unwittingly, the *Times* offers up a new corporate motto for its entire coverage of those critical of the punishment bureaucracy when it quotes its leading source: *"I've never had a conversation with her."*

The closest the article comes to saying anything of substance about Jordan's positions is repeating her general view that "New York City should invest far more in social services while cutting spending on law enforcement." That single comment in a lengthy profile leaves readers ignorant of her extensive platform—and instead suggests that this is the extent of it. Even a brief visit to Jordan's website reveals a range of policy proposals, including alternatives to the punishment bureaucracy relating to sex work, drugs, and mental health treatment, building community-based safety systems to replace some of what police do, removing police from certain mental health situations, halting their surveillance of the subway, ending cooperation between police and immigration authorities, and much more.[13] I don't know Jordan, but it took me four minutes and thirty seconds to find this information and write the previous sentence.

Jordan is a survivor of domestic violence and a Black woman. She and the working-class people and people of color who elected her in Harlem are proposing tangible, often beautiful policies, all of which are backed by evidence. There is no reason to believe that she and they don't care about their collective health and safety. They are not "outside agitators" shipped in from a moon of millionaire faux-anarchists orbiting a distant planet as Fang's all-too-common tirade suggests. But Jordan and the people who voted for her are routinely portrayed in the news as naive dreamers with nothing concrete to offer but platitudes. This should alarm people; by distorting and suppressing views of domestic violence survivors like Jordan using their trauma to envision and create greater safety for everyone, the news impedes rather than enables democratic debate about the role of the punishment bureaucracy in our society.

I sat down at my piano and created a little musical tune called "I've never had a conversation with her" as the copaganda motto for how corporate-owned news covers critique of the punishment bureaucracy. The pattern of not telling people what critics of the punishment bureaucracy are proposing or the evidence behind it characterizes hundreds of news stories that I reviewed from 2020 to 2022 leading up to the midterm elections. In many cases, articles asking whether Democrats were too lenient on crime failed to mention a single non-carceral policy.[14]

This genre of reporting—about the *partisan implications* of critiques without describing those critiques, alternative proposals, or why people advocate them—is one of the most consequential forms of copaganda because it enables a deeper fraud: cultivated ignorance of progressive policies enables the news to claim later, falsely, that progressive policies were tried and failed. Here's an October 2021 example from the *Times* covering calls to "defund" the police:[15]

A Year After 'Defund,' Police
Departments Get Their Money Back

The abrupt reversals have come in response to rising levels of
crime, the exodus of officers and political pressures.

The paper claims that "abrupt reversals" in police budget policy
"have come in response to rising levels of crime." The claim that "police
departments [got] their money back" after an "abrupt reversal" is untrue. Only a tiny number of police agencies saw small reductions, those
rare reductions did not affect operations, and overall spending on police
increased in 2021.[16] But this claim was bolstered by an outright lie about
"rising levels of crime." Recorded crime was *down* in 2021. The FBI estimated that the "violent crime" rate went down by about 3 percent and
"property crime" rate went down by about 6 percent in 2021.[17]

By cultivating ignorance about what defunding police means and
whether it happened, the paper manufactures a false narrative that progressives implemented their policies, which then failed. Most of the article is about Dallas, but it doesn't tell readers that Dallas *did not reduce police
funding at all*.[18] The article claims that a progressive policy, which was
never implemented, caused an increase in crime, which did not happen,
and that therefore funding, which was never cut, is now being restored.

It goes on to suggest that, by adding more cops, cities led by Black
mayors are going back to "prioritizing public safety": "In prioritizing
public safety, Mr. Johnson, a Democrat, had drawn a connection between his approach and that of other Black leaders."

Here, the claim that spending more on police means "prioritizing public safety" is presented as so unarguable that it can merely be
assumed without identifying it as a contested claim, let alone as one
requiring support. As one philosopher of propaganda put it, "Presuppo-
sition can be used to smuggle in content that one would not necessarily
accept if it was presented as the content asserted."[19] Connoisseurs of
copaganda know that this subtle insertion of controversial assumptions
as fact is one of its most prevalent tactics.

It gets worse. In contrast to the article's vague assertions about nonexistent progressive policies being tried and then failing, the article specifies in detail how Dallas police are returning to an "old-school" approach of "hot spot" patrols that flood poor neighborhoods with police. The paper tells readers that "criminologists" agree this makes people safe. As I explain in chapter 7, even pro-police research on "hot spot" policing does not support that assertion, and many experts and more recent randomized control studies find that it does nothing to improve safety.[20] All of this is ignored in the article.

Instead of being engaged, inspired, activated, and able to ask hard questions to learn more and participate in public life, people are left to assume that there isn't a debate, that critics aren't serious, and that there aren't immediate, concrete proposals out there to make their lives better other than more cops, which works great. And to top it off, they are told that, if there are progressive interventions that could help, whatever they are, we've tried those unexplained things, they didn't work, and punishment bureaucrats are back to save us with well-considered interventions that experts universally support.[21]

Copaganda as Obscuring

We have seen how the news uses vague words and insufficient reporting of detail to describe proposed reforms without educating people about what the policies do. Based on my conversations in 2020, for example, none of the Democratic political leaders issuing press releases about finally delivering "accountability" and "transparency" for police after 150 years either knew what specific policies their staffs were proposing, or intended to change anything that would make the punishment bureaucracy accountable to democratic control.

One of my favorite examples is a fawning 2022 *New York Times* profile of Fani Willis, the Atlanta-area district attorney who prosecuted Donald Trump for conspiracy to undermine the 2020 election results.[22] The article ignores what prosecutor offices like hers do systemically:

ruthless prosecution of poor people, mostly for minor offenses. It omits how Willis, like all U.S. prosecutors, oversees a bureaucracy that covers up and benefits from police corruption and ignores corporate crime. The role of such articles is to mislead people about what prosecutors do and therefore what kind of policy changes to support.[23] Many readers will internalize its portrait of Willis as a skilled, brave crusader rather than a ruthless bureaucrat overseeing mass incarceration in the same ways as other contemporary U.S. prosecutors.

The reporter cherry-picks a few high-profile cases to suggest this is a "no nonsense" specialist of uncommon skill and bravery. The article quotes a spokesperson from her office boasting that she has a "90% conviction rate." What does this mean? Who knows! To understand the significance of that number, the reader would need more information. For instance, which cases are charged and which crimes ignored? Does it count the weak cases that are dismissed before trial or only the ones that make it to resolution? Does it include coerced guilty pleas to lesser charges? It's likely, for example, based on similar statistics from other offices, that the conviction rate in low-level cases masks bad or corrupt performance in more serious cases, because one way of getting lots of convictions is to overcharge people or to charge them when their rights were violated by police as a strategy for coercing low-level pleas that protect police against civil liability. Without such context, the phrase "90% conviction rate" is no different than the misleading claims in a used car commercial.

The article only once discusses the substantial problems with her office, and it obscures those concerns by letting Willis avoid and discredit her critics:

"But she's drinking the Kool-Aid," said Mr. Griggs, who added that she was focusing too much on incarcerating poor Black people and not doing enough to address social ills.

In response, Ms. Willis rattled off a list of innovations she had implemented, including changes to alternative sentencing and diversion programs, and a criminal justice class for public school children.

"Mr. Griggs," she said, "don't know what he's talking about."

The paper provides no detail or context to help readers understand these differing perspectives. But, it gives the last word to Willis to dismiss the critic as ignorant.

The *Times* knows that most readers can't know much about the content of "alternative sentencing," "diversion programs," and a "criminal justice class." But they might sound good to a liberal reader skimming the paper over coffee. Many of these "reforms" are fairy tales that make the problems identified by the critic *worse*. "Alternative sentencing" has led to the expansion of discredited programs such as lucrative privatized probation supervision and surveillance, a system that Georgia uses more than any other state on a per capita basis.[24] "Diversion programs" that are run for profit (often with a cut going to prosecutors) often enable officials to arrest, prosecute, jail, and make money off more people. And "criminal justice classes" can be unregulated boondoggles where police indoctrinate young people with propaganda. These "innovations" are usually part of the problem, not the solution to her office prosecuting too many poor and disproportionately Black people for low-level crimes. They don't begin to respond to that critique. Nevertheless, the reporter lets Willis use these inconsequential, irrelevant, and even harmful programs to counter criticisms of her office's role in the ruthless and ineffective mass incarceration of marginalized people.

Readers are left thinking that it was the *critic* who is ignorant and uninformed. This is an insult to the critic, who happens to be the state president of the NAACP. But the newspaper does not permit him space to explain his criticisms or cite evidence for them, making them appear to be unfounded. The most prestigious publication in the U.S. ensures that its readers are less informed than when they began reading the news because they have now been told that reforms they do not understand are fixing criticisms that are never explained.

Such obfuscation typified the wave of articles in 2020 responding to millions of people demanding the transformation of policing. Consider the "reforms" celebrated in Camden, New Jersey.[25] Some outlets sensationally claimed the city had "disbanded" its police department. The *Times* presented Camden's reforms as "the key to the future of policing," with the reporter bragging about the article appearing on page A1 of the Sunday edition:[26]

Could This City Hold the Key to the Future of Policing in America?

As protesters across the country call for police departments to be defunded and dismantled, Camden's experience offers some lessons.

The article used terms like "transform" and "dismantled" and "drastic steps" to suggest that what Camden implemented was "what some activists are calling for elsewhere." In reality, Camden did not "disband" the department; it just fired the police officers and then rehired more cops at lower salaries.[27] This charade produced a police force that was larger than before. It carried out more low-level arrests of poor Black people and separated more Black children from their parents than before. The role of this article and similar ones is to confuse people about what exactly a reform is, present superficial tweaks that reify the status quo as the only realistic changes, and narrow the conception of what is possible.[28] Tens of millions of readers of the *Times* are left unable to distinguish between what happened in Camden and what advocates for defunding the police were proposing.

Instead of describing the content of the changes, the story offers cute anecdotes of police leaders marching with protesters and watching children play basketball. It does not quote the local opponents of the charade or explain their deeper criticisms about the role of police in a highly impoverished city. And it does not include a single sentence explaining their policy proposals. To the contrary, Camden's *expansion* of policing and surveillance is portrayed as "offer[ing] some lessons" for "protestors" calling for police to be "defunded." In a conclusion worthy of *The Onion*, the article ends by depicting a cop letting kids stay on a playground past curfew as he expresses his agreement with one of the happy children that "Black lives matter."

Being Vague Makes Bad Things Possible

Defenders of the punishment bureaucracy cultivate and exploit people's ignorance about it. Time and again, status-quo defenders attack critics of the punishment bureaucracy without explaining *what the defenders are defending.*

Do these status-quo defenders support the war on drugs? Human caging for possessing cannabis, mushrooms, or other scheduled substances? Caging people for sex work? ICE raids? SWAT teams raiding homes at night for drug possession? Do they want more children arrested by armed cops in schools? Do they oppose armed traffic enforcement? Audits of police overtime fraud? Mental-health first responders? Police using facial recognition and license plate readers? Do they support the resources cops spend on tanks, chemical weapons, spying divisions, civil forfeiture, or infiltrating racial justice, environmental, reproductive, and anti-war activist groups? Do they agree with police currently using a plurality of their budgets to cage people for driving on licenses suspended for owing debts, trespassing, shoplifting, protesting, and drug possession? Do they want harsher sentences than every comparable country? Why or why not? The list of *specific* questions they evade is endless.

By ignoring substance, defenders of the punishment bureaucracy suppress discussion about what it does with its money and time. In the process, they avoid having to voice out loud their support for ineffective violence against the most vulnerable people in our society. The last thing they want is a debate about police, prosecutors, and prisons, where they would be compelled to defend the details of authoritarian policy positions. That's why copaganda is so devoid of substance. If they had to spell out the logical consequences of their views, it would horrify the well-meaning people they are trying to manipulate into preserving things mostly as they are.

12

Polls and Making Cops
Look Good

Presentations of public opinion are then often enlisted by the control-
lers as "impartial evidence" of what the public, in fact, believes and
wants. . . . [But] the media play a critical mediating and connecting
role in the formation of public opinion, and in orchestrating that opin-
ion together with the actions and views of the powerful.

-Stuart Hall[1]

Copaganda uses "public opinion" to manufacture "public opinion." The news coverage of a 2022 Loyola Marymount University poll was both revealing and representative.[2] The poll found that 63 percent of conservatives, 68 percent of moderates, and 76 percent of liberals supported "reallocating parts of LAPD's budget to social workers, mental healthcare, and other social services."

Almost 70 percent of those surveyed supported reallocating parts of

Would you support or oppose reallocating parts of LAPD's budget to social workers, mental healthcare, and other social services?

	Liberal	Moderate	Conservative
Strongly support	25.7	16.5	18.7
Somewhat support	49.6	51.5	44.0
Somewhat oppose	17.0	17.5	16.6
Strongly oppose	7.8	14.5	20.7

Source and notes: Thomas and Dorothy Leavey Center for the Study of Los Angeles, Loyola Marymount University. 1,755 adult respondents of the 2022 Police and Community Relations Survey. Response options inverted.

the LAPD budget to social services. That is a stunning repudiation of the punishment bureaucracy. It is difficult to find anything that 70 percent of people in the U.S. support, let alone significant majorities across all demographic groups and political identities.

Would you support or oppose reallocating parts of LAPD's budget to social workers, mental healthcare, and other social services?

Strongly support	21.1
Somewhat support	48.6
Somewhat oppose	17.2
Strongly oppose	13.2

Source and notes: Thomas and Dorothy Leavey Center for the Study of Los Angeles, Loyola Marymount University. 1,755 adult respondents of the 2022 Police and Community Relations Survey. Response options inverted.

Another of the poll's findings is even more interesting. Support for reallocating the police budget to social services is actually higher among people who live with a police officer than people who don't:

Would you support or oppose reallocating parts of LAPD's budget to social workers, mental healthcare, and other social services?

	Police force member in household	No police member in household
Strongly support	32.1	20.2
Somewhat support	43.2	49.0
Somewhat oppose	16.2	17.3
Strongly oppose	8.6	13.6

Source and notes: Thomas and Dorothy Leavey Center for the Study of Los Angeles, Loyola Marymount University. 1,755 adult respondents of the 2022 Police and Community Relations Survey. Response options inverted.

Much could be said about this broad support for reallocation of police funds to social services, but for now let's focus on how the news *covered* the poll. Unsurprisingly, these findings were ignored. *The Los Angeles Times* published an article about the poll and didn't report any of the findings I just mentioned. Instead, the headline declared:[3]

Survey: Most Angelenos have favorable view of
LAPD, despite lingering concerns around bias

The paper distorts the results to give the impression that people "remain generally supportive" of the LAPD, stating that "the public's confidence in the Los Angeles Police Department has improved slightly." Once again, opposition to police is framed as opposition to racial disparities and bias, but it is rarely focused on the idea that police are ineffective at producing a safer society. This false dichotomy is key to maintaining the political narrative that, if you care about safety, you must support the punishment bureaucracy, even if that means some tradeoffs to vague notions of fairness. But look at how the paper distorted the issue of police budgets: "Asked whether they supported a broader proposal to 'defund the police,' however, a strong majority—nearly 69%—said they were either strongly or somewhat opposed to the idea."

The paper's reporting of this result is misleading. It highlights opposition to the word "defund" but suppresses the poll respondents' support for reallocation of resources away from police. In reality, every self-described "defund" campaign I've seen is focused on exactly that: reallocating some money from police budgets to mental health care, non-police emergency response units, housing, education, and other social services. Thus, accurately understood, the poll results document opposition to the label "defund" but *support* for the policy demand. The newspaper thus misleads readers by reporting that people *don't support such demands* when *they do* in overwhelming numbers.

It is hard to overstate the importance of this manipulation. It might be the most important thing in this book. We constantly have fake, uninformed debates that lead to paralysis and confusion instead of implementing effective, popular policies. Journalists and politicians widely ridiculed the term "defund the police," and one of the most common refrains I heard in my conversations with journalists from 2020 to 2022 was that defunding the police was widely unpopular. But the news rarely discussed *what proponents meant by the concept*, their *specific* proposals for changing budget priorities, and why they gained so much traction among marginalized people, health workers, educators, and scholars. Indeed, a closer examination of polling data revealed widespread support for the policy positions in "defund the police" campaigns, especially among marginalized people, including two-thirds of Black voters and Democrats.[4] (Remember the internal survey of Seattle police I discussed earlier, where even police themselves agreed their department was bloated and could be trimmed.) Instead, the news distorts and downplays support among wide swaths of the population to reduce spending on the swollen punishment bureaucracy and redirect it to programs that are more effective at reducing social harm.[5] As a result, people talk past each other on an industrial scale.

News outlets help powerful people concoct a "conventional wisdom" about what people think that is at odds with what people actually think. And, of course, since polling is expensive, who is doing a poll, what is asked, which of its findings are made public or kept secret, and the timing of its public dissemination are influenced by people in particular demographics and with particular incentives, biases, and agendas. The failure of many polls—and, especially, reporting on polls—to ask more meaningful questions based on more specific context is one reason so many journalists and other news consumers so confidently believe that people don't support shifting resources away from the punishment bureacucracy when those changes are widely popular.

Talking Past Each Other

About a year after "defund the police" became a controversial topic, I gave a lecture at a prominent political science department. A group of Ivy League professors took me out to dinner, and we started to discuss "defunding the police." The level of discussion about "defund" was no better than that in the *Los Angeles Times*. Just like news reporters, the professors made no effort to define the terms they discussed, and therefore talked past each other the entire time. Despite being self-described liberals and having strong opinions against "defund," none of them had any facility with the police bureaucracy, its budget allocations and procurement policies, standard features of large police contracts, spending on public relations, surveillance technology, or the history of repression of marginalized people and social movements. Almost everyone kept pointing out that it was a foolish idea to discuss the topic because "the public won't ever support defund." But then I found that their views were so superficially held that their minds were easy to change with a few basic definitions, facts, and evidence.

The conversation mirrored others I had with dozens of journalists in the year after George Floyd's murder. Many of them casually told me that "people don't support defund" and that "progressives will get killed because of defund." But when I asked them what policies progressives were specifically proposing, I got a wide range of mutually exclusive answers. Most strikingly, when I asked them why they were so confident that people rejected "defund" and its associated proposals, the reporters answered that it was the general sense they got about public opinion from *other news stories*. On the rare occasion a reporter found a poll that corroborated their "sense," I pointed out how the poll's questions skewed the results. Then they expressed surprise and agreement at how difficult it was to divine any meaning from the surveys given how the questions were worded and the lack of context provided in them. All of a sudden, they were not so sure that "the public opposed defund" because they saw that it depended on what you asked people.

The same is true of policymakers. I once had a conversation with a conservative local politician who began the conversation saying that they were opposed to defunding police. We walked through a few line items in the police budget and estimated how much money the police spent on drug possession arrests, police overtime, debt-based driver's license suspensions, militarized weaponry, and marketing. The politician was furious that they had never been presented with these budget numbers before and agreed that much of this spending would be better spent on care for their constituents than on police. This more specific conversation resulted in a different outcome than if I had merely asked the politician if they supported reducing the police budget generally or "defunding police."

As these conversations with professors, journalists, and politicians demonstrate, public discourse since the 2020 uprisings about proposals to reallocate some money from police budgets to social investment is encased in layers of erroneous but intentionally manufactured assumptions about what people think. The news media's vague, incoherent, and internally inconsistent discussion of reforms only adds further layers of confusion. The punishment bureaucracy is the beneficiary of this situation in which everyone is confused, confident, and wrong about what other people might want.

Most people don't read polls, only *news reports or headlines about polls*. This coverage typically ignores something: poll results depend on what questions are asked, how they are asked, and what background participants are provided before the answer. Thus, not only are people misinformed about what other people currently think regarding the punishment bureaucracy because of what is asked and how, but neither the polls nor the news coverage provide information about what people would think if they were *differently* informed, much less what they would think about specific proposals or, importantly, how *intensely they would be motivated to come together with other people to do things in the world* to make those things happen or to prevent them from being implemented. Polls therefore don't explain how social movements can begin with a small amount of self-conscious support but then turn into mass struggles that make initially unpopular (or in some cases *seemingly* unpopular) positions common sense.

In virtually every other area of public and private life, reasonable people understand that neither meaningful knowledge nor consequential decisions can be based on such a profound lack of accurate information. If one wanted to predict, for example, how someone will behave in the future or whether a business will be a successful investment or whether a sports prospect will succeed in the major leagues, one must examine the underlying fundamentals of the situation. This includes, for example, how a person or group of people would behave if they possessed certain information as well as the likelihood of them coming into possession of that information. This is why a Friday evening poll showing a candidate leading by ten points is useless to a campaign manager who knows that a catastrophic scandal will be made public on Monday morning.

This is also a reason for optimism. People's daily experience of the world, mass consciousness events like the 2020 uprisings, and the hard work of many people raising awareness about the punishment bureaucracy every day—including vulnerable people, crime survivors, organizers, teachers, dedicated journalists, and scholars—to build shared knowledge about what makes all of our lives better can combine to produce an enduring bulwark against the copaganda that I discuss in this book.

So, we should interrogate whether initial, uninformed "popularity" of vague terms—as measured by people who have the money to conduct a poll that asks particular questions in a particular way—is the best gauge for deciding what change to advocate. For example, few people remember that Martin Luther King Jr. was "unpopular" during his lifetime.[6] As civil rights leader Thomas B. Harvey documents, King had a 75 percent disapproval rating at the time of his death, and 60 percent of Americans said that they opposed the March on Washington when it took place in 1963.[7] The same is true of historical fights against the theft of Indigenous people's land, women campaigning for suffrage, and LGBTQ advocates organizing for same-sex marriage. They were unpopular in polls and attacked by the press for being naive because of their supposed unpopularity. But now most Americans hold those fights in high esteem because social movements can both reveal and change mass consciousness. But copaganda portrays its already distorted "public opinion" as an unchangeable consensus that dooms all possible reforms, making futile the project of significant change. It uses this general cloud of cynicism to consolidate support for the establishment, discredit dissent, and demoralize, deflate, and depoliticize people who might want to lead struggles to make the world better.

News coverage of police budgets is an example of how unserious a discussion can become in a perfect storm of incompetence and incentive to distort. Setting aside people who have a financial interest in the punishment bureaucracy, in eighteen years of working in the punishment bureaucracy I have met very few people who oppose reallocating at least some money from policing, prosecution, and prisons to other social investments that better address the root causes of harm. In fact, this view is commonly held by frontline workers *in the punishment bureaucracy.* It would be even more widely held if the news provided better information. Copaganda is so prevalent because punishment bureaucrats could not in any way justify the current levels of spending if people had full information about their specific expenditures. Polls about public safety are a key tool of their disinformation, and news reporting on polling is a tool of influence, not a device for uncovering a true, static, meaningful, objective will of the masses.

13

The Bad Apple

I can't breathe. I have my ID right here. My name is Elijah McClain. That's my house. I was just going home. I'm an introvert. I'm just different. That's all. I'm so sorry. I have no gun. I don't do that stuff. I don't do any fighting. Why are you attacking me? I don't even kill flies! I don't eat meat! But I don't judge people, I don't judge people who do eat meat. Forgive me. All I was trying to do was become better. I will do it. I will do anything. Sacrifice my identity, I'll do it. You all are phenomenal. You are beautiful and I love you. Try to forgive me. I'm a mood Gemini. I'm sorry. I'm so sorry. Ow, that really hurt. You are all very strong. Teamwork makes the dream work. [Crying.] Oh, I'm sorry I wasn't trying to do that. I just can't breathe correctly. [Vomits due to pressure exerted on his chest and neck.] I can't fix myself. [Vomits again and goes unconscious.]

-Elijah McClain[1]

The male resisted contact, a struggle ensued, and he was taken into custody.

-Aurora Police Department report
concerning Elijah McClain's murder[2]

When the news talks about bad things the punishment bureaucracy does, it downplays their *systemic* nature and singles out "bad apples." Two examples illustrate how copaganda does this: coverage of the police murder of a fourteen-year-old girl in Los Angeles and police marching with protesters during the 2020 protests.

Spinning Police Murder

In December 2021, an LAPD police officer killed fourteen-year-old Valentina Orellana Peralta while she was trying on a dress in a changing room at a Burlington Coat Factory store. The week after, the *New York Times* published two articles that show how police spin the public narrative after a police killing. On the day of the shooting, the headline of the first article blamed a mysterious bullet for killing Valentina:[3]

> **Stray Police Bullet Kills Girl as Officers**
> **Fire at Suspect in Los Angeles Store**

The paper later published a longer article that presented a sensitive portrait of the cop who killed Valentina with a headline emphasizing his progressive views:[4]

> **Officer Whose Bullet Killed a 14-Year-**
> **Old Girl Wanted to 'Change' the Police**

Putting aside that the second headline again blames the bullet, let's focus on how these articles spin police murder. First the background: an LAPD cop named William Dorsey Jones Jr. killed Valentina with an assault rifle when he indiscriminately started shooting at Daniel Elena Lopez, a man having a mental health crisis and wielding a bike lock inside the store. Jones also killed him. These killings were part of a series of almost four dozen police killings in Los Angeles in 2021, including five people that week.

Unlike the paper's coverage of low-level crimes by the poor, the articles avoid using terms like "surge" to describe the increase in Los Angeles police killings. In fact, neither article mentions the other police killings, let alone suggests to readers that this incident was part of a pattern of police killings in Los Angeles. It is an editorial choice to portray an event as isolated rather than to situate it within broader trends. A local grassroots group created this graphic to illustrate the omissions, using the format that the news typically uses to cover "violent crime" not committed by police:[5]

Here are the sources in the first article:

- The police (three times)
- Assistant police chief (twice)
- Police chief
- Assistant police chief (four times)
- Attorney General
- Burlington Coat Factory

Here are the sources selected for the second article after a week of reporting:

- Spokesperson for police union
- Police union lawyer for the cop who killed Valentina
- Person mentored by the cop
- Another person mentored by the cop
- Attorney General
- Professor (former cop, but that is not disclosed)
- Lawyer for Valentina's family
- Police union lawyer for the cop (twice more)

The second article, which came out after the *Times* had a week to decide how to cover the story, reserves the first two and last two positions—the most important in the article—for the police union and the lawyer for the cop. The last line of the article defends police for "following their training and procedure" without treating that claim with skepticism.[6] Unlike the *Times*, local news coverage in *Knock LA* informed readers that Jones had actually disobeyed the commands of other officers on scene. *Knock LA* showed readers what happened based on the various videos of the encounter, and the images undermine the *Times*'s account.

Then things get weirder. The *Times* trots out an "expert"—a Bowling Green State professor who we are told "studies police violence." His opinion is sympathetic to the cop, laying the groundwork for a narrative about how hard the case will be to convict Jones. What doesn't the paper say? The professor is a former cop. Different experts would have expressed the opposite view, pointing to the recklessness of Jones, his disregard of the commands of other officers already on the scene before him, the number of shots he fired, and the position of Elena Lopez when Jones shot him. The *Knock LA* reporters even quoted another active cop, who said: "That is one hundred percent a shooting that should have never happened."

As I explained in chapter 4, police consultants work hard to head off such comments making it into the news. Their crisis management teams select experts and offer them to journalists. It's worth asking why editors did not find it relevant to tell readers that the LAPD employs over twenty-five full-time public relations staff as part of an operation that responds to shootings to control the initial narrative and prevent them from going viral, connects reporters to "experts," and limits which facts are publicly reported.

The *Times* uses its sources to craft a story of Valentina's killing as an isolated tragedy. The article goes out of its way to portray it as an exception, not part of a historical and recent orgy of preventable police violence. Editors chose to print the article without a single source or expert with a critique of police violence *as systemic*. Valentina's killing could have been a moment to deepen popular awareness of intentional policy choices that make the recurrence of such violence preventable, and indeed, they have been prevented in most other countries. Instead, the editors depoliticized a police killing as an exceptional and unfortunate accident.[7]

Then comes the more salacious copaganda. The core of the article offers a sympathetic profile of the shooter as a "good guy" cop who loves children. This is a script the media turns to after police violence: it finds examples of "good cops" doing things like taking presents to kids or playing sports with troubled youth. One classic example is the *Times* coverage of Christopher Schurr, a Grand Rapids, Michigan, cop who in April 2022 killed Patrick Lyoya, a Black man, with a shot to the back of the head while pinning him to the ground. The article features photos of Schurr surrounded by smiling Kenyan children and claiming that he helped "widows and orphans."[8] In the *Times* story about Jones, reporters claim that his social media profile exemplified his commitment to mentoring kids and determination to "confront head-on the issues of racism and policing." This is a stunning misreading of Jones's social media posts. Other journalists who dug into them showed readers that Jones repeatedly defended police brutality and used pro-Trump talking points, including those promoting voter suppression and strange fascist mythologies.[9]

To bolster its portrayal of Jones as a crusader against injustice, the *Times* lifts him up as a paragon of the LAPD's "community policing" efforts. Of course, the paper gives no background on what "community policing" means or its long record of surveillance, brutality, infiltration, and violence in Los Angeles.[10] The term "community policing" is etched into the marble facade at the International Institute for the Glorification of Copaganda for a reason: it is referenced in the news as something vaguely positive, but the news never tells people what it is. Very few laypeople know what "community policing" means, let alone its history. In short, it's a form of counterinsurgency derived from colonial military strategies used to "pacify" native populations, particularly in Africa, the Middle East, and Asia.[11] Its goal is essentially to build allies among a targeted native population to make at least some repressed people trust and support the colonial oppressor so that the oppressor can continue its profitable policies while minimizing unrest by recruiting ambassadors within the repressed community. In 2021, for example, student opposition forced Harvard to cancel a course in which a professor proposed to get students to help him and local police study data on military counterinsurgency tactics they had implemented in Black communities in Massachusetts, in his words, based on strategies developed by "some army buddies of mine who had served in Iraq and Afghanistan."[12] In Los Angeles, well before the *Times* published its articles on Valentina's killing, residents impacted by LAPD violence produced a comprehensive report on the history of "community policing" in Los Angeles. Their history of "community policing" counterinsurgency and its contemporary abuses contradicts the rosy picture gestured at by the *Times*.[13] While their report, *Automating Banishment*, is one of the great community-based histories and analyses of police repression, it's the kind of perspective surgically excluded from the news.

Whatever these obvious flaws with the article's portrayal of Jones, its entire premise is flawed. We cannot understand police violence by delving into the personal motivations and character of a cop who shoots a child trying on a dress. We can only understand recurring police violence by giving people the context that enables them to think *structurally* about why, despite decades of "reform," a summer of uprisings in

2020, and so many "good cops" everywhere, the police shot and killed more people in 2021 than 2020, more people in 2022 than in 2021, more people in 2023 than in 2022, and more people in 2024 than in 2023.[14]

Good Cops Kneeling for Racial Justice

Copaganda frames police violence as the product of "bad apples," which it contrasts with the supposedly benevolent behavior of most police.

Remember Sheriff Swanson in Flint and Chief Acevedo in Houston, whose public grandstanding about racial justice in 2020 I discussed in the introduction? The viral images of these "good cops" were used as an antidote to videos of officers in body armor shooting rubber bullets, launching gas grenades, spewing pepper spray, and swinging batons at protesters and journalists. Liberal leaders and pundits praised police for sympathizing with protesters, and called for more investment in the policing bureaucracy so that the good cops could hold the bad ones "accountable."[15]

During the period when Swanson and Acevedo rose through police ranks to the very top, the U.S. was jailing Black people at six times the rate of South Africa during Apartheid.[16] And in 2020, under their guidance, both Flint and Houston had higher rates of incarceration than the U.S. average—with severe socioeconomic and racial disparities. But Acevedo and Swanson were leading one the most important narrative battles of their generation. Their strategy was to depict most officers as "good cops," and, in times of unrest and crisis over visible police violence, to decry "bad apples" like Derek Chauvin as outliers that they could root out with more money. At the time, Acevedo controlled a nearly $1 billion annual budget—just a fraction of the total policing expenditures in the Houston area, which has about sixty different local police agencies.

In my years as a civil rights lawyer, I have seen virtually the same cycle in city after city: Politicians respond to the fallout from an incident of police violence by pledging various "reforms" that are either meaningless or things the police had been asking for anyway. These pledges are followed by increases in police budgets. Overall police violence then grows, and the cycle repeats.

The federal government took the same approach in 2014 after Michael Brown was killed by police in Ferguson, Missouri. According to a federal lawsuit in which I was one of the lawyers for tens of thousands of disproportionately Black clients, the city averaged 3.6 arrest warrants for every household prior to Brown's killing.[17] Most of these warrants were for unpaid debts to the city. The lawsuit described that, when a person was arrested, their family faced what can only be described as institutionalized ransom: pay arbitrary amounts of cash to the police or let their loved one languish in a cage. Police negotiated and renegotiated for amounts like $100 or $300 with family members each day. People whose families had no money to spare, including my client Keilee Fant, were jailed for days or weeks with no access to a shower, sunlight, their children, or even toothpaste. As public pressure mounted after our investigation and lawsuit, the Department of Justice, which is the largest incarcerating force in the U.S., also sued Ferguson but demanded, as part of its settlement, that the city get more money for police technology, training, and more officers.[18] What does it say when federal bureaucrats see this situation and think, "We need *more* policing"?

Ferguson is not unique. Like thousands of other U.S. cities, it converted its police force into an assembly-line bureaucracy of surveillance, brutality, profit, and family separation. As we all watched police kneeling for cameras in 2020, I couldn't help but think about one of my clients in another case who had spent months away from his wife in an overcrowded jail cell after being charged with driving on a suspended license, which was taken away because the family was too poor to pay old debts. Or another client in a different case who, because she owed fees the police were trying to collect, was sleeping next to a toilet along with many other women on a concrete jail floor covered in feces, blood, mucus, mold, and urine.[19]

This everyday violence is not as visible as the image of George Floyd being suffocated under the knee of a police officer. And although every major police department that I have researched has in recent years had systemic scandals of abuse, lying under oath, and coordinated cover-ups, all of that misconduct pales in comparison to the scope of the daily violence of standard *lawful* policing: one that subjects poor people to mass surveillance and harassment, takes billions of dollars in personal property through civil forfeiture, traps people in abusive jails, coerces plea deals, imposes harsh sentences with no connection to empirical evidence, separates individuals from friends and family, leaves pets to starve alone, and marks tens of millions with a criminal record that closes off opportunities for employment, health care, and housing. Police leaders do not want to talk about the everyday brutality of the punishment bureaucracy. Condemning Chauvin as a "bad apple" is a safer tactic. But it is not "bad apple" police officers who make 10.6 million arrests every year and who, since 1980, have helped quintuple the rate of incarceration in the U.S from its historical average.[20] It is not "bad apple" police officers who purchase tanks and grenade launchers for themselves or who enforce cash bail. It is not "bad apple" officers who criminalize people in poverty for not having places to live or treatment for an addiction. And it is not "bad apple" officers who have made the local jail the largest mental health services institution in almost every major city. This destruction is what "good cops" do in the modern U.S.[21]

The "good cop" rhetoric is so prevalent that the news frames justice and injustice as the result of "good" or "bad" individuals making "good" or "bad" choices. But the punishment bureaucracy was five times smaller per capita for the entirety of American history until 1980, and it is five to ten times smaller in other comparable countries.[22] None of that is the result of individual choices by good or bad individuals.

To see why police push the "good apple" and the "bad apple" narrative, it's helpful to see that they have a hierarchy of public conversations they prefers:

1. Deny any problems.
2. Blame any problems on individual bad cops.
3. Blame any problems on bad units, squads, precincts, or particular police chiefs.
4. Blame any problems on bad police departments.
5. Discuss the role of armed police in a society of deep inequality.

Police will attempt to push public conversations up this hierarchy. When they must acknowledge a problem in a particular instance, if they have their preference, the public will talk only about "bad apple" officers. But it often becomes necessary for police to engage and even encourage public conversations within the other categories, applying the same "bad apple" reasoning to each successively larger group of officers.

Under no circumstances do police want the public to entertain conversations about problems with *policing itself* as a method of social, racial, and economic control. In fact, conversations about each of the other categories are *designed to avoid the deeper conversations*. "Bad apples" can be thrown under the bus, fired, and occasionally even sent to prison. Bad squads and units can be scapegoated and temporarily disbanded, as happened with the cartoonishly corrupt gun squad in Baltimore and the SCORPION Unit after its murder of Tyre Nichols in Memphis.[23] Bad police departments can also be singled out—indeed, one of the remarkable and darkly humorous observations I have made from my years of work across the country is that local clients of mine in each city assume that their local police force is generally recognized as one of the worst nationally. People *assume that police must be better elsewhere*.

When necessary, such as with the LAPD after the Rampart corruption scandal or Ferguson after the 2014 uprisings, police themselves will support this narrative that entire departments are in need of "reform."[24] As noted earlier, after the 2020 uprisings, liberal politicians pointed to Camden, New Jersey, as a model because the town had "disbanded" its police force after repeated police violence, but then left out the part that the city rehired more officers on lower salaries, expanded surveillance contracts, and made even *more* arrests of almost exclusively poor people in the subsequent years for low-level crimes.[25] In this process, it is also common for local or state officials to ask the Department of Justice to investigate an entire police force, as dozens of mayors, governors, and even police chiefs have done in recent years. They do not do this out of a belief that federal intervention will make their police force behave very differently or reduce their power—everyone involved knows that federal intervention will not dramatically change what a police force does in our society. Instead, it's largely a public relations move to reaffirm the legitimacy of the system *generally* and to distract from local energy for more radical solutions. This distraction always happens through federal intervention because of the well-understood, well-trodden path such intervention takes: periods of delay, consulting contracts, recommendation and rationalization of more resources that then becomes court-ordered additional spending, and pacification of liberal residents who are mostly interested in hearing second-hand that *something* is being done.[26]

In this narrative set piece, state and local officials who request federal intervention are asserting that the police force in question is somehow *deviating from standards acceptable to federal bureaucrats* and not acting in basically the same way U.S. police forces always act.[27] It attempts to cast a police force as an outlier from the norm—a "bad apple" in an otherwise legitimate, good-faith system. But this act itself is one of propaganda; it reinforces the idea that nonviolent, democratic standards of U.S. policing exist, and that the department in question is a deviation from that conjured myth.

After years of studying policing, I have found no evidence that any major department is a significant outlier. Every one I have investigated—and that I have seen anyone else investigate—is substantially similar in terms of what they do and do not do. Just as with "bad apple" individual cops, the creation of this category implies that there is a meaningful category of different police forces such that *the mass harms that the prison industrial complex causes are attributable only to the bad ones.*

This kind of scapegoating of police forces is often welcomed by police, not just because it tends to lead to more resources for those "bad" officers, squads, precincts, and departments for "training" and technology, but because talking about the "bad apples" distracts people from asking too many questions like: "Is there something about this bureaucracy, and the social and economic arrangements it protects, that is not amenable to change because its primary function is *not* to promote holistic human safety, equality, and flourishing?"

In this way, the news is engaged in something of an absurdist *Groundhog Day* charade—hundreds of cities are simultaneously and repeatedly, year after year, discussing how violent and unaccountable their police forces are, but the public discourse is not connecting these conversations together because the conversation is only grounded in isolated events.

At the same time, a parallel national conversation flares up every few years about how police are violent and unaccountable, but the public discourse is not connecting this to the conversations that society just had several years before. What might it suggest that each local police bureaucracy in each of thousands of cities and counties have similar policies, similar technology, similar demographic disparities in arrest and surveillance decisions, similar statistics of activity and arrest patterns, similar infiltration by right-wing groups, similar political activity, similar public relations strategies, and similar recurring scandals of corruption and violence? What might it suggest that for the past 125 years, every generation in the U.S. has had a similar conversation in newspaper editorial pages about police corruption, violence against marginalized people, and spying on progressive social movements?

14

The Big Deception

Bruce Wayne, with all the money in the world, can't seem to think of anything to do with it other than to design even more high-tech weaponry and indulge in the occasional act of charity. . . . It never seems to occur to Superman that he could easily end world hunger or carve free magic cities out of mountains. Almost never do superheroes make, create, or build anything. The villains, in contrast, are relentlessly creative. . . .

[Batman and Superman] aren't fascists. They are just ordinary, decent, super-powerful people who inhabit a world in which fascism is the only political possibility.

-David Graeber[1]

What if we were to ask a different question of institutions and activities than the narrow neoclassical question of how efficient they are . . . ? What if we were to ask what kind of people a given activity or institution fostered?

-James C. Scott[2]

The news deceives the public about the motivations of punishment bureaucrats and the processes by which public safety policies come to be. It is copaganda's Big Deception.

The level at which the news discusses the reasons that powerful people pursue public safety policies is superficial, simplistic, and silly. If our theory about why things are happening is wrong, then we won't be able to do much about the things we don't like.

Understanding the Big Deception

The Big Deception mystifies *why* consequential things happen in our society, specifically about how politics and power work. It leads people to assume that punishment policies are the product of reasonable leaders carefully weighing different options rather than of organized interests asserting their power. So, investment in police, prosecutors, and prisons appears to be the natural, good-faith response to "crime" and not, say, a political concession to powerful interest groups.

We see the assumption that punishment policies are pursued for good-faith safety reasons in virtually every aspect of contemporary crime reporting. It shapes the words and phrases used in news stories. It leads reporters to quote officials about their motivations without skepticism or context. It explains the absence of perspectives that posit different reasons for the punishment bureaucracy's policies. Most subtly, it underlies daily editorial decisions that juxtapose things like drug abuse, homicide, youth violence, and homelessness with punishment policies and not, say, housing, public health infrastructure, early childhood education, toxic masculinity, or the isolation and alienation inherent in contemporary monopoly capitalism. In fact, the choice to center police, prosecutors, and prison bureaucrats in discussions about interpersonal harm is itself a form of deception about what their institutions do and why. If the news publishes thousands of stories per year merely mentioning two concepts together—say, sentencing policy and violent crime—people necessarily start to develop a view that they may be, and might be intended to be, causally connected. Conversely, if the news hardly ever juxtaposes two things—say, free medical care and violence—the public may fail to draw any connection between them.

A lack of understanding about why things happen and, thus, how to change them affects the views and behavior of journalists, ordinary people, and people in power. It causes people to:

- Focus our attention on relatively inconsequential issues while ignoring issues of greater significance like material inequality
- Blame the wrong people and institutions for problems
- Spend time and money working on or donating to social change strategies that won't work. Much of the nonprofit world's approach to the punishment bureaucracy is the equivalent of trying to stop oil drilling by presenting Exxon executives a scientific report linking fossil fuels to global warming and then inviting them to a panel discussion about it with snacks afterward
- Design rules, policies, or laws that pay insufficient attention to how existing systems might not be able to implement them as a technical matter despite the intentions behind them
- Promote reforms that entrench the same problems because the causes are not addressed
- Choose careers and jobs that don't satisfy us or advance the things we care about
- Argue about the motivations and character of individual politicians, bureaucrats, or pundits instead of focusing on material North Star goals such as limiting the concentration of wealth and the power of centralized authoritarian bureaucracy
- Focus disproportionately on individual candidates and politicians instead of building effective institutions, relationships, political formations, technologies, and interventions

Before discussing how the news media carries out the Big Deception, let me give you two examples from my life. First, I have spent almost a decade filing lawsuits and otherwise advocating against the cash bail system in the United States. If I believe people in power are genuinely trying to ensure overall safety, equality, and justice, I might adopt a strategy based solely on trying to convince them to pursue more effective policies. I might sit down and explain to legislators and the for-profit bail industry the social-scientific evidence proving that cash bail not only does not promote safety, but leads to more crime, lower rates of court appearance, and staggering economic and public health costs because of the lives destroyed by pretrial detention. Hopefully they would agree, and the bail system as we know it would go away after a few meetings.

However, if I believe that the bail system looks the way it does because it benefits organized interests notwithstanding its ineffectiveness, I might adopt different strategies based on a different theory of change. This might include working on a campaign that combines research, educating the public, base-building, protest, journalism, scholarship, strategic litigation, the arts, and forming coalitions to build organized power that compels those in power to change their policies.

Similarly, having a sound theory of which interests created something we hope to change helps us prepare for predictable responses from those in power. For example, if jail populations decrease, companies and investors who profit off the bail and carceral telecommunications industries might pivot from selling bail bonds or jail phone calls to selling electronic monitoring and drug tests to people released on non-financial conditions. To do this, they may push for the creation of a new pretrial supervision industry if they see the bail industry under threat. Or, because assembly-line pretrial detention is so vital to coercing large percentages of people to plead guilty quickly, police, prosecutors, and judges might attempt to shift from cash-based detention to jailing people on other grounds. For instance, a well-meaning campaign by liberals eliminated wealth-based detention in federal courts in 1984 on the theory that detaining poor people solely because they couldn't pay cash was wrong and ineffective. But, predictably, the "Bail Reform Act" granted more discretion to judges and prosecutors to detain people in more cases for other reasons without using cash—for example by letting prosecutors "presume" detention in drug cases. As a result, overall pretrial detention in federal courts *tripled* over the following four decades, from about 24 percent to over 75 percent of arrested individuals, and the people detained were more disproportionately poor, Black, and immigrant than they were before the "reform."[3]

A second example from my recent experience is my academic study on the history of body-camera copaganda that I summarized in chapter 7. One theory about why body-camera sales exploded after Michael Brown's killing in 2014 was that police and other people in power suddenly became interested in "accountability" and "transparency." It was this theory that the news media spread. In fact, prosecutors, police, and companies had demanded body cameras for years to increase surveillance, compel quick pleas, shield themselves from liability, control the public narrative after police violence, expand facial and voice recognition technology, and rake in profit. But they were unable to convince the government to spend billions on the technology until they came up with the idea to use their own violence to justify it. Understood in this context, the explosion of body cameras was the result of a plan embraced by punishment bureaucrats for reasons diametrically opposed to "accountability" and "transparency."

The following table illustrates how these different worldviews shape political strategy. Worldview 1 is the product of the Big Deception, while Worldview 2 is the product of a root-cause analysis.[4]

The table is simplified to make a crude point: developing an accurate understanding of why things happen and what forces are pushing for them is essential to predicting what will happen and to building a theory of how to change things. Remember three key points as you read my examples of news coverage:

First, in Worldview 1, the strategy is simpler because it assumes that once people in power are informed of the best arguments, they

	Bail	Body cameras
Good faith pursuit of shared values drives policies of punishment bureaucrats (Worldview 1)	Strategy: Describe to the public and people in power that cash bail doesn't make people safe or improve court appearance. → Outcome: government magically develops better systems of pretrial care	Strategy: Describe to the public and people in power that body cams don't reduce police violence, but they do increase police/prosecutor power, societal surveillance, and corporate profit. → Outcome: government magically chooses not to spend billions on police body cameras and body camera corporations voluntarily go out of business.
Profit motives and structural conditions are major driving force of policy (Worldview 2)	Strategy: Uncover structural causes of cash bail problem, do public political education, come up with strategies to build power to fight entrenched interests, create interventions that reduce size and power of opposing forces to prevent against relentless backsliding, stay vigilant because profit-seeking interests and bureaucracies always seek more power. → Outcome: Governments are **forced** to address structural inequalities, imbalances of power, and systems of pretrial care.	Strategy: Uncover structural causes of police violence problem, do public political education, come up with strategies to build power to fight entrenched interests, create interventions that reduce size and power of opposing forces to prevent against relentless backsliding, stay vigilant because profit-seeking interests and bureaucracies always seek more power. → Outcome: Governments are **forced** to address imbalances of power, inequalities, and democratic control over public safety institutions.

will voluntarily improve things. This approach emphasizes rational, good-faith thinking as the foundation of public safety policy and de-emphasizes the role of mapping and contesting power in organizing for social change. The media overwhelmingly relies on Worldview 1, and this leads to brainworms in the minds of news consumers concerning how social change happens. For example, the news often gives credit to a mayor or a governor or a president or a body of elected leaders for enacting a reform. But they omit the organizing, relationship building, strategizing, research, study, investigative journalism, and pressure by groups of people who together changed the political conditions over a period (sometimes years) of hard work that *made* elected leaders do something they otherwise would not have. Focusing on Worldview 1 erases that work—and more accurate conceptions of how progress happens. Virtually no celebrated progressive change in U.S. history took place because people in power wanted to do it—it was the result of building and shifting power.

Second, Worldview 1 privileges a narrow skillset that lawyers and highly educated researchers are trained in, such as written argument and expensive, published studies. I'm all for making the best arguments, investigating the facts, using evidence, doing critical analysis, and publishing research. (Indeed, I wrote this book critical of how the news manipulates us in service of powerful institutions because pursuing knowledge and relentlessly telling the truth is vital to developing informed views, critical thinking, and a population capable of creating a more just world.) But are they the only set of skills necessary or always the most important for social change? What does Worldview 2 say about the skills helpful for changing society? This is more complex. It suggests that you might need organizers—people who understand how to build relationships and power by bringing people together. And courage to pressure powerful institutions in myriad ways (legal and, often, illegal), along with perseverance for long, hard battles. And specialists in critical analysis who can communicate that analysis to educate and inspire sufficiently large numbers of people. And strategists who develop ideas about how different forms of action, resistance, and political education fit together. And people to communicate compelling narratives about what is happening. And experts who understand systems and implementation because you know that you cannot trust the government bureaucracy to implement something, even after a policymaker has been convinced it is a good idea in theory.[5] Implementing ambitious policy change across large institutions is always hard, and this difficult task is made even more daunting when deeply embedded institutional cultures are resistant to it—for example, if it seeks to reduce the power of punishment bureaucrats or put some of them out of a job.

Third, when we develop a more accurate perspective on the causal chain behind why policies come to be, we see that the news media and nonprofit world's push toward thinking about and working on issues in silos is limited. When we are stacked against powerful interests, it's hard to win change by focusing only on, say, bail reform, to the exclusion of other issues. That is because the interests promoting the cash bail system are essentially the same as those promoting police surveillance technology, new prison construction, court-debt collection, and longer sentences. They all fight for these priorities to receive the bulk of bureaucratic budgets. This also means that it's hard to pursue "criminal justice reform" without talking about bigger issues like health care, labor, financial predation, housing, inequality, education, racism, migration, loneliness, trauma, and the environment.

Thus, to fight against the bail system or drug laws or police surveillance, we must move beyond good policy arguments in one area and build a broad political coalition with a social base capable of compelling the powers that be to invest in improving society holistically. We must target bigger-picture features of our society that cannot be fixed by the hyper-specialization pushed by the media, political, and philanthropic trendsetters, which does not foster the power to win big victories.

Daily news overwhelmingly confines itself to Worldview 1. As a result, a lot of well-meaning people spend a lot of time acting as if we are in Worldview 1.

An Example: The War on Drugs

The war on drugs offers a compelling example of the Big Deception. The public statements by politicians about their reasons for launching the drug war bear no resemblance to the actual reasons that they embarked on it. We know this because President Nixon's Assistant for Domestic Affairs admitted it later:

> We knew we couldn't make it illegal to be either against the war or black, but by getting the public to associate the hippies with marijuana and blacks with heroin, and then criminalizing both heavily, we could disrupt those communities. We could arrest their leaders, raid their homes, break up their meetings, and vilify them night after night on the evening news. Did we know we were lying about the drugs? Of course we did.[6]

Nonetheless, for decades the news has reinforced the stated reasons of politicians for the drug war without providing the evidence people could use to develop skepticism about those reasons.

Over fifty years into the war on drugs, the U.S. has spent trillions of dollars to detain tens of millions of people for hundreds of millions of years and separated tens of millions of children from their parents. It has chemically destroyed millions of acres of ecosystems in South America and killed hundreds of thousands of people. It has stopped, searched, sexually violated, and arrested hundreds of millions of people and surveilled the communications of billions of people globally. Through civil forfeiture, it has stolen tens of billions of dollars in private property. And it has deported hundreds of thousands of people. Criminalizing drugs has also denied tens of millions of people therapeutic treatments for cancer, trauma, mental illness, PTSD, chronic pain, and other afflictions. It has kicked millions of families out of public housing and off public benefits, put tens of millions of poor people into a cycle of debt, and cost tens of millions of people their jobs at the cost of hundreds of billions of dollars to the economy.

Despite all these costs, human and financial, as of 2024 prohibited drugs are more potent than ever and overdose deaths have skyrocketed to their highest levels in U.S. history.[7]

People in power who make drug policy are not universally incompetent. They know the above facts. I have rarely encountered a punishment bureaucrat who believes that prosecution, punishment, and prisons are an effective way to reduce drug use, even assuming that is a genuine goal. For example, every major government and academic body has conceded there was no policy or pharmacological basis for the 100-to-1 disparity between punishment of crack cocaine and powder cocaine that became federal law in 1986. The DOJ and Congress nonetheless enforced and reaffirmed such disparate treatment even after they acknowledged that it had no basis. In 2010, after public outcry—including in the scientific, public health, civil rights, and mainstream political circles—Congress reduced the differential to 18 to 1 (another random number it chose for no articulated or justifiable reasons in a bill euphemistically called the "Fair Sentencing Act"), enshrining a still-indefensible disparity for decades to come.[8] Congresspeople will admit in private that the disparate treatment has no basis, just as Nixon officials did.

A U.S. attorney prosecuting my client for a nonviolent drug offense (and seeking a sentence of ten-years-to-life in prison) once confided to me in the parking lot outside the federal courthouse that he knew sending my client to prison and potentially sending their newborn child to foster care would not benefit society. The Big Deception keeps the public from understanding the reasons that the U.S. government sent that prosecutor to that courthouse that day to do it anyway. For decades, news stories have portrayed the drug war as a good-faith effort to reduce drug use. Here is how the *New York Times*, in 1971, described Nixon's efforts when he "tried to get at the problem":

> The Nixon Administration has not been indifferent to the menace of drugs in America. It has tried to get at the problem at the source. It has used its political and economic power to cut off the supply of drugs . . . and it has poured Federal money and manpower into breaking up the drug peddlers in this country.[9]

Here is how the *Times* described the motivations of Governor Nelson Rockefeller in passing some of the most repressive drug laws in history:

> In 1973, Gov. Nelson A. Rockefeller promised the elimination of drug abuse in New York. He believed that the drug treatment programs he had once strongly supported had not worked, so he moved to the other extreme, putting his faith in a . . . law that was the toughest in the country. He predicted it would quickly clear the streets of pushers.[10]

Here is how the *Times*, with no explanation of the U.S. government's role in managing much of the international drug trade, allowed Ronald Reagan to describe the reasons for new federal legislation increasing imprisonment for drugs in 1986: "Mr. Reagan said that the legislation reflected the Government's desire to eradicate illegal drugs." [11]

A lot of well-meaning people didn't appreciate for decades what a failure the drug war was, at least if the measure of failure was not fulfilling its asserted public-health goals. Many people assumed, based on media coverage of drug busts, penalties, and statements by politicians, that more punishment was a *natural* response being pursued in *good faith* by institutions whose primary goal was reducing the supposed harms of drug use.[12]

The news, to this day, portrays baseless policies as genuine attempts to reduce drug use.[13] The assumption underlying news reporting on drugs is that people in power continue to wage the drug war because they believe the social costs are worth the benefits of their policies and because there exist no readily available alternatives. In 2023, for example, the Associated Press reported on Alabama's increased prison sentences for fentanyl, which included new mandatory minimum prison sentences and the possibility of sentencing people to die in prison, by claiming that the new harsh sentences came about "as *lawmakers try to respond* to the deadly overdose crisis." It continued: "Lawmakers in multiple states across the country are looking to increase fentanyl penalties *in an effort to combat* what has been called the deadliest overdose crisis in U.S. history." [14]

The Associated Press portrays these policies as sincere "efforts" to reduce overdoses. The article not only neglects to tell readers about evidence of the failures of these policies and social costs, but treats officials pursuing policies we *know make the problem worse* as though they are trying to help. This is copaganda; it cultivates mythologies about (1) the intentions of powerful people, and (2) how policies are driven by the intentions of particular people in power and not deeper structural conditions.

The focus on asserted intentions distracts from why policies persist despite their failure. Drug use was never a problem that powerful institutions addressed urgently because they cared about the health and well-being of all people. It was not a problem they viewed as so threatening that they calculated the extraordinary human and financial costs and found mass criminalization worth it. Instead, the expansion of the machinery of state power and profit amid social and racial inequalities was, in many overlapping ways, the impetus to search for policies like what became the war on drugs. The war on drugs was a solution in search of a problem.

Notice two consequences of this deception. First, because reporting on drugs omits the evidence about costs and benefits of drug enforcement from each individual news story like the Associated Press article, people in power avoid daily confrontation about why their assertions about their own motivations don't match the evidence. Second, because people are not informed about the institutional benefits of the drug war to certain political, racial, bureaucratic, and financial interests, they don't develop an accurate theory of why the drug war is *still* happening. For example, almost no daily news article on the topic discusses the benefits of current drug policies to private prisons, pharmaceutical companies, police unions, the bail bond industry, the multi-billion-dollar carceral telecommunications industry, probation departments, police and prosecutors (who benefit from every law that gives them the power to selectively threaten certain people with punishment), real estate developers, diversion providers, surveillance companies, and business and property owners in gentrifying areas.

If one believes the news narrative of the good-faith pursuit of public well-being, then it stands to reason that evidence of catastrophic failure would warrant a full reconsideration of the drug war. In that case, you would expect San Francisco mayor London Breed—who recently expanded surveillance and incarceration for drugs and championed an initiative to require drug testing for recipients of public benefits—or the Alabama legislature to say, "Oh my goodness, we didn't realize there was a social science consensus about this for decades. We'll stop the drug war immediately." Presented with the good-faith news framing, many people become convinced either that the policies are the best we have been able to come up with in a difficult situation or that we are just a few more studies, a few more panels at conferences, and a few more expert commissions away from convincing enlightened leaders that they can achieve a better world by adopting different public health interventions.[15] On the other hand, if the above interests were identified in daily stories about drugs, as well as the amount of money and political influence they devote to preserving drug enforcement, people might develop a different view of why those policies persist and a different sense of the strategies that might be useful for someone who wanted to put an end to those policies.

Although the connection between the Big Deception and our views about how to create social change is sometimes hard for people to notice in the crime-reporting context, because of a shift in news coverage in recent years, many people are able to see the same dynamics at play relating to global warming. Most people no longer believe that the problem with tackling global warming is that powerful institutions are not aware of it. But, for example, if the news were to subtly suggest every day for years that Exxon is pursuing more drilling because it cares deeply about global ecological sustainability but does not yet appreciate the impact of drilling on climate change, the news-reading public might develop a different strategy for stopping that drilling than if the news were to suggest that Exxon is pursuing more drilling because it's profitable. *Understanding why institutions act the way they do matters for how we try to change them.*

Falsifying the Motivations of Powerful People

The news perpetrates the Big Deception on two levels. First, it misleadingly simplifies the reasons people in power do things. This distortion pervades news reporting on public safety. Second, on a deeper level, it focuses on short-term individual motivations of people in power instead of the structural conditions in which their decisions occur.

The Big Deception is not limited to copaganda. Almost all corporate advertising engages in some form of the Big Deception, and similarly, it is virtually the *only* job of officials like the White House press secretary or the local mayor's PR team to mislead people about why the president or the mayor did this or that.[16] As shows like *Veep* illustrate in their satire, these government PR jobs regularly involve outright lying, or, if not outright lying, they almost always involve decisions by people in power to emphasize some true things while omitting others. We see this, for example, when officials condemn one country's human rights violations and ignore another's, when officials use flowery freedom rhetoric to justify one military intervention but not another, or when officials emphasize the benefits to the community when approving a real estate development contract but don't mention that the contract went to a billionaire super PAC contributor instead of a community land trust. These are examples in which people in power attempt to influence people's understanding of *why* they are choosing one course of action over another in order to mislead them.

The goal of politicians and punishment bureaucrats is not accurate public understanding of complex issues. This is why they "spin." In my experience, when presented with this point, partisan political operatives concede its truth and justify their spin because they believe that their securing or remaining in power is better for society than if their opponents were in power. As I came to see through interacting with people in these positions, the things politicians and bureaucrats talk about in private concerning why they do things look a *lot* different from their press releases and public statements.

But the news repeats the most blatant forms of this misinformation as *objective news*. A common way the news does this is by asserting without skepticism that the *stated* motivations of powerful people are their *actual* motivations. I'll give you a few examples from New York City.

Expanding Policing to Reduce Crime and Address Social Problems

The *New York Times* published a 2023 article about the strangulation of Jordan Neely on the subway by another rider after Neely suffered a mental health crisis.[17] The paper asserted that Mayor Eric Adams and Governor Kathy Hochul were pursuing a variety of repressive new policies "to reduce crime and the number of people who are mentally ill and living on New York's streets."

The paper did not alert readers to contrary evidence that the reasons for the new policies may have had to do with PR strategy, real estate developers, political demands of police unions, a desire to take attention away from the failure to address material inequalities like affordable housing, and other political and economic factors along the causal chain that operate at a deeper level than the present intentions of two politicians. Nor did the paper provide readers evidence that any of the policies "reduce crime," address homelessness, or improve anyone's mental health. The paper also omitted the evidence that other policies that Hochul and Adams did *not* choose are more effective at achieving the stated goals.

After I drew attention to the problem with portraying these policies as being steered by genuine motivations and discussed it with the *Times*, the paper edited the article (without appending a correction) to assert:

"Both the Adams and Hochul administrations have been using a variety of tactics *they say are meant* to reduce crime."

This was a subtle but important correction: the paper is now reporting these motivations as a *claim* that Adams and Hochul are making, and not as objective truth that is so obvious it cannot be questioned. The difference between writing that the mayor "claimed" to do something because he asserted it would reduce crime and he did something "to reduce crime" is the difference between helping to build a healthy skepticism in the public and helping officials deceive the public about the universe of potential motivations for their actions.

Adams Resurrects Undercover Violence

In 2022, the *Times* covered Eric Adams reinstating corrupt undercover police units and embracing "broken windows" tactics, which target poor people for minor offenses. The article explains such tactics as an "effort to prevent more serious crimes."[18] The article also asserts that Adams resurrected the controversial tactics "in response" to vague concerns that "many found the city to be more dangerous."

These language choices suggest that Adams is reinstating the controversial squads because he thinks they make people safer and as a genuine "response" to the "concerns" of his constituents. The news thus presents a leader sensitive to evidence and to the desires of the people. The strategy is not pursued, to take just a few examples of other potential reasons, because the police union who supported him demanded it, because it would lead to overtime pay for cops, because Adams wanted to present himself a certain way in the media as "tough on crime," or because other political constituencies rely on such squads for gentrification.

Ironically, Adams helped create the propaganda-fueled fantasy world that the article describes him as responding to: New York had near-historic lows of police-reported violent crime but, nonetheless, "many found the city to be more dangerous." The person responsible for these vibes is portrayed as being genuinely "responsive" to the imagined conditions that he himself created for political reasons. In this way, a politician can use misinformation to generate fear, and then the news will say that it was laudable responsiveness to this fear that motivated the politician to act rather than, say, the reasons that led the politician to spread the original misinformation.

Most important, though, are the paper's assertions about the goals of the people who developed and ruthlessly pursued "broken windows" policing. In making the factual claim about the purpose of "broken windows" policing in a single unassuming phrase—"effort to prevent more serious crimes"—the country's "paper of record" erases from history three decades of academic scholarship in the fields of sociology, criminology, history, political science, law, economics, and anthropology about the complex purposes and functions of the strategy to target poor people and people of color for low-level offenses.[19]

This is a pattern. In a previous article about Adams reinstating undercover units months earlier, the paper broadened its claims to cover undercover police *across the country*: "In New York and around the country, police departments have used plainclothes units to attempt to tackle illegal guns and drugs."[20] The news thus assumed that intentional decisions to structure U.S. policing to surveil, brutalize, and cage tens of millions of poor people for low-level offenses—and directing resources away from white-collar crime, drug use by elites, pollution crime, wage theft, tax evasion, public corruption, and sexual assault—were the result of a good-faith effort to make people safer rather than an approach rooted in, say, racism, controlling working-class people, gentrification, or profit.

Policing the Subway

Toward the end of 2022, the *Times* covered a plan to "flood" the subway with police and surveillance cameras.[21] Adams described it as a plan for the "omnipresence" of armed cops and a sort of cleansing from public space of human beings "dealing with mental health issues." The article was titled "New York City Will Increase Police Presence in Subways *to Combat Crime*" and the subheading asserted that "with less than three weeks until Election Day, Gov. Kathy Hochul *is trying to address a troubling series of violent incidents* on the subway" (emphases added).[22] These are controversial and misleading claims. All other potential reasons are again deemed objectively not worth disclosing.[23] It's like reporting that the U.S. invaded Iraq "to spread democracy."

One can contrast how the motivations of punishment bureaucrats are reported with how the asserted motivations of perceived ideological enemies are reported. When Vladimir Putin or Chinese officials are covered, U.S. reporters almost always frame motivations as *assertions* about motivations while using various devices to convey that a reasonable person may be skeptical of them. Thus, they might write something like, "Putin *claims* that the air strike was retaliation for the Ukrainian drone attack," or "Chinese officials *claim* that China is increasing its investment in African infrastructure to reduce poverty." Reporters often follow these qualifications with evidence to the contrary, inviting further skepticism of the motivations of non-allied political elites.[24]

The Costs of Simplifying Motivations

In his 1962 study of propaganda, Jacques Ellul explains that the most effective propaganda is based on true facts, or at least facts that are hard for the target audience to disprove. However, Ellul adds that deception about "intentions and interpretations" is the most pervasive feature of effective propaganda:

> How can one suspect a man who talks peace of having the opposite intent . . . ? And if the same man starts a war, he can always say that the others force it on him, that events proved stronger than his intentions. We forget that between 1936 and 1939 Hitler made many speeches about his desire for peace, for the peaceful settlement of all problems, for conferences. He never

expressed an explicit desire for war. Naturally, he was arming because of "encirclement." And, in fact, he did manage to get a declaration of war from France and England; so, *he* was not the one who started the war.

Propaganda by its very nature is an enterprise for perverting the significance of events and of insinuating false intentions.[25]

How does this work in copaganda? Imagine a news station with a new directive to make more advertising money or to pursue a particular political goal in an election year. Unlike the previous year, this year the broadcast begins each night with a police press conference about a different murder, covering thirty-one murders in January. It would be bad for the news outlet if it turned out that twenty of the murders were not murders and that the victims were still alive. People would trust the station less, and it would have less influence. Good propaganda should be based on true facts. This is why the most effective propagandistic news outlets often perform diligence—or some process that can be seen as diligence—to ensure that certain facts they are reporting are correct if they are the kinds of facts that the public may otherwise be able to discover had been incorrect.

After a month of watching press conferences about truthful murders, viewers become more afraid—they *feel* that there are more murders this year than last year because of *the way the true facts are presented.* This could happen even if there had been double the number of murders the prior year and four times as many murders ten years ago. And once a group of people *feels* this way, it is difficult to make them feel differently by trying to correct their feelings with data, which people have difficulty retaining. As Ellul notes, people act based on how they feel. *This is falsity of interpretation using true facts.*

In our hypothetical press conferences, officials express outrage and promise to make reducing gun violence the number one priority. Police promise to solve the murders, but also note that they may not be able to do everything they need to do if they don't get more funding. In response, each week, politicians at the lectern announce the launch of various new pilot programs to adjust police patrols to reduce murder, along with increasing the potential sentences for homicide, and appointing various high-ranking commanders with lots of medals on their uniforms to run each patrol. After a month of this coverage every night, it is more likely that viewers will believe that officials are doing everything they can about violence and that, if there was anything else they could do, they would be doing it. *This is an example of the falsification of intention using facts.*

Why has falsification of intentions been central to propaganda for over a hundred years? It helps to ask two questions: (1) What benefits do people in power get from distorting their motivations? (2) How do people in power benefit from ordinary people misunderstanding the reasons people in power do things?

In general, powerful people in charge of public safety want us to think (1) that the problems of our society aren't structural; (2) that they share our outrage at these problems; (3) that these problems can be fixed with little tweaks to the existing system rather than radical change; and (4) that they are doing everything they can to fix them. There are many ways powerful institutions benefit from masking their intentions, but one is paramount: it takes attention away from the longer causal chain of reasons for why our society looks the way it does.

People in power benefit from hiding their true motivations in other ways. For one, part of their power lies in them knowing more about how things work than people who might organize against them. They also benefit from distracting the public so that potential opposing forces are unable to determine the most effective opposition strategy. Also, many people might not support the people in power's true intentions and might reject proposals as being motivated by different intentions, such as, say, generating personal wealth after office. Distortion of intentions by focusing on good-faith policy debate also allows institutions to focus advocacy around informing politicians better rather than overthrowing them. Most basically, falsifying intentions matters for some of the same reasons we care about people's motivations in our everyday lives: they are good predictors of future behavior. Thus, if people in power can keep the public thinking that they are making decisions based on the best available evidence, it helps prevent the public from being able to predict their future self-serving behavior.

Understanding propaganda's historical focus on intentions helps us see that, in an unequal and unsafe world that is inconsistent with our values and dreams, it is important to people with power that people without it are distracted from the roots of our problems and uncertain about how to change them. People in power do not want people without power to start thinking about how a world with different social, political, and economic arrangements might be possible.

The distraction of the public from structural problems and material conditions is the most important function of the Big Deception. This is a primary goal of all modern propaganda, and copaganda in particular.

The Biggest Lie

The reasons our society looks the way it does exist along a longer and more complex causal chain than is represented in everyday news. To take one example, a paramount concern for many people is whether their wages are sufficient to meet their needs, but the news does not focus people on the fact that wages in the U.S. would be 4 percent higher (with benefits for health and safety) if the government banned companies from inserting non-compete clauses in worker contracts.[26] When Governor Hochul vetoed a popular bill to ban such agreements in December 2023 after lobbying from Wall Street, the news coverage cited her subjective belief in the need for more nuanced regulation to promote competitive business. The news neither informed people of the causal connection to overall wages nor treated that connection as a daily news story worthy of multiple articles, even though vetoing bills like this is the equivalent of confiscating significant percentages of yearly income from millions of workers.[27] It was useful to deceive workers about the connection between the veto and something they care a lot about, and that society-wide redistribution of wealth from workers to employers could then be obscured as a main driver of the outcome.

In general, the choice to focus on the intentions of powerful people makes it harder for news consumers to understand that underlying conditions determine what choices are available to politicians, which of those options politicians will predictably select, and how entrenched bureaucracy will implement those choices. This is the lie at the heart of the Big Deception. Let's see how it works by looking at different ways of covering a hypothetical news story.

The Conventional News Story

Consider how the news might report a decision by a mayor to authorize a new undercover squad in a gentrifying area. Let's call the mayor "Eric Badams." At one end of the spectrum, one could believe that Badams's decision is made transparently, based on the quality of the arguments supporting it, by an official acting in the best interests of the public. If the policy promises to be good for the community overall by reducing crime, then it will happen. If the policy won't be good for the community, all things considered, then Badams won't do it.

This is closest to how daily news discusses such matters, with a few quotes about the decision from whichever proponents or opponents have the access to get the reporter to quote them. Virtually everyone quoted—including people who disagree with it—will be portrayed as accepting the premise that the government is *trying* to make choices consistent with overall well-being, safety, and shared community values. Only rarely will a news article quote a source arguing that politicians and police are not primarily concerned with public safety but social control to preserve wealth, or that the intentions of politicians are a poor way of understanding what kinds of policy options a mayor like Badams adopts and why.

The Causal Chain

But there are other ways to understand the decision to set up an under-cover police squad. A reporter could think that there are more basic conditions that determine whether any given society creates a unit of armed government bureaucrats who disguise their identity from the public and who are assigned specifically to patrol the poorest areas of a city that have been deliberately segregated based on wealth and skin color.[28] For example, they could report on campaign contributions made by a real estate developer who wanted more undercover police surrounding a new condo-mall development. Or, they could report on the political power of the police union, the police PR budget, and the ability of the police to threaten political opponents through targeted enforcement of low-level laws, surveillance, and planted news stories against any non-compliant politician.[29] They might present facts showing that these interests have influenced similar decisions by decades of mayors since well before Badams was a young feminist poet, his vocation prior to becoming mayor.

On a deeper level, the journalist could explain the decision to create an armed undercover squad for poor neighborhoods by reporting on the economic and cultural forces that lead certain people with certain worldviews to be key aides for mayors making such decisions. Might the content of decisions be influenced by the same factors that determine who is selected for particular roles and what social networks those people come from? Perhaps those groups have preferences, prejudices, financial interests, skills, and gaps in knowledge that lead to certain patterns in the policies they promote? One might even inform news consumers that the chief of staff to Badams went to the same boarding school as the lawyer for the developer.

The journalist could go even deeper. They could point out the forces that paid for the publication of a study by local professors on the economic benefits of selling public land to private developers for new condos, a subsidized stadium, and a shopping mall, as well as the hit the developer's profit might take from visible homelessness in the area. Or they could report that surveillance companies donated to a nonprofit to produce a report on the short-term benefits for property values of installing security cameras in the neighborhood. A reporter might even explain that the calls for this new undercover squad occurred at the same time as calls for similar squads in a hundred other cities. And they could point out that a consortium of global companies was simultaneously trying to secure a new multi-billion-dollar replacement market for a new surveillance technology and cloud-based predictive policing databases originally developed for use by the U.S. military in Afghanistan, and that that consortium's primary market is undercover police units.

A journalist might also explain that the push for such units and for harsher sentencing laws for the contraband those units find on poor people was more significant in areas in which unemployment and poverty had increased in the previous five years. They might observe that increases in policing and prison investments follow increases in inequality and declines in available health care, early childhood education, and affordable housing.[30] When explaining the context to readers, they could note that police presence tends to be higher in non-white communities, and that incarceration generally is higher in more unequal societies.[31]

Finally, on perhaps the deepest level, a journalist could identify how politicians and police deploy various cultural mythologies about safety, whose safety matters, and what forms of inequality and suffering are tolerable. They could note how conceptions of safety differ in various societies, historical periods, election years (as compared with non-election ones), and in cities with conservative or progressive officials. Only rarely does a news story inform news consumers of the facts necessary for them to understand dominant narratives as *socially constructed themes* to advance dominant interests.

If journalists included such facts, the public might start to ask challenging questions. Was Badams's decision to call for the police unit to arrest and detain unhoused people or those with mental health issues the result of genuine concern about their well-being? Does the creation of certain forms of technology or bureaucratic organization create a path toward dependence on certain policing policies? Did affluent people in the neighborhood, who are worried about their property values and ability to shop at the new Whole Foods free of homeless people, lobby Badams to establish the undercover unit? Has the network of schools, professional associations, friendships, favors, and dinner parties combined to make the political preferences of the class of people who own things more consequential than the political preferences of other people?

This hypothetical example demonstrates that certain background conditions determine the context within which institutions make decisions, including the ability of people in power to perceive what decisions are technically and politically feasible. Copaganda obscures that. It encourages news consumers to believe that people in power are working to make people's lives better—even though the interests that control what happens do not support the kinds of big changes necessary to materially improve the safety and well-being of the vast majority of human beings. By focusing on good or bad intentions of individuals in power and not on background material realities along a longer causal chain than the immediate moment of the decision, daily news hides this truth. In my view, this is the most salient thing about public safety and crime reporting in our society.

All the News That's Fit to Omit

One effect of the misplaced emphasis on intentions is that journalists focus on individual policy positions of government officials and political candidates. Contrast this perspective with the approach of military defense contractors, pharmaceutical and medical-device companies, the insurance industry, police unions, or other organized lobbying interests. While these groups spend resources to elect their preferred candidates, they expend far more capital and energy on ensuring that the difference between the range of viable candidates doesn't matter that much to them. These groups understand that *real* power means creating the conditions under which their interests will be significantly served no matter who among the viable candidates is elected. For example:

- Defense contractors establish multi-trillion-dollar programs in hundreds of congressional districts. In this way, contract boondoggles are perpetuated for decades because no congressperson can vote against them. A system in which parts for an aircraft carrier or fighter jet are manufactured in fifty cities is not configured that way because it is the best way to "keep America safe." This, more than any policy argument commonly presented in the news, determines whether these programs exist or not.

- The consulting industry has worked for decades to hollow out government capacity and expertise so that nearly every government function now requires outsourcing contracts to private companies. This arrangement both produces trillions in private wealth—a small fraction of which is then used to purchase the political influence necessary to keep this process going—and reduces the ability of local, state, and national governments to solve problems through public institutions. Private contractors narrow what *kinds of public programs are even possible* by using technological systems, ownership over data, and the integration of those systems with others to block programs that damage their interests.[32]

- Police unions insert contract provisions (often with government accomplices or incompetent political staff who, unlike the unions, are not sophisticated repeat players) that make it illegal or prohibitively costly for subsequent governments to enact certain changes. The same occurs with prosecutor unions, prison guard unions, and probation unions. The punishment bureaucracy thus obscures from the public *the mechanisms it uses to prevent genuine change*. Politicians can keep issuing press releases on their desire for reform, but they know change is not possible without overturning deep institutional arrangements within the punishment bureaucracy. Yet the news rarely discusses these features, which helps explain why we are stuck in endless cycles of abuse and reform rhetoric.[33]

Dominant groups ensure their interests in punishment are served regardless of elections. They create ideological ecosystems to influence conventional wisdom. This includes decades-long efforts to fund university chairs, institutes, think tanks, conferences, retreats, trainings, op-ed writers, fellowships, research papers, awards, and non-profits. Their organizations bankroll campaigns to discipline and expose people who deviate from certain positions. In the conservative movement, the Federalist Society plays this role, but liberals have similar formations. Lawyers, judges, and professors know that they will be attacked by these forces if they take a case, issue an opinion, or write an article that deviates from the consensus. The results are profound distortions to the production of knowledge and debate. This ecosystem shapes what research topics and positions academics avoid in order to secure tenure, what articles journalists feel obligated to write, and what topics news producers skirt or would never think of pitching to keep their jobs. While many dissertations and books have described these background conditions, the news almost never mentions them when explaining any particular story.

Daily news omits the most relevant background conditions and constraints when it explains why politicians propose this or that policy. These underlying social, cultural, bureaucratic, technological, and economic conditions determine which options are available for politicians to choose from; which ones officials perceive as viable to propose; and which ones they conclude are advantageous for retaining power. They also constrain the range of policies that almost any official, no matter their true heart, can pursue. Finally, they shape what kind of person advances to positions of power in institutions, and they foster a shared ideological community among elites that also disciplines their decision-making once in office.

The Big Deception keeps us focused on the qualities or flaws in specific individuals in power or their policy proposal du jour and not focused nearly enough on the conditions in which all people in power operate. With that in mind, we can re-pose the question from earlier: why does the war on drugs exist? It is not because morally good politicians believed it to be the best way to improve public health. But did it happen because morally bad politicians saw that it could give them political advantages? While many people now believe some form of that suggestion after the admissions of Nixon-administration officials, this perspective misses something important: there were economic, political, and racial forces that made it beneficial and profitable to launch the war on drugs. And there were political, administrative, legal, bureaucratic, and technological developments that made something like a "war on drugs" *possible* to implement for politicians. It is *that* longer causal chain that is vital to understanding not just why mid-twentieth-century leaders started the war on drugs, but why subsequent governments have *continued and expanded it*, despite the fact that Richard Nixon left office decades ago. It is impossible to fight meaningfully against the war on drugs, or to accurately cover it as a journalist, without acknowledging the reasons it persists. But it is precisely this context that news reporting omits and distorts.

Instead, daily news outlets like *The New York Times* claim that they are providing "all the news that's fit to print." This pretense to be providing "everything you need to know"—which is a slogan used by outlets— is integral to the tone and thematic content of reporting on these issues. These declarations implicitly suggest what the public does *not* need to know—usually, the social structures, history, and context that lead to crime or other newsworthy events, for that matter. The news therefore makes people less likely to appreciate what they don't know. If there were some other important reason powerful people did something, such as rolling back bail reform or increasing the police budget or adding thousands of cops to the subway and schools, surely it would have been included in the list of things we "need to know." Convincing people that what they have been told in a news report is all they "need to know" is itself an important form of propaganda.

The news bears responsibility for the fact that people are left with the impression that public safety decisions in our society are made far more democratically, and far more on merit, than they are. If the news focused more on the root causes, power relationships, and trends that contextualize the causal chain for any news event, we would fall for political deception less. We would be better able to evaluate the claims of politicians and put less faith in this or that individual person in power. We would be less hyper-focused on electoral politics and more interested in organizing to build collective relationships, economic arrangements, and institutions that change the underlying context within which any public official must operate.[34]

15

Distracting from
Material Conditions

*It is a widespread but fatal trap—precisely, a trap of "liberal opinion"—
to split analysis from action, and to assign the first to the instance of
the "long term," which never comes, and reserve only the second to
"what is practical and realistic in the short term. . . . So, if someone
says to us: "Yes, but given present conditions, what are we to do now?,"
we can only reply "Do something about the present conditions."*

-Stuart Hall[1]

Copaganda distracts people from the material conditions of our society
that both produce and ameliorate crime.

One of my favorite copaganda stories is a 2022 *New York Times* feature about how bicycle theft is plaguing Burlington, Vermont.[2] The
story suggests that bicycle theft by "homeless" people and "meth users"
leads to "violent crime" and "murder." The story is a warning to liberal
readers about what happens when "progressives" and their "hippie . . .
ideals" take control and do terrible things like talk about reducing reliance on police.

The problems with the article are representative of how many news
stories distract from deeper issues of material inequality.[3] First, the article blames "crime" (a rise in "bike theft") on homeless drug users without
discussing poverty, lack of affordable housing, and lack of health care.
Second, it suggests that there has to be a tradeoff between our ideals—
like reducing inequality—and our safety. Third, it takes garden-variety

misinformation about the root causes of crime that Fox News would be proud of and dresses it up for upper-class liberals.

Problems Have Root Causes

Although the specter of homeless encampments full of bike thieves haunts the article, the only mention of affordable housing is the gratuitous introduction of the pro-police mayor as a former "affordable housing developer" (i.e., a person who profited from our society's privatization of insufficient housing for the poor), who complains that someone vandalized the windshield of his Tesla. The paper thereby won the first-ever Copaganda Harry Houdini Award for disappearing the concept of affordable housing from an article about homelessness.

The words "poverty," "inequality," and "wealth" do not appear in the article, nor are those concepts discussed using other words. It's almost as if the epidemic of homelessness in the United States randomly appeared out of nowhere without underlying social policies. The punishment bureaucracy must take unhoused people as a given and then manage their public existence with cops, handcuffs, and cages, without ever asking why people do not have a place to live. News reporting like this confuses millions of readers, who are trained not to associate underlying material conditions with the problems they keep hearing about as "informed" people who read the news. And it depoliticizes us by obfuscating the political and economic battles that determine the course of our lives.

Here's a fact omitted in many articles about growing numbers of poor people living on the street: if the U.S. had remained as equitable as it was in 1975 for the next forty-three years through 2018, the bottom 90 percent of Americans would have earned an extra $47 trillion.[4] Instead, that money went to people already at the top, who use that money, among other things, to influence the political system and to hoard real estate. In 2020, after George Floyd was killed, a nationwide movement demanded reduction in funding of the punishment bureaucracy and an increase in investments to reduce inequality. That same year, the richest 1 percent of Americans gained $4 trillion in wealth.[5] These and other newsworthy factors—including widespread fraud relating to mortgages, foreclosure, rent price-fixing, predatory lending, urban development policies and subsidies, private equity and consolidation of real-property ownership, bankruptcy from medical bills, pension reform, and so on—have contributed to a generational crisis of economic and housing insecurity. In 93 percent of U.S. counties, a minimum-wage salary is not enough to afford a one-bedroom apartment.[6] All of this is left out of articles whipping up a moral panic about unhoused people and "visible disorder."

One of the best illustrations of how such stories contribute to ignorance about inequality is a 2012 study by a Harvard Business School economist. It demonstrated that most people in the U.S. have an inaccurate understanding of inequality.[7] An astonishing 92 percent of people believed that the U.S. should be more equal than it is. But, here's the kicker: they wildly misapprehended how unequal the U.S. was.[8] Almost everyone—of all political parties and backgrounds—wanted more equality than they thought the U.S. had, and they thought the U.S. was already *far more equal than reality.*

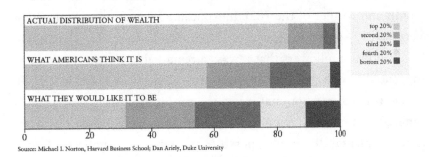

Source: Michael I. Norton, Harvard Business School; Dan Ariely, Duke University

In the "bike thieves" article, the *Times* appears to have intentionally hidden these points about inequality from readers. Here is the elected prosecutor in Burlington describing her interview with the reporter:[9]

Sarah Fair George
@SarahFairVT

I spent over 40 minutes on the phone with the author of this article, talking somewhat incessantly about the housing crisis in BTV and our failure to meet many folks basic needs. Quite astounded that it is not mentioned once in the entire article. Not once.

Omitting the concepts of affordable housing, urban planning, and economic inequality from articles about homelessness is standard practice. The *San Francisco Chronicle*'s coverage of homelessness repeatedly makes it seem like people are homeless because they are mentally ill and use drugs rather than because the city has its greatest crisis of affordable housing in modern history.[10] Growing homelessness is not an accident—it's caused by, among other things, a massive increase in wealth inequality, predatory financial policies, and the corruption of local government politics by real-estate developers.[11]

In one infamous 2021 *Chronicle* story, as the campaign for recalling the district attorney heated up (in part because of his supposed refusal to cage enough people living on the street), the reporter offered a sensitive portrait of a mother whose daughter was struggling with homelessness and addiction on the streets of San Francisco. Noted liberal pundit and winner of the 2021 Inexplicable Promotion of Something Very Bad As Something Very Good Copaganda Award Ezra Klein told his millions of followers that it was "a remarkable piece of reporting" that should force them to "stop scrolling Twitter and read it."[12] The article framed in emotional terms the proposition that the problems suffered by unhoused people in San Francisco were caused by addiction and mental illness as opposed to systemic social policies. To the contrary, the article, using one woman's personal pain, argued that offering too many good things like housing to addicts just makes them too comfortable, and that they wouldn't leave the area or overcome their addiction if things got too nice for them. Through its focus on individual failure and blame, the story weaponized personal tragedy to promote anti-science practices like more prosecution and caging supposedly ungrateful drug addicts, and prohibiting people with an addiction from getting material economic help. This would be like arguing that the solution to journalists being pathologically unable to convey to their readers that problems in our society have root causes should be punishing individual journalists for their addiction to misleading people rather than trying to understand the political, economic, financial, and cultural incentives that lead news outlets to become copaganda addicts and peddlers.

What's the result of the news pushing more cops as a solution to crack down on homeless drug users in perpetuity? A *Chronicle* article from 1992, exactly thirty years before, about the *same* neighborhood in San Francisco called it "an urban nightmare."[13] Police at the time claimed that they had "more cops per square foot" in the Tenderloin neighborhood than any other place and that their crackdown of arrests would yield results on drug use within "another two to three years."

Choosing Between Ideals and Safety

Like so much copaganda, the article about Burlington suggests there has to be a tradeoff between our values and our safety. The idea is that we can have racial justice, economic justice, and civil liberties after George Floyd *or* we can be "safe." The "bike thieves" reporter falsely presents the debate about transferring resources from Burlington police to things that are proven to make people safer as "a clash of ideals and reality."

A clash of ideals and reality

Downtown Burlington is a vibrant cluster of bars humming with live music, cafes hissing with sounds of steamed-milk machines and a Patagonia store with a "Black Lives Matter" sign in the window.

This article is filled with so many toxic tropes that a student working with me became ill with copaganda syndrome after consuming it. To prevent contagion, I won't quote it extensively. But here's the basic message: People dedicated to lessening inequality, saving lives, and creating more connected communities are pollyannish about safety. People who profit from surveillance and human caging deeply care about safety despite evidence that their approach decreases safety. The *Times* represents ordinary people and leaders who base their policy positions on the evidence, which the article withholds, as naive "hippies." Thus, the paper frames our choice as one between, on the one hand, combating material inequality and racism, and, on the other, facing what it calls "reality" and investing in punishment to make us safe.

The article culminates with an attack on Burlington's passage of a modest cap on the number of police officers after the 2020 protests. The paper quotes a source who criticizes "the notion of replacing the police with more social workers" as "predicated on the idea that everyone just wants to get along." The thesis is apparently that some "bike thieves" are evil, and they will hurt other people no matter what, so we must spend exactly the amount of money (or more) on the punishment bureaucracy as each local government in the U.S. happened to allocate in 2022, and the punishment bureaucracy must keep pursuing the same strategies that it has been pursuing to manage interpersonal conflict. Nothing else can keep people safe. Anyone who does not share this view is lost in a fantasyland where everyone just wants to hold hands and sing "Kumbaya."

This thesis is contrary to empirical evidence and authoritarian. It rejects the knowledge accumulated from other societies about meeting people's needs, intervening in cycles of trauma, and fostering stronger social connections. Other wealthy countries that spend a tiny fraction of what we do on police and prisons are *far* less violent than the United States. But the reporter parodies local officials who shifted policies marginally away from investment in policing, and the article does not even let local leaders explain *why* they developed their policies. The reporter provides no evidence for the assertion of a necessary tradeoff between social justice and safety in Burlington, for the premise that both the quantity of harmful behavior and the number of police to manage it happen to be fixed at just the right equilibrium, or for the idea that fairness, equality, and justice aren't consistent with "reality."

The article is also inaccurate on its own terms. The city still had roughly the same size police force as it did before it voted to cap it, and that cap was not the cause of the slight dip in the size of the force. Even after the cap was removed, the city still didn't manage to employ a higher number of cops. And it's not like the city addressed the problems of inequality, housing, and health care—so the article's standard copaganda implication that progressive policies were tried and failed is wrong. The primary policy question, ignored by the article and so many like it, would be whether relatively small reductions in the police force affect the narrow range of harms that the police record and whether municipal resources could be invested in other things at a greater benefit per dollar spent. The article's function is not to deepen public discussion of the best ways to produce safety but to distract people from specific progressive policies and suggest right-wing policies to readers who need to hear those policies in a way that portrays them as enlightened.[14]

Dressing Up Punishment as the Progressive Solution

The article starts with a sensitive, nature-ensconced portrait of the police chief, who is portrayed as cool, thoughtful, and progressive.

We are told that this police chief is some kind of literal Hollywood ideal, having consulted for the hip show *Brooklyn Nine-Nine*, which we are told is "the hit television comedy about a precinct of zany cops who often try to do the right thing." The article assures us

that he is an Obama-loving, racial justice reform-minded person who is just telling it like it is when he insists police are underfunded and understaffed. The message? You can trust this cool guy when he tells you that giving cops more cash will make us safe from the homeless bike thieves.

Having laid the "progressive" foundation, the reporter then lets the police union suggest that bike theft is a gateway crime that will bring unto Burlington a wave of escalating violence.[15] There is little difference between this kind of reporting and what one finds in overtly right-wing media, except that the anecdotes and smiling tone are designed to be persuasive to a different audience who elites have reason to fear might otherwise be interested in hearing about and addressing underlying material conditions. The core message is the same: meeting people's needs, addressing systemic inequalities by improving people's material living conditions, and shifting resources from police to social investments are priorities that demonstrate the dangerous naivete of radicals who aren't living in the "reality" of a world menaced by threats that demand authoritarian control.

Focusing on Tweaks

Focusing on tweaks to the punishment bureaucracy rather than social investments is one of the most important ways copaganda distracts from material conditions. For example, a 2022 *Atlantic* article suggests that various court policies to speed up the mass-incarceration assembly line cause less crime:[16]

IDEAS

The Cause of the Crime Wave Is Hiding in Plain Sight

When the speed of repercussions drops, society loses a key deterrent against unlawful behavior

By Alec MacGillis

The Atlantic published this article in a section it calls "Ideas." The thesis of the article is that "the cause" of "the crime wave" was a backlog in jury trials and other court proceedings.

Before debunking the article's thesis, I want to highlight a few general points that make the article representative of this genre of "tweak-copaganda." First, many articles push policy tweaks within the punishment bureaucracy as solutions to society-wide interpersonal violence. But decades of gold-standard research shows that such tweaks invariably make little difference to public safety when studied later.[17] Why? Because overall levels of social violence are determined to a much greater extent by deeper features of our society and culture. To take one example, the more unequal a society, the greater the social violence.[18] Making slight tweaks to give punishment bureaucrats more power won't ameliorate inequality but instead enforces and preserves it. But the news often identifies issues like a "court backlog" as "*the* cause" for the crime panic of the moment. Every so often, different tweaks become popular among punishment bureaucrats for self-serving reasons (such as officials wanting more funding for courts to process more cases more quickly), and the news will then offer something like a tweak to court backlog policies as the solution to that fear du jour. After that policy tweak inevitably fails to make the U.S. safer, the punishment bureaucracy pivots to another one that will also do little but contribute to the overall expenditures of state repression. But playing whack-a-mole with minor tweak after minor tweak helps powerful people in any given moment avoid the public making linkages between violence and poverty, lack of access to health care, the affordable housing shortage, under-resourced schools, and other root causes. It's easier for reporters to get into the coveted "Ideas" section if they can propose some novel tweak that people in power want as opposed to harping about structural inequality for the umpteenth time.

Second, the news claims that these minor policy tweaks have significant effects on police-reported crime. News stories after the 2020 uprisings are replete with examples: a few more hours of police training, edits to unenforceable police operations manuals, body cameras, small variations in the number or deployment of cops, modest fluctuations in sentencing, tweaks to bail policies, fewer charges for low-level offenses, and so on. The reality is that these things do not play a significant role in affecting society-wide levels of violence. How could they? They in no way address the root causes of interpersonal harm in our society.

Nevertheless, minor tweaks in bureaucratic policy are earnestly dissected by reporters. They are debated in serious publications so vociferously that writers forget to mention things like inequality. The collective result is that the news leads people to overstate the ability of punishment bureaucrats to affect social problems. Pretending that insignificant tinkering with the machinery of authoritarian bureaucracy can make people safer not only distracts people from thinking about root causes, but also traps us all on the hamster wheel of tweaks, constantly in search of the new idea that will change things without having to *change things*.

Fluctuations in punishment policy are not a main driver of violence, and articles overemphasizing such policy tweaks play into an assumption that pervades elite thought like a kind of contemporary cult of flat-earthers. There are many countries with lower rates of homicide, and no one thinks it's because they have harsher mass-incarceration policies. The search for answers to U.S. violence in the weeds of bureaucratic policy is a narrow way of thinking that excludes lessons from most of human history and the contemporary world.

Third, *The Atlantic* fails to distinguish between accountability and "consequences," which it equates mainly with human caging. Much reporting in this area assumes that, because some people think imprisonment is ineffective and harmful, those people are against *accountability* for harm. This common theme leaves the news-consuming public with the vague sense that people who oppose imprisonment as the intervention for violence are somehow not urgently focused on holding people who harm other people accountable. This fallacy ignores an entire wing of practice and scholarship on restorative and transformative justice developed by survivors of violence.[19] Ignoring the success of restorative and transformative justice responses to violence helps the news disguise one of the other root causes of violence: a lack of systemic human connection and relationship that leads to alienation and an inability to work through interpersonal conflict.

We can see each of these themes in *The Atlantic*'s attempt to connect court backlog policies to violence. Let's begin with the title of the article, which asserts that there is a singular "crime wave." This is weird, because although crime was near historic lows in the U.S. at the time of the article's publication, different forms of "crime" were slightly up or down in different areas. Though it invokes "*the* crime wave," the story's anecdotes turn out to be about shootings/murder in two cities. The journalist doesn't address, let alone integrate into his thesis, the more complex picture that many types of police-reported "crime" were fluctuating up and down across the U.S. during the relevant period. This is a sloppy way to start, but it's a lesson in copaganda: when reporters talk about certain policies affecting "crime," they often omit that some kinds of crime are going up and some are going down at any moment without acknowledging that their theory has no explanation for that differentiation. So, for example, say a mayor blames "bail reform" for a rise in shootings but sexual assault and property crime are way down. Did bail reform cause murder but deter sexual assault and property crimes? Why is one crime affected and not others? In reality, the evidence suggests little causal relation between the bureaucratic tweak and *either* crime.

The title is not only making a bold claim that the reporter, Alec MacGillis, has uncovered a scientifically "causal" mechanism for crime, but that he has identified "the" cause. MacGillis's follow-up interview on NPR unspooled to millions more listeners an even more careless iteration of this misinformation about "the cause" of "the crime wave."[20] In solidarity with another person named "Alec," I consulted with a team of theoretical physicists and dictionary authors to award MacGillis and his *Atlantic* editors the 2022 Copaganda Award for Innovation in Quantum Mechanics for their contribution to reimagining the concept of causality.

The paragraph describing the article's thesis belongs in the Copaganda Hall of Fame:

> Criminologists have offered several explanations for the increase, including the rise in gun sales early in the pandemic, changes in police behavior following the protests over the murder of George Floyd, and the social disruptions caused by closures of schools and interruptions in social services. But many people who work in criminal justice are zeroing in on another possible factor—the extended shutdown of so much of the court system, the institution at the heart of the public order.

These two sentences are a good example of a common practice. As we saw earlier in the chapter on experts, MacGillis attributes this wisdom to "criminologists" and "many people who work in criminal justice." By pairing these anonymous groups of sources together, he falsely suggests that these are consensus views within those groups even though they are controversial opinions, and he removes account-ability from whomever he is talking about. Just who are these "crimi-nologists" and "people who work in criminal justice"? As one reads the article, it becomes clear he means "a few pro-police professors" and "prosecutors," respectively.

Two paragraphs later, MacGillis does it again, this time saying that an anonymous consensus of "experts" blames court shutdowns for mur-der: "Above all, experts say, the shutdowns undermined the promise that crimes would be promptly punished." This is key, because one pillar of his thesis is that it is the "swiftness" of punishment "rather than their severity" that matters in deterring crime. MacGillis cites no evidence that people are killing more people because they think they can escape or delay punishment.

The only assertion supported with a citation in this important paragraph is the supposed connection of rising gun sales to mur-der. The link provided goes to another *Atlantic* article, also from the "Ideas" section, called "The Data Are Pointing to One Major Driver of America's Murder Spike," blaming the rise in murders *not* on court backlogs but on more gun sales.[21] That article, by the same former CIA and police consultant I discussed in chapter 5, is also mostly spec-ulation, but it's noteworthy that *The Atlantic* keeps publishing confi-dent claims that contradict one another. Which explanation is it? Is "the cause" of the rise in murders the one that *The Atlantic* asserts now, or the "one major driver" that *The Atlantic* was pushing six months earlier based on "the data"? It's almost as if elite magazines will spew whatever speculation is expedient for whatever political point punish-ment bureaucrats want to make in a particular moment to distract people from root causes.

The copaganda gets more serious when MacGillis attempts to support his sweeping nationwide thesis—that court closures are "the cause" of rising violence and murder—with a few anecdotes and mis-leading numbers from just two cities: Albuquerque and Wichita. As a preface to a horrific anecdote about a person being killed by a cellmate in Albuquerque after the victim had been jailed prior to trial for "nearly 10 months for trying to steal a bottle of tequila with a pocketknife," MacGillis writes: "The link between any one instance of violence and courtroom delays can be hard to prove. But sometimes it couldn't be more obvious."

Here is a translation for readers not yet fluent in copaganda: "I can't give you any evidence of the widespread, causal social phenomenon that I am advocating in a prominent magazine, but let me tell you a story that will make you feel sad."

MacGillis's takeaway from this story is that courts need to move faster; he fails to identify the more obvious, underlying problem: that poverty-based detention of people for petty crimes of desperation in overcrowded jails is inhumane and deadly. In reality, this person was not killed because the court system isn't doing jury trials quickly. He was killed by a judicial system that criminalizes poverty and jails nearly 500,000 presumptively innocent people every night, *before letting them have a jury trial to determine whether they are guilty*, mostly because they cannot access cash.[22]

Even under MacGillis's version of events, the anecdote makes no sense. The hypothesis of his causal argument is that murder was rising because people were *released* before trial and that people generally didn't expect to be punished swiftly. It was *not* that jailing so many people so quickly and for so long would increase the chances of those same people being the victim of crime in jail. But MacGillis was so intent on promoting more expenditures for courts so that they could jail more people more quickly that it didn't even occur to him that this anecdote might better serve a thesis on the illegality of pretrial detention, the criminalization of poverty, the deadliness of police conducting so many custodial arrests, and the brutality of U.S. jails.

After his misinterpretation of the Albuquerque anecdote, MacGillis moves to Wichita. He claims:

Violence had surged in the spring and early summer of 2020, as it had in so many other cities. Wichita police saw a sharp rise in drive-by shootings. And officials noticed something else, said then-police chief Gordon Ramsay: Many suspects arrested in the shootings were defiant, suggesting that nothing would come of the charges against them because the pandemic had shut down most of the court system. Defendants were, as a result, disinclined to take a plea deal. Why plead guilty to avoid a trial when no trials were happening anyway?

This paragraph is full of unsubstantiated claims. When reviewing any argument by punishment bureaucrats, it's helpful to list out the causal chain of assertions, as well as who is making those assertions and what support they offer, because *each* must be true for the argument to retain holistic validity. None of MacGillis's assertions is supported by evidence: "violence had surged" → "police saw a sharp rise in drive-by shootings" → "officials noticed" → "many suspects" were "defiant" → suspects were "suggesting that nothing would come of the charges" because of the pandemic → suspects were "as a result" not pleading guilty.

Aside from its lack of factual support, this thesis reflects ignorance about how the legal system works. One of the main things that coerces people to plead guilty is precisely the immediate consequence of pretrial jailing, and the prospect of a backlog *exacerbates* that coercion by making pretrial jailing last longer. Unsurprisingly, neither MacGillis nor the police chief points to a single example of a shooting suspect "defiantly" refusing a plea deal because they thought they could avoid "consequences" since no trials were happening. In reality, the *opposite* happened: during the period at the beginning of the COVID-19 pandemic that MacGillis discusses, people faced swift and prolonged consequences for even being arrested, let alone convicted. In class-action lawsuits, I and my colleagues represented hundreds of thousands of people confined in many of the country's most crowded jails. People charged with serious violent crimes were largely *detained* prior to trial, and because few trials were happening, they were languishing in increasingly crowded jails under barbaric conditions. They were even more desperate to plead guilty in many cases, especially because of the lack of precautions to protect them from contracting COVID-19. Many of our clients died in jail outbreaks.

People's desperation to plead guilty highlights a key fact MacGillis omits: the vast majority of murder and shooting suspects are detained prior to trial. Being immediately locked up *is* a "swift consequence." And even the smaller number of people released with serious charges face swift consequences, including onerous pretrial surveillance and supervision plus the threat of immediate re-arrest and indefinite detention if they violate any conditions of their pretrial release. For example, it *would* have been consistent with MacGillis's thesis if the police chief had said that police stopped trying to arrest suspects. But that's precisely *not* what the chief said: he said they *were* arresting suspects but that once caught and facing swift pretrial jailing, they were "defiant."[23] Because the article does not include a contrary point of view or relevant facts, readers of *The Atlantic* might not be able to see how its own anecdotes and arguments contradict its thesis.

Back in Albuquerque, MacGillis's main source is a fearmongering prosecutor who emphasizes low-level crimes. MacGillis writes: "A person charged with a crime, he told me, "doesn't see any consequence of it. They're released back into the community."

This claim is false. Even a cursory perusal of Albuquerque's court system at the time reveals many people punished for many crimes, and many people being detained even prior to formal punishment. Nor does releasing presumed innocent people in low-level cases have any necessary connection to a backlog. Most importantly, neither the prosecutor nor MacGillis offers an example of a shooting or murder suspect who didn't face "consequences." One would think that, in a national publication, someone making an ambitious causal claim about the origins of crime could show a single example in support of that claim. Instead of presenting evidence of a single person who shot someone not facing "consequences" because of a backlog, MacGillis tells us that a few dozen fewer jury trials were happening. Pay attention to that: a major magazine article pitched as having discovered "the cause" of "the crime wave" across the U.S. is reduced to a claim about *a few dozen fewer jury trials* over a period of many months in Albuquerque and Wichita.

As is often the case when one reads copaganda closely, the article doesn't include evidence to support its "causal" argument about Albuquerque and Wichita, let alone the United States. In fact, MacGillis says Wichita resumed jury trials in July 2020, but "by the end of 2020, homicides were up sharply in Wichita." How does this fit with his thesis? We are not told. Later, he claims that Wichita "bucked" a national trend and saw "9 percent" fewer homicides. But another thing MacGillis elides is that this appears to be a decrease of only five homicides in a time span that does not align with his causal theory. Even so, *The Atlantic* bases a *causal* claim regarding an important area of social policy on a handful of homicides from one cherry-picked city.

Perhaps most damning, there are lots of other crimes other than shootings and murders, though they get no mention from MacGillis. In many places, including those with court backlogs, those crimes were down in the same period. How does MacGillis's new scientific theory about court backlogs reducing "swift consequences" explain this? He doesn't mention it.

MacGillis appears to have been hoodwinked. The first time I heard the "backlog" argument was from former Houston police chief and copaganda stormtrooper Art Acevedo. Every time I talked to him or saw him interviewed, he harped on the need to get more money to speed up courts and reduce the "backlog." I then heard this argument from many sheriffs and prosecutors before it filtered its way up into the vaunted world of *Atlantic* "Ideas" through the punishment bureaucracy's public relations networks.

What's really going on? Why did people bring this theory to MacGillis for publication? The punishment bureaucracy is obsessed with "efficiency" for its own institutional reasons. Remember, no other society transfers so many human beings from their families, schools, homes, jobs, churches, and civil society and locks them behind the bars of government-run jails, even before convicting them of anything. To carry this out, punishment bureaucrats must make the legal system's formal commitment to "due process" as ruthlessly efficient as possible, even if that means overriding nominal constitutional protections. This means they need most individuals to either plead guilty as quickly as possible or the case to be dismissed. If people fight their cases, many of these cases will not result in conviction but will take extraordinary resources for court-appointed lawyers, motions, defense investigators, and jury trials—this combination would mean that even if only 10 percent of cases resulted in jury trials, it would break the system. So, bureaucrats want to coerce more guilty pleas, secure more quick convictions, and generate more fines, fees, and profits at each stage. Courts, prosecutors, and sheriffs constantly seek larger budgets by invoking "backlogs" even though this situation is actually caused by their own choice to prioritize so many arrests and prosecutions for low-level crimes. Keep in mind what we discussed earlier: only 5 percent of all police arrests are for "violent crimes," and that punishment bureaucrats have, over the last several decades, routinely chosen to arrest more people for marijuana possession than all "violent crime" combined.

So, does *The Atlantic* think readers will believe a supposed national increase in shootings and murders—but *not* many other serious crimes, which are apparently immune from the "causal" mechanism MacGillis has uncovered—was caused by the delay of a few dozen criminal jury trials for mostly low-level crimes in two cities? Probably not. But that's not the way copaganda like this works. When we read something, most of us later remember only a general, simplistic impression. Think about, for example, how someone might describe an article they read last week to a friend at a dinner party. After glancing at the headline, reading only part of it, or even reading the whole thing in a few minutes, that person was left with an overall impression, leading them to tell their friend:

"There's a court backlog around the country that's causing murder because there aren't consequences for people committing crimes. We have to give courts and prosecutors more money so they can clear it."

Toward the end of the article, MacGillis allows a public defender to offer a different perspective:

> She said that the solution to the backlogs was not simply to try to push through as many cases as quickly as possible. Prosecutors, she said, should rethink whether it was really necessary to bring so many cases in the first place, and should divert more people accused of nonviolent crimes into alternative, community-based resolution programs.
>
> Back in Albuquerque . . . [the prosecutor] said he could see the case for such rethinking, but legislators would have to take that on. For his office, the immediate challenge remained working through a backlog.[24]

How MacGillis handles this disagreement is revealing. He gives the last word to the prosecutor, and he doesn't correct the prosecutor's false statement that this is an issue "legislators would have to" resolve. The point the public defender made is that *these* prosecutors, like police and prosecutors across the U.S., have themselves created backlogs by continuing to insist on flooding the courts with historically unprecedented numbers of low-level cases, which constitutes the modern phenomenon of mass criminalization. They don't have to do that. They have discretion to decide which of the many crimes to prosecute and which to not prosecute. They do this every day when they ignore the crimes of the wealthy, or the crimes committed by police and jail guards.

This article is not an outlier. Many people and institutions who produce news are so under the ideological hold of the punishment bureaucracy that they parrot its assumptions and myths. Chief among these myths is the idea that tweaks in the policies of prosecutors and courts have substantial, observable, and immediate effects on violence when, in reality, our safety is almost entirely determined by the material features of our society.

Most reporters do not boast in an "Ideas" section that they have uncovered "the cause" of national crime trends—but their reporting conveys the same basic deception. Many juxtapose two phenomena to suggest a causal relationship without necessarily making the claim explicitly. For example, a September 2023 *Atlanta Journal-Constitution* article reports a decrease in homicides in Atlanta, explaining: "The shift follows Mayor Andre Dickens' efforts aimed at combatting violence, particularly among youths, with activities like the City's Midnight Basketball League."[25] This is absurd. The decrease in homicides was not just in Atlanta but *nationwide*, and there is no evidence that the national decline could have had anything to do with a small basketball program co-run with the Atlanta Police Department as a counterinsurgency operation. But the use of the phrase "the shift follows" was designed to *make people think* that the Atlanta mayor and police had caused fewer murders—that they had uncovered the secret to reducing crime that other cities had not, and that the secret was to pay more money to armed police to host basketball games. Later in the same article, the police are quoted saying something totally different: that the reduction in murder is due to their "drugs, guns and gangs" approach, which the paper does not explain or question.

A similar false causality is evident in a March 2022 *Boston Globe* article about how young people organized to remove armed police from their schools.[26] The story featured a copaganda all-timer: "Since then, the schools have witnessed an alarming number of attacks." The paper's use of "since then" and "alarming" conveys that things have gotten worse because the kids got the police out of the schools—that there is a *causal connection* between fewer cops and increases in crime. But five paragraphs later, we learn that data shows crime has gone *down* in the schools! And the article further omits the empirical evidence that police do not make schools safer.[27]

When the news suggests some kind of causal relationship to explain a crime statistic, ask yourself: Is the statistic being offered by the punishment bureaucrat a reliable one? What is the long-term trend of this statistic, not just the short-term one? Is the asserted shift happening in other places, or is it unique to the place being described? If you're being offered an explanation that is place-specific or time-specific, does that make sense given what's happening with the same measurement in other places or with the timing of the supposed cause? Is the thing identified in the explanation capable of causing the problem at this magnitude? What material causes might be at work that are not being presented?

Homelessness

The distraction from material conditions and exaggeration of the positive impact of tweaks in repressive policies is exemplified by how the news covers homelessness. As we saw in Burlington, news stories about "homelessness" rarely discuss the economic conditions that cause it. For instance, the *New York Times* ran an article about the New York City mayor's plan to "remove people with severe, untreated mental illness from the city's streets and subways."[28]

The mayor's plan called for thousands of punishment bureaucrats to involuntarily hospitalize unhoused people even if the person "posed no threat to others."[29] The article on homelessness and mental illness is notable for what is missing: it does not contain a single mention of the economic causes of homelessness. It does not discuss poverty, inequality, urban planning, economic policies, or affordable housing. It does not report on any alternative and effective policies that would address these issues in a non-punishment fashion, such as cash transfer programs for people at risk of losing their housing.[30] Nor does it recount the root causes of mental illness or how divestment from mental health care and preventive health care in general has deprived those in crisis of treatment. And, it doesn't refer to any of the multiple proposals to build that care infrastructure. A person reading this article would leave their interaction with the news uninformed about either the causes of the problems or the range of cost-effective solutions politicians could implement. The only constant is punishment.

A similar 2021 Associated Press article on homelessness claimed in its headline, "San Francisco's Vaunted Tolerance Dims amid Brazen Crimes."[31] It features a gentrifier who moved to San Francisco from Seattle "in search of more sunshine." The article portrays the city's people as compassionate liberals who have been pushed over the edge into favoring government repression by the "feeling" of disgust with homeless drug users on the street. As the gentrifier put it: "I'm over it." Describing various anecdotes of homelessness, the article contains not a single word on profit, wealth inequality, affordable housing, health care, racism, or capitalism.

I built a little shrine to these "homelessness happens for no reason" stories in the basement of the Copaganda Safe Injection Site I run. Reporters can come in and consume copaganda in a safe environment, surrounded by abstract oil paintings of California Governor Gavin Newsom destroying the earthly belongings of unhoused people.[32]

The cumulative effect of such articles is that people consuming news become actively less informed because they believe that serious problems have no discernible cause rooted in the ways our society is organized. The unrelated, superficial "solutions" the news promotes, like conducting sweeps on park benches, solve nothing and only make conditions worse for the unhoused. But news consumers are left thinking that people in power are trying their best to explore elusive solutions to problems as intractable as nuclear fission or how to sustain life on Mars. The *Times* article dresses up Mayor Adams's plan for mass detention of New York's homeless in just this fashion: "Mr. Adams has received criticism from some progressive members of his party for clearing homeless encampments. . . . The mayor has defended his focus on public safety."

To the *Times*, Adams's move to clear the places people sleep while destroying their earthly possessions constitutes not an empirically ineffective and unconstitutional program of state violence for which governments across the U.S. get continually sued. It is part of a good-faith "focus on public safety."

While the article describes Adams's policies toward the homeless and mentally ill as "tough on crime" policy needed to address "growing disorder" with "aggressive measures," here's how the paper described people who oppose the government disappearing homeless people: "Left-leaning advocates and officials who dominate New York politics say that deploying the police as auxiliary social workers may do more harm than good."

Setting aside the dubious assertion that the city's politics is "dominated" by anything resembling an organized left, look at how the position of the "left-leaning" opponents on homelessness is caricatured. Their view, which is grounded in evidence and constitutional law, is portrayed as shaky and ambivalent (more cops as opposed to more housing "may" do more harm on the issue of homelessness, who could know?), in contrast to the mayor's confident assertions that he is conquering crime and disorder.

Similarly, when New York politicians implemented the massive expansion of police "omnipresence" and surveillance I described earlier, the *Times* referred to the plan as "the latest in a series of efforts" to address the problems, which it called "stubborn" and "difficult for elected leaders to address."[33] Who are the sources that want us to think society has been trying hard to fix the problems of homelessness and mental illness?

- The governor (two paragraphs)
- NYC mayor (three paragraphs)
- The governor (two more paragraphs)
- Head of police union (three paragraphs)

- Politician who endorsed far-right Republican governor candidate (two paragraphs, complaining that the policies aren't authoritarian enough)
- NYPD commissioner
- NYC mayor (two more paragraphs)

The article calls the problems of homelessness and mental illness "stubborn" because "the violence has persisted" despite numerous prior investments in more police and surveillance, but it does not explain why the government *keeps trying a strategy that hasn't worked* or who benefits from that failed strategy. In this way, the news can help people in power obscure that they are not addressing the root causes of the problems they decry in stump speeches.

This is a symbiotic relationship between authoritarian politicians and the media: they collude in convincing the public to accept repression instead of improvements in material conditions. Time and again, the same policies of control, violence, and profit are implemented to "solve" a problem like homelessness, and time and again the news portrays the problem as impervious to the best efforts of the greatest minds among us. Nothing new or transformative is tried at scale, and the problem persists. Copaganda allows politicians to portray homelessness or mental illness as "a problem that has seemed intractable" despite the best efforts of well-meaning and compassionate leaders.[34] Effective and widely known solutions to these problems exist. But when one attempts to solve any problem by trying things that have been repeatedly disproven, *any problem will seem intractable.*

The coverage of homelessness and mental illness illustrates one of the most important themes in this book: copaganda convinces people that, sadly, much to our discomfort as caring people, there is no way to solve the serious problems of our society. Having reluctantly come to that conclusion, we now have to expand authoritarian measures to manage those problems through violence. We wish we didn't have to do this, but we've tried everything else. Eric Adams said it best to Fox News:[35]

"They say the definition of insanity is to do the same thing repeatedly, but expect different results."

Repression as "Care"

An emerging vanguard of copaganda is rebranding repressive policies as compassionate. Politicians around the country are increasingly using the concept of "care" to describe policies of violence that jail unhoused people and criminalize people for their mental illness. The news coverage of California's "CARE Court" offers a prime example. In 2022, with great media fanfare, new California legislation created a new bureaucracy called the "CARE Court," which stands for Community Assistance, Recovery and Empowerment Court.

As a Human Rights Watch report documents, the law created a costly new court system in every county of the state.[36] It gave the courts more power to coerce treatment, specifically targeting people with mental illness and unhoused people. Ultimately, it is backed with the power of judicial orders, the threat of conservatorship (in which people lose power to make decisions over their lives and bodies), and the inherent power of the government to use violence to enforce its orders.

To legitimize this authoritarian grab, punishment bureaucrats framed the plan as "care." This rhetoric can confuse the public by making expansion of the courts difficult to distinguish from what progressives are proposing—the expansion of investments in systems of care. This obfuscation tricks people into thinking that those in power are working to solve the big problems that affect the most vulnerable people in our society. What the CARE law did *not* do is provide any new housing or treatment capacity.[37] In fact, the CARE Court will actually hurt Californians in need of housing who are *not* diagnosed with mental illness, because it requires counties to prioritize CARE Court participants for services and placement without increasing the overall number of available places to live or the accessibility of services.

The governor's push for the CARE Court came amid a growing crisis in California in which rising inequality and an acute shortage of affordable housing is causing record homelessness. At the same time, underfunding of health care has led to a dearth of programs with trained personnel and infrastructure to care for people in crisis. Instead, cities have criminalized poverty, homelessness, and mental illness, including making it illegal to sit, lie down, or sleep in public. With the number of unhoused people rising further during the COVID-19 pandemic, the state's political establishment and media became obsessed with "disorder" on public streets. In 2022, a sense of urgency among members of California's political elite to appear to be doing something about homelessness and mental illness led to the passage of the governor's CARE Court plan by a vote of 38–0 in the State Senate and 62–2 in the Assembly.

Like other tweaks to the bureaucracies of coercion, the CARE Court deflects energy away from working for deeper changes in material conditions. Instead of confronting this dynamic, the news enabled it, quoting various officials claiming that the law is about "preserving self-determination," ensuring "self-sufficiency," and "empowering" people. The punishment bureaucrats named the new initiative the "CARE" court so that every time TV, radio, or newspapers covered their proposal, it would convey the impression that a benevolent government was hard at work helping people in need.

It worked. For example, the *San Diego Union Tribune* editorial board naively described the impetus behind the law, essentially parroting the governor's claims that "the proposal builds off the recognition that existing laws have fallen short of helping thousands of often homeless Californians who suffer from mental illness."[38]

This is copaganda that can best be summed up as follows: *There may not be a home for you to live in, but there's now a judge who can order you to live there.* If a bill provides no new housing and no new programs to help people in mental health crises, then it does not address homelessness or mental illness. But it does empower the government to shuffle people out of sight using force, and a lot of people will draw salaries from the creation of a new court bureaucracy. Only a profoundly lost bureaucracy would pass a bill targeting homelessness that doesn't provide any new homes. Only a concerted propaganda effort can portray as "compassionate" a coercive government intervention that medical experts say is inhumane and ineffective. Only the most cynical political elite would portray using threats of violence to force involuntary treatment as "preserving self-determination."

Painting Repression as Something Repressed People Want

The tactic of laundering repression through sympathetic characters or language is complemented by another one: selectively giving voice to marginalized people who support punitive policies. One of my favorite historical examples of this phenomenon is a 1942 *New York Times* article entitled "Japanese Enjoys Internment," about a Japanese man detained with other "enemy aliens" who reported that "he had been treated so well, he told the authorities, that he felt his wife and children should be interned to enjoy the same comforts and privileges."[39] A 2022 *New York Times* article offers several examples of how this tactic functions in contemporary copaganda:[40]

Democrats Face Pressure on Crime From a New Front: Their Base

Not long ago, the party was focused on police reform, but rising fears of violence, especially among communities of color, have led candidates to change course.

The article's thesis is that a supposedly new pro-police turn by Democrats has come in response to the needs and demands of "communities of color." This copaganda recasts Democratic support for the punishment bureaucracy as a commitment to listening to the most vulnerable people. In one of the most revealing paragraphs in recent copaganda history, the article asserts:

The candidates and elected officials pushing the party to address crime more aggressively are largely people of color. Candidates are motivated not mainly by fear of Republican attacks,
but rather by mounting outcry from the Black, Hispanic, and
Asian American communities bearing the brunt of a national
crime wave.

The article's quoted sources are a lesson in crafting copaganda:

- Person worried about crime at a political rally for pro-
  establishment candidate in Maryland
- Pro-establishment Democratic candidate
- Pro-police Democratic mayor
- Pro-establishment Democratic candidate #2
- Pro-establishment Democratic candidate #3
- Pro-establishment Democratic candidate #4
- Suburban voter at same rally worried about "disorderly and
  dangerous" young people
- Government official at same rally who had supported the
  Republican governor
- "Centrist" political organization Third Way
- Pro-police Democratic mayor #2
- Pro-police Democratic mayor #3
- Pro-establishment Democratic candidate #3 (again)
- Pro-establishment Democratic candidate #2 (again)

The selective curation of sources helped concoct several related
myths: (1) Democrats were "changing course"; (2) the small number of
non-white officials and candidates were the ones driving this change;
(3) these powerful people were actually motivated by ordinary people of
color; and (4) all of this beautiful democracy in action was caused by "a
national crime wave." The reporter did not quote *anyone* with a different
view or tell readers that violent crime was actually at near-historic lows.

The two "ordinary voters" quoted were people attending a political rally for a pro-police, corporate-funded candidate. There was no effort to introduce readers to candidates, organizers, voters, crime survivors, and people of color who are working on alternative approaches to community safety that do not rely on expanding the punishment bureaucracy.

Take the foundational assertion in the subheading: that it was "rising fears of violence" that "have led" certain elements in the Democratic Party to recently "change course." The premise is that public sentiment is the cause of recent policy shifts by Democratic candidates who are being responsive and accountable to their base, rather than a PR campaign to stoke fear that pushes the other way. In fact, the paper's claim is bolder: it was the Democratic Party's sensitivity to the concerns of "communities of color" that motivated these supposed pro-police shifts.

The *Times* erases other explanations as to why Democratic Party leaders might want to boost police: it's a policy favored by wealthy donors who fund their campaigns; police unions give them money and have a lot of power to threaten them if they act against police interests; expanding the punishment bureaucracy serves the interests of people who own things; police surveillance and repression are profitable to powerful political interests; increasing the means of disciplining movements for social, racial, economic, global, and environmental justice felt important to corporate Democrats after unprecedented mass uprisings; the party leaders ideologically agree with expanding the punishment bureaucracy themselves, regardless of their constituents' desires; and so on.[41] Instead of exploring these reasons, the article insists that the pro-punishment wing of the party is driven by its unfailing commitment to the most vulnerable: "In Democratic strongholds like Maryland, a rise in violent crime has pushed the party's candidates to address the issue of public safety in newly urgent terms." To underscore this, the article adds that Democratic candidates such as future corporatist governor Wes Moore are merely *responding* to calls for a crackdown coming from "largely people of color": " 'You need to listen to what people are telling you,' Mr. Moore said."

There is no doubt that if these marginalized communities were calling for wealth redistribution, universal health care, and a constitutional right to housing, the same corporate-funded politicians would oppose such demands. They certainly would not immediately draft bills to fund them. How did politicians and the news treat marginalized communities' demands for the reallocation of police funds to social programs in 2020? So much for the idea that politicians respond to the priorities of their most oppressed constituents.

Adam Johnson has thoroughly analyzed the *Times*'s use of "communities of color" to justify mass-incarceration policies.[42] As Johnson points out, articles like this one conflate Black communities caring about violence with those communities supporting more investments in "policing, more enforcement of petty crimes, and tougher sentences." In the eyes of the news, Black voters caring about violence "becomes a policy preference for more bloated police budgets, greater enforcement of broken windows, and more people in jail." In virtually none of the articles does the paper even try to support this connection; it is simply assumed.

Accurate reporting on this issue would require engaging with the polling that Black communities consistently want investments in *material* things, support non-punishment policies that reduce violence, and, by huge supermajorities, want to *reduce* incarceration.[43] It would require grappling with the evidence about which kinds of investments increase safety. It would require engaging with the historical and political economic forces that have led U.S. society to offer its poorest communities only one option—punishment—as a supposed solution to material deprivation and inequality. And it would require engaging with the reality that no community is monolithic and that political and media elites have worked hard for a long time to spread misinformation about crime and safety and promote leaders among marginalized populations who do their bidding.[44]

In the ongoing effort to get readers to feel good about expanding punishment, selective representation of the views of certain marginalized people pervades mainstream news. But in the 2022 *Times* article about the political rally in Maryland, the portrayal of how U.S. politics works is ludicrous. A reader is left with the impression that national politics is a place where politicians are immediately responsive to the expressed desires of the most vulnerable people. The *Times* launders a corrupt political system by pretending that it diligently responds to the needs of the vulnerable.

The centerpiece of the article is a dissembling portrait of the corporate-backed Black Democratic candidate in Maryland. Complete with photos of him, the article makes assertions about how officials and candidates "of color" are the ones leading the charge "to address crime more aggressively." This is factually inaccurate given that most Democrats pushing such policies are not candidates of color, but it also betrays a willful blindness to the connections, social status, and sheer wealth it takes to become a serious candidate for major political office. Anyone working in these political circles understands that virtually no candidate is viable if they cannot milk enough cash out of wealthy people. Eric Adams, for example, was showered with cash by the real estate industry and raised over four times the campaign war chest of his closest opponent. It is not an accident that, among many "candidates of color" who do *not* support such policies, elites are *choosing candidates of color who support their agenda*. It is a good way to inoculate themselves against progressive criticism and advance their interests at the same time.

The article's thesis that Democrats have made a policy shift toward supporting increased policing is odd for another reason: it's false. As numerous scholars have documented, the Democratic Party has been at the forefront of policies expanding the punishment bureaucracy for over fifty years, including often using candidates of color to do so.[45] Incredibly, the paper makes no effort to identify a single Democratic Party policy that has recently changed. Think for a moment about what that reveals about the decision to publish such an article.

Instead, the article falsely suggests that certain politicians once had anti-police policy positions that they have now abandoned for pro-police positions. No examples are provided. The reality is that police budgets were at record highs and the U.S. remained the world leader in incarceration, and Democrats, as always, were leading promoters of both.

Finally, the article is an exemplary specimen of the false dichotomy that copaganda sets up between safety and our values, which can be used to distract from the need to improve material conditions. The article dismisses "left-leaning Democrats" who are worried that police are "irreparably biased." But it also says that "demands for safer neighborhoods from voters of color have made it impossible for Democrats to keep talking around the issue." Translation? The most vulnerable people care about bias, but they care more about safety, which is mutually exclusive.

This parody of the truth creates an alternate reality for news consumers: Policy positions of elites originate from the hearts and minds of the most vulnerable people. The most vulnerable people care about injustice, but they care more about safety, and we cannot give them both. A political party of elites adapts itself to the organic, unmanipulated will of the most vulnerable people, magnanimously permitting itself to be led by candidates who represent those marginalized people. Even though evidence demonstrates that a policy doesn't reduce violence, elites do it anyway, not because it produces profit and ensures their power, but because the most powerless people demand it. Even though everyone cares mostly about improving their material conditions, no one ever mentions or addresses that. In other words, a well-functioning democracy.

16

Resisting Copaganda

Freedom is the freedom to say that two plus two make four. If that is granted, all else follows.

-George Orwell[1]

The upshot after all these words from all these news stories is that a lot of unspeakable but preventable harm continues to happen every day, and policies no one can justify are called justice. Copaganda, the poisonous spider, weaves its web almost everywhere we turn for information about the world—even in the darkest corners of our collective imagination. But a specter haunts the punishment bureaucracy: the truth. An honest examination of the connection between our professed collective values and the evidence would not support anything like the current policies of mass incarceration for profit. This is why a lot of people spend a lot of money going to great lengths to create copaganda. It takes considerable effort to get so many people thinking that two plus two make five.

I am writing this book on copaganda at a time when domestic and global authoritarianism are advancing rapidly—making it all the more urgent that we work together to fortify our minds against relentless pressure to give up the glimmer of hope, the seedling of faith in other humans, and the will to say what is true that enables us to whisper in the growing cacophony of every room: *two plus two make four.*

Where Do We Go from Here?

If our world continues to be highly unequal, we will continue to be bombarded with copaganda to justify using the punishment bureaucracy to

manage and control that inequality. But like any effort to confront injustice, doing something about copaganda involves learning as much as
we can about how it works and coming together to organize with others.

I do not purport to have answers to the difficult questions posed by
the symbiotic conspiracy between the punishment bureaucracy and the
news media to manipulate how we see the world, but I can offer some
reflections based on my own experiences. In this chapter, I sketch some
thoughts on things we can do, alone and together, to combat copaganda,
even in the context of consolidated ownership of mass media outlets.
First, I'll share some resources I created for news consumers, students,
organizers, advocates, journalists, and public officials. They are not intended to be exhaustive, but examples of the kinds of resources that any
of us can create and use to put pressure on punishment bureaucrats and
the news outlets who help them spread copaganda. After that, I'll list a
few tips on things I try in my own life.

A Guide for Posing Questions to Punishment Bureaucrats and Politicians

Police, prosecutors, and prison officials rarely talk about what they
do. This is a failure both of journalism and governance. For example, in almost no public hearing or local news story are punishment
bureaucrats forced, or even politely asked, to answer questions about
the bulk of what their departments, agencies, and employees do with
their time and money. Here is a short list of questions that any ordinary person, any journalist, any advocate, and any public official could
ask *any* police chief, in *any* city at *any* time, in *any* public hearing or
media interview:

Ask them about who they choose to investigate and arrest:

• Why do you choose not to arrest bosses for wage theft, but you
  choose to arrest poor people for shoplifting?

- Why do you choose to devote almost all your undercover resources to drug busts and not to undercover investigations of white-collar crime, sexual assaults on university campuses, or police corruption?
- Why do arrests for drug possession make up the plurality of your arrests for several decades?
- Why do you choose not to investigate and arrest people who own polluting businesses for illegal dumping of chemicals? What surveillance operations do you have devoted to monitor air and water pollution violations? How many undercover informants do you currently have working to investigate illegal dumping of chemicals into the air or water?
- If state law criminalizes abortion or other access to reproductive care, do you intend to have your officers investigate, surveil, and place chains on people for any of these offenses? What about if, in the future, state law criminalizes contraception or sodomy?

Ask about the assumptions underlying these enforcement decisions:

- Do you have any reason to believe that, contrary to nationwide empirical evidence, usage of illegal drugs is higher in poor neighborhoods than in wealthier neighborhoods or higher among Black people than white people in this city? If drug use in this city is not different than what the available nationwide data shows, why do you focus your narcotics operations, undercover narcotics operations, and arrests on these groups almost exclusively?[2]
- Why do you think that armed police officers are the socially optimal first responder to mental health incidents, and do you have evidence to back up that position?
- Do you believe that armed police officers are the most cost-effective way to deal with vehicular traffic code enforcement, and do you have evidence for that position? What percentage of your police budget is devoted to traffic enforcement, including overtime payments to officers for appearing in court for tickets?

• Does the fact that about 90 percent of the people arrested by your department are too poor to afford an attorney say anything about the kinds of crimes that you choose to investigate?

Ask them about accountability:

• Can you provide a list of each officer who has been investigated for having lied in the past ten years in a police report, in an application for a warrant, on any department paperwork, in video footage, in testimony, to a prosecutor, or to a superior concerning any employment incident? When an officer was determined to have lied, what consequences did they face?
• Do you agree that you should be terminated from your job if you provide the public false, incomplete, or misleading information to any of these questions?

Ask them about money:

• How many officers are paid either full-time or part-time to do any form of public relations, including but not limited to: direct contact with reporters, social media, video production, participation in neighborhood message boards or listservs, tracking and researching public opinion, collecting information on favorable or unfavorable journalists, conducting or contracting for focus groups on police messaging, any form of lobbying, and intervention with victims' families to control press access to them?
• Which surveillance technology are you employing that has not been disclosed to the city council? How much are you spending on such technology? How frequently are you deploying Stingray or similar devices to capture cellular phone information of unsuspecting residents?
• Who are the top ten highest-paid cops in the city, including both

regular and overtime pay? What internal protocols and investigations have you initiated to audit or prevent against the national epidemic of overtime and sick-leave fraud by police?[3]

- What equipment used by police was purchased with donations from police foundations, and who are the donors to those foundations?
- Can you list all private grants and donations that pay for anything used by officers in the department, including but not limited to technology, weapons, artificial intelligence, and predictive policing software?
- Can you provide a list of the top fifty most valuable contracts your department (or the municipal government acting on behalf of the department) has signed with private vendors for procurement, along with the amount of the contract, relevant contract documents, and whether the bidding process was competitive? What evidence is there that these vendors have a history of successful performance, that they lack financial conflicts of interest, and that their products provide value for public money?

These are just some questions that could be asked of police chiefs, sheriffs, mayoral staff, and, with some tweaks, prosecutors. Members of city council or county boards of supervisors with oversight authority, as well as the news media and ordinary members of the public, are entitled to ask these questions, and to persist until they get comprehensive, truthful answers in the public record. Think about what it says that something like this does not typically happen in any city.

Building a culture and a public archive of adversarial questioning of punishment bureaucrats and the auditor-controllers who are supposed to be overseeing the bureaucrats' spending should be seen as an essential component of both democratic civic engagement and ethical news coverage. And there are many other questions to ask. Perhaps you can add your own to the list.

A Guide for Reading and Writing About Crime

I put together a few contextual statements for journalists to insert into their stories or for readers to think about and insert for themselves when they consume the news. The following are statements that can be inserted directly into virtually every news article that talks about crime, public safety, "crime data," "crime rates," "crime surges," or a "crime wave." Inserting these factual statements would immediately improve the accuracy and completeness of any reporting on crime. Think of these, which are based on information discussed earlier in this book, as an exercise to supplement the news as you're reading it, as a thought exercise for how perception can change based on what information is presented or excluded, and as the beginning of a list you can develop on your own for a wide range of topics covered in public safety reporting. Think of it also as a tool in organizing and putting pressure on news outlets to change how they present information:

When the story is about crime in general:

- "Property crime data reported by the police excludes most property crime, including wage theft by employers (which costs workers an estimated $50 billion per year, more than three times more than all police-reported property crime); tax evasion, which steals about $1 trillion every year (which is more than sixty times all police-reported property crime); and corporate fraud, which steals about $830 billion each year (which is over fifty times more than all police-reported property crime)."[4]
- "Violent crime data reported by police excludes nearly all the violent crimes committed by punishment bureaucrats, which experts estimate to include several million physical and sexual assaults each year.[5] Given their magnitude, including the crimes by government

employees, official crime statistics could change the direction of crime trends reported by police at any given time."[6]

- "Despite recent short-term fluctuations in police-reported crime, overall levels of police-reported violent and property crime remain at near-historic forty-year lows."[7]

- "Violence is generally lower in societies that spend less money on police, prosecutors, and prisons and that spend more money on health care, treatment, early childhood education, youth activities, poverty reduction, and wellness."[8]

- "According to experts who have studied the empirical evidence, investments in early childhood education, health care, housing, treatment, and poverty reduction are more cost-effective ways of reducing crime than investments in prisons, prosecutions, and police."[9]

- "The vast majority of sexual assault and gender-based violence is not reported to police and never makes it into official 'crime rates' because most survivors of such violence determine that police, prosecutor, and prison bureaucracies are not an appropriate, viable, safe, or effective way to address that harm."[10]

- "Most violent and sexual crimes involve people who know each other, not strangers. Police commit about one-third of all stranger-homicides in the U.S."[11]

- "U.S. police spend only about 4 percent of their time on what they categorize as violent crime. Such crimes account for only 5 percent of the arrests that police make. For many years until recent legalization in dozens of states, the police made more arrests for marijuana possession than for all violent crime combined. With marijuana legal in almost half the states, marijuana possession arrests are still about half of all arrests for all violent crime combined."[12]

- "The U.S. confines people to jail cells at six times its own historical average, five to ten times as much as other comparable countries, and imprisons Black people [at] six times the rate of South Africa during Apartheid."[13]

- "Police-reported property crime rates exclude civil forfeiture seizures by police (which roughly equal all reported burglary combined), a significant percentage of which are illegal."[14]
- "The vast majority of crimes—such as air and water pollution crimes, police perjury, prosecutor obstruction of justice, government corruption, corporate fraud, and bribery—are not reported to police and not pursued by prosecutors, and they don't show up in police-reported crime rates. Crime rates capture a small subset of police-reported crimes committed mostly by the poor, and mostly exclude crimes committed by the wealthy."[15]
- "Across the U.S., there have been scandals of police departments manipulating reported crime rates to promote a political agenda."[16]
- "Many of the greatest threats to community public safety are not defined as crimes. The process of determining which harms are criminalized and which are not is a political process that has more to do with who has power than an objective evaluation of which activities are the most significant threats to public safety."

When the story quotes a police officer, prosecutor, or expert:

- "Police officials have been shown to make false and misleading statements to the media in order to mislead the public."
- "Prosecutors have been shown to make false and misleading statements to the media in order to mislead the public."
- "The mayor/governor/senator/president/lobbyist has a history of making claims about the reasons behind their public safety proposals that turn out to be incomplete and inaccurate."
- "The professor offered as an expert in this article or used as a source on background is a [*insert appropriate label*: former police officer, former prosecutor, consultant who profits from consulting with police departments]."
- "Police unions across the U.S. consistently support far-right politicians and platforms. The Fraternal Order of Police, which bills itself

as the largest police union in the world, endorsed Donald Trump for president in 2020 and 2024. It has not endorsed a Democrat for president in the twenty-first century."[17]

When the story is about the type or severity of punishment:

- "Based on the available evidence, sentences of incarceration have no measurable, specific deterrent effect on future crime, and incarceration appears to slightly increase crime in the future owing to the criminogenic effects of incarceration. Among sentences of incarceration, research shows that longer sentences have no additional specific deterrent effect at all. Similarly, there is no strong evidence on police-reported crime of either general deterrence or incapacitation associated with existing levels of imprisonment, let alone evidence that imprisonment at existing levels is the socially optimal method of preventing police-reported crime."[18]
- "Based on the available evidence, criminal punishment is not an effective way to mitigate problems of substance abuse. After fifty years of increased drug criminalization, illegal drugs are more widely available and more potent than ever, and overdose deaths are at an all-time high."[19]
- "Every year in custody reduces a person's life expectancy by two years."[20]
- "Because of the massive numbers of people the U.S. puts into prisons, the overall life expectancy of the average U.S. resident is 1.8 years lower than it would be if the United States had incarceration rates comparable to its own pre-1980s levels or those of other countries."
- "Based on the available research, incarceration is not a socially beneficial let alone socially optimal response to [*insert topic here:* domestic violence, theft, sexual assault, murder, mental illness, homelessness, drug use, etc.]."

This is just a preliminary list, and I hope that you can share it with people who read about or cover crime and safety. Develop more statements of your own whenever you see new research or a news claim that lacks sufficient context. Send those suggestions to friends, colleagues, and local journalists. Turn these fact sheets into living documents that are updated, crowdsourced, used as talking points, and shared as public goods in your community.

There are many ways in which people with different experiences, skills, and access can use tools like these or prepare their own tools. I've gotten notes from teachers, professors, students, retirees, and incarcerated people who are leading lessons and reading groups about copaganda to deepen their collective understanding. Unsurprisingly, high school students in particular love dissecting copaganda as a way of building critical analysis skills! People could come together both formally and informally to set up their own copaganda accountability groups to discuss and respond to local copaganda together. Even small groups of people collaborating regularly could make a difference in both public awareness and in local reporting where they live—and it would be educational and fun to build those relationships and skills together.

Some more organized groups have already done a great deal. A group of people in the heavily policed Skid Row community in Los Angeles, working through the Los Angeles Community Action Network (which serves the unhoused community in Skid Row) and its Stop LAPD Spying Coalition (to whom all royalties of this book will be donated), have pioneered effective resistance to copaganda. For example, they produced one of the great modern resources of counter-copaganda in their free online publication *Automating Banishment: The Surveillance and Policing of Looted Land*. It is a testament to the wealth of knowledge about historical and contemporary local policing that small but committed groups of people can obtain through collective study, public records requests, frontline documentation, interviews, primary sources, persistence, and deep relationship with and accountability to those most harmed by the punishment bureaucracy. The purpose of this collective work is to reject the dominant narratives and indoctrination of corporate and government copaganda. Throughout history, effective resistance to injustice has been rooted in collective study—that is, ordinary people getting together to learn from and teach one another. This can often involve learning from personal experiences of people most targeted by powerful institutions and engaging with primary sources of information not mediated through mass-controlled media. Such a practice of collective learning helps communities become more responsive to the latest innovations of corporate and bureaucratic repression and the lies about them, because they have cultivated healthy mutual habits and relationships. This is important because, in the same manner as an evolving virus, the punishment bureaucracy uses established propaganda tactics with new twists at different cultural moments in history to smuggle and disguise similar injustices with new bespoke labels tailored to the zeitgeist. Moreover, the core principles of resistance to copaganda are similar to the skills, habits, and relationships necessary for resisting other kinds of propaganda, such as propaganda supporting the military-industrial complex or colonization, border violence, apartheid, ecocide, and genocide.

Fortifying Our Own Minds

One thing I have learned is that the most effective strategy at all times and in all places—in court, in politics, and in life—is centering your heart with the most vulnerable people and animals and ecosystems, and then relentlessly telling the truth about what you see. The failure of many liberals in journalism and politics to do this is the source of much of the authoritarian danger we face now. Many people I meet in journalism, academia, nonprofits, and politics are constantly engaging in elaborate games to justify not telling the truth. They do focus groups and message testing and decide to support stuff they used to abhor. But the bar for lying—to yourself and to others—is extremely high. It's rarely met.

But to do this, we have to take steps every day to maintain our ability to know what the truth is. We can take steps in our daily lives to fortify our minds against the relentless attempts all around us to make us okay with a world that could so easily be so much healthier and safer for so many people. We can put ourselves in a position to fight against

the cynicism, complacency, lack of imagination for a better world, isolation, factual inaccuracies, and arrogance that living in our society—and
especially consuming its most prominent daily news sources—breeds.
There is no single answer for how to do this, but I want to share a few
things I do in my own life.

1. Getting Information from a Range of Sources

Most of us should consume far less, if any, daily news. There is a
reason scholars of propaganda have found that the most avid mainstream news consumers are among the least informed but most confident people. Because our minds are a great but impressionable treasure,
and because it is one of the things in the world over which we have the
most control (not total control, but some), what we decide to expose our
minds to matters. The following are examples of better sources of information to consume, instead of daily "news," to learn about happenings
in the world:

• Long-form journalism, magazine articles, in-depth investigations,
  newsletters by specialists, reports by trusted organizations, podcasts
  (such as the fantastic media criticism and propaganda analysis podcast
  Citations Needed or the exceptional podcast *The Dig*, which explores
  important critical ideas, scholarship, and social movements in depth),
  and videos that take the time to delve more deeply into issues, including patterns and trends. You'll ultimately learn more "facts" than you
  might have seen in the daily mainstream news, and you'll have better context for them. Take the time you would have spent reading or
  watching news and consume a longer piece on an issue that is interesting to you instead. Build a network of information sources you trust by
  seeing who other people you think highly of are following or citing;
  by reading the bibliographies of books you like; and getting recommendations from people whose critical thinking you admire (such as,
  importantly, people who like cats).

- Books. This is a personal matter that is *not* objective, but I have found the following books, among many others, to be important to me in understanding copaganda and the forces behind it: David Graeber's *Utopia of Rules*, Stuart Hall et al.'s *Policing the Crisis*, Kristian Williams's *Our Enemies in Blue* (introduction by Andrea Ritchie), Jacques Ellul's *Propaganda*, Stop LAPD Spying Coalition's *Automating Banishment*, Angela Davis's *Are Prisons Obsolete?*, Edward Herman and Noam Chomsky's *Manufacturing Consent*, James Baldwin's *Collected Essays*, Orisanmi Burton's *Tip of the Spear*, Shulamith Firestone's *The Dialectic of Sex*, Peter Gelderloos's *Anarchy Works*, and Jerry Mander's *Four Arguments for the Elimination of Television*.
- If you need to consume daily news, consume daily news produced by sources that do not have a business model connected to large corporations. Don't read the *New York Times* or similar news outlets as a way of understanding daily developments in the world, unless for the specific purpose of understanding what people in power are talking about and what they want people to be thinking. Whatever you do, don't go on neighborhood listservs to talk about crime unless it is to promote this book.
- Film: The following films, among many others, are a good introduction to some of the issues discussed here: *Let the Fire Burn, Manufacturing Consent, Network, Beyond Bars, 3,000 Years and Life*, and *Anchorman* (just kidding).
- Listen to and learn from the people most harmed by the punishment bureaucracy. Correspond with people in jails and prisons, send them books, and visit them. Mariame Kaba has compiled an excellent list of resources to help you.[21]

2. Filling Our Lives with Deep Relationships

Who we surround ourselves with is the most important thing in our development as critical thinkers and in amassing the strength to

keep doing things in the world even though it can be scary and drain-
ing to go up against powerful institutions. We need people who inspire
and excite us, people who push us, people who hold us accountable to
our values. One of my mentors, Lani Guinier, used to call the latter
group her "personal board of directors"—people who are there to hold
us when we need to be held, but also to confront us when we need to be
confronted. People who can make sure that we always stay alive to the
injustices of the world, never get used to them, and have the support to
challenge them whatever way we can and to do it as strategically and as
humbly as possible. Many problems that seem intractable when we face
them alone become less so when we are in relationship with others. (For
example, several trusted people helped me turn unhinged rants about
daily news into this book.)

Maintaining these relationships can be difficult in a world of at-
omization and busyness, and in a world that often prioritizes other
kinds of personal relationships. It takes diligence and planning to
build and sustain a cadre and to plan regular gatherings for the purpose of deepening bonds and providing space for collective study. It's
worth it.

3. Art, Music, Poetry, and Theater

Art, music, poetry, theater, and other forms of expression expand our minds, expose us to different stimuli, and keep us tethered
to what it means to be human. The arts help us see truths about
other people's experiences in ways that reading a news article cannot, and they make us better news consumers. Being exposed to great
artistic expression helps us never lose sight of the beauty and insight
and weirdness human beings are capable of, and what we're fighting
for when we try to have a world in which all people can have what
they need to flourish and to pursue their own delights and fancies.
The arts are one of the best ways to counter copaganda's power to

make unimaginable brutality seem like common sense, and to make commonsense improvement of people's material conditions seem unimaginable.

4. Get Involved! Care About Something!

Getting involved is the most important thing one can do. Much of the most important learning and growing we do as human beings comes about through collective spaces and action. This can be through mutual aid that helps vulnerable people in our communities; reading and study groups; volunteering with a community bail fund or participatory defense hub; or joining a library, school board, or CourtWatch program (more on that below).

For example, take the work of Silicon Valley De-Bug in San Jose. They have pioneered a community organizing model called "participatory defense," in which people facing charges, their family members, and others in the community come together in that time of crisis to use individual cases as an opportunity to build shared, accessible knowledge for non-lawyers about what is happening in seemingly complex legal proceedings and also cultivate community knowledge about the punishment bureaucracy generally. Working together, the families and community members can help teach each other what to expect, watch court proceedings to identify when things are not being done legally or fairly by police, prosecutors, jails, or judges, and prepare background information about families that could be helpful for the court in reaching more appropriate decisions on pretrial release, at trial, or at sentencing. Volunteers can also observe courts, document their findings, and work with lawyers, journalists, organizers, and academics to analyze and disseminate those findings. They are now helping to develop participatory defense hubs across the country that anyone can join.

Finally, there is a growing movement of CourtWatch programs in which volunteers sign up to observe and document what happens in court. Over the years, we have worked closely in our civil rights work with volunteers from CourtWatch programs in Pittsburgh, Prince George's County (Maryland), New Orleans, and New York City, among others. In each place, community members created places where people who care about documenting and telling their neighbors what the punishment bureaucracy is doing can come together, learn a lot, educate others, and have fun in the process. My mother joined the local CourtWatch program when she retired, and the process changed how she and many other volunteers understand our legal system and our society, simply by watching proceedings and documenting them for others to see. She and the other volunteers developed a skepticism about and understanding of the punishment bureaucracy far different from what they had developed through decades of news consumption. And, there are many ways to get involved that are not nearly as formal as these examples.

Everyone has a role to play in combating copaganda. We can support independent, non-corporate-owned forms of news and build our own decentralized networks that connect people and give people information about what is happening in the world. And teachers, nurses, doctors, social workers, community organizers, public defenders, mutual aid groups, civil rights lawyers, public health researchers, data scientists, environmental scientists, immigration experts, survivors of government violence, family members of those survivors, and all of us can intervene in existing methods of news production. Everyone has skills and experiences to offer. It can start as a regular lunch with a local reporter, editor, or producer to start educating them about what you see every day. Unlike police, social workers, survivors of violence, teachers, and public defenders may not get the budget for relentless behind-the-scenes organizing of journalists, but organizations exist to help you and your colleagues figure it out as you tackle your other important life obligations and work. For example, I joined with leading scholars and journalists to take insights like those in this book to form the Center for Just Journalism.[22] The Center has dedicated staff who can connect local organizers and journalists to data, analysis, story ideas, and experts across a range of safety and crime issues; provide research reports to make news stories more accurate and informative; distribute resources for understanding crime data and reporting; and develop curricula for teachers in high school, college, and journalism schools to train a new generation of more critically minded journalists and news consumers.

Even on your own or with a few committed colleagues or friends, you can organize, build relationships with, and help politically educate journalists. You can make including a broader range of perspectives the path of least resistance rather than only quoting police and prosecutors. People who understand the harm and ineffectiveness of the punishment bureaucracy and who are working to build alternative systems of support and care can make our collective voices harder to ignore.

When people come together to study, investigate, and report on things they see happening in their community, they usually find ways of improving what they find. Participating in whatever way you are mentally and physically able to is a way of obtaining and sharing with other people crucial information about our society's commitment to its values.

———————

Shortly before finishing this book, I was talking with one of the children in Flint, Michigan, whom I am representing in the civil rights case that I mentioned in the introduction. The case is against the sheriff and the private-equity owned telecommunications industry, alleging a conspiracy to profit from banning family visits in jail. We were discussing why so few people in Flint and across the country knew that many jails had banned hundreds of thousands of people in jail and their loved ones from hugging, holding hands, or looking into each other's eyes. She then said something I will never forget. She explained that working on the case was exciting for her not just because it meant that people cared about what was happening to her family, but also because it meant there were "adults who care about *something.*"

She told me that she dreams of a career in early childhood education, even though she says she doesn't personally like little kids. But, she explained, it's a big problem for our society that adults don't listen to children. What I think she identified in us adults is a dulling of our senses and our spirits. She saw something like what Jacques Ellul saw decades earlier: being an adult in a heavily propagandized society often means becoming addicted to the substance that is killing your brain and losing your resolve to care. Copaganda is part of a deeper project of preserving the way things are and making us all okay with it. It turns things about our society that should shock us to the core into things we do not even notice, into things we meet with a million isolated shrugs and a sense of helplessness, or, perhaps in the end, into things we celebrate and crave like fiends. The final nail in the copaganda coffin is that we view this process as becoming "informed."

I think my client was hitting on a profound lack of skepticism, curiosity, and resolve; and therefore, a lack of seriousness about what matters. Most of all, we must fight copaganda by maintaining a never-ending interest in the world, being especially attentive to what life is like for the most vulnerable among us. We have never learned enough, we never have all the answers, we have never seen all the cool things we can see, and we can never let our guard down. The world can always be made better by finding someone else with integrity, holding their hand, and singing: "If two plus two equals four, all else follows."

Notes

Introduction: What Is Copaganda?

1 *Malcolm X with Dick Gregory at the Audubon Ballroom*, THE COMPLETE MALCOLM X (Dec. 13, 1964), [https://perma.cc/UY8N-AJYZ].

2 *See Flint, Genesee County, MI: Right to Hug*, CIVIL RIGHTS CORPS (last visited June 3, 2024), [https://perma.cc/3DNU-SGXJ]; Sarah Stillman, *Do Children Have a Right to Hug Their Parents?*, NEW YORKER (May 13, 2024), https://www.newyorker.com /magazine/2024/05/20/the-jails-that-forbid-children-from-visiting-their-parents.

3 Jay Croft, *A Sheriff Put Down His Baton to Listen to Protestors*, CNN (May 31, 2020), [https://perma.cc/XP9B-LR9P].

4 In the most recent contract negotiated by Swanson, the sheriff's office switched from Securus to the next largest jail telecom provider, GTL, which our lawsuit alleges had offered the sheriff and the county more money. *Genesee, MI Visitation Scheduling*, GENESEE CTY. MICH., https://geneseecountymi.gtlvisitme.com/app (last visited Dec. 29, 2023).

5 After our lawsuit, the sheriff admitted to NBC Nightly News anchor Lester Holt on national television that the jail had eliminated family visits to make money, agreed that it was wrong and unjustified, and vowed to let families visit each other again. *See* Dan Slepian, Kenzi Abou-Sabe, & Alexandra Chaidez, *Denied the "Right to Hug: In Many U.S. Jails, Video Calls Are the Only Way Detainees Can See Loved Ones* (June 20, 2024), https://www .nbcnews.com/investigations/many-us-jails-video-calls-are-only-way-detainees-can-see -loved-ones-rcna158048.

6 *Police Chief Acevedo Wants to Give Police Escort for George Floyd's Funeral*, ABC 13 (June 1, 2020), [https://perma.cc/57XF-LQ4B]; *George Floyd Protests*, KHOU-11 (May 31, 2020, [https://perma.cc/63U5-WWKQ]; Michael Scheidt, *EBR Sheriff Gautreaux and District Attorney Hillar Moore Comment on Death of George Floyd*, BATON ROUGE PROUD (June 2, 2020), [https://perma.cc/G4WS-WBNL]; Teresa Mathew, *More Than 40 People Have Died in the East Baton Rouge Jail. Will Voters Oust the Sheriff?*, APPEAL (Oct. 9, 2019), [https://perma.cc/9NDC-W8V3]; Katie Lusso (@KatieLusso), TWITTER (June 1, 2020), [https://perma.cc/5BV8-4XKA]; Li Cohen, *Video Shows NYPD Vehicles Driving into Protesters in Brooklyn*, CBS NEWS (May 31, 2020), [https://perma.cc/6MKV-LVHG]; *One Perfect Moment: Georgia National Guard, Protesters Dance the "Macarena,"* FOX 5 (June 5, 2020), [https://perma.cc/6NM9-SN76]. *See, e.g.,* Shant Shahrigian, *Mayor de Blasio Praises NYPD Officers Who Took a Knee in Solidarity with NYC Protesters*, DAILY NEWS (June 1, 2020), [https://perma.cc/84Y4-MVJ9].

7 *See* LA. REV. STAT. ANN. § 22:1065.1(A); Teresa Mathew, *More Than 40 People Have Died in the East Baton Rouge Jail. Will Voters Oust the Sheriff?*, THE APPEAL (Oct. 9, 2019), https://theappeal.org/more-than-40-people-have-died-in-custody-of-the-east-baton -rouge-jail-will-voters-send-the-sheriff-packing.

8 Mike Hixenbaugh, *Houston's Police Chief Wins National Praise—but Faces Local Anger over Shootings and Transparency*, NBC (June 4, 2020, 4:23 PM), [https://perma .cc/4JB9-B84Y]. The year before, Acevedo's officers killed two people in a fraudulent search warrant execution and tried to cover it up. Brittney Martin & Eli Rosenberg, *Two People Were Killed in a Botched Drug Raid. Investigators Say the Official Story Is a Lie*, WASH. POST (July 26, 2019, 2:52 PM), https://www.washingtonpost.com/nation/2019/07/26 /two-people-were-killed-botched-drug-raid-investigators-say-official-story-was-lie/; Art Acevedo (@ArtAcevedo), TWITTER (Apr. 16, 2020, 8:59 AM), [https://perma.cc /YN6Q-S6BL]; Scott Shackford, *Texas Judge Tells Woman Given $3,500 Bond for Misde-meanors She's "Job Security,"* REASON (Nov. 18, 2016, 4:02 PM), [https://perma.cc/4KRM -N5VU].

9 ASHLEY NELLIS, SENT'G PROJECT, MASS INCARCERATION TRENDS 2 (Jan. 2023), [https://perma.cc/NSB5-M7JN] ("The number of people in prison began a marginal decline in 2010 and thus far has not reversed course"); Jasmine Heiss et al., THE SCALE OF THE COVID-19-RELATED JAIL POPULATION DECLINE 1 (Aug. 2020), [https://perma.cc /SMG5-3Z9E].

10 Larry Buchanan et al., *Black Lives Matter May Be the Largest Movement in U.S. History*, N.Y. TIMES (July 3, 2020), https://www.nytimes.com/interactive/2020/07/03/us /george-floyd-protests-crowd-size.html.

11 PATRICK MURRAY, MONMOUTH U. 6 (June 2, 2020), [https://perma.cc/3ZNF -E8BB].

12 *See* EDWARD S. HERMAN & NOAM CHOMSKY, MANUFACTURING CONSENT: THE POLITICAL ECONOMY OF THE MASS MEDIA (1988). *See also generally* MICHAEL PARENTI, INVENTING REALITY: THE POLITICS OF THE MASS MEDIA (1986).

13 *See* Alec Karakatsanis, *Alec's Copaganda Newsletter* [https://perma.cc/4MFG -VWL3].

14 *See* Bruce Western & Becky Pettit, *Mass Imprisonment, in* PUNISHMENT AND INEQUALITY IN AMERICA 11, 14–15 (ed. Bruce Western, 2006); Lani Guinier & Ger-ald Torres, THE MINER'S CANARY: ENLISTING RACE, RESISTING POWER, TRANSFORMING DEMOCRACY 263 (2002).

15 Emily Widra, *Incarceration Shortens Life Expectancy*, PRISON POLICY INITIATIVE (June 26, 2017), [https://perma.cc/2TJ9-JD63].

16 *See generally* Our Work, CIVIL RIGHTS CORPS, [https://perma.cc/Y5GT-223H] (last visited Dec. 31, 2023).

17 I set forth an analysis of the punishment bureaucracy in the first essay of my book *Usual Cruelty*. Alec Karakatsanis, *The Punishment Bureaucracy, in* USUAL CRUELTY 13 (2019).

18 Timothy Williams, *Marijuana Arrests Outnumber Those for Violent Crimes, Study Finds*, N.Y. TIMES (Oct. 12, 2016), https://www.nytimes.com/2016/10/13/us/marijuana -arrests.html. *See* Corey Rayburn Yung, *How to Lie with Rape Statistics: Americas Hidden Rape Crisis*, 99 IOWA L. REV. 1197, 1246 (2014) (By 2010, major U.S. cities had backlogs of tens of thousands of untested rape kits); Chris Gilligan, *States Struggle with Rape Kit Backlogs Despite Funding Efforts*, U.S. NEWS (June 20, 2023, 5:02 PM), [https://perma .cc/8C4M-QTCM] (Police departments were forgoing or slowing rape investigations

while they spent money on low-level arrests); *Sheriff Warns LA County Cuts Will Eliminate Sexual Assault Investigations Unit*, CBS L.A. (June 30, 2020, 3:49 PM), [https://perma.cc /U2RG-D97Z]; Letta Tayler & Elisa Epstein, *Legacy of the "Dark Side,"* H.R. Watch (Jan. 9, 2022), [https://perma.cc/KVU8-TUC8]; William D. Cohan, *A Clue to the Scarcity of Financial Crisis Prosecutions*, N.Y. Times (July 21, 2016), https://www.nytimes .com/2016/07/22/business/dealbook/a-clue-to-the-scarcity-of-financial-crisis-prose cutions.html. *See* Allie Grasgreen, *Dealing (with) Drugs at Elite Colleges*, Inside Higher Ed (Feb. 15, 2011), [https://perma.cc/L9LX-46MS]; Brad Heath, *Investigation: ATF Drug Stings Targeted Minorities*, USA Today (July 20, 2014, 3:40 PM), [https://perma.cc/Y22T -K4WZ].

19 Worth Rises, The Prison Industry: How It Started. How It Works. How It Harms. (2020), [https://perma.cc/KAE8-KQJF]. This ecosystem allows punishment bureaucrats to profit massively. Noam Scheiber et al., *How Police Unions Became Such Powerful Opponents to Reform Efforts*, N.Y. Times (last updated Apr. 2, 2021), https:// www.nytimes.com/2020/06/06/us/police-unions-minneapolis-kroll.html; *Jobs We Do: Probation and Parole*, Am. Fed'n of State, Cnty, & Mun. Emps. [https://perma .cc/2GT5-DFVM] (last visited Aug. 1, 2023); Whitney Benns, *Unholy Union: St. Louis Prosecutors and Police Unionize to Maintain Racist State Power*, 35 Harv. BlackLetter L. J. 39 (2019).

20 Brady Meixell & Ross Eisenbrey, *An Epidemic of Wage Theft Is Costing Workers Hundreds of Millions of Dollars a Year*, Economic Policy Institute (Sept. 11, 2014), [https://perma.cc/88YU-PDN7]; Laura Davison, *Tax Cheats Are Costing the U.S. $1 Trillion a Year, IRS Estimates*, Bloomberg (Apr. 13, 2021, 12:26 PM), https://www .bloomberg.com/news/articles/2021-04-13/tax-cheats-are-costing-u-s-1-trillion-a -year-irs-estimates?leadSource=uverify%20wall; Charles Duhigg, *Clean Water Laws Are Neglected, at a Cost in Suffering*, N.Y. Times (Sept. 12, 2009), https://www.nytimes .com/2009/09/13/us/13water.html; Alan Neuhauser, *100,000 Americans Die from Air Pollution, Study Finds*, U.S. News (Apr. 8, 2019), [https://perma.cc/85VF-SEME]; Alexandra Thompson & Susannah N. Tapp, Bureau Just. Stat., U.S. Dept. Just., NCJ 307089, Criminal Victimization, 2022, 6, 8 (2023).

21 The FBI's Uniform Crime Reports and the Bureau of Justice Statistics' (BJS's) National Crime Victimization Survey are the two primary sources the U.S. government uses to track crime. *Crime Data Explorer*, Crime Data Explorer, https://cde .ucr.cjis.gov/LATEST/webapp/#/pages/explorer/crime/crime-trend (last visited Jan. 1, 2023); Alexia Cooper & Erica Smith, Bureau Just. Stat., U.S. Dept. Just., NCJ 236018, Homicide Trends in the United States, 1980–2008 2 (Nov. 2011). *See also* Alexandra Thompson & Susannah N. Tapp, Bureau of Just. Stat., U.S. Dept. of Just., NCJ 305101, Criminal Victimization, 2021 1 (2021); *see also* Alexandra Thompson & Susannah N. Tapp, Bureau of Just. Stat., U.S. Dept. of Just., NCJ 307089, Criminal Victimization, 2022 1 (2022) ("The last three decades saw an overall decline in the violent victimization rate from 79.8 to 23.5 per 1,000 from 1993 to 2022").

22 *Crime*, Gallup, [https://perma.cc/N49M-AU9F] (last visited Jan. 1, 2023).

23 Joshua Klugman, *Quantifying Police Killings*, QMISS BLOG (TEMPLE UNIVERSITY) (July 14, 2020), [https://perma.cc/HW4W-WYLC].

24 Don Stemen, VERA INST. JUST., *The Prison Paradox* (July 2017), [https://perma.cc/M4KG-78TT]; Philip Bump, *Over the Past 60 Years, More Spending on Police Hasn't Necessarily Meant Less Crime*, WASH. POST (June 7, 2020), https://www.washington post.com/politics/2020/06/07/over-past-60-years-more-spending-police-hasnt-nec essarily-meant-less-crime/.

25 THEA SEBASTIAN ET AL., CIVIL RIGHTS CORPS, GETTING SMART ON SAFETY (2024), https://www.futures-institute.org/getting-smart-on-safety-evidence-on-non -carceral-investments-that-work-to-prevent-violence-harm.

26 Police have a long and violent history of repressing social movements for equality. *See generally* KRISTIAN WILLIAMS, OUR ENEMIES IN BLUE: POLICE AND POWER IN AMERICA (2015); SIDNEY L HARRING, POLICING A CLASS SOCIETY (2017); FRANK DONNER, PROTECTORS OF PRIVILEGE: RED SQUADS AND POLICE REPRESSION IN URBAN AMERICA (1992). *See also, e.g.*, JULES BOYKOFF, THE SUPPRESSION OF DISSENT (2013) (explaining how the state and mainstream media have historically quashed U.S. social movements including mid-century communists, the Black Panther Party, indigenous movements, and modern-day globalization critics); Ryan Grim & Jon Schwarz, *A Short History of U.S. Law Enforcement Infiltrating Protests*, INTERCEPT (June 2, 2020, 2:12 PM), [https://perma.cc/ZJ99 -V95B]; Todd Gitlin, *The Wonderful American World of Informers and Agents Provocateurs*, NATION (June 27, 2013), https://www.thenation.com/article/archive/wonderful-ameri can-world-informers-and-agents-provocateurs/ (describing historical police infiltration of the labor movement); OVERSIGHT & REV. DIV., OFF. OF THE INSPECTOR GEN., A REVIEW OF THE FBI'S INVESTIGATION OF CERTAIN DOMESTIC ADVOCACY GROUPS (2010), https://www.nytimes.com/interactive/projects/documents/justice-department-inspec tor-general-report?ref=politics (describing police infiltration and disruption of organizing for anti-war efforts, animal liberation, environmental justice, and workers' rights). One recent example are the "terrorism" and RICO charges for forest defenders, legal observers, and bail fund charity employees fighting against the demolition of a forest to build a "faux city" for police "training" near Atlanta. After police killed a leading forest defender, many others were arrested, seemingly for attending a music festival, and many more were arrested in a sprawling conspiracy indictment that attempts to criminalize them for anarchist political beliefs. *See* Timothy Pratt, *"Alarming and Absurd": Concern as "Cop City" Activists Charged with Racketeering*, GUARDIAN (Sept. 7, 2023), [https://perma .cc/W6RB-X9S5].

27 *How the Cold War Shaped First-Person Journalism and Literary Conventions*, CITATIONS NEEDED PODCAST, (Sept. 22, 2021), https://citationsneeded.medium. com/episode-144-how-the-cold-war-shaped-first-person-journalism-and-literary -conventionss-42bf68ccaef; Gabe Levine-Drizin, *In the '90s the U.S. Government Paid TV Networks to Weave "Anti-Drug" Messaging into Their Plot Lines. Here Are the Worst Examples*, THE COLUMN, Dec. 27, 2021), https://www.columnblog.com/p /in-the-90s-the-us-government-paid.

28 Kiersten Willis, *Spike Lee Paid over $200k by NYPD to Lead Program to Improve Relationship Between Cops and Community*, ATL. BLACK STAR (Aug. 18, 2018), [https://perma .cc/GBQ5-YUSW].

1. What Is Crime News?

1 NOAM CHOMSKY, PIRATES AND EMPERORS, OLD AND NEW, vii (1st ed. 1986).

2 James Baldwin, "The Devil Finds Work," *in* BALDWIN: COLLECTED ESSAYS 504 (Toni Morrison, ed.) (1998).

3 KTLA 5 Weekend Morning News (@KTLAWeekendAM), TWITTER (Mar. 9, 2022, 1:56 PM), [https://perma.cc/LCJ8-AV33]. *See also* CENTER FOR JUST JOURNALISM, BUILDING A BETTER BEAT (2023), [https://perma.cc/7YZL-TXMB] (citing studies showing how the news overrepresents both white victims and Black perpetrators of crime).

4 David Wallace-Wells, *Ten Million a Year*, 43 LONDON REV. BOOKS, Dec. 2021, [https://perma.cc/UU6R-RTQD].

5 *See Defendants Charged in Criminal Cases*, BJS, https://www.bjs.gov/fjsrc/var .cfm?ttype=one_variable&agency=AOUSC&db_type=CrimCtCases&saf=IN (last visited Jan. 2, 2023). *See also* Duhigg, *supra* introduction, note 20. *See generally Prosecution of Federal Pollution Crimes*, DOJ [https://perma.cc/9A4K-V5XK] (last visited Jan. 2, 2023).

6 *See, e.g.*, Wallace-Wells, *supra* chapter 1, note 4; Marina Bolotnikova, *America's Car Crash Epidemic*, Vox (Sept. 19, 2021), [https://perma.cc/MY4M-565V]; *Decrease in U.S. Health Insurance Coverage Led to 25,180 Deaths*, OPEN ACCESS GOV. (Oct. 29, 2020), [https://perma.cc/HY6C-2V68]; Vandana Tripathi, *How Many U.S. Deaths Are Caused by Poverty, Lack of Education, and Other Social Factors?*, COLUMBIA PUB. HEALTH Now (July 5, 2011), [https://perma.cc/52SG-W3HK]; David Cecere, *New Study Finds 45,000 Deaths Annually Linked to Lack of Health Coverage*, HARV. GAZETTE (Sept. 17, 2009), [https://perma.cc/E4UQ-ULYX]; Melissa Denchak, *Flint Water Crisis: Everything You Need to Know*, NRDC (Nov. 8, 2018), [https://perma.cc/YP6X -7XMG]. *See also* Annie Nova, *Unaffordable Rents Are Linked to Premature Deaths, Princeton Study Finds*, CNBC (Dec. 19, 2023, 11:35 AM), [https://perma.cc/PY7R -UARL]; Gum-Ryeong Park et al., *How Do Housing Asset and Income Relate to Mortality? A Population-Based Cohort Study of 881,220 Older Adults in Canada*, 314 SOC. SCI. & MED. 115429 (2022).

7 *See, e.g.*, *More Than 100 Children Illegally Employed in Hazardous Jobs, Federal Investigation Finds*, U.S. DEPT. LABOR (Feb. 17, 2023), [https://perma.cc/WA7P-SSDC].

8 Amanda Mull, *The Great Shoplifting Freak-Out*, ATLANTIC (Dec. 23, 2021), [https:// perma.cc/GT78-CYXF]; Meixell & Eisenbrey, *supra* introduction, note 20; Amy Traub, *The Steal: The Urgent Need to Combat Wage Theft in Retail*, DĒMOS (June 12, 2017), [https://perma.cc/VW4K-4NJC]; Aila Slisco, *California Gov. Gavin Newsom Promises to Boost Police Funding amid Shoplifting Wave*, NEWSWEEK (Nov. 23, 2021), [https://perma .cc/38TV-ENZQ]. Politicians across the country are *years* behind even recovering money stolen from workers. Arcelia Martin, *Texas Workforce Commission Years Behind on Recovering*

Back Wages for Workers, Report Finds, DALLAS MORNING NEWS (Aug. 9, 2023, 1:30 PM), [https://perma.cc/WME8-UHAA].

9 Genevieve Carlton, *Wage Theft, the $50 Billion Crime Against Workers,* Working: Then & Now (Apr. 17, 2023), [https://perma.cc/4MP5-BJ5G].

10 NAT'L LOW INCOME HOUS. COAL., OUT OF REACH: THE HIGH COST OF HOUSING (2018).

11 Erin McCormick et al., *Revealed: The "Shocking" Levels of Toxic Lead in Chicago's Tap Water,* GUARDIAN (Sept. 21, 2022), [https://perma.cc/MB5X-RAWP]; Adam Johnson, *Media Indifference to Report on Deadly Chicago Water Contamination an Object Lesson in How Crime Is Socially Constructed,* REAL NEWS NETWORK (Sept. 30, 2022), [https://perma.cc/C5RA-4S7Z].

12 *Attorney General Bonta Calls on Nation's Largest Banks to Eliminate Overdraft Fees,* CAL. DEPT. JUST. (Apr. 6, 2022), [https://perma.cc/T8LY-HZHU]; *CFPB Orders Atlantic Union Bank to Pay $6.2 Million for Illegal Overdraft Fee Harvesting,* CONSUMER FIN. PROT. BUREAU (Dec. 7, 2023), [https://perma.cc/SQ3X-278T]; *CFPB Research Shows Banks' Deep Dependence on Overdraft Fees,* CONSUMER FIN. PROT. BUREAU (Dec. 1, 2021), [https://perma.cc/25JB-TU2K] (estimating overdraft and non-sufficient funds revenue totaled $15.47 billion in 2019); *Uniform Crime Report: Property Crime,* FBI (2019), [https://perma.cc/Y2V2-SYDT] (estimating total losses from property crimes in 2019 at $15.8 billion).

13 *Robbery,* FBI, [https://perma.cc/JN8B-CEEZ] ("In 2019 . . . robberies accounted for an estimated $482 million in losses.") (last visited Jan. 2, 2023).

14 Alexander Dyck et al., *How Pervasive Is Corporate Fraud?,* REV. ACCT. STUD. (2019), [https://perma.cc/3BKE-THH2].

15 Tripathi, *supra* chapter 1, note 6.

16 Nat'l Hous. L. Project, *Survey of Legal Aid Attorneys,* NHLP (July 2020), [https://perma.cc/K44F-5ZUU].

17 Neel Dhanesha, *The Massive, Unregulated Source of Plastic Pollution You've Probably Never Heard Of,* Vox (May 6, 2022, 6:00 AM), [https://perma.cc/A4LY-LTQ4]; David Gelles, *She's on a Mission from God: Suing Big Oil for Climate Damages,* N.Y. TIMES (July 19, 2023), https://www.nytimes.com/2023/07/19/climate/climate-lawsuit-puerto-rico.html; Reed Abelson & Margot Sanger-Katz, *"The Cash Monster Was Insatiable": How Insurers Exploited Medicare for Billions,* N.Y. TIMES (Oct. 8, 2022), https://www.nytimes.com/2022/10/08/upshot/medicare-advantage-fraud-allegations.html; Maureen Tkacik, *Born to Die,* AM. PROSPECT (Apr. 26, 2023), [https://perma.cc/5QZ8-FF8Y]. Not only are these violations not regularly reported as dangerous crimes, but the polluters are rewarded with billions of dollars in public subsidies to do the pollution. Dylan Baddour, *Gulf Coast Petrochemical Buildout Draws Billions in Tax Breaks for Polluters,* AM. PROSPECT (Mar. 19, 2024), [https://perma.cc/DDX2-PBTK].

2. The Volume of Crime News

1 Clarence Darrow, The Story of My Life, 356 (1932) (quoting Lewis Lawes, a prison warden at Sing Sing Correctional Facility).

2 Basis for Actual Knowing, *Stefano Harney and Fred Moten—Propositions for Non-Fascist Living—Video Statement—October 2017*, Vimeo (Oct. 15, 2017), https://vimeo.com/238275888.

3 Mitch Smith, *As Applications Fall, Police Departments Lure Recruits with New Tactics*, N.Y. Times (Dec. 25, 2022), https://www.nytimes.com/2022/12/25/us/police-officer-recruits.html; Chelsia Rose Marcius, *N.Y.P.D. Officers Leave in Droves for Better Pay in Small Towns*, N.Y. Times (Dec. 9, 2022), https://www.nytimes.com/2022/12/09/nyregion/new-york-police-department-attrition.html; James Barron, *Why Police Officers Are Leaving*, N.Y. Times (Dec. 14, 2022), https://www.nytimes.com/2022/12/14/nyregion/nypd-pay-work-costs.html.

4 I worked with the Center for Just Journalism to prepare a resource for journalists and news consumers on the issue: Center for Just Journalism, Building a Better Beat (2023), [https://perma.cc/7YZL-TXMB]. Moreover, the news overrepresents anecdotes of individual violent crimes while failing to examine the social causes of crime. Kenneth Dowler, *Comparing American and Canadian Local Television Crime Stories: A Content Analysis*, 46 Canadian J. Criminology & Crim. Just. 573, 574 (2004). Also, the volume of violent crime reporting is more related to demographics than actual crime rates. Jae Hong Kim, *The Influence of Community Structure on Crime News Coverage*, 28 Comm. & Soc. 97, 107–8 (2015) (finding that, as areas become more urbanized and ethnically diverse, local news reports on more sensational and violent crime than is proportional to FBI crime statistics).

5 Philip Bump, *What's the Non-Obvious Reason Fox News Is Talking About Crime More?*, Wash. Post, graph, "Mentions of topic relative to first six months of 2022" (Oct. 26, 2022), https://www.washingtonpost.com/politics/2022/10/26/crime-midterm-elections-news-coverage-fox-news/.

6 Tyler Monroe & Rob Savillo, *Fox's Coverage of Violent Crime Dropped After the Midterms*, Media Matters, graph "Violent Crime Segments on Fox News" (Nov. 17, 2022, 2:49 PM), [https://perma.cc/VY5A-E8Y9].

7 Fola Akinnibi & Raeedah Wahid, *Fear of Rampant Crime Is Derailing New York City's Recovery*, Bloomberg (July 29, 2022), https://www.bloomberg.com/graphics/2022-is-nyc-safe-crime-stat-reality/.

8 Jamil Hamilton & Alana Sivin, *Freedom, Then the Press, Volume II: New Data, Same Tricks*, FWD.us (Dec. 15, 2022), [https://perma.cc/LG9U-HUPQ].

9 Lisa Kashinsky, *Horton Case Linked Newspaper and President*, Eagle-Tribune (Dec. 6, 2018), https://www.eagletribune.com/news/merrimack_valley/horton-case-linked-newspaper-and-president/article_9d153aa5-bc8e-573d-9521-a9dd65f4db1f.html; John Pfaff, *Op-Ed: The Never-Ending "Willie Horton Effect" Is Keeping Prisons Too Full for America's Good*, L.A. Times (May 14, 2017), https://www.latimes.com/opinion

/op-ed/la-oe-pfaff-why-prison-reform-isnt-working-20170514-story.html; Beth Schwarzapfel, *Willie Horton Revisited*, MARSHALL PROJECT (May 13, 2015), [https://perma.cc/86NX-QXJK].

10 Lyanne Melendez, *Man Seen Stealing from SF Walgreens in Viral Video Last Year Arrested, Accused of Shoplifting at CVS*, ABC-7 (July 18, 2022), https://abc7news.com/sf-retail-theft-walgreens-cvs-shoplifting-video/12059659/ [https://perma.cc/86 NX-QXJK].

11 *See* Carolyn Said, *What Walgreens Isn't Saying*, S.F. CHRONICLE (Oct. 23, 2021), https://www.sfchronicle.com/sf/article/More-than-meets-the-eye-to-Walgreens -S-F-16555962.php; Eric Westervelt, *Behind the Loud Pushback Against Progressive District Attorneys Across the Country*, NPR (Nov. 26, 2021, 4:24 PM), [https://perma .cc/2B8J-X3YF].

12 Steven Keehner, *Shoplifting Is Big News; Stealing Millions from Workers Is Not*, FAIR (July 19, 2021), [https://perma.cc/HJ3D-MJPL].

13 Nathaniel Meyersohn, *"Maybe We Cried Too Much" over Shoplifting, Walgreens Executive Says*, CNN (Jan. 7, 2023), [https://perma.cc/NUD5-BYVJ]; Susie Neilson, *A Viral Video Has Everyone Talking About San Francisco's "Shoplifting Surge,"* S.F. CHRON. (June 26, 2021), https://www.sfchronicle.com/crime/article/Is-shoplifting-rising-in-San-Francisco-Here -s-16272907.php [https://perma.cc/FMK8-RWKY]; Hope Corrigan, *Why Is Walgreens Really Closing Stores in San Francisco?*, QZ (Oct. 21, 2021), [https://perma.cc/7VAX-AMB4]; Rachel Swan et al., *Is Shoplifting Forcing Walgreens to Cut Back in S.F.?*, S.F. CHRON. (Oct. 18, 2021), https://www.sfchronicle.com/sf/article/Is-shoplifting-forcing-Walgreens-to-cut-back-in-16536960 .php; Mike Masnick, *Retailers Are Blaming the Internet for a Retail Theft Surge That Might Not Be Happening; Media Is Helping Them Out*, Techdirt (Dec. 28, 2021), [https://perma.cc/96AY -T7JY]; Ernesto Lopez et al., *Shoplifting Trends: What You Need to Know*, COUNCIL ON CRIM. JUST. (Nov. 2023), [https://perma.cc/T8AF-TRCG]; Eduardo Medina, *Retail Group Retracts Startling Claim About "Organized" Shoplifting*, N.Y. TIMES (Dec. 8, 2023), https://www.nytimes.com/2023/12/08/business/organized-shoplifting-retail-crime -theft-retraction.html ("The National Retail Federation had said that nearly half of the industry's $94.5 billion in missing merchandise in 2021 was the result of organized theft. It was likely closer to 5 percent"); Thea Sebastian & Hanna Love, *Retail Theft in US Cities: Separating Fact from Fiction*, BROOKINGS INST. (Mar. 6, 2024), [https://perma.cc /L6MY-5G3V].

14 SF CHRON. via INTERNET ARCHIVE WAYBACK MACHINE, https://web.archive.org /web/20211122025826/https://www.sfchronicle.com/ (capture from Nov. 22, 2021, last visited Jan. 2, 2024).

15 Eric Levenson & Cheri Mossburg, *"This Has Been Out of Control." San Francisco's Chain Drug Stores Have a Shoplifting Problem*, CNN (June 17, 2020), [https://perma.cc /Q8YN-RSHW]; Dan Simon, *San Francisco Confronts Surging Crime, Drugs and Homelessness as It Tries to Bounce Back from Covid-19*, CNN (June 23, 2021), [https://perma .cc/2R8A-LY72].

16 NYPD News (@NYPDnews), TWITTER via INTERNET ARCHIVE WAYBACK MACHINE (Feb. 16, 2022, 4:50 PM), https://web.archive.org/web/20220217005528

/https://twitter.com/NYPDnews/status/1494111945183711235; Edward Ongweso Jr., *NYPD Proudly Poses with Seized Diapers, Baby Shampoo*, VICE (Feb. 17, 2022), [https:// perma.cc/T77Q-8LXS].

17 ANATOLE FRANCE, THE RED LILY (1894).

18 Robert Channick, *Rising Crime Scaring Some Visitors Away from Michigan Avenue and Other Chicago Destinations During Crucial Holiday Shopping Season*, CHI. TRIB. (Dec. 11, 2021), https://www.chicagotribune.com/business/ct-biz-downtown-chicago -crime-holiday-shopping-20211211-jpjij34llfffifk6cu5av5bnfkq-story.html; Don Thompson, *DAs, Retailers Say California Needs Tougher Retail Theft Law*, AP (Dec. 3, 2021, 6:58 PM), [https://perma.cc/LG7A-P9GA]; Michael Corkery & Sapna Maheshwari, *Thefts, Always an Issue for Retailers, Become More Brazen*, N.Y. TIMES (Dec. 3, 2021), https:// www.nytimes.com/2021/12/03/business/retailers-robberies-theft.html.

19 CHI. POLICE DEPT., 2021 ANNUAL REPORT 77 (2021), [https://perma.cc/2J9Z -8WEL].

20 Christine Hauser & Michael Christopher Brown, *Sifting Through the Train Thefts of Los Angeles*, N.Y. TIMES (Jan. 19, 2022), https://www.nytimes.com/2022/01/19/us/la -train-tracks-cargo-thieves.html.

21 City News Service, *Newsom Vows to End "Third-World" Freight Train Robberies in Los Angeles*, TIMES OF SAN DIEGO (Jan. 21, 2022), [https://perma.cc/6LDT-BWNX].

22 Letter from George Gascón, Dist. Att'y, L.A., to Adrian Guerrero, Gen. Dir. Pub. Aff's., Union Pac. R.R. Co. (Jan. 21, 2022), [https://perma.cc/8N7T-LY4E].

23 Rachel Swan, *Is an International Crime Operation Targeting the Bay Area's Wealthiest Cities with "Burglary Tourism?*," S.F. CHRON (Mar. 16, 2022, 7:08 PM), https://www .sfchronicle.com/crime/article/Is-an-international-crime-operation-targeting-the -16987327.php.

24 Lauren Kaori Gurley, *Child Labor Violations Soared in Fiscal 2023*, WASH. POST (Oct. 19, 2023), https://www.washingtonpost.com/business/2023/10/19/child-labor -violations-2023/.

25 A.M. Rosenthal, *We Told You So*, N.Y. TIMES (Oct. 25, 1988), https://www .nytimes.com/1988/10/25/opinion/on-my-mind-we-told-you-so.html.

26 *See* Alec Karakatsanis (@equalityalec), TWITTER (June 29, 2022), https://x.com /equalityAlec/status/1542299660810743808 (describing the background of the community campaign in West Hollywood to reduce the amount of money paid to the sheriff's department for deputies under a lucrative and fraudulent contract with the city).

27 Lucia Moses, *Inside the New York Times' New Push Notifications Team*, DIGIDAY (Nov. 3, 2015), [https://perma.cc/D45Z-YEEW]; Liz Spayd, *Why'd You Do That? How the Times Decides to Send News Alerts*, N.Y. TIMES (Aug. 25, 2016), https://www.nytimes .com/2016/08/25/public-editor/whyd-you-do-that-how-the-times-decides-to-send-news -alerts.html?_r=0.

28 *See* Brian X. Chen, *Apps That Blast Out Crime Alerts Don't Have to Rattle You*, N.Y. TIMES (May 29, 2019) https://www.nytimes.com/2019/05/29/technology/personaltech /neighborhood-crime-apps.html; David Ingram & Cyrus Farivar, *Inside Citizen*, NBC NEWS (June 2, 2021), [https://perma.cc/PCM2-DE92].

3. Moral Panics and the Selective Curation of Anecdote

1 Quoted in STUART HALL ET AL., *infra* chapter 3, note 8 at 75.

2 Livia Gershon, *How Crime Stories Foiled Reform in Victorian Britain*, JSTOR DAILY (Oct. 27, 2021), [https://perma.cc/GUG5-MMT8]. Adam Johnson has written powerfully about the "fare evasion" moral panic. *See The Evergreen, Cop-Curated, Anti-Poor, Faux Investigative "Fare Evasion" Story*, COLUMN (Oct. 4, 2022), [https://perma.cc/Q32A-98ZV]. In 2022, New York officials declared poor people evading fares on *public* transit to be a "threat to the spirit" of a "sacred" place. O Mazariego, *The MTA Will Try to Crackdown on Fare Evasion, Has Cost Them $500 Million So Far*, HIPHOPWIRED (Apr. 27, 2022), [https://perma.cc/235H-JFMB]. Journalists followed suit, printing numerous investigations and stories about fare evasion. *See, e.g.*. Michael Gold & Erin Woo, *What Other Cities Can Teach New York About Homelessness on Transit*, N.Y. TIMES (Apr. 4, 2022), https://www.nytimes.com/2022/04/04/nyregion/homeless-people-subway-transit-systems.html (as part of a plan to address homelessness on subways, "police officers made 719 arrests, issued 6,828 summonses—the vast majority for fare evasion" in a single month); Clio Chang, *Buses Have Been Free Before*, CURBED (Feb. 22, 2022), [https://perma.cc/7UKF-5R8A]; Natalie Duddridge, *MTA Stations Unarmed, Private Guards at Subway Entrances to Stop Would-Be Fare Evaders*, CBS News (Oct. 27, 2022, 12:51 PM), [https://perma.cc/4HUU-PQJD]. As the frenzy over the issue increased, Washington, DC, reporters set up cameras to catch people evading fares. Victoria Sanchez (@VictoriaSanchez), TWITTER (Oct. 5, 2022, 7:17 AM), [https://perma.cc/7CBJ-ZSWL]. Predictably, NYPD reported a 103 percent increase in fare evasion arrests from 2021 to 2022. Fola Akinnibi, *Arrests for Low-Level Crimes Climb Under NYC Mayor Eric Adams*, BLOOMBERG, table titled "Growing Focus" (Aug. 30, 2022, 9:00 AM), https://www.bloomberg.com/news/articles/2022-08-30/nyc-s-rise-of-low-level-arrests-worry-critics-of-broken-windows-era.

3 During a four-month period in 1993, the local news media in Denver embarked on a campaign to create fear about a supposed wave of gang violence by teenagers. It led the Democratic governor to call an emergency legislative session, promising to crack down on Black youth with an "iron fist." Local news outlets published hundreds more stories about murder than the previous year, when murder had been higher. Although violent crime in Colorado was declining, the panic led to draconian new laws that dismantled the juvenile system in Colorado and dramatically expanded the imprisonment of children. *See* LynNell Hancock, *When Denver Lost Its Mind over Youth Crime*, NEW REP. (Nov. 23, 2021), https://newrepublic.com/article/164419/denver-lost-mind-youth-crime-wave-panic.

4 One of the most alarming recent examples of the news disseminating untrue police claims about drugs that led to general panic and fear is the bizarre moral panic over fentanyl exposure. Hundreds of news stories from 2018 to 2023 generated a panic that police officers were experiencing fentanyl overdoses simply through coming into contact with the substance on the job. Brian Mann, *Cops Say They're Being Poisoned by Fentanyl. Experts Say the Risk Is "Extremely Low,"* NPR (May 16, 2023, 6:15 PM), [https://perma.cc/3GQ7-6ZF7]. As the Center for Just Journalism explored in its study of the systemic "breakdown in journalistic standards" in reporting about fentanyl exposure, this myth has been

repeatedly and comprehensively debunked by scientists and medical professionals as lacking scientific plausibility. *Fentanyl Exposure: Myths, Misconceptions, and the Media*, Center for Just Journalism, [https://perma.cc/NFN9-GQUT] (last visited June 10, 2024). But the debunked myth feeds into general copaganda tropes such as that policing is a dangerous profession, even though it is not close to being among the most dangerous jobs in the U.S., and that marginalized people or people using certain illegal substances exhibit uncontrollable, animalistic strength that both require armed responses and justify the inevitable violence that ensues against them. The concept of "excited delirium," invented by police, is one such example. Amy Larson, *"Excited Delerium" Attributed to Another Man's Death in Contra Costa County*, KRON-4 (May 9, 2023, 9:18 PM), [https://perma.cc/N7NH-AFAB]; Danielle Kurtzleben, *Being a Police Officer Is Dangerous. These Jobs Are More Dangerous*, VOX (Aug. 22, 2014, 12:00 PM), [https://perma.cc/9A7V-223L].

5 *California Increases Efforts to Combat Organized Retail Theft Ahead of Busy Holiday Shopping Season*, OFF. GOV. NEWSOM (Nov. 15, 2022), [https://perma.cc/Z2RA-7ST6]; *California to Make Largest-Ever Investment to Combat Organized Retail Crime*, OFF. GOV. NEWSOM (Sept. 12, 2023), [https://perma.cc/9JWT-C7QL]. The same thing happened across the U.S. For example, in 2024, because of the supposed "spike" in retail theft, the governor of New York proposed $45 million for a special police "smash and grab" unit, more prosecution, increased prison sentences, and cash for business owners. *See, e.g.*, Kathy Hochul, *As Larceny Offenses Spike, Governor Hochul Proposes Major Expansion of Resources to Fight Retail Theft and Keep New Yorkers Safe*, OFF. GOV. HOCHUL (Feb. 14, 2024), available at [https://perma.cc/8AQR-TG9N].

6 Mihir Zaveri, *Prosecutions for Fire Safety Violations Dropped by 98% in New York City*, N.Y. TIMES (Oct. 5, 2022), https://www.nytimes.com/2022/10/05/nyregion/fire-code-prosecutions-nyc.html?action=click&module=Well&pgtype=Homepage&section=New%20York.

7 Kimiko de Freytas-Tamura, *"Devastated": 15 Fire Victims Are Mourned at Bronx Service*, N.Y. TIMES (Jan. 16, 2022), https://www.nytimes.com/2022/01/16/nyregion/bronx-fire-funeral.html.

8 I had been analyzing copaganda for a couple of years by the time I read *Policing the Crisis* in full. It profoundly deepened my understanding of the issue. HALL ET AL., POLICING THE CRISIS.

9 *Id.*, 182.

10 *Id.*, 182.

11 Alice George, *The 1968 Kerner Commission Got It Right, But Nobody Listened*, SMITHSONIAN MAG. (Mar. 1, 2018), [https://perma.cc/2UF3-NPSD].

12 MARK FISHMAN, MANUFACTURING THE NEWS, at 8 (2014).

13 In this period, when I observed that overall crime was still down, some journalists claimed that murder was the only reliable statistic because all of the others could be easily manipulated by police.

14 German Lopez, *A Shift in Crime*, N.Y. TIMES (Sept. 23, 2022), https://www.nytimes.com/2022/09/23/briefing/crime-rates-murder-robberies-us.html.

15 Caroline Hicks, *Police in Charlotte Investigating 13 Homicides So Far This Year, Making*

October Deadliest Month This Year, WBTV-3 (Oct. 22, 2021, 4:55 PM), [https://perma.cc/4TTW-4H8Z].

16 Nigel Duara, *A Veto for the "Mandela" Bill That Sought to Limit Solitary Confinement in California*, CAL MATTERS (Sept. 26, 2022), [https://perma.cc/DA7K-RHDQ].

17 *Solitary Confinement Should be Banned in Most Cases, UN Expert Says*, U. NATIONS (Oct. 18, 2011), [https://perma.cc/LP4A-5F43].

18 *See, e.g.*, Martin Kaste & Brandt Williams, *Police Departments Try to Walk the Line Between Reform, Public Safety*, NPR (Dec. 9, 2020), [https://perma.cc/H8GG-3BWY].

19 Martin Kaste, *Shootings Spiked During the Pandemic. The Spike Now Looks Like a "New Normal,' "*NPR (Aug. 29, 2022, 6:00 AM), [https://perma.cc/R65Y-T7SE].

20 *FBI Releases 2022 Crime in the Nation Statistics*, FBI (Oct. 16, 2023), [https://perma.cc/6MGE-K345].

21 Andy Friedman & Mason Youngblood, *Nobody Defunded the Police: A Study*, REAL NEWS NETWORK (Apr. 18, 2022), [https://perma.cc/ZM8P-YFCF].

22 Grace Manthey et al., *Despite "Defunding" Claims, Police Funding Has Increased in Many U.S. Cities*, ABC NEWS (Oct. 16, 2022, 8:34 AM), [https://perma.cc/U89L-236G].

23 Teo Popescu, *Did Seattle Defund the Police? Five Graphs Explain This Enduring Myth* (Apr. 4, 2024, 11:00 AM), [https://perma.cc/EM7Z-X6YC] ("In fact, the department has consistently received more funding for hiring than it can spend.") *See also* Mina Barahimi Martin, *Follow the Money: 2022*, ACLU of Washington (Nov. 15, 2022), [https://perma.cc/BN5V-3SCF].

24 Seattle Police Crime Dashboard, https://www.seattle.gov/police/information-and-data/data/crime-dashboard.

25 JACQUES ELLUL, PROPAGANDA: THE FORMATION OF MEN'S ATTITUDES 53 (1965).

26 Neel Dhanesha, *The Massive, Unregulated Source of Plastic Pollution You've Probably Never Heard of*, VOX (May 6, 2022), [https://perma.cc/A4LY-LTQ4]; CENTER FOR CLIMATE INTEGRITY, THE FRAUD OF PLASTIC RECYCLING (2024), [https://perma.cc/G8DC-PZLF].

27 Ashley Parker (@AshleyRParker), TWITTER (Mar. 3, 2023, 11:22 AM), [https://perma.cc/G9JT-97EU].

28 GALLUP, *supra* introduction, note 22.

29 Jeffrey M. Jones, *More Americans See U.S. Crime Problem as Serious*, GALLUP (Nov. 16, 2023), https://news.gallup.com/poll/544442/americans-crime-problem-serious.aspx.

30 ELLUL, *supra* chapter 3, note 25 at vi.

4. Policing Public Relations

1 James C. Scott, *The Uses of Disorder and "Charisma," in* Two CHEERS FOR ANARCHISM (2012), [https://perma.cc/UNZ8-4LMJ].

2 Geoffrey Cubbage, *Analysis: Chicago Outspends and Outstaffs NYC, LA on Communications and Public Relations*, BGA POLICY (Oct. 18, 2022), [https://perma

.cc/2JET-NYA3]; *Budget—2024 Budget Ordinance—Positions and Salaries*, Chi. Data Portal (Nov. 21, 2023), [https://perma.cc/M2NN-MP63].

3 *See* Will Jarrett, *Supervisors Grill SFPD on Media Spin Doctoring*, Mission Local (May 5, 2022), [https://perma.cc/C3WQ-L8ES].

4 Maya Lau, *Police PR Machine Under Scrutiny for Inaccurate Reporting, Alleged Pro-Cop Bias*, L.A. Times (Aug. 30, 2020, https://www.latimes.com/california/story/2020-08-30 /police-public-relations.

5 Chris Gelardi, *Meet the Cops Running the NYPD's 86-Member Public Relations Team*, New York Focus, (May 14, 2024), https://nysfocus.com/2024/05/14/nypd -dcpi-tarik-sheppard-protests-pr.

6 Alec Karakatsanis, *Police Departments Are Spending Millions on "Copaganda,"* Real News Network (July 21, 2022), [https://perma.cc/GHP7-WTY3]; LA County Sheriffs (@LASDHQ), Twitter (May 4, 2022), [https://perma.cc/AL22-AQ5J].

7 St. John Barned-Smith, *Houston Police Department's Rainbow Cruiser Raises Eyebrows but Ready to Go for Pride Parade*, Hous. Chron. (June 23, 2017), https://www.houston chronicle.com/news/houston-texas/houston/article/Houston-Police-Department-s -rainbow-cruiser-11243917.php; Avianne Tam, *NYPD Unveils Rainbow-Themed Vehicle Before City's Gay Pride March*, ABC News (June 23, 2016), [https://perma.cc/77X9 -U85G]; Lizzie Chadbourne, *NYPD'S "Autism Awareness" Squad Car Is Nothing but a Publicity Stunt*, Truthout (Apr. 28, 2023), [https://perma.cc/3YN9-4GM9]; Tony Plohetski, *How Austin Police "Gay Pride" Patrol Car Almost Wasn't*, Austin Am. Statesman (Sept. 25, 2018), https://www.statesman.com/story/news/2016/09/15/how-the-austin-police -gay-pride-patrol-car-almost-wasnt/10058302007/.

8 10th District—Ogden (@ChicagoCAPS10), Twitter (Apr. 13, 2021, 1:59 PM), https://twitter.com/ChicagoCAPS10/status/1382030803404738566 [https://perma.cc/35 7W-7FQR].9 *See, e.g.,* Alec Karakatsanis (@equalityalec), Twitter (Aug. 23, 2022, 2:16 PM), [https://perma.cc/9TF3-YNJE] (depicting correspondence between Jess Montejano of the public relations firm Riff City and Brooke Jenkins, San Francisco's district attorney).

10 @journo_anon, Twitter via Internet Archive Wayback Machine (Dec. 6, 2021, 2:40 PM), https://web.archive.org/web/20211206224107/https://twitter.com/journo _anon/status/1467987424215109634 (full document production available at https://www .documentcloud.org/documents/21116909-p54916_sfpd_production_1).

11 To take just one well-reported example, after the protests of 2020, Crime Stoppers in Houston became a prominent, multi-million-dollar player in a campaign to target progressive judicial and county officials, as well as policies perceived as making the punishment bureaucracy more lenient. To do this, it used not only large state grants, but also money from the local DA and assessments charged to poor people in criminal cases. David A. Fahrenthold & Keri Blakinger, *How a Crime-Fighting Institution Took a Partisan Turn*, N.Y. Times (Apr. 21, 2022), https://www.nytimes.com/2022/04/21/us/politics/crime -stoppers-houston.html?partner=slack&smid=sl-share.

12 *See* Ericka Cruz Guevarra et al., *When Police Need PR Help, Many Turn to One Firm in Vacaville*, KQED (Dec. 6, 2021), [https://perma.cc/UC6Z-GC7A]. This is a difficult

thing to quantify comprehensively, because there is a lot of coordinated police activity "on the beat" in the community and on social media that is not counted as a formal part of the "public relations" budget. For example, during the recall election of "progressive" district attorney Chesa Boudin in San Francisco, local government officials reported to me that officers routinely (and illegally, in violation of California election law for publicly paid employees) campaigned for the recall on the job. Often, police inaccurately told people that they could not investigate certain crimes or make certain arrests under the current prosecutor, and that this wouldn't change unless he were recalled.

13 Alec Karakatsanis (@equalityalec), Twitter (May 5, 2022, 1:59 PM), [https://perma.cc/U8ZS-6WAE] (depicting texts between the San Francisco Police Department's director of strategic communications and a local reporter). *See also* Radley Balko, *The Bogus Backlash Against Progressive Prosecutors*, Wash. Post (June 14, 2021), https://www.washingtonpost.com/opinions/2021/06/14/bogus-backlash-against-progressive-prosecutors/.

14 Sheba Turk (@ShebaTurk), Twitter (Sept. 28, 2022, 6:57 AM).

15 Glen Stellmacher, *Derailing the Defund: How SPD Manipulated the Media Narrative Around the 2020 Protests*, Real Change News (July 19, 2023), [https://perma.cc/342N-KKDN].

16 When the scandal was uncovered with public information requests for internal emails three years later, the public media outlet retracted the op-ed. *See* Antonio Oftelie, *Seattle, Be Wary of Defunding Police Without Building Bridges*, Crosscut via Internet Archive Wayback Machine (Aug. 3, 2020), https://web.archive.org/web/20230415022413/https://crosscut.com/opinion/2020/08/seattle-be-wary-defunding-police-without-building-bridges. *See also* M. David Lee III, *What Crosscut Learned from a Public Records Request by Real Change*, Crosscut (Aug. 1, 2023), [https://perma.cc/K9P6-FVU3].

17 When journalist Radley Balko did a quick internet search, he found thirty such stories in just the two previous years before he decided that he had done enough searching to make his point. Radley Balko, *For Police PR Flacks, Quack Lives Matter*, Watch (Jan. 31, 2023), [https://perma.cc/KJ8U-W2JE].

18 *See generally* Tim Franklin et al., The Local News Initiative at Northwestern, The State of Local News 2023: Vanishing Newspapers, Digital Divides, and Reaching Underserved Communities (2023), [https://perma.cc/U5XZ-8ANN]; Margaret Sullivan, *What Happens to Democracy When Local Journalism Dries Up?* Wash. Post (Nov. 30, 2021), https://www.washingtonpost.com/magazine/2021/11/30/margaret-sullivan-the-local-news-crisis/.

19 *See* Stop LAPD Spying Coalition (@stoplapdspying), Twitter (Mar. 8, 2021, 12:07 PM), [https://perma.cc/JV6Q-8ZJG] (depicting an email from LAPD Lieutenant Stacey Vince "approving" a draft of a law professor's book on big-data policing; *Statements in Support of NYU Law Students Demanding Accountability from the NYU Policing Project*, Stoplapdspying (May 10, 2022), [https://perma.cc/Z42Z-UAKK] (addressing student responses to Barry Friedman's dual role as New York University's founder of the Policing Project and endorser of Axon policing products).

20 A similar phenomenon applies to which crimes authorities look for. For example,

President Ronald Reagan transferred thousands of federal agents from investigating white-collar financial crimes to pursuing the "war on drugs," and the FBI under Presidents Bill Clinton and George W. Bush oversaw still-further declines in its white-collar crime -fighting investigations. Antitrust enforcement now has hundreds fewer employees. For example, the staff of the Federal Trade Commission is down 40 percent since the 1970s, and the Department of Justice Antitrust Division lost 25 percent of its staff between 2013 and 2023. Filippo Lancieri et al., *The Political Economy of the Decline of Antitrust Enforcement in the United States*, 85 Antitrust L. J. (Oct. 2023), [https://perma.cc/Y6YW-29S9]. The result is that the government—and the media—doesn't find out about a wide range of white-collar crimes that they used to be aware of.

5. Whose Perspective? How Sources Shape the News

1 Ellul, *supra* chapter 3, note 25 at 237–38, quoting Jean Rivero, *Technique de Formation de L'opinion Publique*, L'opinion Publique (1957).

2 *"We Can't Guarantee Your Safety": Head of LAPD's Police Officers' Union Warns Tourists Away*, KCAL (Dec. 7, 2021, 9:47 PM), [https://perma.cc/9VUA-V7W6].

3 Ali Watkins & Troy Closson, *Shootings Rise in New York, Coloring Perceptions of City's Safety*, N.Y. Times (Apr. 6, 2022), https://www.nytimes.com/2022/04/06/nyregion /shootings-new-york-city-safety.html.

4 Jeong Park, *After Stealing $19,000 Worth of Watches, Suspects Flee West Hollywood in a Rolls Royce*, L.A. Times (May 8, 2022), https://www.latimes.com/california/story/2022-05-08 /after-stealing-19-000-worth-of-watches-suspects-flee-west-hollywood-in-a-rolls-royce.

5 Hauser & Brown, *Sifting Through the Train Thefts of Los Angeles.*

6 Compare, e.g., David Helps, *What Actually Killed Breonna Taylor*, Nation (Mar. 16, 2022), https://www.thenation.com/article/society/breonna-taylor-gentrification/; *with* Bill Hutchinson, *"Breonna Taylor Is Now Attached to Me for the Rest of My Life," Sgt. Jon Mattingly Says in Exclusive Interview*, ABC News (Oct. 21, 2020), [https://perma.cc/F4 B9-YD65].

7 *See* Stuart Schrader, *The Lies Cops Tell and the Lies We Tell About Cops*, New Rep. (May 27, 2021), https://newrepublic.com/article/162510/cops-lie-public-safety-defund -the-police; Mark Joseph Stern, *The Police Lie. All the Time. Can Anything Stop Them?*, Slate (Aug. 4, 2020, 11:51 AM), [https://perma.cc/L9ZT-JP9R]; Wendy Ruderman, *Crime Report Manipulation Is Common Among New York Police, Study Finds*, N.Y. Times (June 28, 2012), https://www.nytimes.com/2012/06/29/nyregion/new-york-police-department-ma nipulates-crime-reports-study-finds.html; Joseph Goldstein, *"Testilying" by Police: A Stubborn Problem*, N.Y. Times (March 18, 2018), https://www.nytimes.com/2018/03/18 /nyregion/testilying-police-perjury-new-york.html; Nicolas Bogel-Burroughs & Frances Robles, *When Police Lie, The Innocent Pay. Some Are Fighting Back.*, N.Y. Times (Aug. 28, 2021), https://www.nytimes.com/2021/08/28/us/false-police-statements.html; Nia T. Evans, *Blue Lies Matter*, Bost. Rev. (Feb. 22, 2022), [https://perma.cc/K3ZD-VBTM]; Eric Levenson, *How Minneapolis Police First Described the Murder of George Floyd, and What We Know Now*, CNN (Apr. 21, 2021), [https://perma.cc/UL29-BWAL]; Natasha

Korecki, *What Chicago's Ultimate Bad Cop Taught Me About Police Reform*, Politico (June 15, 2020, 4:30 AM), [https://perma.cc/YW69-CJSG]. Shawna Chen, *Uvalde Mayor Says He Fears "Cover-Up" of Deadly School Shooting*, Axios (July 5, 2022 [https://perma.cc/7S2Q -9SSY]. This is a particular problem in breaking news stories, where initial police versions of events can go viral—or can prevent a story that would have gone viral had the truth been known from going viral—even though those initial versions can be wild fabrications. *See, e.g.*, Robert Mackey, *Survivors of a Deadly Attack on a Portland Protest Were Victimized Twice: First by the Gunman, Then by the Police*, Intercept (Feb. 23, 2022), [https://perma.cc /SK88-B9P2]; Ashley Parker & Justine McDaniel, *From Freddie Gray to Tyre Nichols, Early Police Claims Often Misleading*, Wash. Post (Feb. 17, 2023), https://www.washingtonpost .com/nation/2023/02/17/police-shootings-false-misleading/.

8 Neil MacFarquhar, *Murders Spiked in 2020 in Cities Across the United States*, N.Y. Times (Sept. 27, 2021), https://www.nytimes.com/2021/09/27/us/fbi-murders-2020 -cities.html.

9 *Peter A. Winograd*, UNM Sch. L., [https://perma.cc/3UG7-B3Z7] (last vis- ited Jan. 5, 2023); John Acosta, *New Mexico Has the Second-Highest Police Shooting Rate in the U.S.—Is It Ready to Change?*, Guardian (May 6, 2021, 6:00 AM), [https://perma.cc /AG8D-9DPJ].

10 *Compare* Ryan Boetel, *ABQ Study: Fewer People in Jail Equals More Time*, ABQ J. via Internet Archive Wayback Machine (Oct. 12, 2016, 11:53 PM), https://web .archive.org/web/20190910080645/https://www.abqjournal.com/865409/fewer-people-in -jail-equals-more-crime.html; *with* Stemen, *The Prison Paradox*; *and* sources cited in chap- ter 9, note 45.

11 Sam Levin, *"No Progress" Since George Floyd: US Police Killing Three People a Day*, Guardian (Mar. 30, 2022, 6:00 AM), [https://perma.cc/PE8W-4ED2].

12 *About Us*, Datalytics, [https://perma.cc/N2BU-HKE5] (last visited Jan. 5, 2024) (noting that Asher had also worked for the Defense Department).

13 Ali Winston, *Palantir Has Secretly Been Using New Orleans to Test Its Predic- tive Policing Technology*, Verge (Feb. 27, 2018, 3:25 PM), https://www.theverge.com /2018/2/27/17054740/palantir-predictive-policing-tool-new-orleans-nopd.

14 Jeff Asher, *Murder Rose by Almost 30% in 2020. It's Rising at a Slower Rate in 2021*. N.Y. Times (Sept. 22, 2021), https://www.nytimes.com/2021/09/22/upshot/murder -rise-2020.html.

15 *See* Alec Karakatsanis (@equalityalec), Twitter (Sept. 27, 2021, 1:53 PM), [https:// perma.cc/3UBY-XS2H]; Alec Karakatsanis (@equalityalec), Twitter (Sept. 22, 2021, 1:38 PM), [https://x.com/equalityAlec/status/1440732126882586641].

16 As scholars of propaganda have pointed out, there is a strategy behind presenting an "expert" while hiding conflicts of interest: it invokes an expert's "calling—the disin- terested pursuit of knowledge—not his position or his representativeness, to confer on his statements objectivity and authority." Hall et al., *supra* chapter 3, note 8 at 58 (internal alterations and quotations omitted).

17 *Compare* Ali Watkins, *After Murders "Doubled Overnight," the N.Y.P.D Is Solv- ing Fewer Cases*, N.Y. Times via Internet Archive Wayback Machine (Nov. 26, 2021,

3:00 AM), https://web.archive.org/web/20211126081416/https://www.nytimes.com/2021
/11/26/nyregion/nypd-murder-clearance-rate.html; *with* the revised article: Ali Watkins, *Murders Increased During the Pandemic. Did They Also Get Harder to Solve?*, N.Y.
TIMES (Dec. 2, 2021), https://www.nytimes.com/2021/11/26/nyregion/nypd-murder
-clearance-rate.html.

18 This is a widespread copaganda tactic across news outlets. *See, e.g., Did Syracuse
Police Arrest Boy, 8, over Stolen Chips? Viral Video Explained*, CNY CENTRAL (Apr. 19, 2022),
[https://perma.cc/9Z6V-BQGH] (local news not disclosing expert's police-officer background while the expert downplayed police violence against an eight-year-old accused of
stealing a bag of chips).

19 German Lopez, *Examining the Spike in Murders*, N.Y. TIMES (Jan. 18, 2022), https://
www.nytimes.com/2022/01/18/briefing/crime-surge-homicides-us.html.

20 It seems that the reporter did not understand how to read the research graphs he
was relying on, did not contemplate various effects of lockdowns, and did not understand
that the causal connections between the pandemic and murder need not be immediate for
there to be a relationship. *See* Alec Karakatsanis (@equalityalec), TWITTER (Jan. 20, 2022,
10:45 AM), [https://perma.cc/VNN6-QRK5].

21 Bizarrely, reasons offered for rising murder from the September 2021 article—such
as "bail reform"—disappeared as conceivable explanations even though the paper asserted
them as explanations of the same phenomenon just a few months previously.

22 Julie Hollar, *NYT Twists Stats to Insist We Need More Policing*, FAIRNESS & ACCURACY
IN REPORTING (Jan. 27, 2022), [https://perma.cc/8BD9-E9WA].

23 *See* Alec Karakatsanis (@equalityalec), TWITTER (Jan. 20, 2022, 10:45 AM), [https://
perma.cc/WHP3-JNC8]. Back in 2016, Rosenfeld was also busy offering "three possible
explanations" for a small, short-term rise in homicide, although back in 2016, he con-
tended baselessly that the reasons were fewer people in prison, the opioid epidemic, and
the "Ferguson Effect." *See* Kelly Moffitt, *What's driving up homicides in the U.S.? UMSL's
Rick Rosenfeld revisits the "Ferguson Effect,"* ST. LOUIS PUBLIC RADIO (June 15, 2016), https://
www.stlpr.org/show/st-louis-on-the-air/2016-06-15/whats-driving-up-homicides-in-the
-u-s-umsls-rick-rosenfeld-revisits-the-ferguson-effect.

24 German Lopez, *Police and the Alternatives*, N.Y. TIMES (Mar. 6, 2022), https://www
.nytimes.com/2022/03/06/briefing/crime-solutions-ukraine-war-books.html [https://perma
.cc/ZRU2-YDBD].

25 John E. Eck et al., *Adding More Police Is Unlikely to Reduce Crime: A Meta-Analysis of
Police Agency Size and Crime Research*, TRANSLATIONAL CRIMINOLOGY, Spring 2017, at 14.

26 There has been a subtle strategy shift among some punishment bureaucrats and
liberal pundits: argue for *both* more policing for the "short term" and more social
investment in marginalized people for the future. Such pundits know that the political will exists only to do the former and that doing the former will make doing the
latter more difficult. So, pairing more money for the punishment bureaucracy with
vague calls for something unlikely to happen at some unspecified time later—such as
massively reducing inequality—provides a progressive sheen to bolstering repressive
investments.

27 German Lopez, *A Violent Crisis*, N.Y. Times (Apr. 17, 2022), https://www.nytimes.com/2022/04/17/briefing/violent-crime-ukraine-war-week-ahead.html.

28 Jeff Asher & Ben Horwitz, *How Do the Police Actually Spend Their Time?* N.Y. Times (Nov. 8, 2021), https://www.nytimes.com/2020/06/19/upshot/unrest-police-time-violent-crime.html.

29 This is reminiscent, for example, of the numerous punishment bureaucrats who avoid basic questions about why most police time on drugs is spent on marijuana offenses by insisting on only ever discussing fentanyl. The carefully selected terrain of argument is one way that a rotating cast of punishment zealots keeps public focus off aspects of the system that would be wildly unpopular, but which are revealing about its true goals.

30 German Lopez, *The Perils of Legalization*, N.Y. Times (Apr. 25, 2022), https://www.nytimes.com/2022/04/24/briefing/drug-legalization-opioid-crisis-week-ahead.html.

31 Two of the supposedly neutral experts (who are pro–drug war zealots) Lopez identifies in his recent stories joined together in December 2023 to publish a rant in *The Atlantic*'s "Ideas" section, in which they argued, contrary to available evidence, for the continued criminalization of drugs to send a "message" to drug users. They argued that criminalization must be a good idea because drug users were responsible for other criminal offenses that "in many cities go unpunished today," a claim that has no basis. *See* Keith Humphreys & Jonathan Caulkins, *Destigmatizing Drug Use Has Been a Profound Mistake*, Atlantic (Dec. 12, 2023), https://www.theatlantic.com/ideas/archive/2023/12/destigmatizing-drug-use-mistake-opioid-crisis/676292/.

32 Hannah L.F. Cooper, *War on Drugs Policing and Brutality*, 50 Substance Use & Misuse, 1188 (2016).

33 *Kassandra Frederique: Executive Director*, Drug Policy Alliance, [https://perma.cc/GR6T-Z3CR] (last visited Jan. 6, 2023).

34 German Lopez, *From Portland to Portugal*, N.Y. Times (Aug. 4, 2023), https://www.nytimes.com/2023/08/04/briefing/portugal-portland-decriminalization-overdoses.html.

35 *See* Courtney Vaugh, *New Research Finds No Link Between Measure 110 and Overdose Deaths*, Port. Mercury (Sept. 27, 2023, 8:35 AM), [https://perma.cc/65AQ-XGJF].

36 Drug Policy Alliance, *Oregon Set to Recriminalize Drugs, Return to Failed Approach of Arresting, Jailing People for Possession*, press release (Mar. 1, 2024), [https://perma.cc/6SET-UNKG]

37 German Lopez, *Murders, on the Decline*, N.Y. Times (June 26, 2023), https://www.nytimes.com/2023/06/26/briefing/murder-rate.html.

6. Academic Copaganda

1 Hall et al., *supra* chapter 3, note 8 at 242.

2 James Baldwin, *No Name in the Street*, in Baldwin: Collected Essays 357 Toni Morrison, ed.) (1998).

3 Christopher Lewis & Adaner Usmani, *The Injustice of Under-Policing in America*, 2 Am. J. L. & Equal. 85, 85 (2022).

4 It was also unclear to me from the data whether many school-based cops (often labeled "resource officers") are included. This represents a small part of broader classifica tion problems across different police administration systems.

5 Prem Thakker, *Uninvited and Unaccountable: How CBP Policed George Floyd Protests*, INTERCEPT (Sept. 21, 2023), [https://perma.cc/K38F-U8TU].

6 Another expert pointed out to me a separate oversight: the work week in many of the comparison countries is shorter than the U.S. work week, and also, U.S. police log significantly more hours than that in overtime pay. So, the choice to measure the number of cops instead of estimating the total hours of policing is likely further skewing the results.

7 Heather Ann Thompson, *Rescuing America's Inner Cities? Detroit and the Perils of Private Policing*, HUFFINGTON POST (Aug. 25, 2014), [https://perma.cc/X7AM-TFBM].

8 *See* https://metrospd.org/about-the-agency-1.

9 Amelia Pollard, *The Rise of the Private Police*, PROSPECT (Mar. 3, 2021), [https:// perma.cc/LWR4-7NEJ].

10 Robin Washington, *Is Philando Castile the Ultimate Casualty of Driving While Black?*, MARSHALL PROJECT (July 11, 2016), https://www.themarshallproject.org /2016/07/11/is-philando-castile-the-ultimate-casualty-of-driving-while-black; Shannon Van Sant, *Philando Castile's Mother Wipes Out School Lunch Debt, Continuing Son's Leg- acy*, NPR (May 7, 2019), https://www.npr.org/sections/thesalt/2019/05/07/721142955 /philando-castiles-mother-wipes-out-school-lunch-debt-continuing-son-s-legacy.

11 *See* sources cited *infra* chapter 9, note 45.

12 Chris Hacker et al., *Police Departments Sell Their Used Guns. Thousands End Up at Crime Scenes*, CBS News, [https://perma.cc/8626-DRS8] (last visited June 10, 2024).

13 Conor Friedersdorf, *Police Have a Much Bigger Domestic-Abuse Problem Than the NFL Does*, ATLANTIC (Sept. 19, 2014), https://www.theatlantic.com/national/archive /2014/09/police-officers-who-hit-their-wives-or-girlfriends/380329/.

14 *Disturbing Data Shows How Often Domestic Violence Turns Deadly*, PBS (Dec. 10, 2018), https://www.pbs.org/newshour/show/disturbing-data-shows-how-often-domestic -violence-turns-deadly.

15 *See generally* MARIAME KABA & ANDREA RITCHIE, NO MORE POLICE: A CASE FOR ABOLITION (2022); ALEX S. VITALE, THE END OF POLICING (2017); Brian Root, *Why More Police Funding Is No Route to Public Safety*, H.R. WATCH (June 21, 2022, 12:00 PM), [https:// perma.cc/7845-ACU6]; Susan Nembhard et al., *Understanding the Harms of Police Vio- lence Can Help Build Community Safety*, URBAN INST. (Apr. 19, 2022), [https://perma.cc /Y6PS-HEUK].

16 *See supra* introduction, note 26.

17 NYPD Chief of Patrol (@NYPDChiefPatrol), TWITTER (May 4, 2024), [https:// perma.cc/6LFQ-CUVV].

18 See http://bit.ly/police-repression.

19 Teamsters JC 16 (@TeamstersJC16), TWITTER (Jan. 19, 2021, 2:39 AM), https:// twitter.com/TeamstersJC16/status/1351434027308347392 [https://perma.cc/E3J2-CF8A].

20 *See, e.g.,* Stop LAPD Spying Coalition, *Racial Terror and White Wealth in South*

Central, Automating Banishment: The Surveillance and Policing of Looted Land, [https://perma.cc/2CL7-4UWG] (last visited Jan. 6, 2024).

21 Renee Bracey Sherman, *People Who Have Abortions vs. the Police*, Nation (June 23, 2022), https://www.thenation.com/article/society/abortion-police/.

22 Naomi Murakawa, *Say Their Names, Support Their Killers: Police Reform After the 2020 Black Lives Matter Uprisings*, 69 UCLA L. Rev. 1430, 1430 (2023). *See also, e.g.*, Sam Levin, *White Supremacists and Militias Have Infiltrated Police Across US, Report Says*, Guardian (Aug. 27, 2020), [https://perma.cc/7VBL-5XJR]; Will Carless, *Hundreds of Cops Are in Extremist Facebook Groups. Why Haven't Their Departments Done Anything About It?*, Reveal (Sept. 30, 2019), [https://perma.cc/E4LX-F6PP]; Editorial Board, *Extremists in Uniform Put the Nation at Risk*, N.Y. Times (Nov. 13, 2022), https://www.nytimes.com/2022/11/13/opinion/us-police-military-extremism.html.

23 *See, e.g.*, *2022 PBA of Georgia Endorsed Candidates*, SSBPA (Aug. 29, 2022), [https://perma.cc/A98P-L37P]; *Law Enforcement Speech*, CHI. FOP, [https://perma.cc/C5ZE-8LKN] (last visited Jan. 7, 2023); *Endorsements*, Nicole Malliotakis, [https://perma.cc/72C8-3VHM] (last visited Jan. 7, 2023); *Stefanik Endorsed by the New York State's Fraternal Order of the Police*, Elise for Congress (Oct. 7, 2022), [https://perma.cc/CW3P-78BS].

24 *See, e.g.*, Franke Stoltze, *LA Sheriff's Deputies Search Home of Supervisor Sheila Kuehl, as Well as LA Metro and Others*, LAist (Sept. 14, 2022, 6:46 PM), [https://perma.cc/AJY3-WG9J]; Kate Cagle, *Outgoing Compton Mayor Alleges Fraud by Sheriff's Department*, Spectrum News 1 (May 31, 2021, 7:22 AM), [https://perma.cc/J6SP-6RBA]; Amanda Holpuch, *Arrest Violated County Official's Free Speech Rights, Judge Rules*, N.Y. Times (Jan. 18, 2024), https://www.nytimes.com/2024/01/18/us/ohio-niki-frenchko-arrest.html.

25 In the professors' initial framing of their argument, an increase in police would be more effective in reducing crime than an increase in prisons. This is unremarkable, because they agree with the literature that more imprisonment does not reduce crime at all. But comparing the policy of expanding police with a knowingly ineffective policy says nothing about whether more police are preferable to *other* policies. The point of comparison for their plan shouldn't be *bad* policies; it should be other good policies.

26 To take political action against a prosecutor in St. Louis who police perceived to be progressive, officers began refusing to testify, even in murder cases. Jeremy Kohler & Ryan Krull, *Detective Sabotaged His Own Case Because He Didn't Like the Prosecutor. The Police Department Did Nothing to Stop Him*, Propublica (Oct. 10, 2023) [https://perma.cc/W3LC-QDCV].

27 *See generally*, Stuart Schrader, Badges Without Borders: How Global Counterinsurgency Transformed American Policing (2019).

28 Lewis & Usmani, *supra* chapter 6 note 3 at 88. Although the professors dismiss increased investments in social programs to redress inequality as unrealistic, they assume that reducing the U.S. prison population by "2 million" prisoners is feasible. They never explain how it is feasible, and, as noted above, they do not even notice a glaring problem: the police bureaucracy their proposal would make more powerful is one of the main technical and political drivers of mass imprisonment.

29 *Id.* at 96-97.

30 Email chain between Christopher Lewis, Adaner Usmani, and Alec Karakatsanis on file with The New Press.

31 Eck et al., *supra* chapter 5, note 25; Sebastian ET AL., *supra* introduction note 25. In fact, in their reply to me, Lewis and Usmani take it a step further and, without discussing any of the scholarly evidence on police alternatives, argue: "There are no feasible social policy alternatives that can prevent crime nearly as efficiently as policing." *See* Christopher Lewis & Adaner Usmani, Reply to Alec Karakatsanis, Nov. 12, 2022, https://perma. cc/5L8E-U6D7.

32 Yuki Noguchi, *How Police Violence Could Impact the Health of Black Infants*, NPR (Nov. 13, 2020, 5:01 AM), [https://perma.cc/A5EE-Z45J]; Joscha Legewie, *Police Violence and the Health of Black Infants*, SCI. ADVANCES 1–8 (Dec. 2019).

33 *See* People's City Council—Los Angeles (@PplsCityCouncil), TWITTER (Apr. 6, 2022, 7:25 PM), [https://perma.cc/XW3B-KXAZ].

34 Aleen Brown & John McCracken, *Documents Show How a Pipeline Company Paid Minnesota Millions to Police Protests*, GRIST (Feb. 9, 2023), [https://perma.cc/7QVB-EKU8].

35 Alex Vitale & Alec Karakatsanis, *Why More Cops Are the Last Thing We Need*, CRIME REP. (Nov. 10, 2022), [https://perma.cc/U7SX-UVBP]; Christopher Lewis & Adaner Usmani, *Reply to Alec Karakatsanis*, Nov. 12, 2022 [https://perma.cc/5L8E-U6D7].

36 In addition to ignoring almost every point I made, the professors also fabricate arguments I did not make. For example, the professors say that I complained about their calculations because I think that "homicide overestimates the rate of serious crime." *Id.*, 5. That was not an argument I made, but it does illustrate a form of avoiding substantive engagement, common to academic copaganda, in which a scholar creates and responds to straw-person arguments that were not made.

37 Lewis and Usmani assert that any policy effort at redistribution "will happen at the federal level" because state and local governments "cannot do much about concentrated disadvantage." So, they say, they are only offering advice on what local governments can do with the thing they control: police. This is a controversial claim that contradicts several broad areas of research. Local and state governments can implement a number of non-police alternatives to reduce inequality and crime, expand health care, improve education, and strengthen community cohesion. *See Evidence on Non-Carceral Safety Investments*, C.R. CORPS, [https://perma.cc/58M9-YU44] (last visited Jan. 9, 2024).

38 Charles Lane, *Why More Police Might Be the Key to Real Criminal Justice Reform*, WASH. POST (Nov. 30, 2022, 7:00 AM), https://www.washingtonpost.com/opinions /2022/11/30/police-criminal-justice-reform/?_pml=1.

39 *See* San Francisco Deputy Sheriffs' Association (@SanFranciscoDSA), TWITTER (Feb. 21, 2023, 10:20 PM), https://x.com/SanFranciscoDSA/status/1628233245728067584 [https://perma.cc/Y65T-RBA8] (referring to it as the MIT study because the journal in which it was published was a collaboration with MIT).

40 Reihan Salam & Charles Fain Lehman, *We're Underfunding the Police*, ATLANTIC (Mar. 8, 2023), https://www.theatlantic.com/ideas/archive/2023/03/underfunding-police -violent-crime/673314/[https://perma.cc/T54R-P67U].

41 Before accusing me of censorship for criticizing their article in detail and then declining to respond to my criticisms, one of the professors, ironically, signed the *"Harper's* Letter on Justice and Open Debate," which decries a culture of "restriction of debate" and calls for more "open debate." *A Letter on Justice and Open Debate*, HARPER'S MAG. (July 7, 2020), [https://perma.cc/8UUZ-RUSR].

42 *See* Dissent Collective (@DissentCollectv), TWITTER (Nov. 9, 2022, 2:10 PM), [https://perma.cc/Y72W-63HF].

43 Alex S. Vitale, *Campus Police Are Among the Armed Heavies Cracking Down on Students*, Nation (May 9, 2024), https://www.thenation.com/article/archive/campus-police-arresting-student-protesters/.

44 Alec Karakatsanis (@equalityalec), TWITTER (Jan. 18, 2023, 11:52 AM), [https://perma.cc/YEC6-PZ9M].

45 Alvaro de Menard, *What's Wrong with Social Science and How to Fix It: Reflections After Reading 2,578 Papers*, FANTASTIC ANACHRONISM (Sept. 11, 2020), [https://perma.cc/ZT84-CWQ4].

46 Megan T. Stevenson, *Cause, Effect, and the Structure of the Social World*, 103 B.U. L. REV. 2001, 2001 (2023).

7. How Bad Academic Research Becomes News

1 BARBARA EHRENREICH, FEAR OF FALLING: THE INNER LIFE OF THE MIDDLE CLASS 53 (1985). Banfield was the mentor of James Q. Wilson, whom former NYPD commissioner William Bratton credited as the intellectual force behind "broken windows" policing. Richard Bernstein, *James Q. Wilson: Fertile Thinker, Friend of Facts*, N.Y. TIMES (Aug. 22, 1998); *see generally* Harcourt, *infra* chapter 14, note 19.

2 Matthew Yglesias, *Some Thoughts on Police*, TWTEXT, [https://perma.cc/4CT7-KXLX] (last visited Jan. 9, 2023).

3 Matthew Yglesias, *The End of Policing Left Me Convinced We Still Need Policing*, Vox (June 18, 2020, 3:50 PM), [https://perma.cc/X2CZ-PD9G]; *Protestors' Anger Justified Even If Actions May Not Be*, MONMOUTH U. (June 2, 2020), [https://perma.cc/3ZNF-E8BB].

4 *See, e.g.*, Matt Ford, *The Missing Statistics of Criminal Justice*, ATLANTIC (May 31, 2015), https://www.theatlantic.com/politics/archive/2015/05/what-we-dont-know-about-mass-incarceration/394520/. The quality of available data, conditions for studying it, complex phenomena with many causes, possibility for manipulation and corruption, and relatively low number of studies make answering questions about the impacts of policing more fraught in many respects than, say, studying the effects of drinking more alcohol, eating more fish, smoking, consuming sugar, salt, or butter, and so on. And even in the latter categories of inquiry, researchers are constantly coming out with new studies revising previous understandings. *See, e.g.*, Susan Dominus, *Is That Drink Worth It to You*, N.Y. TIMES, (June 15, 2024), https://www.nytimes.com/2024/06/15/magazine/alcohol-health-risks.html (describing, to the chagrin of people who had begun to drink red wine for health benefits, new research suggesting that alcohol is worse for people than

previously thought). All of this makes the level of certainty declared by small and insular groups of pro-police criminologists worthy of particular skepticism.

5 *See* Eck et al., *supra* chapter 5, note 25.

6 Bruce G. Taylor et al., *The Effects of Community-Infused Problem-Oriented Policing in Crime Hot Spots Based on Police Data*, J. OF EXPERIMENTAL CRIMINOLOGY 20 (Dec. 2022). Much of the "consensus" referred to by pro-police journalists stems from a group of pro-police studies about flooding "high crime" areas with police. But, setting aside their many flaws, even the pro-police studies on which most public claims are based, overall, show "small and inconsistent" effects on police-reported crime on their own terms. *See, e.g.*, Pamela Buckley et al., *Does Hot Spots Policing Reduce Crime? An Alternative Interpretation Based on a Meta-analysis of Randomized Experiments* (2023), [https://perma.cc/PX7P-6SDK]. More importantly, the studies generally discuss only effects in the short term, limited to a small geographic area, and do not purport to evaluate long-term effects of increased policing on crime or society. Finally, as discussed later, the studies (which other studies contradict) do not purport to measure whether reductions in crime on a particular street or corner are due to unique features of police (such as their being armed and violent) or whether the same benefits could be achieved by other kinds of people being present.

7 *See, e.g.*, Aaron Vansintjan, *What Nobel Laureate Elinor Ostrom's Early Work Tells Us About Defending the Police*, SHAREABLE (June 16, 2020), [https://perma.cc/V9LY-VKNN].

8 *See, e.g.*, Jonathan Klick & Alexander Tabarrok, *Using Terror Alert Levels to Estimate the Effect of Police on Crime*, 48 J. L. ECON. 267 (two pro-police scholars cited by Yglesias himself finding that, despite Yglesias's claim that "investments in policing pay off in reduced violent crime," "violent crimes show no response to increased police presence," even in their short-term study).

9 *See generally* Nathan J. Robinson, *How Should Values Influence Social Science Research?* CURRENT AFF'S (July 10, 2020), [https://perma.cc/987Z-77TK].

10 Note an especially egregious example of Yglesias's pro-cop distortion: some of the studies he cites find policing associated with modest drops in car theft, other property crime, or overall "crime," which Yglesias mischaracterizes as "violent crime." That is an elementary error that undermines his argument, because generic "crime" involves things like drug consumption, trespassing, traffic arrests, and other "crimes" that are primarily identified through selective policing. An additional issue is that Yglesias takes aim at complex, internally contested social movement calls by waging a proxy war against a single book, *The End of Policing* by sociologist Alex Vitale, as if a single book stands in for an entire social movement and intellectual history spanning several fields of study. *See* ALEX VITALE, THE END OF POLICING (2017).

11 Ruderman, *supra* chapter 5, note 7; Ben Poston, *FBI Crime-Reporting Audits Are Shallow, Infrequent*, MILWAUKEE J. SENT. (Aug. 18, 2012), [https://perma.cc/D2HS-TVLP]; Matt Hamilton, *LAPD Captain Accuses Department of Twisting Crime Statistics to Make City Seem Safer*, L.A. TIMES (Nov. 6, 2017), https://www.latimes.com/local/lanow/la-me-ln-lapd-crime-stats-claim-20171103-story.html?_gl=1*sc8swp*

_gcl_au*NDg4NDczMzQwLjE3MDQ1MDczMzg. *See, e.g.,* U.S. Dept. of Just. C.R. Div. & U.S. Att'y's Off. Dist. of N.J., Investigation of the Newark Police Department (July 22, 2014), [https://perma.cc/7DZV-6B52].

12 Take the City of Newark, New Jersey: the DOJ found that 93 percent of the tens of thousands of police-pedestrian stops lacked justification—every unjustified police stop, search, and arrest is an illegal assault. Investigation of the Newark Police Department, *supra* chapter 7, note 11.

13 The Department of Justice estimates that about 4 percent of prisoners are sexually assaulted each year (excluding all other physical assaults), meaning about 95,000 individuals. The majority of sexual assaults are by government officers. Allen J. Beck et al., Sexual Victimization in Prisons and Jails Reported By Inmates, 2011–12, NCJ 241399 (2013); *see also* Thomas Ward Frampton, *The Dangerous Few: Taking Seriously Prison Abolition and Its Skeptics*, 135 Harv. L. Rev. 2013, 2046 (2022) ("Extrapolating from this data, the study's lead author estimated that nearly 200,000 people were sexually abused in American detention facilities in 2011 . . . [compared to] 243,800 outside of prison.") (quotations and emphasis removed).

14 Theorists including Ruth Wilson Gilmore, Angela Davis, Alex Vitale, and Mariame Kaba reframe the entire set of problems we should be discussing and working to address if we care about everyone's safety. *See generally* Transform Harm, www.transform harm.org (last visited Jan. 9, 2024) (collecting sources on reducing violence).

15 For an in-depth discussion of how this works, with specific examples, *see* Alec Karakatsanis, *The Punishment Bureaucracy: How to Think About "Criminal Justice Reform,"* 128 Yale L. J. F. 848, 848 (2019), an essay that can also be found in my book *Usual Cruelty.*

16 *American Police*, Throughline: NPR (June 4, 2020, 12:08 AM), [https://perma.cc /KK7V-K4SQ]; Jeremy Scahill, *Occupied Territory: Why Chicago's History Matters for Today's Demands to Defund Police*, Intercept (July 4, 2020, 8:00 AM), [https://perma .cc/N5DR-WCVZ].

17 Asher & Horwitz, *supra* chapter 5, note 28; Speri, *Police Make More Than 10 Million Arrests a Year, but That Doesn't Mean They're Solving Crimes*, Intercept (Jan. 31, 2019, 12:32 PM), [https://perma.cc/KN9P-ULCB].

18 *See Free to Drive*, Free to Drive, [https://perma.cc/PB8V-F4TQ] (last visited Jan. 9, 2024).

19 Williams, *Marijuana Arrests Outnumber Those for Violent Crimes, Study Finds.*

20 Cameron Kimble & Inimai M. Chettiar, *Sexual Assault Remains Dramatically Underreported*, Brennan Center for Justice (Oct. 4, 2018), [https://perma.cc /K66Y-MJ3V]; Jeff Asher, *Why We Can't Be Sure if Violent Crime Is on the Rise*, Five-ThirtyEight (Dec. 7, 2017, 10:00 PM), [https://perma.cc/AP2L-KEFJ].

21 Sebastian et al., *supra* introduction note 25.

22 The largest available survey of (mostly) pro-police researchers, compiled by a prominent pro-police professor, found that significantly larger numbers of those researchers believe that increasing "social services budgets" like "housing, health, and education" will improve public safety than researchers who believe that increasing police budgets will

improve public safety. *See* CRIMINAL JUSTICE EXPERT PANEL, POLICING AND PUBLIC SAFETY (2021), [https://perma.cc/5VXC-W8VN]. Even among the group of researchers who skewed pro-police, about 40 percent did not believe that increasing police would improve safety—far from a "consensus."

23 *See* THE FEMINIST ON CELLBLOCK Y, CNN (2018).

24 Andrea King Collier, *The Black Panthers: Revolutionaries, Free Breakfast Pioneers*, NAT. GEO.: THE PLATE (Nov. 4, 2015), [https://perma.cc/T4C6-9958].

25 Daniel McMillen et al., *Do More Eyes on the Street Reduce Crime? Evidence from Chicago's Safe Passage Program*, 110 J. URBAN ECON. 1 (2019).

26 Tomaz Capobianco, *Traffic Mimes in Bogotá*, THIS CHANGES EVERYTHING, [https://perma.cc/6545-KJB4], (last visited Jan. 10, 2024).

27 Christopher Blattman et al., *Civilian Alternatives to Policing*, SocArxIv (Dec. 12, 2023), [https://perma.cc/N3BD-7QBS].

28 Eric Reinhart, *Moving from Crisis Response to Crisis Prevention in U.S. Mental Health Systems*, STAT (Feb. 8, 2024), [https://perma.cc/JQ6N-HPXV]; Thomas S. Dee & Jaymes Pyne, *A Community Response Approach to Mental Health and Substance Abuse Reduced Crime*, 8 SCI. ADVANCES 1 (2022).

29 Alec Karakatsanis, *What Does It Mean to Be a "Good Cop"?*, SLATE (June 8, 2020, 12:59 PM), [https://perma.cc/7FMT-D66B].

30 Aaron Chalfin & Justin McCrary, *Are U.S. Cities Underpoliced? Theory and Evidence*, 100 REV. OF ECON. & STATS. 167, 167 (2018).

31 BECK ET AL., *supra* chapter 7, note 13. (government estimates of sexual assaults on incarcerated individuals).

32 *See, e.g.*, Megan Stevenson and Sandra G. Mayson, *Pretrial Detention and the Value of Liberty*, 108 VA. L. REV. 709 (2022) (using sophisticated survey responses to show that people would rather be the victim of violent crime than endure various forms of standard government treatment, such as short or medium terms of pretrial detention). For example, even a lawful arrest, which would otherwise meet the legal definition of a kidnapping if done without sufficient cause, involves putting metal chains on a person and taking them away forcibly to a dangerous place where any number of bad things may happen to them in the following days. These are costs that must be weighed against any asserted benefits of using human caging as a response to an ostensible social problem.

33 *See, e.g.*, World Health Organization, CREATING SUPPORTIVE CONDITIONS TO REDUCE INFECTIOUS DISEASES IN PRISON POPULATIONS (Nov. 6, 2023), [https://perma.cc/5AZC-LPYT]; Eric Reinhart and Daniel L. Chen, *Incarceration and Its Disseminations: COVID-19 Pandemic Lessons from Chicago's Cook County Jail*, 39 HEALTH AFFAIRS (June 2020).

34 Baynard Woods & Brandon Soderberg, *Credible Messengers*, INTERCEPT (July 26, 2020, 9:00 AM), [https://perma.cc/NJP8-3D9S].

35 Jonathan Ben-Menachem, *Getting a Traffic Ticket Makes You Less Likely to Vote, Research Finds*, WASH. POST (Sept. 15, 2022), https://www.washingtonpost.com/politics/2022/09/15/driving-while-black-voting-rates/.

36 Chalfin & McCrary, *supra* chapter 7, note 30 at 167.

37 *Id.*, 184.

38 Jacob Kaplan & Aaron Chalfin, *More Cops, Fewer Prisoners?*, 18 CRIMINOLOGY & PUB. POL'Y 171, 171 (2019). When I asked Chalfin's co-author over email about how to account for this controversial claim that is not supported by the citations or the literature, he blamed Chalfin for handling that "lit review" portion of the article, which discusses the supposed state of prior research.

39 *See* Alec Karakatsanis, *The Body Camera: The Language of Our Dreams*, 4 YALE JOURNAL OF LAW & LIBERATION 1, 35-37 (2024), available at https://bpb-us-w2.wpm ucdn.com/campuspress.yale.edu/dist/f/4764/files/2024/07/Alec-Karakatsanis_The -Body-Camera-FINAL.pdf. Who funds research and why matters for what research is produced. In addition to funding by the surveillance industry, police foundations, and the massive grants available from prosecutorial agencies like the Department of Justice, the largest philanthropic funder of research on the punishment bureaucracy is Arnold Ventures, which took an authoritarian turn after hiring controversial economist and pro-police zealot Jennifer Doleac as "Executive Vice President of Criminal Justice." (Disclosure: the same philanthropists behind Arnold Ventures donated generously for many years to the civil rights work of the organization I founded, Civil Rights Corps, until abruptly cutting off all donations to our work with no explanation after Arnold Ventures hired Doleac.) Doleac has been quoted publicly making the spurious claim that "there is a strong consensus in the literature that hiring more police reduces crime." *See* CRIMINAL JUSTICE EXPERT PANEL, *supra* chapter 7, note 22. Arnold Ventures has funded some good research over the years prior to Doleac's hiring, but the relevant point here is that a small collection of entities carries enormous influence in decisions regarding which research about police, prosecutors, and prisons gets funded and which does not.

Apart from the influence of money on research, professional networks and confidential data-sharing agreements also give police influence over academic research. Chalfin's own academic work, for example, repeatedly relies on controversial former police chief William Bratton, and reviewing the acknowledgment and bibliography sections of pro-police research reveals close collaboration by nearly every level of the policing bureaucracy and an almost total failure of engagement with critical literature. In general, the routine failure of pro-police research to cite contrary evidence or to respond to meta-scholarship on conceptual and methodological flaws in their research design are red flags indicating a bubble of groupthink.

One of the consequences of this groupthink is the pervasive dissemination of controversial, weak, or flat-out erroneous factual claims as conventional wisdom. For example, Yglesias cites prominent Princeton professor Patrick Sharkey, one of the most well-funded and influential pro-police sociologists. (Both Sharkey and Chalfin have received funding from Arnold Ventures.) Sharkey, who has produced some rigorous work on other topics such as alternatives to policing, has repeatedly parroted baseless claims about police reducing crime in the mass media. Writing in the *Washington Post* shortly after the murder of George Floyd—and citing only a couple of the same discredited studies Yglesias relies on for propositions that those studies do not support—Sharkey declared: "One of the most robust, most uncomfortable findings in criminology is that putting more officers on the street leads to less violent crime." *See* Patrick Sharkey, *Why Do We Need the Police?*, WASH. POST (June 12, 2020), https://www.washingtonpost.com/outlook/2020/06/12/defund-police-violent-crime/?arc404=true. Four years later, in *Harper's Magazine*, he was even more strident: "We have strong evidence in the social sciences indicating that when you have more police officers on the street, it reduces violent crime. *There's just no way to argue that claim.*" (emphasis added). Ras Baraka et al., *Crime and Punishment: Can American Policing Be Fixed?*, HARPER's Mag. (Nov. 30, 2023), https://harpers.org/archive/2024/04/crime-and-punishment-5/. Not only does Sharkey disregard the flaws with the pro-police research and ignore the research finding the contrary, but he tells lay readers that there is "no way to argue" against him. This kind of anti-intellectual attitude pervades the small bubble of pro-police researchers. Sharkey's repeated platforming in corporate media is a reminder of what it takes to be an academic with access to elite news production. It's not primarily about a good-faith search for the truth, careful claims backed by rigorous study, and so on. It often comes down to whether a professor is willing to say things that people in power want them to say, even if those things stretch any reasonable interpretation of their own research and even if they are contrary to available evidence.

40 *See, e.g.*, Megan Stevenson (@MeganTStevenson), TWITTER (July 15, 2020 5:38 PM), [https://perma.cc/68FX-HN2S] (discussing systemic conflicts of interest stemming from cozy police relationships at the University of Chicago Crime Lab, probably the most influential and controversial of the pro-police academic copaganda operations).

41 Another example is a much-publicized article by Chalfin in which he and several colleagues purported to find that adding more police decreases homicide (except in cities with large Black populations). *See* Aaron Chalfin et al., *Police Force Size and Civilian Race*, 4 AM. ECON. REV. 139 (2022). There are many flaws with the study (including bad data, faulty methodology, misstatement of the findings in prior research, and unsupported claims), but one is most relevant here. The narrow research question in the study was about the effect of more police on police-recorded homicides, which Chalfin and his co-authors defined to *exclude* essentially all killings by police and all deaths in jail or prison of people arrested by police. Even setting that study design aside, when discussing the findings later in the paper and publicly, the authors slipped into making unsupported claims about overall "lives saved," the number of police required to "save one life," and the overall "public safety returns to an increase in police manpower." This was odd because their own research found that adding more police significantly increases the number of low-level arrests, and a wide range of research finds that more such arrests, jailing, and imprisonment increases death, harms public health in many ways, fosters more discrimination, and leads to more police violence (which also, in turn, causes more death). *See infra* chapter 9, note 45. (discussing short-, medium-, and long-term effects of increased jailing on death, crime, and public health). *See also generally* VERA INSTITUTE, THE SOCIAL COSTS OF POLICING (2022), [https://perma.cc/U5FN-JM24]. Additionally, other research shows, to take just a few examples of the many collateral effects that lead to increased death, that policing has significant negative health consequences on diabetes, obesity, Black maternal health, and infant mortality. *See, e.g., supra* chapter 6, note 32; Abigail A. Sewell, *The Illness Associations of Police Violence: Differential Relationships by Ethnoracial Composition*, 32 SOCIOLOGICAL

Forum (2017). This practice of extrapolating from discrete measurements based on the deaths that police record as "homicides" to make broad claims about the complex effects of police on overall life and death across multiple, complex mechanisms is a quintessential example of how researchers and journalists can spread misinformation.

8. Keywords of Copaganda: Smuggling Ideology into the News

1 Leo Tolstoy, Anna Karenina (1878) (translated by Nathan Haskell Dole).

2 Letter from James Baldwin to Angela Y. Davis (Nov. 19, 1970), [https://perma.cc/XRR8-UT5J].

3 Troy Closson, *Queens Prosecutor Long Overlooked Misconduct. Can a New D.A. Do Better?*, N.Y. Times (Jan. 27, 2021), https://www.nytimes.com/2021/01/27/nyregion/melinda-katz-queens.html.

4 Another similar example are the bail reforms advertised by many prosecutors. One study evaluating the outcomes of so-called "progressive" prosecutors surrounding bail reform makes a strong argument that *no* "progressive" prosecutor has effected bail reforms from their office that meaningfully has changed the lives of poor people accused of crimes. *See* Sarah Gottlieb, *Progressive Façade: How Bail Reforms Expose the Limitations of the Progressive Prosecutor Movement*, 81 W&L L. J. 1 (2024).

5 Jacob Kaye, *Law Professors Sue City, DA Katz*, Queens Daily Eagle (Nov. 10, 2021), [https://perma.cc/56S3-9T68].

6 *How Can You Destroy a Person's Life and Only Get a Slap on the Wrist*, N.Y. Times (Dec. 4, 2021), https://www.nytimes.com/2021/12/04/opinion/prosecutor-misconduct-new-york-doj.html.

7 Jonah E. Bromwich, *After Spate of Shootings, Manhattan D.A. Takes Tougher Stance on Guns*, N.Y. Times (Jan. 26, 2022), https://www.nytimes.com/2022/01/26/nyregion/alvin-bragg-gun-violence.html?referringSource=articleShare.

8 A 2021 Associated Press article is an example of a related phenomenon: suggesting that a particular reform that punishment bureaucrats don't like is more consequential than it is. The AP article suggests that police were powerless to stop Portland from becoming "lawless" after the legislature passed a relatively toothless law that placed minor restrictions on police use of rubber bullets and chemical weapons. The new law did not stop police from arresting people for crimes, didn't hold them accountable for misconduct or reduce their budget, and didn't even prohibit them from using military or chemical weapons. The law was so toothless that the Portland police themselves had *supported* it. But the news article suggested that this meaningless law was responsible for Portland descending into anarchy by rendering police powerless against crime. Sara Cline, *"Lawless City?" Worry After Portland Police Don't Stop Chaos*, AP (Oct. 15, 2021), [https://perma.cc/AZ3N-PY5Y].

9 Steve Eder et al., *As New Police Reform Laws Sweep Across the U.S., Some Ask: Are They Enough?*, N.Y. Times (Oct. 10, 2021), https://www.nytimes.com/2021/04/18/us/police-reform-bills.html.

10 David Leonhardt, *Can Policing Change?*, N.Y. Times (Apr. 20, 2021), https://www

.nytimes.com/2021/04/20/briefing/walter-mondale-vice-president-rwanda-genocide
.html.

11 The Oxford Pocket Dictionary of Current English, *Sweeping*, Encyclopedia
.com, [https://perma.cc/NV65-PBYS]; The Oxford Pocket Dictionary of Current English,
Overhaul, Encyclopedia.com, [https://perma.cc/2ZNH-BGPY].

12 Nicholas Fandos et al., *The House Passes a Policing Overhaul Bill Named for George
Floyd, Whose Death Spurred Nationwide Protests*, N.Y. Times (Mar. 29, 2021), https://www
.nytimes.com/2021/03/04/us/george-floyd-act.html.

13 The word "aim" is used a lot in news coverage to characterize the goal of a particular proposal. For example, when President Biden announced a "Safer America Plan," CBS News described it as "aimed at fighting crime and reducing gun violence across the U.S.," even though no details were available that would have enabled a reasonable understanding of the plan, and ultimately, it turned out that nothing in any of the related proposals would have made much of a difference. *See* CBS News (@CBSNews), Twitter (Aug. 30, 2022, 3:53 PM), [https://perma.cc/X5YE-6JBA].

14 Katie Benner et al., *Inside a Near Breakdown Between the White House and the Police*, N.Y. Times (Feb. 2, 2022), https://www.nytimes.com/2022/02/02/us/politics/policing
-white-house-law-enforcement.html.

15 Noam Chomsky, The Common Good 43 (1998).

16 Norimitsu Onishi, *Police Announce Crackdown on Quality-of-Life Offenses*, N.Y. Times (Mar. 13, 1994), https://www.nytimes.com/1994/03/13/nyregion/police-announce
-crackdown-on-quality-of-life-offenses.html.

17 Corey Kilgannon, *Plan Tests Tense Relationship Between N.Y.P.D. and Mentally
Ill People*, N.Y. Times (Dec. 5, 2022), https://www.nytimes.com/2022/12/05/nyregion
/mental-health-plan-nypd.html. While the *New York Times* chooses not to put the term "quality of life" in quotes, other outlets, like *Bloomberg*, have started to do so. *See* Fola Akinnibi, *Arrests for Low-Level Crimes Climb Under NYC Mayor Eric Adams*, Bloomberg (Aug. 30, 2022), https://www.bloomberg.com/news/articles/2022-08-30/nyc-s
-rise-of-low-level-arrests-worry-critics-of-broken-windows-era?sref=IUm3fzs0.

18 Brandon Soderberg & Andy Friedman, *Media Outlets Can't Stop Describing Violence as "Officer-Involved" Incidents*, HuffPost (Jan. 14, 2022), [https://perma.cc/TU9B
-CN6M].

19 Jonathan Moreno-Medina et al., *Officer-Involved: The Media Language of Police Killings* (Nat'l Bur. of Econ. Rsch., Working Paper No. 30209), [https://perma.cc/9NMA-8UER].

20 *APD: SWAT Standoff Ends with House Fire, 14-Year-Old Killed*, KOB-4 (July 13, 2022, 8:46 AM), [https://perma.cc/5ACC-QPL7]; *APD Standoff Ends in House Fire, 1 Dead*, ABQ J. (July 7, 2022), [https://perma.cc/PH5A-C6GY].

21 Austin Fisher, *"APD Was 'Mistaken' About Federal Warrant for the Man Targeted in
SWAT Raid*," Source NM (July 12, 2022), [https://perma.cc/JCM8-U2H5].

22 Marcius, *supra* chapter 2, note 3.

23 *See* Smith, *supra* note 3, chapter 2.

24 *See* Alec Karakatsanis (@equalityalec), Twitter (Feb. 21, 2022, 3:07 PM), [https://
perma.cc/Q3WC-B5W8].

25 Ben Grunwald, *A Large-Scale Study of the Police Retention Crisis*, Duke Law School Public Law & Legal Theory Series No. 2024-41 (2024).

26 It also happened amid the greatest crackdown on access to reproductive healthcare in modern history—a plan hindered in some states only by not having the police resources to track people and providers—along with rising far-right authoritarianism; a plethora of laws and executive actions to deploy cops to arrest voters; expanded police investments in tracking biometrics, movement of vehicles, and other surveillance using algorithms and big data; and high-profile searches of the homes and offices of elected leaders and oversight officials who were voicing criticism of police.

27 Glenn Thrush, *Justice Dept. Considers Early Release for Female Inmates Sexually Abused Behind Bars*, N.Y. TIMES (Dec. 13, 2022), https://www.nytimes.com/2022/12/13 /us/politics/federal-prison-sexual-abuse.html.

28 I recommend Eugene Debs's prison memoir *Walls and Bars*, written in 1926, for its description of the federal bureau of prisons bureaucracy, even when it was orders of magnitude smaller than it is today.

29 *See, e.g.*, Keri Blakinger et al., *Texas Corrections Officers Quit in Droves, Prisons Get Even More Dangerous*, MARSHALL PROJECT (Nov. 1, 2021), [https://perma.cc/L8QU-SX3R].

30 Jolie McCullough, *Almost 600 Texas Youths Are Trapped in a Juvenile Prison System on the Brink of Collapse*, TEX. TRIB. (Aug. 2, 2022), [https://perma.cc/WX69-QSBS]. To its credit, the article did include a brief reference to the fact that some advocates have pushed for closing the facilities. But it then misleadingly made it appear that all "advocates" wanted increased budgets for the child-caging facilities. Much of the reporting that blames horrific conditions on "understaffing" does not even mention the possibility that fewer people should be confined at all.

31 One morning, as I was writing this chapter, an almost identical article about "dangerous levels" of "understaffing" in the children's jail near where I live appeared in my local news in Washington, D.C. Jenny Gathright & Colleen Grablick, *Why Is My Child Always on Lockdown?*, DCIST (July 21, 2023, 11:32 AM), [https://perma.cc/98CM -HZPG]. Then, a few months later, on the day I was implementing comments from my editor to this chapter of the manuscript, *another* article came out about an "extreme shortage" of prison guards in Wisconsin that failed to mention the concept of mass incarceration at all. Mario Koran & Justin Mayo, *10 Guards, 900 Inmates and the Dire Results of Warnings Ignored*, N.Y. TIMES (Feb. 2, 2024), https://www.nytimes.com/2024/02/02/us /wi-prison-staffing-shortage.html.

32 JAMIE BISSONETTE, WHEN THE PRISONERS RAN WALPOLE: A TRUE STORY IN THE MOVEMENT FOR PRISON ABOLITION (2008); *see also* Peter Gelderloos, *Anarchy Works* (2010), [https://perma.cc/T5N8-76KQ].

33 Alec Karakatsanis, *Police Departments Spend Vast Sums of Money Creating "Copaganda,"* JACOBIN (July 20, 2022), https://jacobin.com/2022/07/copaganda -police-propaganda-public-relations-pr-communications.

34 Paul Waldman, *When Everyone Wanted to Be "Tough on Crime,"* AM. PROSPECT (Aug. 13, 2013), [https://perma.cc/X5VX-ELVQ].

35 Arit John, *A Timeline of the Rise and Fall of "Tough on Crime" Drug Sentencing*, Atlantic (Apr. 22, 2014), https://www.theatlantic.com/politics/archive/2014/04/a-timeline-of-the-rise-and-fall-of-tough-on-crime-drug-sentencing/360983/.

36 Astead W. Herndon, *They Wanted to Roll Back Tough-on-Crime Policies, Then Violent Crime Surged*, Union-Bulletin (Feb. 18, 2022), https://www.union-bulletin.com/seattle_times/they-wanted-to-roll-back-tough-on-crime-policies-then-violent-crime-surged/article_e93077a3-8a12-52e6-ab93-b42c0b0cd428.html; Katie Glueck & Ashley Southall, *As Adams Toughens on Crime, Some Fear a Return to '90s Era Policing*, N.Y. Times (Mar. 26, 2022), https://www.nytimes.com/2022/03/26/nyregion/broken-windows-eric-adams.html.

37 Editorial Board, *Biden's Pathetic Anti-crime Package Is an Empty Press Release*, N.Y. Post (July 21, 2022, 5:53 PM), [https://perma.cc/PY6N-9JWS].

38 *Soft-On-Crime Policy Emboldens Criminals to Commit More Dangerous Crimes*, Wash. Examiner (July 29, 2022, 9:01 PM), [https://perma.cc/R86G-NY6Q].

39 Daniel S. Nagin et al., *Imprisonment and Reoffending*, 38 Crime & Just. 115, 120 (2009).

40 *See* Center for Just Journalism, Bail Reform: What to Know and Where to Go for More (2023), [https://perma.cc/9ARD-U8VE] (summarizing studies on the topic).

41 Center for Just Journalism, Deterrence and Incapacitation (2023), [https://perma.cc/9UL6-HTF7].

42 Sebastian et al., *supra* introduction note 25.

43 *See* Sebastian et al., *supra* introduction note 25; Kevin Drum, *An Updated Lead-Crime Roundup for 2018*, Mother Jones (Feb. 1, 2018), [https://perma.cc/A7C2-868D]; Jessica T. Simes & Jaquelyn L. Jahn, *The Consequences of Medicaid Expansion Under the Affordable Care Act for Police Arrests*, Plos One, 1–15 (Jan. 2022); Econ. Opportunity Inst., The Link Between Early Childhood Education and Crime and Violence Reduction, Opp. Inst. [https://perma.cc/Y983-BFLD] (last visited Jan. 11, 2024); *see also* Monica Deza et al., *Losing Medicaid and Crime*, National Bureau of Economic Research, Working Paper 32227 (2024), [https://perma.cc/XL3V-AY93]; Jorge Luis García et al., *Early Childhood Education and Crime*, 40 Infant Mental Hlth. J. 141, 141 (2019); Anders et al., *The Effect of Early Childhood Education on Adult Criminality: Evidence from the 1960s Through 1990s*, 15 Am. Econ. J. 37, 37 (2023).

44 Karakatsanis, *supra* chapter 7, note 15. Setting aside the indifference to crimes of the wealthy, punishment bureaucrats mostly ignore even the kinds of interpersonal violence that they themselves purport to care about. They solve very few murders, and the rate of solving them is declining to historic lows. Abené Clayton, *"Far from Justice": Why Are Nearly Half of U.S. Murders Going Unsolved?*, Guardian (Feb. 27, 2023, 1:00 PM), [https://perma.cc/5JWQ-82WM]. They ignore the vast bulk of certain crimes such as child sexual assault, sexual assault on college campuses, sexual assault generally, domestic violence, and crimes committed by jail guards, prison guards, and police. Not only do punishment bureaucrats not investigate most sexual assaults, but they are frequent perpetrators of them. So,

its unsurprising that, for decades, police across the U.S. didn't bother to test hundreds of thousands of rape kits. We are talking about millions of serious felony assaults in these ignored categories—and an even larger number of which are never reported to the punishment bureaucracy because many survivors do not trust punishment bureaucrats to redress their harms. That is a damning indictment of the existing bureaucracy as a mechanism for producing a safer society. If your goal were to cease these violent harms, the fact that the bureaucracy with more funding than any in world history isn't even capable of *learning about*, let alone helping to redress the social conditions that cause them, these crimes should be a moment of reckoning.

45 Josh Dulaney, *Oklahoma Sheriff, Commissioner, Accused of Discussing Killing a Reporter and Returning to Black Hangings*, The Oklahoman (Apr. 16, 2023), https://www .oklahoman.com/story/news/2023/04/16/oklahoma-sheriff-and-commissioner-accused -of-racism-and-threats/70119918007/.

46 Nicole Gonzales Van Cleve, Crook County: Racism and Injustice in America's Largest Criminal Court, 54 (2016).

47 Dan Baum, *Legalize It All*, Harper's Mag. (Apr. 2016), https://harpers.org /archive/2016/04/legalize-it-all/.

48 Sharon LaFraniere et al., *Tech Consultant Arrested in San Francisco Killing of Cash App Creator*, N.Y. Times (Apr. 13, 2023), https://www.nytimes.com/2023/04/13/us /bob-lee-cash-app-killing.html#:~:text=%E2%80%9CThis%20is%20the%20danger %20of,police%20solved%20it%20so%20quickly.

49 One of the authors of the article about the murder of the tech executive is also one of the most unaccountable purveyors of copaganda in San Francisco in the last several years: the former *New York Times* San Francisco bureau chief Thomas Fuller. He repeatedly made false or recklessly misleading claims in nationally published articles. *See* Thomas Fuller, *San Francisco's Shoplifting Surge*, N.Y. Times (May 21, 2021), https:// www.nytimes.com/2021/05/21/us/san-francisco-shoplifting-epidemic.html?smid=tw -share; Thomas Fuller, *In Landslide, San Francisco Forces Out 3 Board of Education Members*, N.Y. Times (Feb. 16, 2022), https://www.nytimes.com/2022/02/16/us/san-francisco -school-board-recall.html. In each of these instances, Fuller fanned the flames of a supposed "crime wave" by poor people in San Francisco, and in the shoplifting article, relying on personal anecdotes and feelings, he even suggested as fact that a (fabricated) rise in low-level retail theft may be linked to legislation passed in California to reduce lengthy prison sentences for low-level nonviolent crimes—a claim that is, at this point in the state of the research, like climate science denial.

50 *See, e.g.*, Federal Bureau of Investigation, Relationship of Victims to Offenders (2019), [https://perma.cc/65A5-KWPW].

51 Christian Leonard, *"Enormous Rise" in San Francisco Overdose Deaths in 2023*, S.F. Chronicle (Apr. 27, 2023, 7:55 AM), https://www.sfchronicle.com/sf/article/drug -overdose-deaths-2023-17904060.php.

52 Stuart Hall et al., *supra* chapter 3, note 8 at 221–22.

53 Hiroki Tabuchi, *Texas to New Jersey: Tracking the Toxic Chemicals in the Ohio Train*

Inferno, N.Y. TIMES (Apr. 17, 2023), https://www.nytimes.com/2023/04/17/climate/train
-fire-palestine-plastics-pvc.html.

54 Hanna Dreier, *As Migrant Children Were Put to Work, U.S. Ignored Warnings*, N.Y.
TIMES (Apr. 17, 2023), https://www.nytimes.com/2023/04/17/us/politics/migrant-child
-labor-biden.html.

55 Glenn Thrush, *Justice Dept. Presses Local Courts to Reduce Fines*, N.Y. TIMES
(Apr. 20, 2023), https://www.nytimes.com/2023/04/20/us/politics/justice-dept-courts
-fines.html. *See* 18 U.S.C. § 242 (which makes it a federal felony to intentionally violate
constitutional rights).

56 Adam Johnson, *Our "Fines Only" Approach to Child Labor Exploitation Exposes
Tough on Crime Crowd's Double Standard*, COLUMN (Aug. 29, 2023), [https://perma.cc
/NH3Z-C6YQ].

57 In many mainstream news stories, companies, business trade organizations, and
police are presented as experts on "crime" to be quoted for their expertise and not as seri-
ally recidivist criminal perpetrators. During the "shoplifting" panic of 2021 and 2022, for
example, numerous business executives were quoted for expert opinions on theft or otherwise quoted as victims of shoplifting in articles that failed to mention their long histories
of stealing wages from low-income workers.

58 Christopher Wildeman, *Incarceration and Population Health in Wealthy Democracies*,
54 CRIMINOLOGY 360, 374 (2016).

59 Peter Hermann, *Man Fatally Shot in Fort Totten Area of Northeast Washington*, WASH.
POST (Apr. 6, 2022, 1:58 PM), https://www.washingtonpost.com/dc-md-va/2022/04/06
/shooting-homicide-dc/.

60 David Channen, *Twin Cities Area Sees Surge in Carjackings, Putting Drivers on Edge*,
STAR TRIB. (Nov. 13, 2021, 3:36 PM), https://www.startribune.com/twin-cities-area
-sees-surge-in-carjackings-putting-drivers-on-edge/600116335/.

61 Fuller, *supra* chapter 8, note 49.

62 Emma Tucker & Mark Morales, *New York City Crime Wave Continues into 2022
as City Rolls Out Safety Plan*, CNN (Mar. 5, 2022, 3:00 AM), [https://perma.cc/5ACJ
-W6N7].

63 Andrew Siff, *Surge in NYC Subway Crime Sets City on Edge: Breaking Down the Numbers*, NBC-4 (Oct. 13, 2022, 5:07 AM), [https://perma.cc/CT3D-T2JM].

64 The terms "wave" and "surge" are sometimes applied to other social phenomenon
and used in the media as metaphors in non-crime stories, especially in regard to immigrants. I'm not arguing that they are exclusively used as crime metaphors, just that there
are reasons to believe that they are harmful and inappropriate in that context. *See also*,
e.g., OTTO SANTA ANA, BROWN TIDE RISING: METAPHORS OF LATINOS IN CONTEMPORARY
AMERICAN PUBLIC DISCOURSE (2002) (explaining how the language used to describe Latinos in the *Los Angeles Times* portrays immigrants as invasive outsiders, and the ways this
language furthers anti-Latino legislation in California).

65 Elliot Young, (@elliottyoungpdx), TWITTER (Dec. 4 2022), https://x.com/elliott
youngpdx/status/1599540292340056064.

66 Sara Sun Beale, *The News Media's Influence on Criminal Justice Policy: How Market-Driven News Promotes Punitiveness*, 48 Wm. & Mary L. Rev. 397, 397 (2006).

9. Copaganda Against Change

1 Michel Foucault, Discipline and Punish 268 (1979).

2 *See* Sam Levin, *Teacher and Cousin of Black Lives Matter Founder "Tased to Death" by LAPD*, Guardian (Jan. 12, 2023, 1:00 PM), [https://perma.cc/PYD8-CLEN].

3 Nicholas Bogel-Burroughs et al., *L.A.P.D. Severely Mishandled George Floyd Protests, Report Finds*, N.Y. Times (March 11, 2021), https://www.nytimes.com/2021/03/11/us/lapd-george-floyd-protests.html.

4 Kim Barker et al., *In City After City, Police Mishandled Black Lives Matter Protests*, N.Y. Times (March 20, 2021), https://www.nytimes.com/2021/03/20/us/protests-policing-george-floyd.html.

5 For those who need a reminder of what police violence is, consider watching this compilation of videos from the spring and summer of 2020 depicting police violence in cities across the country. *See* @JordanUhl, Twitter (May 30, 2020, 10:19 PM), [https://x.com/JordanUhl/status/1266917228752056320].

6 *See, e.g.*, Human Rights Watch, New York Police Planned Assault on Bronx Protesters (2020), [https://perma.cc/75L3-CPUY].

7 *See, e.g.*, *Against the Romance of Community Policing*, Stuart Schrader (Aug. 20, 2016, 4:37 PM), [https://perma.cc/F876-47HB]; Dept. of the Army, Civil Disturbance Operations 2-17–2-18 (2005), [https://perma.cc/3Z8F-AP6C].

8 The violence beamed into living rooms around the country helped to galvanize support for the Voting Rights Act of 1965, which President Johnson signed that August, but there is much less awareness about the way it was used to strengthen police. President Lyndon B. Johnson, *Special Message to the Congress on Law Enforcement and the Administration of Justice* (Mar. 8, 1965), [https://perma.cc/S5UW-8FTE].

9 Kristian Williams, Our Enemies in Blue 94 (2015) (quoting Robert Fogelson).

10 *See, e.g.*, Kevin D. Walsh, N.J. Off. of the State Comptroller, The High Price of Unregulated Private Police Training to New Jersey (Dec. 6, 2023), [https://perma.cc/Q48R-F2QM].

11 *See* Do Not Resist (Vanish Films, 2016); Alain Stephens, *The "Warrior Cop" Is a Toxic Mentality. And a Lucrative Industry*, SLATE (June 19, 2020, 6:00 AM), [https://perma.cc/VW9R-V69P]. *See generally* Radley Balko, Rise of the Warrior Cop (2013); Robert Klemko, *Much of America Wants Policing to Change. But These Self-Proclaimed Experts Tell Officers They're Doing Just Fine*, Wash. Post (Jan. 26, 2022), https://www.washingtonpost.com/national-security/2022/01/26/police-training-reform/; Edith Garwood, *With Whom Are Many U.S. Police Departments Training? With a Chronic Human Rights Violator—Israel*, Amnesty Int'l (AUG. 25, 2016), [https://perma.cc/6JU3-2RMF]; *Police Exchange Program Itinerary*, Deadly Exchange, [https://perma.cc/3NV2-H7TR] (last visited Feb. 14, 2024); Meg O'Connor, *Phoeniz Police Wantonly Use Violence and Violate Civil Rights, DOJ Finds*, The Appeal, (June 13, 2024), https://

theappeal.org/phoenix-police-doj-civil-rights-investigation-announcement/?utm
_source=social&utm_medium=twitter (describing how the Phoenix Police Department
trains its officers that "escalation is de-escalation.").

12 SCHRADER, *supra* chapter 9, note 7.

13 Sometimes elites openly celebrated police criminal violence, as the New York City
mayor did after police deliberately ran over racial justice protestors in 2020. Mehdi Hasan,
Bill de Blasio Needs to Resign. By Defending Police Violence, He Has Betrayed New Yorkers,
INTERCEPT (May 31, 2020), [https://perma.cc/U68D-5JBK].

14 *See generally Senate Select Committee to Study Governmental Operations with Respect
to Intelligence Activities*, U.S. SENATE (Apr. 29, 1976), [https://perma.cc/D8E3-Y3K6]. *See
also* Sahil Singhvi, *Police Infiltration of Protests Undermines the First Amendment*, BRENNAN
CENTER (Aug. 4, 2020), [https://perma.cc/4LF3-XFDH].

15 *SEE* GERALD CHALEFF, AN INDEPENDENT EXAMINATION OF THE LOS ANGELES
POLICE DEPARTMENT 2020 PROTEST RESPONSE (2021), [https://perma.cc/8YDJ-HMKY].

16 Bogel-Burroughs et al., *supra* chapter 9, note 3.

17 *Gerald Chaleff*, DATA COLLAB. FOR JUST., [https://perma.cc/F8T7-6YAT] (last visited Jan. 11, 2024).

18 Shakeer Rahman (@Sh4keer), TWITTER (March 12, 2021, 12:23 PM), [https://
perma.cc/PBL3-UN3N].

19 Bogel-Burroughs et al., *supra* chapter 9, note 3.

20 Shakeer Rahman (@sh4keer), TWITTER (March 12, 2021, 12:23 PM), [https://
perma.cc/H7KB-3X2X].

21 Shakeer Rahman (@Sh4keer), TWITTER (March 12, 2021, 12:23 PM), [https://
perma.cc/6DNL-UD4Z].

22 KRISTIAN WILLIAMS, *supra* chapter 9, note 9 at 248 (2015). *See generally* DONNER,
PROTECTORS OF PRIVILEGE.

23 In his classic book *1984* (Signet Edition, 1983 at 35-36), Orwell wrote:

> For some reason they were nicknamed memory holes. . . . As soon as Win-
> ston had dealt with each of the messages, he clipped his . . . corrections to
> the appropriate copy of *The Times* and pushed them into the pneumatic tube.
> Then, with a movement which was as nearly as possible unconscious, he crum-
> pled up the original message and any notes that he himself had made, and
> dropped them into the memory hole to be devoured by the flames.
>
> What happened in the unseen labyrinth . . . he did not know in detail, but
> he did know in general terms. As soon as all the corrections which happened
> to be necessary in any particular number of *The Times* had been assembled
> and collated, that number would be reprinted, the original copy destroyed,
> and the corrected copy placed on the files in its stead. This process of continu-
> ous alteration was applied not only to newspapers, but to books, periodicals,
> pamphlets, posters, leaflets, films, sound-tracks, cartoons, photographs—to
> every kind of literature or documentation which might conceivably hold any
> political or ideological significance. Day by day and almost minute by minute
> the past was brought up to date.

24 Dan Monk, *Kroger Paid Employee Bonuses in March, Asked for Money Back in April*, WCPO (June 2, 2023), [https://perma.cc/EW6C-CRXL].

25 Jim MacKinnon, *Victim Identified After Timber Top Apartment Units Evacuated for Carbon Monoxide*, Akron Beacon J. (Oct. 21, 2022), [https://perma.cc/4R3P-TE9K].

26 *Carbon Monoxide Detectors (Now Required by the OFC)*, Ohio Dept. Comm., [https://com.ohio.gov/divisions-and-programs/state-fire-marshal/code-enforcement /technical-bulletins-and-advisory-documents/carbon-monoxide-detectors-now -required-under-ohio-fire-code] (last visited Jan. 11, 2024); *see also, e.g.*, Title 9, Chapter 93.99(C) Akron Municipal Code (making violation of Ohio Fire Code a misdemeanor crime in the city).

27 Another favorite example of mine is when the *San Francisco Chronicle* described various forms of theft and fraud by the San Francisco 49ers as "diverting millions of dollars" that "should have been shared with local taxpayers." Lance Williams & Ron Kroichick, *49ers Offer Santa Clara Sweetheart Deal to Resolve Levi's Stadium Management Fight*, S.F. Chron. (Aug. 10, 2022, 12:46 PM), https://www.sfchronicle.com/sports/49ers /article/49ers-offer-Santa-Clara-sweetheart-deal-to-17363120.php.

28 *See, e.g.*, Jessie Singer, There Are No Accidents (2022); David Graeber, The Utopia of Rules 161 (2015) (Graeber observes similarities in how the news media discusses mass shootings and nineteenth-century slave revolts, which are described as "either individual insanity or inexplicable malice," divorced from their structural causes).

29 *See, e.g.*, Eric Schmitt & Helene Cooper, *Pentagon Acknowledges Aug. 29 Drone Strike in Afghanistan Was a Tragic Mistake That Killed 10 Civilians*, N.Y. Times (Nov. 3, 2021), https://www.nytimes.com/2021/09/17/us/politics/pentagon-drone-strike-afghanistan .html.

30 *See* Alec Karakatsanis (@equalityalec), Twitter (Sept. 23, 2022, 12:16 PM), [https:// perma.cc/WC2E-5E4P].

31 Ernesto Londoño & Daniel Politi, *"Terror": Crackdown After Protests in Cuba Sends a Chilling Message*, N.Y. Times (July 28, 2021), https://www.nytimes.com/2021/07/28 /world/americas/cuba-protests-crackdown-arrests.html.

32 Paul Mozur et al., *"An Invisible Cage": How China Is Policing the Future*, N.Y. Times (June 25, 2022), https://www.nytimes.com/2022/06/25/technology/china-surveillance -police.html.

33 I summarize here the arguments I make in my academic study on body cameras. *See* Alec Karakatsanis, *The Body Camera: The Language of Our Dreams*, 4 Yale Journal of Law & Liberation 1, 35-37 (2024), available at https://bpb-us-w2.wpmucdn .com/campuspress.yale.edu/dist/f/4764/files/2024/07/Alec-Karakatsanis_The-Body -Camera-FINAL.pdf.

34 *See id.* at 13. There are hundreds of private police foundations across the U.S. collectively—at least according to the small number of publicly available records—that funnel at least $461 million to police. This money comes from some of the most prominent companies in the U.S.—including Chevron, Shell, Target, Walmart, Microsoft, and others—and from many individual donors who, by donating through intermediaries, are able to mask their identities. *See* Katya Schwenk, *The Police Have a Dark Money Slush*

Fund, Lever News (March 29, 2024), https://www.levernews.com/the-police-have-a-dark
-money-slush-fund/ [https://perma.cc/9FMJ-6THN].

35 *See id.*

36 *Transcript: Mayor Eric Adams Appears Live on CNN's "CNN This Morning,"* NYC.
gov (Jan. 30, 2023), [https://perma.cc/3UXT-MWMD]. Contrary to Adams's assertions,
it was not the body cameras that provided the most revealing angles of the Nichols murder. *See* Rick Rojas & Jesus Jiménez, *As Officers Beat Tyre Nichols, a Crime-Fighting Camera
Watched over Them*, N.Y. Times (Feb. 1, 2023), https://www.nytimes.com/2023/02/01/us
/skycop-camera-tyre-nichols-memphis.html [https://perma.cc/HV9G-BYEL] (explaining how a Memphis SkyCop surveillance camera installed on a nearby utility pole captured "an unobstructed bird's-eye view" of officers beating Nichols while the officer's body
cameras "were often jostled, pointed away, or dark.").

37 Fascinating new research by economists, led by Bocar Ba, has quantified this idea:
"In the three weeks following incidents triggering BLM uprisings, policing firms experi-
enced a stock price increase of seven percentage points relative to the stock prices of non-
policing firms in similar industries." The economists continued:

> In particular, firms producing surveillance technology and police account-
> ability tools experienced higher returns following BLM activism-related
> events. Furthermore, policing firms' fundamentals, such as sales, improved
> after the murder of George Floyd, suggesting that policing firms' future per-
> formances bore out investors' positive expectations following incidents trig-
> gering BLM uprisings.

Bocar Ba et al., *Market Response to Racial Uprisings* (2023), available at https://www
.dropbox.com/scl/fi/fmz3oa4tdsq6idftdfmvt/marketresponse_aug2023.pdf?dl=0&rlkey=7
jku89c6degkj04t7mrk94s5k.

38 For an introduction to how the cash bail system works, *see* Alec Karakatsanis, *Justice for the Rich, Money Bail*, Appeal (July 18, 2018), [https://perma.cc/EQS3-5RSX].

39 *See, e.g.*, Stephanie Wykstra, *Bail Reform, Which Could Save Millions of Unconvicted
People from Jail, Explained*, Vox (Oct. 17, 2018), [https://perma.cc/T9TF-VS3M].

40 *See, e.g.*, Elaine Hennig and Jay Jenkins, Texas Center for Justice & Equity,
Materially Misleading: How the Houston Chronicle's Coverage of Bond Mis-
informs the Public (Apr. 2022), [https://perma.cc/M35M-QGAN]; Laura Bennett
and Jamil Hamilton, FWD.us, Freedom, Then The Press: New York Media and Bail
Reform (Apr. 2021), [https://perma.cc/J5F7-LE8Q].

41 O'Donnell v. Harris Cnty., Texas, 251 F. Supp. 3d 1052, 1106 (S.D. Tex. 2017), *aff'd
as modified*, 882 F.3d 528 (5th Cir. 2018), and *aff'd as modified sub nom*, O'Donnell v. Harris
Cnty, 892 F.3d 147 (5th Cir. 2018).

42 Andrew Schneider, *Harris County's Misdemeanor Bail Reforms Are Working, a New
Report Finds*, HOUS. PUB. MEDIA (March 3, 2022, 3:35 PM), [https://perma.cc/NFE3
-LXS8]. *See also* Alec Karakatsanis (@equalityalec), Twitter (Mar. 7, 2022, 3:19 PM),
[https://perma.cc/Q6CE-RNAL].

43 Urquidi v. City of Los Angeles, No. 22-STCP-04044, slip op. (Cal. Super. Ct.
May 16, 2023), [https://perma.cc/S4SH-AG3K].

44 Nat'l Conf. State Legislatures, *Road to Reform: State Approaches to Addressing Debt-Based Driver's License Suspensions* (Mar. 21, 2024), [https://perma.cc/K4UU-RSGP].

45 Léon Digard & Elizabeth Swavola, *Justice Denied: The Harmful and Lasting Effects of Pretrial Detention*, VERA INST. J. (Apr. 2019), [https://perma.cc/ZP3Z-W4RQ]; Steve Coll, *The Jail Health-Care Crisis*, NEW YORKER (Feb. 25, 2019), https://www.newyorker.com/magazine/2019/03/04/the-jail-health-care-crisis; Joseph A. Bick, *Infection Control in Jails and Prisons*, 45 CLIN. INFECTIOUS DISEASES 1047, 1047 (2007); Emily Widra, *No Escape: The Trauma of Witnessing Violence in Prison*, PRISON POLICY INITIATIVE (Dec. 2, 2022), [https://perma.cc/5HQA-KEXE]; Beck et al., *supra* chapter 7, note 13; Paul Heaton et al., *The Downstream Consequences of Misdemeanor Pretrial Detention*, 69 STANFORD L. J. 711, 711 (2017); Megan Stevenson, *Distortion of Justice*, George Mason Legal Studies Research Paper No. LS 18-30 (2016); *Pretrial Criminal Justice Research*, ARNOLD FOUND., [https://perma.cc/M72Y-4SYE] (last visited Jan. 11, 2024). *See also* INDEP. MONITOR. *O'DONNELL V. HARRIS CTY.* DECREE, MONITORING PRETRIAL REFORM IN HARRIS COUNTY, SEVENTH REPORT OF THE COURT-APPOINTED MONITOR (2024), [https://perma.cc/WJY7-28CB]; Terry-Ann Craigie & Ames Grawert, *Bail Reform and Public Safety*, BRENNAN CENTER FOR JUSTICE (2024), https://www.brennancenter.org/our-work/research-reports/bail-reform-and-public-safety (analyzing data from dozens of jurisdictions and concluding that "there is no reason to believe that bail reform has led to increased crime").

46 VERA INST. JUST., NEW YORK, NEW YORK (July 2019), [https://perma.cc/XZJ2-WZDK].

47 *See* BENNETT & HAMILTON, *supra* chapter 9, note 40.

48 Emma G. Fitzsimmons, *New York City Will Increase Police Presence in Subways to Combat Crime*, N.Y. TIMES (Oct. 22, 2022), https://www.nytimes.com/2022/10/22/nyregion/nyc-subway-police-combat-crime.html.

49 *See, e.g., During Questioning in Albany, NYPD Commissioner Shea Backtracks on Bail Reform Law as Big Reason for Gun Violence*, CBS N.Y. (Oct. 14, 2021, 6:43 PM), [https://perma.cc/P72V-UUW2].

50 Jennifer Gonnerman, *Before the Law*, NEW YORKER (Sept. 29, 2014), https://www.newyorker.com/magazine/2014/10/06/before-the-law.

51 Jamiles Lartey, *New York Rolled Back Bail Reform. What Will the Rest of the Country Do?*, MARSHALL PROJECT (Apr. 23, 2020), [https://perma.cc/7R5S-B7DS]; Joseph Spector & Anna Gronewold, *New York Democrats Pare Back Nation-Leading Bail Reform amid Crime Wave*, POLITICO (Apr. 11, 2022), [https://perma.cc/5PM6-Z8DC].

52 *See* Greg Groogan, *Harris County DA Calls for Public Pressure on Judges Releasing Violent Offenders*, Fox 26 (Oct. 5, 2021), [https://perma.cc/K37W-DCD7]; Dustin Dorsey, *San Jose Police, Mayor Angered After Homicide Suspects Released due to Bail Reform Law*, ABC 7 (Dec. 1, 2021), [https://perma.cc/2W5M-PHMJ]; Clare Amari, *Wisconsin Debates Cash Bail Changes in Wake of Waukesha Parade Tragedy—as Some States Ditch the System Entirely*, PBS WISC. (Jan. 18, 2022), [https://perma.cc/W5LT-Z4V5]; *Behind Police Leaders' Claims That Bail Reform Is Responsible for Surge in Violence*, CNN (Aug. 15, 2021, 2:11 PM), [https://perma

.cc/QVQ3-L236]; Anthony Johnson, *New Jersey Lawmakers Push to Amend Bail Reform Laws amid Spike in Gun Violence*, ABC 7 (Feb. 8, 2022), [https://perma.cc/6T7Y-MCWZ].

53 Ashley Parker (@AshleyRParker), TWITTER (Mar. 3, 2023, 11:22 AM), [https://perma.cc/ND83-NFK2]. *See It's a Shame It Came to This, but D.C. Should Rewrite Its Criminal Code*, WASH. POST (March 3, 2023), https://www.washingtonpost.com/opinions/2023/03/03/biden-congress-dc-criminal-code-nullify/.

54 *See Washington, DC Crime Incident Dashboard*, POWER BI [https://perma.cc/MDY2-AZ9M] (last visited Jan. 11, 2024). Even if one were to focus on murder, as some pundits did, murder went down by 10 percent in 2022, and at the time of Parker's tweet, there were nine more murders in 2023 than at the same time the previous year in a city of over 700,000 people. Every murder is an unspeakable tragedy, but this statistic is not a basis for claiming "crime is out of control."

55 James Hohmann (@jameshohmann), TWITTER (Mar. 3, 2023, 11:17 AM), [https://perma.cc/4CA9-DLUW].

56 President Biden (@POTUS), TWITTER (Mar. 2, 2023, 3:33 PM), [https://perma.cc/C4CF-QDED].

57 Apparently relying on Fox News misinformation, Biden and some Democrats complained that the law would reduce sentences people get for carjacking. The code revisions would not, in practice, decrease sentences for carjackings. *See* Mark Joseph Stern, *Why Biden Stabbed D.C. in the Back*, SLATE (March 3, 2023, 1:19 PM), [https://perma.cc/ME5L-CJKA].

58 *See* Karakatsanis, *supra* chapter 7, note 15. (reviewing the data from various sources).

59 Tom Cotton (@TomCottonAR), TWITTER (Mar. 2, 2023), https://x.com/TomCottonAR/status/1631430564405280772.

10. Progressives Want a Pro-Crime Hellscape

1 Martin Luther King Jr., *Letter from a Birmingham Jail* (Apr. 16, 1963), [https://perma.cc/BT46-SEYY].

2 Shane Goldmacher, *Progressive Backlash in California Fuels Democratic Debate over Crime*, N.Y. TIMES (June 8, 2022), https://web.archive.org/web/20220608092218/https://www.nytimes.com/2022/06/08/us/politics/california-voters-democrats-crime.html/.

3 Olivia Truffaut-Wong, *Celebrities Can't Stop Endorsing Rick Caruso for L.A. Mayor*, CUT (Nov. 8, 2022), https://www.thecut.com/2022/11/celebrities-endorsing-rick-caruso-for-la-mayor.html.

4 Jeremy B. White, *Prosecutor Races Test California's Patience for Crime Policies*, POLITICO (Mar. 13, 2022), https://www.politico.com/news/2022/03/13/california-attorney-general-race-bonta-00011434.

5 Mark Z. Barabak, *How a Progressive Bay Area Prosecutor Was Reelected While San Francisco Tossed Its Liberal DA*, L.A. TIMES (June 30, 2022), https://www.latimes.com/politics/story/2022-06-30/criminal-justice-reform-movement-district-attorneys-diana-becton.

6 David DeBolt, *Alameda County District Attorney Election Results: Pamela Price Leads*, OAKLANDSIDE (June 7, 2022, 9:00 PM), [https://perma.cc/N4RC-SESN].

7 *What to Watch in the June 7 Primaries*, BOLTS MAG. (June 7, 2022), [https://perma .cc/3QNW-WQY6]. Jeremy B. White, *Prosecutor Races Test California's Patience for Crime Policies*, POLITICO (March 13, 2022), [https://perma.cc/W4AY-TU3Z].

8 *See* Eric Ting, *New Poll of Chesa Boudin Recall Shows Closer, but Still Bleak, Race for San Francisco DA*, SF GATE (May 16, 2022), https://www.sfgate.com/politics/article /Chesa-Boudin-recall-closer-poll-shows-17177181.php. *See also San Francisco Survey Results*, PUBLIC POLICY POLLING (May 13–14, 2022) (full original poll on file with The New Press.) In the public policy poll that came out in mid-May before the June election, 48 percent of respondents said they would vote "yes" for a recall and 38 percent said they would vote "no." However, the poll shows support for many specific Boudin policies. These include creating an office of worker protection (55 percent in favor), creating an innocence commission (65 percent versus 12 percent opposed), not prosecuting children as adults (46 percent in favor versus 30 percent opposed), and ending money bail (39 percent in favor versus 30 percent opposed).

9 Piper French, *The Billionaire-Funded Campaign Trying to Recall SF's Progressive DA Chesa Boudin*, IN THESE TIMES (Apr. 18, 2022), [https://perma.cc/8ZJG-SB7V]; Dario McCarty, *Big Donors Fueled High Profile Recall of Progressive San Francisco District Attorney Chesa Boudin*, OPEN SECRETS, (July 7, 2022), [https://perma.cc/72R9-RZ8Z].

10 Boudin received more votes in his favor in the recall election than he had received first-place votes in the first round of ranked choice voting in the election that he won to get into office, and he received more votes against recall than he did first-, second-, or third-choice votes combined in 2019.

11 After the criticism, this paragraph was replaced with a paragraph that undermines the original thesis of the article, but which attempts to make that thesis anyway based on unnamed "strategists" and the baseless factual assertion that "fears of public safety were central drivers" of the results. The new paragraph reads: "Two elections in two cities, of course, do not fully capture the dynamics of an issue as complex as crime politics. And even on Tuesday, the left did not only suffer losses in prosecutor contests but scored a few victories. But the sheer fact that fears for public safety were central drivers in such heavily Democratic bastions is an ominous sign for the party in November, strategists in both parties said." *See* N.Y. TIMES VIA INTERNET ARCHIVE WAYBACK MACHINE, https://web.archive .org/web/20220608092218/https://www.nytimes.com/2022/06/08/us/politics/california -voters-democrats-crime.html/ (last visited June 4, 2024).

12 *See supra* introduction, note 21.

13 *See, e.g.*, Jon Henley, *Adopting Rightwing Policies "Does Not Help Centre-Left Win Votes*," GUARDIAN (Jan. 10, 2024), [https://perma.cc/7BBZ-FMPB] (studying decades of empirical research from different countries to demonstrate that center-left parties do worse in elections if they adopt more right-wing policies and validate right-wing narratives).

14 *See* Jon Hurdle and Jonah E. Bromwich, *Victory in Philadelphia Buoys Supporters of Progressive District Attorney*, N.Y. TIMES (May 19, 2021), https://www.nytimes .com/2021/05/19/us/krasner-vega-philadelphia.html.

15 A thorough explanation can be found here: Chris Stein, *Republicans Claim Democrats Can't Keep Us Safe—Crime Data Disagrees*, GUARDIAN (June 30, 2023, 6:00 PM), [https://perma.cc/2RF2-4MRXI]. *See also* David Menschel (@davidinpdx), TWITTER (Apr. 7, 2022, 4:21 PM), [https://perma.cc/F6E8-R38U].

16 In talking about the relative differences in coverage, I'm not suggesting that news outlets don't cover the wins of those seeking to challenge the punishment bureaucracy at all. They sometimes write election stories covering such wins. But I am arguing that the volume, intensity, framing, and prominent placement of the coverage is different. Most starkly, the pronouncements from "strategists" and "experts" about what one isolated progressive victory means for the country are different than such pronouncements about a progressive loss.

17 Jonathan Weisman & Shawn Hubler, *6 Takeaways from Tuesday's Election*, N.Y. Times (June 8, 2022), https://www.nytimes.com/2022/06/08/us/politics/california-primaries-boudin-caruso-bass.html.

18 *See* Alexander Burns, *Democrats Face Pressure on Crime from a New Front: Their Base*, N.Y. TIMES (June 3, 2022), https://www.nytimes.com/2022/06/03/us/democrats-crime-gun-violence.html.

19 Anna Tong, *Think Chesa Boudin Is Letting Criminals Roam Free? You Have No Idea, Because SF's Court Records Are a Mess*, S.F. CHRON. (Sept. 25, 2021), https://www.sfchronicle.com/opinion/openforum/article/Think-Chesa-Boudin-is-letting-criminals-roam-16486133.php.

20 After I published an essay on this *New York Times* article, the paper altered the article, without an official correction, to correct falsities I identified and to add an entirely new source. My analysis was based on the original article, not any subsequent, unacknowledged changes the paper has made in response to criticism.

21 Sridhar Pappu (@SridharPappu), TWITTER (May 22, 2022, 10:47 PM), [https://perma.cc/2MD7-WNX2].

22 NOAM CHOMSKY: LITERARY CENSORSHIP, ANDREW MARR INTERVIEW, YOUTUBE (Feb. 14, 1996, posted Dec. 9, 2021), https://www.youtube.com/watch?v=pV85306K64w ("If you believed something different, you wouldn't be sitting where you're sitting").

23 Anastasia Valeeva & Weihua Li, *Rifles, Tasers, and Jails: How Cities and States Spent Billions of COVID-19 Relief*, MARSHALL PROJECT (Sept. 7, 2022), [https://perma.cc/6RFA-T8WA]; Sam Levin, *California Cities Spent Huge Share of Federal COVID Relief Funds on Police*, GUARDIAN (Apr. 7, 2022, 6:00 AM), [https://perma.cc/5HM6-69V2]; John Byrne, *Chicago Mayor Lori Lightfoot Spent $281.5 Million in Federal COVID-19 Relief Money on Police Payroll*, CHI. TRIB. (Feb. 18, 2021, 12:25 PM), https://www.chicagotribune.com/politics/ct-chicago-lightfoot-covid-19-police-spending-20210217-uohx77y36nblrf2526whoedkgi-story.html.

24 Copaganda enforcement officials have classified Weisman as a "copaganda super predator" because of the "surge" in his "organized copaganda operation" in recent years.

25 ISAAC BRYAN ET AL., MILLION DOLLAR HOODS, THE PRICE FOR FREEDOM: BAIL IN THE CITY OF L.A. (2017), [https://perma.cc/X2T9-PCVW].

26 GPS electronic surveillance allows bureaucrats to affix a device on people's bodies to monitor their movements and to exclude them from large geographic areas of the city.

Use of the technology, which mainly targets the county's poorest people, had expanded over 5,000 percent from 2015 to 2021 in Los Angeles. ALICIA VIRANI, UCLA SCH. OF L., PRETRIAL ELECTRONIC MONITORING IN LOS ANGELES COUNTY: 2015 THROUGH 2021 (2022), [https://perma.cc/SNZ9-929M].

27 Kevin Rector, *A Korean Man's Shocking Killing on Streets of L.A. Sends His Daughter Searching for Answers*, L.A. TIMES (June 29, 2022, 5:00 AM), https://www.latimes.com/california/story/2022-06-29/la-me-father-slain-daughters-search-for-answers.

28 Los Angeles Times (@latimes), TWITTER (June 30, 2022), [https://perma.cc/UNZ9-M3G2].

29 The recall efforts in San Francisco and Los Angeles began as soon as new district attorneys were elected and *before* any time had passed to evaluate crime trends. That fact disproves the article's suggestion that recall activists were open-minded and only turned on the prosecutors after they evaluated their new policies. After all, according to police statistics, violence in both places was lower than under prior more authoritarian prosecutors. The political and profiteering nature of both recalls is one reason there were no recall efforts of more authoritarian prosecutors in the past when crime was higher. Including these truths would have undermined the public's belief in the stated motivations of recall activists. Of course, they want people thinking their pre-planned recall was a reasoned, deliberative, and organic community response to "violence" and not a political ploy to eliminate an official who had promised to charge police officers, landlords, and local companies with crimes and to reduce certain features of the highly profitable punishment bureaucracy assembly line.

30 Matthew Chayes (@chayesmatthew), TWITTER (Dec. 15, 2021, 9:01 AM), [https://perma.cc/Z7BS-9VRJ].

31 ELLUL, *supra* chapter 3, note 25.

32 Heather Knight, *Why a Progressive Prosecutor Just Left D.A. Chesa Boudin's Office and Joined the Recall Effort*, S.F. CHRON. (Oct. 27, 2021, 6:04 PM), https://www.sfchronicle.com/sf/bayarea/heatherknight/article/She-s-a-progressive-homicide-prosecutor-who-16556274.php.

33 *See* Megan Cassidy and Mallory Moench, *Who Will Replace S.F. District Attorney Chesa Boudin? Here's Who Is on the Short List*, S.F. CHRON. (July 5, 2022), https://www.sfchronicle.com/bayarea/article/chesa-boudin-recall-17166010.php.

34 David Greenwald, *Chronicle Calls Her a "Progressive Prosecutor" but in 2019 the Vanguard Covered Brooke Jenkins Committing Egregious Prosecutorial Misconduct*, DAVIS VANGUARD (Oct. 25, 2021), [https://perma.cc/9N3H-9YBV]; Bob Egelko, *DA Brooke Jenkins Committed Misconduct in Case That Launched Her Recall Efforts, Courts Find*, S.F. CHRON. (Aug. 30, 2023, 1:20 PM), https://www.sfchronicle.com/politics/article/brooke-jenkins-misconduct-18338499.php; Lana Tleimat, *DA Jenkins Committed Misconduct in Murder Trial, Court of Appeals Finds*, MISSION LOCAL (Aug. 29, 2023), [https://perma.cc/4TBF-45WK]; *see, e.g., State Bar Complaints Filed Against SF Interim D.A. Jenkins by Retired Judge*, KTVU-2 (Oct. 13, 2022, 8:58 PM), [https://perma.cc/AY5Z-NVB5]; Jonah Owen Lamb, *Claim Accuses San Francisco District Attorney of Lying to Protect Cop*, S.F. STAND. (Aug. 24, 2023, 7:50 PM), [https://perma.cc/286Q-VR3C]; *Public Defender Accuses SF DA of Violating Juvenile Records Law*, KTVU Fox-2 (Jan. 11, 2023, 11:41 AM), [https://perma.cc/S88A

-UAS4]. *See also* Peter Calloway (@petercalloway), Twitter (Aug. 24, 2023), [https://perma.cc/V2E6-8QYC]; Peter Calloway (@petercalloway), Twitter (Jan. 12, 2023, 9:33 PM), [https://perma.cc/NP6G-S9E7]; Alec Karakatsanis (@equalityalec), Twitter (June 1, 2022, 12:19 PM), [https://perma.cc/H9M7-ULYG].

35 Christien Kafton, *San Francisco DA Cracks Down on Drug Dealers; Public Defender Calls Policies "Regressive,"* KTVU (Aug. 4, 2022), [https://perma.cc/ZS2L-88SJ].

36 Sean Hannity (@seanhannity), Twitter (July 18, 2022, 11:02 PM), [https://perma.cc/A3MA-ZHLH].

37 Alice B Toklas LGBTQ Democratic Club (@AliceLGBTQDems), Twitter (May 9, 2022, 3:46 PM), [https://perma.cc/4F78-X6CG].

38 Jonah Owen Lamb, *Is San Francisco DA Obstructing Police Shooting Probes? Watchdog Says Yes,* S.F. Stand. (Dec. 13, 2023, 9:00 AM), [https://perma.cc/RZ8X-69SP].

39 David Menschel (@davidminpdx), Twitter (July 7, 2023, 7:18pm), [https://perma.cc/ZS2L-88SJ]; David Menschel (@davidminpdx), Twitter (May 31, 2023), [https://perma.cc/AP6G-8RLF]. Not only was San Francisco less safe while spending far more on the war on drugs, but the office was so incompetently managed that Jenkins managed to convict fewer people of drug dealing in her first year on the job than Boudin had in the year prior. Joe Lancaster, *1 Year After Chesa Boudin's Recall, Is San Francisco Safer Under His Successor's More Punitive Policies?,* Reason, https://reason.com/2023/07/12/1-year-after-chesa-boudins-recall-is-san-francisco-safer-under-his-successors-more-punitive-policies/.

40 Scott Talley, *This Wayne County Assistant Prosecutor Says "Thank You" by Giving Back to Her Community,* Det. Free Press (Dec. 4, 2021, 7:01 AM), [https://perma.cc/W2HU-X68M].

41 *See* Lindsay Ballant (@lindsayballant), Twitter (March 25, 2022, 6:20 PM), [https://perma.cc/6FGP-9NLU]. Ballant's tweet cites *NYC's Small Landlords Say They're Suffering Too,* Fox 5 (July 14, 2021), [https://perma.cc/SNS8-GQG3]; Ryan Mills, *Small-Time Landlords Struggle to Keep the Lights on as "Devastating" Eviction Moratorium Continues,* Nat'l Rev. (Apr. 5, 2021, 6:30 AM), [https://perma.cc/XNP5-JAMY]; Liel Leibovitz, *The DSA Comes for Immigrant Landlords of Color,* Tablet (March 23, 2022), [https://perma.cc/XB5J-F3RQ]; Howard Husock, *Biden's Illegal Eviction Ban Is Destroying People Like Lincoln Eccles,* N.Y. Post (Aug. 13, 2021), [https://perma.cc/ZW3Z-EXUZ].

42 Editorial Board, *The San Francisco District Attorney Saga Set Back Criminal Justice Reform,* Wash. Post (June 12, 2022, 8:00 AM), https://www.washingtonpost.com/opinions/2022/06/12/chesa-boudin-san-francisco-recall-criminal-justice-reform-setback/.

43 I followed the news coverage of San Francisco closely because I became friends with Chesa Boudin years before when he was a public defender. We worked together to represent indigent people who could not pay enough cash to get out of jail. Boudin sat with me when I argued the case of Kenneth Humphrey in the Court of Appeal, although Boudin had left the case and been elected district attorney by the time we won the case in the California Supreme Court. It was a landmark ruling striking down the cash bail system as it was practiced every day in California. I had also asked Boudin to serve on the board of Civil Rights Corps when it was founded in 2016, which he did until he ran for district attorney.

44 *See* SFPD Crime Dashboard: https://www.sanfranciscopolice.org/stay-safe/crime

-data/crime-dashboard. These trends were relatively stable. Even setting aside the 2022 crime declines under Boudin, both property crime (down 11 percent) and violent crime (down 19 percent) decreased between 2019 and 2021. *See* Peter Calloway (@petercalloway), TWITTER (Apr. 1, 2022), [https://perma.cc/U58Y-YX4F].

45 Jon Skolnik, *GOP Billionaires Bankroll Effort to Recall SF's District Attorney*, TRUTHOUT (June 7, 2022), [https://perma.cc/KG76-NQCX]. *See, e.g.*, Mallory Moench & Kevin Fagan, *Drug Dealers in the Tenderloin Come Out in Force at Night. What Can S.F. Do to Stop the Chaos?*, S.F. CHRON. (Apr. 4, 2022, 5:45 PM), https://www.sfchronicle .com/sf/article/drug-dealers-in-the-tenderloin-come-out-in-force-17049710.php (ignoring that crime rates were *down* in the Tenderloin at the time of the article's writing). *See also* Alec Karakatsanis (@equalityalec), TWITTER (Apr. 2, 2022, 11:53 AM), [https://perma .cc/FJH4-MY55] (collecting examples of misinformation from the *Chronicle*).

46 Roni Caryn Rabin, *Overdose Deaths Reached Record High as the Pandemic Spread*, N.Y. Times (Nov. 17, 2021), https://www.nytimes.com/2021/11/17/health/drug-overdoses -fentanyl-deaths.html.

47 Peter Calloway (@petercalloway), TWITTER (Apr. 1, 2022), https://twitter.com /petercalloway/status/1510032531629826049.

48 James Hohmann, *Boudin's Recall Proves Democrats Have Lost the Public's Trust on Crime*, WASH. POST (June. 8, 2022, 6:21 AM), https://www.washingtonpost.com /opinions/2022/06/08/chesa-boudin-recall-san-francisco-crime/.

49 Roger Berkowitz, Hannah Arendt Center for Politics and Humanities, available at https://hac.bard.edu/amor-mundi/on-fake-hannah-arendt-quotations-2024-08-04.

50 Adam Johnson, *4 Major Plot Holes in the "Organized Crime Rings Are Closing Walgreens!" Narrative*, COLUMN (Oct. 15, 2021), [https://perma.cc/XH7R-TTKD]. *See also supra* chapter 2, note 13.

51 Eric Ting, *New San Francisco Ad Blasts Chesa Boudin over Drugs. There's Just One Problem.* SFGATE (May 5, 2022), [https://www.sfgate.com/politics/article/Chesa-Boudin -recall-ad-branded-lie-17150379.php].

52 Nellie Bowles, *How San Francisco Became a Failed City*, ATLANTIC (June 8, 2022), https://www.theatlantic.com/ideas/archive/2022/06/how-san-francisco-became-failed -city/661199/. *See* Chris Herring (@cherring_soc), TWITTER (June 16, 2022, 3:58 PM), [https://perma.cc/8W36-F997] (summarizing the article's major false claims and omissions about homelessness in San Francisco, including using incorrect statistics). *See also* Yasha Levine, *Private Islands, Forgotten California Oligarchs, and Jewish Converts. Say Hello to Our Ruling Class*, WEAPONIZED IMMIGRANT (Nov. 19, 2021), https://yasha.substack .com/p/private-islands-forgotten-california [https://perma.cc/KE8W-XPN2].

53 Amanda Agan, *Prosecuting Low-Level Crimes Makes Us Less Safe*, WASH. POST (Apr. 6, 2021), https://www.washingtonpost.com/outlook/2021/04/06/misdemeanor -prosecution-future-crime/.

54 *We Recommend Alexandra Mealer for Harris County Judge*, HOUS. CHRON. (Oct. 14, 2022, 1:37 PM), https://www.houstonchronicle.com/opinion/endorsements/article/mealer -hidalgo-harris-county-endorsement-17504659.php.

55 Harris County (Houston area) is essentially run by five people who make up the

Harris County Commissioners Court, which acts as both the executive *and* the legislature. The county is bigger than twenty-five states, and the county judge heads the court.

56 Adam Zuvanich, *Houston Violent Crime Dropped by 10 Percent in 2022, Police Survey Shows*, Hous. Pub. Media (Feb. 3, 2023), [https://perma.cc/YCE2-UL9V].

57 *See* sources cited *supra* chapter 8, note 43.

58 The editorial briefly attempted to criticize the progressive incumbent, but none of the criticisms make sense. It half-heartedly blames the progressive incumbent for what are problems caused by organized right-wing forces. For example, the article blames the incumbent for the fact that two Republican commissioners boycotted meetings, preventing a quorum to pass legislation. The editorial board asks, rhetorically: "But would they have tapped the nuclear option had earnest attempts been made to listen to their concerns and broker compromise?" This is like primarily blaming a person for being [stabbed] after not giving up their wallet when a person with a knife on the street demands it. The board next blames the incumbent for several staffers who were indicted by the right-wing district attorney, but omits that its own reporting established that the indictments were a small part of a politically motivated and unprecedented assault on local democracy by the district attorney. Before her landslide election defeat in 2024, the district attorney attempted to prosecute many of her progressive enemies who accomplished misdemeanor bail reform, including a sitting judge who supported reform (another prosecutor office rejected those charges after the Harris County prosecutor was forced to recuse herself). The charges were far-fetched based on [evaluations] of the allegations that I and other current and former defense attorneys conducted. The prosecutor also raided offices of political opponents, forced county employees to attend politically motivated grand jury proceedings, and threatened county budget officials and low-level county staff working on "criminal justice reform." *See* Jen Rice & Neena Satija, *"Don't Cross Her": How DA Kim Ogg Has Repeatedly Aimed Her Power at Harris County Officials*, Hous. Chron. (Sept. 23, 2023, 9:31 PM https://www.houstonchronicle .com/news/investigations/article/kim-ogg-harris-county-power-18334282.php?sid =616ec6db8cd15f31fd623fec&ss=A&st_rid=13525bf1-6af6-48b4-a2be-38be 18320a54&utm_source=newsletter&utm_medium=email&utm_term=news&utm_cam paign=HC_BreakingNews. The environment in Harris County was as lawless and authoritarian as I have ever seen in any local legal system, and the lack of mention about any of these things is revealing.

59 Bowles, *supra* chapter 10, note 52. Annie Lowrey, *The People vs. Chesa Boudin*, Atlantic (May 19, 2022), https://www.theatlantic.com/ideas/archive/2022/05/chesa-boudin -recall-san-francisco-crime/629907/; Benjamin Wallace-Wells, *Why San Francisco Fired Chesa Boudin*, New Yorker (June 8, 2022), https://www.newyorker.com/news/the-politi cal-scene/why-san-francisco-fired-chesa-boudin; Jonathan Chait, *Boudin and the Debacle of Urban Left-Wing Politics*, Intelligencer (June 9, 2022), https://nymag.com/intelligencer /article/chesa-boudin-recall-san-francisco-crime-left-liberals-defund-democrats.html.

60 *See supra* chapter 10, note 47.

61 Megan Brenan, *Record-High 56% in U.S. Perceive Local Crime Has Increased*, Gallup (Oct. 28, 2022), [https://perma.cc/7R4D-MJMW].

11. What We Don't Know *Can* Hurt Us

1 Aldous Huxley, foreword to Brave New World, xv (1932).

2 Annie Karni & Stephanie Lai, *Law Enforcement Funding Package Splits Democrats Ahead of Midterm Elections*, N.Y. Times (Sept. 19, 2022), https://www.nytimes.com/2022/09/19/us/politics/police-democrats-congress-midterms.html.

3 *See* Letter to Speaker Pelosi, Leader Hoyer, Chair Nadler, Whip Clyburn, and Other Members of Congress (Aug. 11, 2022), [https://perma.cc/4CFW-CCBT].

4 Lluvia Botello & Kerry Allen, *House Passes Public Safety Legislation to Support Mental Health and Violence Prevention*, NACCHO (Sept. 23, 2022), [https://perma.cc/Z8RZ-V83F].

5 *2023 Police Violence Report*, Mapping Police Violence, [https://perma.cc/2M2N-3XKB] (last visited Feb. 14, 2024).

6 Emma G. Fitzsimmons, *Anxious New Yorkers Worry Whether Eric Adams Is the Man for the Moment*, N.Y. Times (Aug. 9, 2022), https://www.nytimes.com/2022/08/09/nyregion/eric-adams-nyc.html. By the end of 2023, Adams was down to 28 percent approval. Emily Ngo, *Eric Adams' Job Approval Rating Tumbles to 28 Percent*, Politico (Dec. 6, 2023, 7:03 PM), [https://perma.cc/733E-R2NW].

7 Karni & Lai, *supra* chapter 11, note 2. The paper appended a "correction" to the bottom of the article that says that the article "misstated" the position of the groups, who "are not pressing for passage of the package in its current form." This is also problematic, because the body of the article makes it seem like "the package" being discussed consisted only of the police funding bills and that there could have been some amendments to change their "current form" that could have convinced the groups to support the bills. In actuality, the "package" included funding bills for non-police safety alternatives, and *those* were the parts of the package that civil rights groups supported.

8 Glen Stellmacher, *Derailing the Defund: How SPD Manipulated the Media Narrative Around the 2020 Protests*, Real Change News (July 19, 2023), [https://perma.cc/342N-KKDN].

9 Glenn Greenwald (@ggreenwald), Twitter (July 28, 2023, 1:14 PM), [https://perma.cc/N5XB-9FPF].

10 Fang railed against "[George] Soros" and other progressive philanthropists, suggesting that they were behind the protests and then raved about marauding bands of "anarchists" leading all the "violent protests" against police in cities across the country. He also falsely claimed, parroting a widely debunked right-wing conspiracy theory, that the protesters in various cities were not from communities where demonstrations happened.

11 One good place to start is the archive available here: *Welcome*, Transform Harm: A Resource Hub for Ending Violence, [https://perma.cc/47CD-X5NQ].

12 Katie Glueck, *Staunch Critic of the N.Y.P.D. Grapples with Deaths of 2 Officers*, N.Y. Times (Jan. 26, 2022), https://www.nytimes.com/2022/01/26/us/politics/kristin-richardson-jordan-nypd.html.

13 *Policy & Legislation: Full Platform*, Kristin in Harlem, [https://perma.cc/QGH7-SL8Q].

14 *See, e.g.*, Luis Ferré-Sadurní & Jesse McKinley, *How "Defund the Police" Roiled*

Competitive Races in New York, N.Y. Times (Dec. 13, 2020), https://www.nytimes
.com/2020/11/06/nyregion/election-nyc-defund-police.html?action=click&module=
Spotlight&pgtype=Homepage.

15 J. David Goodman, *A Year After "Defund," Police Departments Get Their Money Back*, N.Y. Times (Oct. 10, 2021), https://www.nytimes.com/2021/10/10/us/dallas-police
-defund.html.

16 Grace Manthey et al., *Despite "Defunding" Claims, Police Funding Has Increased in Many U.S. Cities*, ABC (Oct. 16, 2022), [https://perma.cc/U89L-236G].

17 *See* data cited in the FBI's Crime Data Explorer *supra* introduction, note 21. (showing rate of violent crime declining from 398 to 387 per 100,000 and property crime declining from 1,958 to 1,832 per 100,000).

18 Stacy Rickard, *Dallas City Council Approves $4.35B Budget, Millions Going Toward Adding Dallas Police Officers, New Equipment*, Spectrum News (Oct. 9, 2021), [https://
perma.cc/Q38L-WAAD].

19 Jason Stanley, How Propaganda Works 138 (2015).

20 *See supra* chapter 7, note 6.

21 *See, e.g.*, Ana Kasparian (@AnaKasparian), Twitter (Mar. 22, 2022, 8:38 PM), [https://perma.cc/6P4H-ZK3Z].

22 Richard Fausset, *In Atlanta, a Local Prosecutor Takes on Murder, Street Gangs and a President*, N.Y. Times (Sept. 12, 2022), https://www.nytimes.com/2022/09/12/us/fani-t
-willis-trump-atlanta.html.

23 For a detailed description of what her office and other prosecutors offices actually do, see Karakatsanis, *supra* introduction, note 17.

24 *See* Leah Wang, *Punishment Beyond Prisons 2023: Incarceration and Supervision by State*, Prison Policy Initiative (May 2023), [https://perma.cc/RCX2-676M]. *See generally* Vincent Schiraldi, Mass Supervision: Probation, Parole, and the Illusion of Safety and Freedom (2023).

25 Joseph Goldstein & Kevin Armstrong, *Could This City Hold the Key to the Future of Policing in America?*, N.Y. Times (July 12, 2020), https://www.nytimes.com/2020/07/12
/nyregion/camden-police.html.

26 Kevin Armstrong (@KevinGArmstrong), Twitter (July 12, 2020, 10:17 AM), [https://perma.cc/567A-DPW7].

27 Brendan McQuade, *The Camden Police Department Is Not a Model for Policing in the Post–George Floyd Era*, Appeal (June 12, 2020), [https://perma.cc/BE3G-6U67].

28 *See, e.g.*, Nellie Bowles, *Abolish the Police? Those Who Survived the Chaos in Seattle Aren't So Sure*, N.Y. Times (Aug. 7, 2020), https://www.nytimes.com/2020/08/07/us
/defund-police-seattle-protests.html.

12. Polls and Making Cops Look Good

1 Hall et al., Policing the Crisis 63.

2 Loyola Marymount U., Police Data Brief: 2022 Police and Community Relations Survey (2022), [https://perma.cc/SJ3E-GY3R].

3 Libor Jany, *Survey: Most Angelenos have favorable view of LAPD, despite lingering concerns around bias*, L.A. Times, (Sept. 28, 2022), https://www.latimes.com/california /story/2022-09-28/survey-most-angelenos-support-lapd.

4 Murakawa, *supra* chapter 6, note 32.

5 Lauren Goldstein et al., Overall Findings from Messaging Research on Reimagining Public Safety (2022), [https://perma.cc/8TMY-5AGB].

6 Harry Enten, *Americans See Martin Luther King Jr. as a Hero Now, but That Wasn't the Case During His Lifetime*, CNN (Jan. 16, 2023, 5:01 AM), [https://perma.cc /KDZ6-JWYF].

7 *See generally* Thomas B. Harvey (@tbh4justice), Twitter (March 2, 2022, 6:40 PM), https://twitter.com/tbh4justice/status/1499167860140044292. *See also* Derecka Purnell (@dereckapurnell), Twitter (March 2, 2022, 5:52 PM), [https://perma.cc/4BLS-ALZK].

13. The Bad Apple

1 Dan Evon, *Are These Elijah McClain's Last Words on Police Video?*, Snopes (Feb. 21, 2021), [https://perma.cc/A3JM-58GK].

2 *Critical Incident in the 1900 Block of Billings St (Elijah McClain Case)*, City of Aurora (June 22, 2020, 12:27 PM), [https://perma.cc/JJ5P-Y6EZ].

3 Michael Levenson, *Stray Police Bullet Kills Girl as Officers Fire at Suspect in Los Angeles Store*, L.A. Times (Dec. 23, 2021), https://www.nytimes.com/2021/12/23/us/girl -fatally-shot-police-los-angeles.html. *See also* Radley Balko, *The Curious Grammar of Police Shootings*, Wash. Post (July 14, 2014, 1:04 PM), https://www.washingtonpost.com/news /the-watch/wp/2014/07/14/the-curious-grammar-of-police-shootings/; Rob Beschizza, *NYT Declares "Bullet" Killed 14 Year Old Girl, Not the Cop That Fired It*, BoingBoing (Jan. 5, 2022, 11:50 AM), [https://perma.cc/4CH4-EM7N].

4 Jill Cowan et al., *Officer Whose Bullet Killed a 14-Year-Old Girl Wanted to "Change' " the Police*, N.Y. Times (Dec. 31, 2021), https://www.nytimes.com/2021/12/30/us/los -angeles-police-burlington-shooting-william-dorsey-jones.html.

5 People's City Council—Los Angeles (@PplsCityCouncil), Twitter (Dec. 24, 2021, 5:39 PM), [https://perma.cc/9T86-JGAC].

6 Cerise Castle & Jon Peltz, *LAPD Officer William Dorsey Jones Jr. Kills Two People, Including 14-Year-Old Valentina Orellana Peralta*, Knock LA (Dec. 30, 2021), [https:// perma.cc/FW69-HZP5].

7 *See also* Julia Métraux, *How Police Work the Media When Civilians Die in Custody*, Mother Jones (Aug. 10, 2023), [https://perma.cc/G7FC-K425].

8 Kim Barker et al., *The Driver, The Officer, and the Deadly Traffic Stop in Grand Rapids*, N.Y. Times (May 18, 2022), https://www.nytimes.com/2022/04/27/us/patrick-lyoya -christopher-schurr-traffic-stop.html.

9 Castle & Peltz, *supra* chapter 13, note 6. *Deleted Tweets for LAPD Officer Jones*, RENTRY, [https://perma.cc/R53K-GTZ7] (last visited Jan. 12, 2024).

10 Stop LAPD Spying Coalition, *supra* chapter 6, note 20.

11 *See, e.g.,* Schrader, *supra* chapter 6, note 27 and chapter 9, note 7.

12 Avriel Epps-Darling (@kingavriel), Twitter (Jan. 22, 2021, 12:35 PM), [https://perma.cc/7XBC-NYLN].

13 Stop LAPD Spying Coalition, *Community Policing = Policing of Community,* Automating Banishment, [https://perma.cc/K7JQ-5HLG] (last visited Jan. 12, 2024).

14 *See supra* chapter 11, note 5.

15 Shant Shahrigian, *Mayor de Blasio Praises NYPD Officers Who Took a Knee in Solidarity with NYC Protesters,* Daily News (June 1, 2020, 11:31 PM), [https://perma.cc/84Y4-MVJ9]; Christy E. Lopez, *George Floyd's Death Could Have Been Prevented If We Had a Police Culture of Intervention,* Wash. Post (May 29, 2020, 6:43 PM), https://www.washingtonpost.com/opinions/the-killing-of-george-floyd-underscores-why-we-need-a-police-culture-of-peer-intervention/2020/05/29/a54ee178-a1e7-11ea-b5c9-570a91917d8d_story.html.

16 Lani Guinier & Gerald Torres, The Miner's Canary: Enlisting Race, Resisting Power, Transforming Democracy 263 (2002).

17 *Ferguson, MO: Debtors' Prisons,* Civil Rights Corps, [https://perma.cc/73HP-3XNC].

18 *See General Inmate Population Reports,* Bureau of Prisons, [https://perma.cc/2LSN-G8NN] (last visited Jan. 12, 2024); Justice Dept. & City of Ferguson, Mo. Resolve Lawsuit with Agreement to Reform Ferguson Police Dept. & Mun. Ct. to Ensure Const. Policing, Dept. Just. (March 17, 2016), [https://perma.cc/KWQ4-A93Q]; Jim Salter & Eric Tucker, *Ferguson Missed Deadlines in Deal with Justice Department,* AP (Jan. 27, 2017, 8:50 PM), [https://perma.cc/S9Z3-QDSB].

19 *See, e.g.,* Gates v. Cook, 376 F.3d 323, 333 (5th Cir. 2004) (describing prison cells "covered in feces, urine and dried ejaculate"); Steve Coll, *The Jail Health-Care Crisis,* New Yorker (Feb. 25, 2019), https://www.newyorker.com/magazine/2019/03/04/the-jail-health-care-crisis; Alysia Santo, *Prison Rape Allegations Are on the Rise,* Marshall Project (July 25, 2018, 8:00 AM), [perma.cc/NVJ6-VFRM]; Dave Gilson, *What We Know About Violence in America's Prisons,* Mother Jones (July 2016), [https://perma.cc/BHX5-D3VL].

20 Wendy Sawyer & Peter Wagner, *Mass Incarceration: The Whole Pie 2020,* Prison Policy Initiative (March 24, 2020), [https://perma.cc/GX2N-8SV2].

21 Matt Ford, *America's Largest Mental Hospital Is a Jail,* Atlantic (June 8, 2015), https://www.theatlantic.com/politics/archive/2015/06/americas-largest-mental-hospital-is-a-jail/395012/.

22 *Criminal Justice Expenditures: Police, Corrections, and Courts,* Urban Inst., [https://perma.cc/GGU2-JPHS] (last visited Jan. 12, 2024).

23 *See* Baynard Woods & Brandon Soderberg, I've Got a Monster: The Rise and Fall of America's Most Corrupt Police Squad (2020).

24 *Rampart Scandal Timeline,* PBS [https://perma.cc/8DFR-6H6P].

25 Brendan McQuade, *The "Camden Model" Is Not a Model. It's an Obstacle to Real Change,* Jacobin (July 4, 2020), https://jacobin.com/2020/07/camden-new-jersey-police-reform-surveillance; Sidney Fussell, *What Disbanding the Police Really Meant in Camden, New Jersey,* Wired (July 1, 2020), https://www.wired.com/story/disbanding-police-really-meant-camden/.

26 This is not to say that federal intervention can never have any positive effects. Although the impact of federal intervention is generally exaggerated and often makes the problems worse by increasing investment in the policing bureaucracy, it can sometimes mandate policies that reduce police violence and corruption, validate the experiences of marginalized people, and bring other benefits. I focus here, however, on its common copagandistic attributes and the role it plays in public narrative to prevent more radical change.

27 @OLAASM, Twitter (June 11, 2020, 12:52 PM), [https://perma.cc/46X3-EBUF].

14. The Big Deception

1 David Graeber, Utopia of Rules 211–18 (2015).

2 James C. Scott, Two Cheers for Anarchism 67 (2012).

3 Alison Siegler, Freedom Denied: How the Culture of Detention Created a Federal Jailing Crisis 21–22 (2022), [https://perma.cc/9AZW-WKN6].

4 Chart courtesy of the amazing Nika Soon-Shiong.

5 You may also need effective methods of conflict resolution, mutual aid, care, and protection from corporate and police adversaries. See, e.g., Amanda Alexander, *Nurturing Freedom Dreams: An Approach to Movement Lawyering in the Black Lives Matter Era*, 5 Howard Hum. & C.R. L. Rev. 101 (2021).

6 Baum, *supra* chapter 8, note 47.

7 *See Overdose Deaths: Behind the Numbers*, Drug Policy Alliance, [https://perma.cc/MBP9-CR6V] (last visited June 4, 2024).

8 Alec Karakatsanis, *Why US v Blewett Is the Obama Justice Department's Greatest Shame*, Guardian (July 23, 2013).

9 James Reston, *Nixon, Drugs and the War*, N.Y. Times (June 2, 1971), https://www.nytimes.com/1971/06/02/archives/nixon-drugs-and-the-war.html.

10 Tom Goldstein, *The Rockefeller Drug Law*, N.Y. Times (May 14, 1979), https://www.nytimes.com/1979/05/14/archives/the-rockefeller-drug-law-after-6-years-officials-question-its.html.

11 Gerald N. Boyd, *Reagan Signs Anti-Drug Measure, Hopes for 'Drug-Free Generation,'* N.Y. Times, (Oct. 28, 1986), https://www.nytimes.com/1986/10/28/us/reagan-signs-anti-drug-measure-hopes-for-drug-gree-generation.html.

12 *See, e.g.,* Seth Mydans, *Agents Seize 20 Tons of Cocaine in Raid on Los Angeles Warehouse*, N.Y. Times (Sept. 30, 1989), https://www.nytimes.com/1989/09/30/us/agents-seize-20-tons-of-cocaine-in-raid-on-los-angeles-warehouse.html.

13 *See, e.g.,* Anna Tong & Josh Koehn, *DA Boudin and Fentanyl: Court Data Shows Just 3 Drug Dealing Convictions in 2021 as Immigration Concerns Shaped Policy*, S.F. Stand. (May 17, 2022, 2:04 PM), [https://perma.cc/5866-36JR].

14 Kim Chandler, *Alabama Lawmakers Approve Harsher Penalties for Fentanyl*, AP (Apr. 6, 2023, 6:35 PM), [https://perma.cc/4N7C-4GT9] (emphases added). There are some exceptions to this deceptive reporting, and those exceptions prove how easily drugs could be covered differently as a public health issue. *See, e.g.,* Noah Weiland & Margot Sanger-Katz, *Overdose Deaths Continue Rising, with Fentanyl and Meth Key Culprits*, N.Y.

Times (May 11, 2022), https://www.nytimes.com/2022/05/11/us/politics/overdose
-deaths-fentanyl-meth.html.

15 Ironically, the federal government rejected a recommendation in the 1970s by a heavily stacked "law enforcement" commission to *not* criminalize marijuana.

16 Most companies want consumers to believe that their products are provided for some good moral reason or to meet some need. In 2020, I saw two TV commercials in a row that illustrate this phenomenon. The first was a Chick-fil-A ad about how the company had created a rewards card because, out of a concern for public health, it wanted to help frontline medical workers. (Note: Chick-fil-A produces unhealthy food, has a history of unhealthy practices, and no reasonable corporate executive could believe that a customer rewards card is the best way for the company to help frontline workers. Customer reward cards are a profit-seeking branding strategy common in corporate strategic playbooks.) The very next ad was from T-Mobile, announcing to customers that it had merged with another behemoth telecom company, and that the *reason* for the merger was so it could help customers better. Here was a profit-maximizing, monopoly-pursuing mega-corporation trying to get its audience to believe that the reason for its behavior was genuine care for them.

17 Hurubie Meko et al., *No Arrest in New York Subway Chokehold Death, and Many Want to Know Why*, N.Y. Times (May 4, 2023), https://www.nytimes.com/2023/05/04 /nyregion/subway-chokehold-arrest-decision.html.

18 Michael Gold, *Panic in the Brooklyn Subway: Police Hunt Gunman Who Shot 10*, N.Y. Times (Apr. 12, 2022), https://www.nytimes.com/2022/04/12/nyregion/shooting-subway -sunset-park.html. The original article bolstered this copaganda by omitting that violent crime was near historic lows. An amended version of the article included that correct context and shifted to say that Adams was acting "in response" to the *perception* of rising crime rather than actual crime. The paper concocted nearly identical copaganda after the SCORPION Unit murdered Tyre Nichols in Memphis, claiming that the unit was created to fight crime. *See* Alec Karakatsanis (@equalityalec), Twitter (Feb. 7, 2023), [https:// perma.cc/7VUJ-DJMK].

19 *See, e.g.*, Bernard E. Harcourt, Illusion of Order: The False Promise of Broken Windows Policing (2002); Ngozi Kamalu & Emmanel Onyeozili, *A Critical Analysis of the "Broken Windows" Policing in New York City and Its Impact*, 11 Afr. Am. J. Criminology & Just. Studies 71 (2018); Daniel O'Brien et al., *Broken (Windows) Theory: A Meta-analysis of the Evidence for the Pathways from Neighborhood Disorder to Resident Health Outcomes and Behaviors*, 228 Soc. Sci. & Med. 272 (2019).

20 Troy Closson, *Can Adams Rebuild, and Rein In, a Notorious N.Y.P.D. Unit?*, N.Y. Times (June 22, 2023), https://www.nytimes.com/2022/01/05/nyregion/eric-adams -nypd-anti-crime-unit.html.

21 Fitzsimmons, *supra* chapter 9, note 48.

22 *Id.*; *see also* Alec Karakatsanis (@equalityalec), Twitter (Oct. 24, 2022), [https:// perma.cc/4ZFQ-AL72].

23 This kind of reporting pervades coverage of pro–punishment bureaucrat politicians like Adams and Hochul. The *Times* asserted in another article that Adams "has spent much of his first year in office seeking to reduce crime and disorder in the city." Jeffery C.

Mays & Nicole Hong, *Hochul and Adams Envision "New New York." Getting There Is the Trick*, N.Y. TIMES (Dec. 14, 2022), https://www.nytimes.com/2022/12/14/nyregion /adams-hochul-ny-plan.html. And the *Washington Post* asserted that Hochul "signed stricter bail laws as a way to address crime." Alexi McCammond, *Being "Tough on Crime" Isn't an Appeal to White Voters*, WASH. POST (Apr. 8, 2024), https://www.washington post.com/opinions/2024/04/08/democrats-crime-hochul-2024-biden/. In 2023, a *Spectrum News* television reporter asserted that the NYPD under Adams increased lucrative armed police surveillance and overtime and in public schools "because of persistent teen violence." *NYPD Chief of Patrol Discusses Youth Crime, Smoke Shops*, SPECTRUM NEWS (Feb. 19, 2023, 7:45 PM), [https://perma.cc/6UWC-CMLL].

24 This is part of a systemic problem in mainstream journalism that accepts as given what are pervasive myths. For example, the *New York Times* asserted as *fact* that military veterans in the U.S. who were engaged in recent military occupations were "trying to spread democracy." Dave Phillips, *"I Just Can't Stand By": American Veterans Join the Fight in Ukraine*, N.Y. TIMES (March 5, 2022), https://www.nytimes.com/2022/03/05/us /american-veterans-volunteer-ukraine-russia.html. In another example, Reuters and the Associated Press asserted that the purpose of Biden's call for 100,000 more cops was "for fighting and preventing crime" and for "crime prevention." *See* Alec Karakatsanis (@equalityalec), TWITTER (July 21, 2022, 8:20 PM, [https://perma.cc/PAS8-C8JW]; Alec Karakatsanis (@equalityalec), TWITTER (July 21, 2022, 6:21 PM). These are controversial claims about which university seminars are taught and books are written to contest. But entire fields of investigative journalism and critical academic study (and sometimes global consensus in the non-Western world) are casually erased in a few words.

25 ELLUL, *supra* chapter 3, note 25 at 57–58; *see also id.* at 52 ("The most generally held concept of propaganda is that it is a series of *tall stories*, a tissue of lies, and that lies are necessary for effective propaganda. . . . This concept leads to two attitudes among the public. The first is: 'Of course we shall not be victims of propaganda because we are capable of distinguishing truth from falsehood.' Anyone holding that conviction is extremely susceptible to propaganda, because when propaganda does tell the 'truth,' he is then convinced that it is no longer propaganda; moreover, his self-confidence makes him all the more vulnerable to attacks of which he is unaware.").

26 *See, e.g.*, Axel Gottfries & Gregor Jarosch, *Dynamic Monopsony with Large Firms and Noncompetes*, NAT'L BUREAU OF ECON. RESEARCH, Working Paper No. 31965 (2023).

27 Luis Ferré-Sadurní, *Hochul Vetoes Ban on Noncompete Agreements in New York*, N.Y. TIMES (Dec. 22, 2023), https://www.nytimes.com/2023/12/22/nyregion/kathy -hochul-veto-noncompete.html.

28 One could do the same analysis with SWAT teams. When the LAPD created the country's first "SWAT" team in 1969, its first target was the Black Panthers headquarters containing five children, three women, and five adult men, which it attacked with 350 officers and military weapons. Matthew Fleischer, *50 Years Ago, LAPD Raided the Black Panthers. SWAT Teams Have Been Targeting Black Communities Ever Since*, L.A. TIMES (Dec. 8, 2019, 3:00 AM), https://www.latimes.com/opinion/story/2019-12-08/50-years -swat-black-panthers-militarized-policinglos-angeles. Today, there are tens of thousands

of raids every year by SWAT teams across the country, the vast majority of which target poor people and people of color.

29 Good investigative journalism gets at these complexities, which is one reason it is so vital to any notion of democratic participation.

30 As Michelle Alexander pointed out in *The New Jim Crow*, during the Clinton administration, federal funding for public housing decreased by $17 billion and federal funding for prisons increased by a little over the same amount ($19 billion). Michelle Alexander, The New Jim Crow: Mass Incarceration in the Age of Colorblindness 72 (2010).

31 For reading generally on the political economy of prison expansion and carceral bureaucracy, I recommend Judah Schept's excellent book *Coal, Cages, Crisis*, which discusses the construction of hundreds of new prisons built in rural Appalachia between 1980 and 2000. I also recommend Ruth Wilson Gilmore's classic *Golden Gulag*, about similar phenomena in California and beyond.

32 This is one reason that allied forces after World War II handed lucrative contracts to IBM despite the corporation's central role in Nazi crimes against humanity. IBM made unprecedented amounts of money using *the very same machines* to help allied governments as it had just used to help the Nazis. Edwin Black, IBM and the Holocaust: The Strategic Alliance Between Nazi Germany and America's Most Powerful Corporation (2012). *See also* Alec Karakatsanis (@equalityalec), Twitter (Feb. 9, 2023, 12:25 PM), [https://perma.cc/U8YY-8R7K] (describing the parallels between modern and historical propaganda). *See generally* Mariana Mazzucato & Rosie Collington, The Big Con: How the Consulting Industry Weakens Our Businesses, Infantilizes our Governments, and Warps Our Economies (2024).

33 In just one example, newspaper editorials have called for reforms to the cash bail system and to conditions inside the Los Angeles County jail for over 100 years. *See, e.g.,* Keri Blakinger (@keribla), Twitter, (May 21, 2023), [https://perma.cc/8ZNN-ZZFM].

34 I recommend the work of Gar Alperovitz, especially his short, fun book *America Beyond Capitalism*, for a discussion of simple, feasible, creative ways of democratizing ownership in our society.

15. Distracting from Material Conditions

1 Hall et al., *supra* chapter 3, note 8 at ix–x.

2 Michael Corkery, *The Bike Thieves of Burlington, Vermont*, N.Y. Times (Nov. 12, 2022), https://www.nytimes.com/2022/11/12/business/burlington-police-stolen-bikes.html.

3 Other problems with the article include the lack of an evidentiary basis to blame meth for the problems described; that it provides no evidence that the police department "reformed" itself; that it presents no evidence that any problem described is unique to Burlington's policy choices; that it provides no evidence that bike theft has increased substantially; that it leaves out some significant facts about the recent history of the local police that might tell a different story about why people don't want to work there; and that the paper's social media accounts absurdly claimed that the bike theft problem was

a window into "a world of violence and despair that lurks below the city's surface." *See* Kate O'Neill (@okatherine), Twitter (Nov. 12, 2022, 1:12 PM), [https://perma.cc/C8SR -PZ9Y] (describing shortcomings in the article); Emily W, *Jon Murad's NYPD Career Deserves More Scrutiny*, Rake (Dec. 22, 2021), [https://perma.cc/53NX-V3AY] (calling for further investigation into Jon Murad's background); New York Times (@nytimes), Twitter (Nov. 12, 2022, 10:25 AM), [https://perma.cc/DVV7-3YTB]. Other smart commentators have described additional ethical and journalistic problems with the article. *See, e.g.*, Michael Hobbes (@RottenInDenmark), Twitter (Nov. 14, 2022, 8:37 AM), [https://perma.cc/E3RK-LAPF].

4 Carter C. Price & Kathryn A. Edwards, Trends in Income from 1975 to 2018, [https://perma.cc/659Q-QRQ4].

5 Alexandre Tanzi, *The Wealth Gains That Made 2020 a Banner Year for the Richest 1%*, Bloomberg (March 22, 2021), https://www.bloomberg.com/news/articles/2021-03-22/the-wealth -gains-that-made-2020-a-banner-year-for-the-richest-1?leadSource=uverify%20wall.

6 Nat'l Low Income Housing Coal., Out of Reach (2023), [https://perma.cc /XBZ7-VL2X].

7 Politizane, Wealth Inequality in America, YouTube (Nov. 20, 2012), https:// www.youtube.com/watch?v=QPKKQnijnsM.

8 David Gilson & Carolyn Perot, *It's the Inequality, Stupid*, Mother Jones (March 2011), [https://perma.cc/HQ7C-Q9RU].

9 Sarah Fair George (@SarahFairVT), Twitter (Nov. 12, 2022, 5:15 PM), [https:// perma.cc/PA7Z-UFXY].

10 *See, e.g.*, Heather Knight, *She Set Out to Save Her Daughter from Fentanyl. She Had No Idea What She Would Face on the Streets of San Francisco*, S.F. Chron. (Dec. 3, 2021, 8:52 AM), https://www.sfchronicle.com/projects/2021/rescuing-jessica-san-fran cisco-fentanyl-addiction/.

11 *Deals for Developers*, NPR, [https://perma.cc/34R4-S7TV] (last visited Jan. 12, 2024).

12 Ezra Klein (@ezraklein), Twitter (Dec. 2, 2021, 10:53 PM), [https://perma.cc /M3T7-464X].

13 *See* Gil Duran (@gilduran76), Twitter (Aug. 7, 2022), [https://perma.cc /RNY8-KR7S].

14 The article unwittingly provides profound evidence against its own thesis: the most effective local response so far to the ostensible bike theft problem, according to the article itself, has been a spontaneous and organized collective of residents who band together to help get people their bikes back.

15 The article also includes two anecdotes in which the police told crime victims they were too busy to help them. The reporter presents no evidence that police in Burlington "don't have time" to help crime victims because they "have their hands full." Since 2020, I have tracked similar false claims by cops in news coverage in other cities when progressive reforms were discussed—and officials in several cities told me that they uncovered coordinated police-union campaigns after 2020 to tell crime victims something to this effect when officers respond to calls. The *Times* makes no attempt to tell its readers that threatening work

stoppages has historically been a *political* tactic cops use to attack progressive politicians and to increase police budgets. *See, e.g.*, Susie Neilson, *Are S.F. Police Behaving Differently Under Brooke Jenkins Than Under Chesa Boudin? Study Finds Immediate Shift*, S.F. CHRON. (Nov. 2, 2022), https://www.sfchronicle.com/crime/article/brooke-jenkins-sf-policing-17550839.php.

16 Alec MacGillis, *The Cause of the Crime Wave Is Hiding in Plain Sight*, ATLANTIC (July 19, 2022), https://www.theatlantic.com/ideas/archive/2022/07/covid-court -closings-violent-crime-wave/670559/.

17 Megan T. Stevenson, *Cause, Effect, and the Structure of the Social World*, 103 B.U. L. Rev. 2001 (2023) ("most reforms and interventions in the criminal legal space are shown to have little lasting effect when evaluated with gold standard methods").

18 RICHARD WILKINSON & KATE PICKETT, THE SPIRIT LEVEL: WHY EQUALITY IS BETTER FOR EVERYONE (2009).

19 *See* DANIELLE SERED, UNTIL WE RECKON: VIOLENCE, MASS INCARCERATION, AND A ROAD TO REPAIR (2021); *Restorative Justice*, TRANSFORM HARM, [https://perma.cc/7K2F -TG9J] (last visited Jan. 12, 2024).

20 *Pandemic Court Closures Could Be Driving High Crime Rates*, NPR (July 24, 2022), [https://perma.cc/AY6D-K23M].

21 Jeff Asher & Rob Arthur, *The Data Are Pointing to One Major Driver of America's Murder Spike*, ATLANTIC (Jan. 10, 2022), https://www.theatlantic.com/ideas/archive/2022/01 /gun-sales-murder-spike/621196/.

22 Emily Widra, *New data and visualizations spotlight states' reliance on excessive jailing*, PRISON POLICY INITIATIVE (Apr. 15, 2024), https://www.prisonpolicy.org/blog/2024/04/15 /jails_update/.

23 Something else potentially consistent with the police chief's claim would have been an assertion that the bail system was improperly releasing people in Kansas charged with the most serious crimes, such that people could show their defiance by repeatedly violating serious criminal laws. The article provides no evidence of this, and it would be contrary to what I have seen and read about the functioning of the bail system there.

24 In an example of a different perspective on the backlog issue, officials in Harris County, Texas, commissioned a public safety review of what to do with its court backlog in 2020, and the recommendation was to dismiss less serious cases and focus on serious ones. Holly Hansen, *Report Urges Harris County to Begin Widespread Dismissal of "Non-Violent" Felony Charges*, TEXAN (June 26, 2020), https://thetexan.news/issues /criminal-justice/report-urges-harris-county-to-begin-widespread-dismissal-of-non -violent-felony-charges/article_b11a2445-06d5-562f-8c7e-4f2f7a3be9ae.html.

25 Alexis Stevens, *Homicide Pace Continues to Slow in Atlanta*, ATL. J-CONST. (Sept. 25, 2023), [https://perma.cc/YZN3-HQCR].

26 Ivy Scott, *After Police Officers Were Phased Out of Boston's Public Schools, Violent Incidents Raise Public Safety Concerns*, BOS. GLOBE (March 23, 2022, 12:26 PM), https://www.bostonglobe.com/2022/03/23/metro/police-officers-were-phased-out -bostons-public-schools-during-pandemic-families-wonder-what-that-means-public -safety/#:~:text=Since%20then%2C%20the%20schools%20have,have%20experienced %20during%20the%20pandemic.

27 SENTENCING PROJECT, THE FACTS ABOUT DANGERS OF ADDED POLICE IN SCHOOLS (2011), [https://perma.cc/QBZ6-6J3C].

28 Andy Newman & Emma G. Fitzsimmons, *New York City to Involuntarily Remove Mentally Ill People from Streets*, N.Y. TIMES (June 20, 2023), https://www.nytimes .com/2022/11/29/nyregion/nyc-mentally-ill-involuntary-custody.html.

29 It is the same approach that the San Francisco mayor used when she issued an emergency declaration that suspended various democratic laws and shut down a life-saving overdose center, supposedly to deal with the "crisis" of homelessness and drug use. Thomas Fuller et al., *San Francisco Mayor Declares State of Emergency to Fight City's "Nasty Street,"* N.Y. TIMES (Dec. 17, 2021), https://www.nytimes.com/2021/12/17/us/san-francisco-state -of-emergency-crime.html.

30 *See, e.g.*, David Calnitsky & Pilar Gonalons-Pons, *The Impact of an Experimental Guaranteed Income on Crime and Violence*, 68 SOC. PROBLEMS 778 (2021); Nancy Stedman, *Cash Transfer Programs Are Growing More Common in the U.S. as Studies Show They Improve People's Health*, PENN LEONARD DAVIS INT. HEALTH ECON. (Aug. 30, 2023), [https://perma .cc/8FN3-9GRQ]; Megan Greenwell, *Universal Basic Income Has Been Tested Repeatedly. It Works. Will America Ever Embrace It?*, WASH. POST (Oct. 24, 2022, 9:50 AM), https://www .washingtonpost.com/magazine/2022/10/24/universal-basic-income/.

31 Olga R. Rodriguez & Janie Har, *San Francisco's Vaunted Tolerance Dims amid Brazen Crimes*, AP (Dec. 12, 2021, 12:44 AM), [https://perma.cc/LX2J-3MVM].

32 *See* Alec Karakatsanis (@equalityalec), TWITTER (Aug. 13, 2024), https://x.com /equalityAlec/status/1823358349393711462 (showing photo of Newsom personally sweeping homeless encampments and noting that Newsom's private photographer costs the State of California about $200,000 per year).

33 *See* Fitzsimmons, *supra* chapter 9, note 48.

34 The article allows Adams and other politicians to frame custodial arrests with metal chains by agents with guns (which would meet the legal definition of armed kidnapping if a private person carried it out) as an act of compassion despite their choice not to invest in the far more effective work of building systems of genuine prevention and care.

35 Stephanie Pagones, *NYC Mayor Adams, Police Slam Bail Reform Policies amid Arrests of Repeat Offenders: "Definition of Insanity,"* Fox (Aug. 3, 2022), [https://perma .cc/2LYA-SBHW].

36 H.R. Watch, *Human Rights Watch Urges a No Vote on CARE Court (SB 1338)*, H.R. WATCH (Aug. 15, 2022), [https://perma.cc/2UQY-ZKAU].

37 Nicole Nixon & Chris Nichols, *Newsom Signs CARE Court Bill, Paving Way for Court-Ordered Treatment Plans*, CAPRADIO (Sept. 14, 2022), [https://perma.cc/TB44 -QZTX]. California has, over the years, appropriated additional money for some housing and treatment programs, but all elected officials involved acknowledge that the programs are insufficient and that they are entirely separate from the CARE court system.

38 *They're Big Newsom Wins, but Questions Remain on CARE Court, Diablo Canyon Nuclear Plant*, S.D. UNION TRIB. (Sept. 1, 2022), https://www.sandiegouniontribune .com/opinion/editorials/story/2022-09-01/newsom-diablo-canyon-care-court-mentally -ill-homeless; Heather Knight, *Gavin Newsom Has a Bold New Mental Health Plan, Inspired*

by the Misery on S.F. Streets. Will It Work?, S.F. Chron. (March 3, 2022), https://www
.sfchronicle.com/sf/bayarea/heatherknight/article/Gavin-Newsom-Care-Court-mental
-health-16973070.php.

39 Nathan J. Robinson (@NathanJRobinson), Twitter (May 28, 2024, 11:47 AM),
[https://perma.cc/36EY-38TE] (citing *Japanese Enjoys Internment*, N.Y. Times, Jan. 13,
1942, at 5, archived at https://timesmachine.nytimes.com/timesmachine/1942/01/13/85
017030.html?pageNumber=5).

40 Burns, *supra* chapter 10, note 18.

41 Stop LAPD Spying Coalition, *Real Estate and Capitalist Crisis*, Automating Banishment, [https://perma.cc/YAY2-B98D] (last visited Jan. 12, 2024). *See also* Karakatsanis,
supra introduction, note 17.

42 Adam Johnson, *NYT'S "Black Voters Want More Cops" Reporting Genre Cynically
Conflates Desire for Public Safety with Demands for More Policing, Longer Sentences*, Column
(June 3, 2022), [https://perma.cc/YU6G-XAQJ].

43 Fwd.US, Black Voters Want More Safety and More Justice (March 2024),
[https://perma.cc/HGA6-FQ92] (rigorous national polling showing that 84 percent of
Black voters want to reduce jail and prison populations, with supermajorities supporting a
variety of popular progressive reforms.)

44 This news tactic is reminiscent of a 2022 story in which Amazon was caught in
internal emails strategizing how to portray progressive policy proposals as harmful to
"Communities of Color." Amazon and the *Times* both understand something important:
a good way of justifying brutal, unequal policies is to tell liberals that "communities of
color" want them. Emily Birnbaum, *Amazon Urges Consultant to "Push" Message from
Minority Groups*, Politico (June 3, 2022, 3:24 PM), [https://perma.cc/TWK3-CNY6].

45 *See* Naomi Murakawa, The First Civil Right: How Liberals Built Prison
America (2014).

16. Resisting Copaganda

1 George Orwell, Nineteen Eighty-Four at 69 (1949).

2 *See* Chris Hamby & Michael Forsythe, *Behind the Scenes, McKinsey Guided Companies at the Center of the Opioid Crisis*, N.Y. Times (June 29, 2022), https://www.nytimes
.com/2022/06/29/business/mckinsey-opioid-crisis-opana.html.

3 *See* Graham Rayman, *Hundreds of Rikers Island Correction Officers Caught Abus-
ing Sick Leave Policies During COVID Staffing Crisis: "Just Completely Dysfunctional,"* N.Y.
Daily News (Jan. 23, 2022, 10:00 PM), [https://perma.cc/4MSR-YB4D]; *State Police: 22
Troopers Implicated in Overtime Scandal Will Be Disciplined*, WBUR (July 10, 2020), [https://
perma.cc/E5K3-QA5J].

4 *See supra* introduction, note 20. A separate analysis of just 134 companies
found that they hid $1.2 trillion in offshore tax havens in the two decades before 2018.
Navodhya Samarakoon, *The Effect of the Closure of the Double Irish Arrangement on the
Location of U.S. Multinational Companies' Profits*, SSRN (July 1, 2023), [https://perma
.cc/26Z4-TGFM].

5 *See, e.g.,* BECK et al., *supra* chapter 7, note 13; (estimating that about 4 percent of incarcerated people, or around 95,000 individuals, are sexually assaulted each year, and the majority of sexual assaults are by government officials); Floyd, et al. v. City of New York, et al., CENTER FOR CONSTITUTIONAL RIGHTS, [https://perma.cc/7QJD-WDQ8] (last visited Jan. 14, 2024); *Stop and Frisk Data*, NYCLU OF N.Y., [https://perma.cc/632F-NXYD] (last visited Jan. 14, 2024); U.S. DEPT. OF JUST. C.R. DIV., *supra* chapter 7, note 11. (finding that at least 93 percent of police assaults in Newark were illegal).

6 These crimes are vast and diverse. *See* Hayley Miller, *Black Realtor and His Client Handcuffed by Police During House Tour in Michigan,* HUFF POST (Aug. 8, 2021, 2:17 PM), [https://perma.cc/ZAZ9-Y8LY]; U.S. DEPT. OF JUST. C.R. DIV., INVESTIGATION OF THE FERGUSON POLICE DEPT. (March 4, 2015), [https://perma.cc/JB2V-UMLT]; *Justice Department Reaches Agreement with the City of Miami and the Miami Police Department to Implement Reforms on Officer-Involved Shootings,* DEPT. OF JUST. (Feb. 25, 2016), [https://perma.cc/R959-WLY4].

7 *See* FBI Crime Data Explorer, *supra* introduction, note 21.

8 *See* WILKINSON & PICKETT, *supra* chapter 15, note 18

9 *See supra* introduction, note 25 and chapter 8, note 43.

10 *See* Thompson & Tapp *supra* introduction, note 20.

11 *See supra* introduction, note 23 and chapter 8, note 50.

12 Asher & Horwitz, *supra* chapter 5, note 28.

13 *See supra* introduction, note 14.

14 *See, e.g.,* Christopher Ingraham, *Law Enforcement Took More Stuff from People Last Year Than Burglars Did,* WASH. POST (Nov. 23, 2015), https://www.washingtonpost .com/news/wonk/wp/2015/11/23/cops-took-more-stuff-from-people-than-burglars-did -last-year/; J. Justin Wilson, *New Report Finds Civil Forfeiture Rakes in Billions Each Year, Does Not Fight Crime,* INST. FOR JUST. (Dec. 15, 2020), [https://perma.cc/J53Q-G78Y].

15 *See supra* introduction, note 20.

16 *See supra* chapter 5, note 7.

17 Tom Jackman, *Fraternal Order of Police Union Endorses Trump,* WASH. POST (Sept. 16, 2016, 3:14 PM), https://www.washingtonpost.com/news/true-crime/wp/2016/09/16/fraternal -order-of-police-union-endorses-trump/.

18 *See supra* chapter 8, note 41.

19 *See* Drug Policy Alliance, *supra* chapter 14, note 7.

20 Wildeman, *supra* chapter 8, note 58. *See also* Emily Widra, *Incarceration Shortens Life Expectancy,* PRISON POLICY INITIATIVE (June 26, 2017), [https://perma.cc/J4H5-DMEP].

21 *9 Solidarity Commitments to/with Incarcerated People for 2021,* https://docs.google .com/document/d/1ByMHRNbsntdyziubfPJq7vDzxiBFEqroxzCUgKsxp9E/edit [https://perma.cc/73ZJ-QFKD] (last visited Jan. 12, 2024).

22 *About Us,* Center for Just Journalism, [https://perma.cc/3EMZ-9P5T] (last visited Jan. 12, 2024).

Acknowledgments

I first thank my parents, whose unconditional support has been the key to whatever I have done throughout my entire life. I hope I do things useful enough in the world to justify only having one child. I also thank my grandmother for being the only person to read a lot of what I write, and for somehow reading all of the civil rights cases I work on. I am writing these acknowledgments from the upstairs bedroom in your house, Grandma.

I also want to thank my lifelong companions from the Sequoia School. You are each more special to me than I can convey, and together you are a home. Everything in here is shaped by what you teach me every day.

And to D+K: you are my special helper-friends for good. I'm excited for what life will bring us.

I owe a great debt to my editor Ashley Smith and to the brilliant Tanya Coke and Diane Wachtell from the New Press for their help conceiving, editing, and bringing forth this book into the world. And to the incomparable Naomi Murakawa, whose scholarly excellence, insights, editing, and kindness were essential and inspiring in making this book what it is. I also owe a great deal to the individuals who provided exceptional research assistance, including Jacob Ali-Wertheimer, Lily Bou, Susan Li, Natalie Murphy, Dylan Onderdonk-Snow, Byron Raco, and Craig Toennies.

I want to thank all of the amazing people at The New Press who helped with this book, including Nia Abrams, Haajar Abu Ismail, Ellen Adler, Keshav Bansal, Maury Botton, Jess Cheng, Julia Fink, Fran Forte, Gia Gonzales, Mary Beth Jarrad, Kevin Mercado, Lina Munar, Sharon Swados, Rachel Vega-DeCesario, and Derek Warker.

I would also like to thank Laura Bennett of the Center for Just Journalism; Chesa Boudin of Berkeley Law; Adam Johnson of *The Column*

Acknowledgments

and the *Citations Needed* podcast; Shakeer Rahman of Stop LAPD Spying Coalition; and Elizabeth Rossi, Katherine Hubbard, Quinita Ennis, Danielle Dupuy-Watson, and all of my colleagues at Civil Rights Corps who have given me ideas and/or much-needed support as I was writing this book and whose work has helped to deepen our understanding of copaganda. I also thank the many hundreds of people on social media who have sent (and who continue to send!) me examples of copaganda every day; and the dozens of anonymous reporters, editors, producers, professors, and government officials who regularly provide me the inside scoop, many of whom helped me with this book at some professional risk. I also thank Bill Ayers, Alex Baron, Lindsay Bradley, Peter Calloway, Gina Clayton-Johnson, Salil Dudani, Paul Engler, Krish Gundu, Thomas Harvey, Raj Jayadev, Sarah Leonard, Wade McMullen, David Menschel, Gabe Newland, Oren Nimni, Ellie Olsen, Jeanne Segil, Aviva Shen, Liz Simons, Lex Steppling, Megan Stevenson, Sarah Stillman, Zoë Towns, Julia Udell, Robert Vargas, Madhvi Venkatraman, and Alex Vitale for the many conversations that helped me understand better what I was trying to write about and why it matters.

Finally, I thank Nika Soon-Shiong. Your genius, support, criticisms, work ethic, laughter, and courage were an inspiration for me every day in writing this book. I have never encountered anyone who has pushed me harder, and never anyone who I cared so much about believing in what I do.

I dedicate this book to all my clients who have been killed by the punishment bureaucracy while we fought your cases. Your courage has always given me the energy I need every day to keep going, even when the fight feels impossible. I also write this book for all the students, young journalists, and junior faculty afraid to speak up about pervasive intellectual and moral flaws in what passes for elite education, journalism, and scholarship. If you relentlessly tell the truth, and if you do so with grace, humility, humor, and a smile, the group of people you will assemble in your little corner of the world will be more powerful than you could ever dream of.

Index

Index

Index

Index

Index

Index

Index

Index

Index

Index

Index

Index

About the Author

Alec is the founder of Civil Rights Corps. Alec has pioneered constitutional civil rights cases to challenge the size, power, profit, and everyday brutality of the punishment bureaucracy across the United States. These legal challenges have helped to free hundreds of thousands of people from confinement in jail cells, returned tens of millions of dollars to indigent people and families, blocked billions in government spending on state violence, prevented hundreds of thousands of illegal convictions, prevented the separation of tens of thousands of families, and transformed the way the punishment bureaucracy handles fines, fees, and bail across the United States. Alec has also worked with directly impacted communities across the country to design innovative new legal, advocacy, and narrative strategies for challenging widespread illegal and harmful practices of prosecutors, police, probation officers, judges, and private companies who work with them to profit from the punishment bureaucracy.

Alec is the author of the book *Usual Cruelty*, which his grandmother likes. He appears widely in television, radio, podcasts, documentary films, and loving debates with friends. He also lectures widely about the punishment bureaucracy, typically giving more than 100 lectures, speeches, interviews, and workshops per year, including training thousands of lawyers in how to dismantle the injustices of the punishment bureaucracy every day in courtrooms across the United States.

Alec was awarded the 2016 Trial Lawyer of the Year Award and the 2023 New Frontier award by the John F. Kennedy Presidential Library. Other honors include the Stephen B. Bright Award for contributions to indigent defense in the South. His work at Civil Rights Corps challenging the money bail system in California—alongside his colleague Katherine Hubbard—was honored with the Champion of Public Defense Award by the National Association of Criminal Defense Lawyers.

About the Author

Alec graduated from Yale College with a degree in ethics, politics, and economics; and Harvard Law School, where he was a Supreme Court chair of the Harvard Law Review. Before founding Civil Rights Corps, Alec was a civil rights lawyer and public defender with the Special Litigation Division of the Public Defender Service for the District of Columbia; a federal public defender in Alabama, representing impoverished people accused of federal crimes; and co-founder of the nonprofit organization Equal Justice Under Law.

Alec is interested in genuine holistic safety for everyone and ending human caging, surveillance, police, the death penalty, borders, war, and inequality. He also likes playing the piano and soccer, collecting rocks, singing, growing flowers, creating mosaics from dried flowers, repeating the same jokes until they become funny, writing bad poetry, and making weird paintings on large pieces of wood and metal.

A Note About Royalties

All royalties from this book are donated. As with my first book, *Usual Cruelty*, I have required that the publisher donates all royalties to a nonprofit organization doing essential work relating to the subject matter. The royalties from this book will be donated to the Los Angeles Community Action Network and its Stop LAPD Spying Coalition. This is a community organization based in the Skid Row neighborhood of Los Angeles that does some of the most important work I am aware of on challenging the unjust and ineffective punishment bureaucracy and the propaganda that sustains it.

Publishing in the Public Interest

Thank you for reading this book published by The New Press; we hope you enjoyed it. New Press books and authors play a crucial role in sparking conversations about the key political and social issues of our day.

We hope that you will stay in touch with us. Here are a few ways to keep up to date with our books, events, and the issues we cover:

- Sign up at www.thenewpress.com/subscribe to receive updates on New Press authors and issues and to be notified about local events
- www.facebook.com/newpressbooks
- www.twitter.com/thenewpress
- www.instagram.com/thenewpress

Please consider buying New Press books not only for yourself, but also for friends and family and to donate to schools, libraries, community centers, prison libraries, and other organizations involved with the issues our authors write about.

The New Press is a 501(c)(3) nonprofit organization; if you wish to support our work with a tax-deductible gift please visit www.thenewpress.com/donate or use the QR code below.